# Mark Twain and Male Friendship

# MARK TWAIN AND MALE FRIENDSHIP

*The Twichell, Howells, and Rogers Friendships*

Peter Messent

OXFORD

UNIVERSITY PRESS

2009

# OXFORD
## UNIVERSITY PRESS

Oxford University Press, Inc., publishes works that further
Oxford University's objective of excellence
in research, scholarship, and education.

Oxford   New York

Auckland   Cape Town   Dar es Salaam   Hong Kong   Karachi
Kuala Lumpur   Madrid   Melbourne   Mexico City   Nairobi
New Delhi   Shanghai   Taipei   Toronto

With offices in
Argentina   Austria   Brazil   Chile   Czech Republic   France   Greece
Guatemala   Hungary   Italy   Japan   Poland   Portugal   Singapore
South Korea   Switzerland   Thailand   Turkey   Ukraine   Vietnam

Copyright © 2009 by Peter Messent

Published by Oxford University Press, Inc.
198 Madison Avenue, New York, New York 10016

www.oup.com

Oxford is a registered trademark of Oxford University Press

Library of Congress Cataloging-in-Publication Data
Messent, Peter B.
Mark Twain and Male Friendship : the Twichell, Howells and Rogers
Friendships / Peter Messent.
p. cm.
Includes bibliographical references and index.
ISBN 978-0-19-539116-9
1. Twain, Mark, 1835–1910—Friends and associates.   2. Authors,
American—19th century—Biography.   3. Twichell, Joseph Hopkins,
1838–1918—Friends and associates.   4. Howells, William Dean,
1837–1920—Friends and associates.   5. Rogers, Henry Huttleston,
1840–1909—Friends and associates.   6. Male friendship—United
States—History.   I. Title.
PS1333.M47 2009
818'.409—dc22
[B]
2009001727

3   5   7   9   8   6   4   2

Printed in the United States of America
on acid-free paper

# Acknowledgments

I owe thanks to a number of Twain scholars for their help at various stages of this book. Lou Budd and Peter Stoneley read the whole manuscript late on, and their willingness to perform this (thankless) task, valuable feedback, and the positive and generous nature of their responses are all greatly appreciated. Both must, in fact, be doubly thanked. Lou had already read and commented on a number of the chapters at an earlier stage, and Peter had previously read over a former version of chapter 6. Thanks, too, to Steve Courtney—the author of the new biography, *Joseph Hopkins Twichell: The Life and Times of Mark Twain's Closest Friend*—for his extremely generous help as I researched the Twichell papers, and for his comments on draft versions of the chapters on the Clemens-Twichell relationship. Thanks also to Vic Fischer and Robert H. Hirst for their (equally generous) assistance in identifying and checking material in the Mark Twain Papers and, along with the rest of their team, in making me feel so welcome as I did my research there. Bob and the scholars working with him know just about everything there is to know about Clemens, and share that knowledge with both enthusiasm and exceptional generosity. They—and all the academics and specialists I mention here—have been the very model of collegiality. Neda Salem, also a member of the Mark Twain Papers and Project, deserves special mention. She was endlessly patient and helpful when I was working in Berkeley as she sought out the many letters, manuscripts, and files I asked to see, and on several occasion saved my bacon in finding material that I could not exactly reference. She also answered my e-mail queries with exemplary speed and efficiency. Other members of the Twain community who helped me at various stages of the book include Hal Bush, David H. Fears, Shelley Fisher Fishkin, Forrest Robinson, and Barbara Schmidt. My brother, Philip Messent, who works in the field of family therapy, offered valuable feedback from a very different professional angle on a version of chapter 6. The comments of one of my immediate colleagues,

Graham Thompson, who read over a draft version of chapter 1, were very helpful indeed. Another colleague, John Fagg, assisted me with just the right bibliographical information as I wrote (briefly) on George Bellows in chapter 7. My thanks too to Carolyn Longworth of the Millicent Library, Fairhaven, particularly for sending me copies of the two Dias books referenced in my work on Henry H. Rogers. I also thank the librarians at the Beinecke Rare Book & Manuscript Library at Yale, the Houghton Library of the Harvard College Library, and the Connecticut State Library Archives for their help. (In the case of all the research centers I used—and where relevant—I would like to recognize, and give thanks for, the permissions to publish that have been granted me). I acknowledge, too, the support of my colleagues in the School of American and Canadian Studies at the University of Nottingham (England), and especially of the then Head of School, Judie Newman. I am lucky to work in such an intellectually stimulating environment. I would also like to thank Brendan O'Neill (assistant editor) and Gwen Colvin (production editor), of Oxford University Press—together with any others involved—for their enthusiastic assistance in preparing this book for publication. Any faults in this book are mine alone, and should not be laid at the door of any of the above.

I received funding as I worked to complete this book and acknowledge that gratefully here. The British Academy awarded me a number of small grants enabling me to conduct my archive research in the United States. I also thank the Arts and Humanities Research Council for a matching leave that proved crucial in helping the book to completion. Earlier versions of chapters 3, 5, and 6 appeared in *Nineteenth-Century Literature*, Blackwell's *A Companion to Mark Twain*, and *Arizona Quarterly* respectively. I am grateful to the relevant publishers for permission to reprint them here.

My field of study gives me the opportunity to acknowledge some of my own close male friendships. I am aware that these, too, are subject to the types of conditioning factors noted in the friendships examined in this book, but this does not affect their importance or their worth. I was fortunate, at an early stage in my life, to have made good friends at school who have remained close—despite occasional periods of relatively little contact or communication—throughout adulthood. John Clements in particular has been the best of friends: loyal, unselfish, and charismatic both in and outside his work (as a clinical psychologist in the caring services). As we get older, so we get tamer in certain ways, and maybe our previous late-night, and bourbon-fueled, conversations happen only rarely now. But, whatever the occasion, we can always relax in each other's company—surely the very sign of close friendship—and always enjoy our time together. Roger Kelly, Joe Khan, Martin Kimber, Jim MacDonald, and Mike Willson complete this particular round-up of ex-Wimbledon College friends. From my University days at Manchester I have stayed close to Phil Melling, fanatic Wigan rugby league supporter and—impressively—founding organiser (with his wife Sue) of Study Guatemala, a charity providing free education to disadvantaged children in that country. I must also mention Godfrey Kearns, who taught Phil and me at University, and who remains a good friend, though we see each other far too infrequently. I have been lucky, as I have suggested, in my University Department colleagues, particularly David Murray who—in all my time at Nottingham (some thirty-five years)—has been a supportive, warm-hearted, and witty close friend. He has changed my view of Liverpool F. C. supporters. Richard King, Peter Ling, and Douglas Tallack, too, have been good friends and colleagues. Along with Dave, their contribution to my own education over the years, and to the discipline of American Studies, has been considerable. My brothers, Andy and Phil, have become ever closer and more important to me, especially following the deaths of our parents, John and Rosa. Along with my dear sister Mary and cousin Alex Anderson, they too have been highly supportive in all aspects of my life. I am pleased to think of my son William—now in his thirties and a talented and generous young man—as a friend too. Other past close friends—Peter Morris and Charles Gregory (Greg)—are now dead, but remain much missed. John Harvey is very much alive and still writing his excellent crime fiction. It is impossible to list all those others who fall into the category of friends: I hope those not mentioned will not cross me from their address books.

Finally, I must acknowledge the importance of my immediate family. Alice, my daughter, and Sam, her husband, along with William, are of course very special to me, as are my stepdaughters Leah and Ella. I am proud of them all. But I dedicate this book to Carin, my long-suffering but loving wife—with all my love.

# Contents

# Mark Twain and Male Friendship

# Introduction

[Y]our mouth . . . [Clemens wrote, speaking of the problems of autobiographical dictation to a stenographer] . . . won't say . . . a sluice of
intimately personal, & particularly private things . . . to any but a very
close personal friend, like Howells, or Twichell, or Henry Rogers.
—Henry Nash Smith and William M. Gibson, eds., *Mark Twain-
Howells Letters*, 845.

lose friendships can be difficult to sustain. Their nature changes with
time and with the distance that also often intervenes. William Dean
Howells—in the late nineteenth century, the most important literary figure
in America—writes on exactly this topic in an essay called "Storage."
I quote at some length:

Save in some signal exception, a thing taken out of storage cannot be
established in its former function without a sense of its comparative
inadequacy. . . .
I have lately been privy to the reunion of two old comrades who are
bound together more closely than most men in a community of interests, occupations, and ideals. During a long separation they had kept
account of each other's opinions as well as experiences; they had
exchanged letters, from time to time, in which they opened their
minds fully to each other, and found themselves constantly in accord.
When they met they made a great shouting, and each pretended that
he found the other just what he used to be. They talked a long, long
time, fighting the invisible enemy which they felt between them. The
enemy was habit, the habit of other minds and hearts, the daily use of
persons and things which in their separation they had not had in
common. . . . [T]hough they live in the same town, and often dine at
the same table, and belong to the same club, yet [the old friends] have
not grown together again.[1]

3

Howells here is perceptive about male friendship and its loud bonhomie—a sign of fellowship that can indicate real intimacy, or cover over its lack in sheer good-humored noise. He is perceptive, too, in noting the "community of interests, occupations, and ideals" on which friendships depend, and the conjunction of minds and hearts, persons and things, that—when regularly exercised—keep them strong.

We might, however, puzzle a little over what "things" have to do with friendship, but can find an answer in a practical example in Howells's own relationship with Clemens, and the typewriter bought by the latter (presumably) to facilitate his work. The first mention of the machine comes in a typed letter to Howells written by Clemens in capital letters (the only type available) on December 9, 1874. I quote selectively:

> I DON'T KNOW WHETHER I AM OGING TO MAKE THIS TYPE-WRITING MACHINE GO OR NTO,: THAT LAST WORD WAS INTENDRED FOR N-N<u>OT</u>: BUT I GUESS I SHALL MAKE SOME SORT OF A SUCC SS OF IT BEFORE I RUN IT VERY LO G. I AM SO THICK-FINGERED THAT I MISS THE KEYS.
> YOU NEEDNT A SWER THIS; I AM ONLY PRACTICING TO GET THREE: A<u>NOTHER</u> <u>SLIP</u>-<u>UP</u> <u>THERE</u>-:...BLAME MY CATS BUT THIS THING REQUIRES GENIUS IN ORDER TO WORK IT JUST RIGHT.
> YOURS EVER,
> MARK.[2]

Clemens had bought one of the very first commercial typewriters, marketed by the Ilion (New York) Remington Company in the July of that year. The purchase was unsurprising given his life-long interest in technology and new inventions, especially as they applied to his occupation as a writer. Both he and Howells, indeed, were key figures in the professionalization of writing in the post-Civil War years, in the complex adaptation of culture to the capitalist market, with Clemens as the more enthusiastically innovative of the two.

Howells answered his friend's letter two days later, saying, "I have your printed letter of yesterday. Fire away; and when you get tired of the machine, lend it to me." Clemens follows up on this suggestion on the fourteenth of December, when he concludes another typed letter:

> I GUESS I SHALL HAVE TO AFFLICT YOU WITH THE MACHINE BEFORE LONG; IT IS MOST TOO TEARI G ON THE MIND FOR
> YOURS EVER,
> MARK.

By June 25, 1875, though, the machine had been passed on (evidently swapped for a saddle) to Clemens's publisher, Elisha Bliss, where—as its former owner told Howells—it is "grimly pursuing its appointed mission, slowly & implacably rotting away another man's chances for salvation."

But it seems Bliss, too, must have given up on the machine and handed it on (presumably on Clemens's directions) to Howells, who writes on November 5 of the same year:

My dear Clemens:
   The type-writer came Wednesday night, and is already beginning to have its effect on me. Of course it doesn't work: if I can persuade some of the letters to get up against the ribbon, they wont get down again without digital assistance.... I don't despair yet of sending you something in its beautiful hand writing—after I've had a man out from the agent's to put it in order. It's fascinating, in the meantime, and it wastes my time like an old friend.[3]

According to Clemens's later account of this "infernal" machine in the autobiographical dictations, Howells later gave him back the typewriter and (after a number of unsuccessful attempts) he finally passed it on elsewhere.[4]

This correspondence suggests the connection between "things" and the friendships that frame their use. It might be judged marginal to my main concerns were it not for its illustration of aspects of the Clemens-Howells relationship. It highlights Clemens's wit, focusing on the comic exchange between the man and a machine that in theory is there to aid, but in practice plagues, him. (The potentially problematic nature of—and loss of agency and control inherent in—the move from the hand-inscribed manuscript of an earlier and more intimate mode of literary production to the new technologies of the mass marketplace are also relevant here.[5]) It shows Howells's ability to collude with, and thus extend, the joke that Clemens launches. It suggests, too, the gentler quality of Howells's humor in comparison to Clemens's hyperbolic tendencies (where the malevolent instrument threatens to unbalance the mind itself). More generally, it conveys the sense of easy camaraderie and understanding—of minds and outlooks in tune—which is so noticeable in the majority of their forty-year friendship and correspondence.

In "Storage," Howells refers to friendships that do not withstand the tests of time and absence. His own relationship with Clemens—despite ups and downs and fallow periods—appears, though, to have done so. In *My Mark Twain*, written immediately following Clemens's death in 1910, Howells speaks of his friend's sometimes unpredictable, willful but spontaneous behavior, and refers to his wife Olivia's "low, despairing cry of, 'Oh Youth!'" when this occurred. He then adds his assent to the accuracy of her chosen term: "He was a youth to the end of his days, the heart of a boy with the head of a sage."[6] He notes Clemens's absolute honesty, "his essential fineness, his innate nobleness," and the "jubilant" time they had working together on the aborted Colonel Sellers play. He judges Clemens "the most serious, the most humane, the most conscientious of men," recollects "the intense talk, with the stories and the laughing" that marked his visits to the Howells family, and speaks of "the intensity with which he pierced to the heart of life."[7] Howells does not draw back from listing Clemens's faults too, but the depth of his affection and respect for his dead friend comes through clearly in the piece.[8]

This is, however, a commemorative work, and—as Goodman and Dawson point out—possibly "exaggerates the intimacy" between Howells and Clemens, and "distorts [his] more complicated responses" to their friendship.[9] Howells's acute sense of loss for Clemens, though, also permeates his private correspondence of the time. He writes to Frederick Duneka, on the day before the death: "It wrings my heart to think of Clemens dying." While a letter written to Joe Twichell the following July reads: "When Clemens died I felt *desolate*, as I never had before; he had been such a world-full friend."[10]

In this book I focus on the three exceptional male friendships in Clemens's life—those that meant most to him, and stayed strong over a very considerable length of time: in two of the cases, over forty years. The first of these—chronologically speaking—was with Howells, a friendship that began with the latter's favorable 1869 review of Clemens's first travel book, *The Innocents Abroad*, and their consequent meeting when Clemens visited the *Atlantic Monthly* office to thank him. The two men's personal compatibility played a significant part in the making of a lifelong relationship. This was built initially on Howells's recognition of Clemens's literary worth and his warm interest in Clemens's career, but would come to involve both a close family friendship and a variety of professional collaborations—most of which, to the comic delight of both men, ended in failure.

The second friendship was with Joseph Twichell—the "Dear Old Joe" to Twichell's "Dear old Mark" in their long friendship and correspondence.[11] Clemens came to know Twichell (I develop the fuller story of all these relationships later in the book) on his early visits to Hartford, Connecticut: the town where he would spend his happiest family years. Twichell, the local Congregationalist minister and an ex-Civil War chaplain, supported and gave spiritual advice to Clemens as he courted his future wife, Olivia Langdon.[12] He then became Clemens's pastor and close friend when the Clemens family settled in Hartford. And, despite Clemens's gradual move away from any type of formal religious commitment, and growing rejection of traditional Christian notions of the Deity, their relationship lasted right through to Clemens's death. A December 22, 1903, letter Twichell wrote to him—following two recent deaths that included one of Joe's "cherished college friends"—looked back over their friendship to speak (somewhat prematurely as it so happened) of their final parting. Clemens could be nostalgic at times, but Twichell far outdid him in this respect. So his account of the two funerals leads him to their own relationship:

Our regiment in the marching column of life is fast melting away. Yes, indeed, Mark "It will soon be good-bye with us" as you said on my souvenir of your Birth-day party. Well, "the past, at least, is secure," and I hope the future too. Lately I went with a funeral to Bloomfield. En route we crossed the old road by which we used to travel to Talcott

Mountain. And again I saw those two young fellows plodding merrily along, swapping stories, exchanging no end of lively talk, full of their manifold themes of common interest, feeling the years before them. My! My! *what* good times they had! An[d] *now*—Can it be that the play is so nearly played out? . . . Never before did I feel so mortal as now. Yet I do hope to set eyes on you again—all of you—before we quit this planet. . . .

Ever affectionately Yours

Joe.[13]

When the play was, for Clemens, finally played out just over six years later on April 21, 1910, Twichell's response to his death (followed by the unexpected body blow of his wife Harmony's sudden death three days later) took the form of silent but clearly intense grief.[14] His journal entry of the time reads: "Apr 21. Our beloved friend Mark Twain dies at Redding [Connecticut]. The sorrow caused was soon to be followed by one nearer still. Little can be said of either in this diary."[15]

The third friendship on which I focus is that between Clemens and Henry H. Rogers, who was—when Clemens first came to know him—vice president of the Standard Oil Company, and one of the country's richest and most powerful businessmen. A pamphlet by Elbert Hubbard called *Little Journeys to the Homes of Great Business Men: H. H. Rogers* (written in 1909, the same year that Rogers died), is filtered, as the title suggests, through a romantic and celebratory lens.[16] But the tone and content suggest Rogers's standing for those who admired his achievements as a businessman:

> The life of H. H. Rogers was the complete American romance. He lived the part—and he looked it. . . . H. H. Rogers had personality. Men turned to gaze at him on the street; women glanced, and then hastily looked, unnecessarily hard, the other way; children stared. The man was tall, lithe, strong, graceful, commanding. His jaw was the jaw of courage; his chin meant purpose; his nose symboled [sic] intellect, poise and power; his brow spelled brain.
>
> He was a handsome man. . . . In him was the pride of the North American Indian and a little of the reserve of the savage [though he is described elsewhere in the piece as "of straight New England stock"]. His silence was always eloquent. . . . With friends he was witty, affable, generous, lovable. H. H. Rogers was the ideal executive.
>
> He did not decide until the evidence was all in; he listened, weighed, sifted, sorted and then decided. And when his decision was made, the case was closed.[17]

It is tempting to quote more of such extraordinary prose. It is enough, though, to say that this one-sided view was more than matched by others who saw Rogers, in the words of his great-grandson Michael D. Coe, as "a kind of Darth Vader in the business world," the equal of any of his fellow "robber barons" in rapacious and often dubious commercial activities.[18]

Rogers prompted hyperbolic responses from his turn-of-the-century contemporaries, emphasizing the two different sides of the man. So Thomas Lawson described him in 1905 as "relentless, ravenous, pitiless as a shark" in business, but "away from the spirit of dollar making...one of the most charming and lovable human beings I have ever encountered."[19] Peter Krass suggests similarities here with Clemens himself:

> It was obvious that they shared certain qualities, namely that there were two sides to both of them. There was Twain the humorous raconteur and Clemens the obsessive businessman. There was Henry Rogers the civic-minded socialite and "Hell Hound" who would squash any business obstacle. Both were charming, enjoyed off-color jokes, and relished...their leisure time. Most importantly, Clemens was not blind to Rogers's tough business side....The fact that Rogers was forthright earned Clemens's respect; the oilman was not a hypocrite.[20]

Clemens's relationship with Rogers came, though, much later than the Howells and Twichell friendships—when, in 1893, Rogers stepped in to help Clemens with his (acute) business difficulties. Rogers fiercely defended Clemens's financial corner and—as detailed later—ensured an eventual recovery that would have been extremely unlikely without his help. From then, until Rogers's death on May 19, 1909, Clemens effectively placed himself in Rogers's financial charge.

Despite the relatively late blossoming of this friendship, and its origin in business matters, it seems to have been the most important of Clemens's male friendships in these years. As Gregg Camfield comments, "Clemens's connections with Rogers from 1893 to Rogers's death...were among the strongest he had with anybody....[I]n Rogers, he found one of the very few men whom he considered a peer as a conversationalist and humorist."[21] After Olivia's death he adopted Rogers's family almost as an extension of his own, and was particularly close to his son Harry (Henry H. Rogers, Jr.) and to Mary, Harry's wife.[22] On November 21, 1900, Clemens would inscribe a photograph to Rogers, "To Henry H. Rogers From his oldest & best friend, Mark Twain."[23] He heard of Rogers's death from daughter Clara on his arrival at Grand Central Station on a visit to New York for financial advice from his friend. Evidently "stricken and deeply troubled," he was taken to the Grovesnor Hotel. His biographer and companion, Albert Bigelow Paine, described him as having "a helpless look, and he said his friends were dying away from him and leaving him adrift."[24]

I focus on the three friendships with Howells, Twichell, and Rogers for a number of reasons. They were, of course, not the only male friendships in Clemens's life. So, for instance, he would keep in touch with boyhood friend and fellow riverboat pilot, Will Bowen, and—addressing him in a letter of February 6, 1870, as "My First, & Oldest & Dearest Friend"—would write to him of his feelings about their shared past in a remarkably open manner.[25] Clemens's Nevada mining and journalism days were predominantly lived in male company, and he began his lifelong friendship there with Joseph T. Goodman, editor of the *Virginia City Territorial Enterprise*. In Nevada, too, he met and quickly bonded with visiting lecturer and humorist, Charles Farrar Browne (Artemus Ward)—an important professional influence until Browne's early death in 1867.

Clemens's friendships could always be volatile, and this was especially true of Bret Harte, a literary mentor in his California days. That friendship famously collapsed following Harte's stay with Clemens's family in Hartford in late 1876. In June 1878, hearing Harte had been appointed to a consulship in Germany, he would describe him to Howells as "a liar, a thief, a swindler, a snob, a sot, a sponge, a coward, a Jeremy Diddler... brim full of treachery."[26] The extravagant tone of Clemens's language is a reminder that while he was the most loyal of friends, he could also (if he felt he had been let down or betrayed) be the fiercest and most unforgiving of enemies. It may be that Clemens was keen to throw off the influence of those who had once been seen as his literary betters, for he also fell out with a second Californian literary friend, the publisher of his first book of short stories, Charles Henry Webb.[27] Clemens did, though, remain friends with minor poet Charles Warren Stoddard, who would accompany him to England as his personal secretary on his November 1873 visit.

There were other friendships, too, made at each stage of Clemens's busy and varied life. Though never especially close, Charles Jervis Langdon was a member of his fraternal circle on the 1867 *Quaker City* excursion. That relationship would result in Clemens then meeting his future wife, Charles's sister Olivia, back home—when the Langdon family was visiting New York City. Dan Slote was another one of "the boys" (as "Mark Twain" calls his group of like-minded and irreverent companions in *The Innocents Abroad*) whose friendship would remain important in the years following the trip.[28] This was, though, another relationship that would eventually go belly-up. Clemens did enjoy one successful business venture with Slote. The New York City stationary firm in which the latter's family had a stake (Slote, Woodman & Company) published and distributed "Mark Twain's Patent Self-Pasting Scrap Book"—the only one of Clemens's numerous inventions that had any real success.[29] But Clemens later invested heavily in a new engraving process that promised radical improvements to the printing industry, joining Slote (who held the original patent) in setting up the Kaolotype Engraving Company to run the business. It seems, however, that Slote, and the German metallurgist (Charles Sneider) who was involved in the development of the process, were swindling their partner. Their relationship consequently and irretrievably broke down. Following that breakdown, Clemens remorselessly harassed Slote and threatened legal action against him. Partly as a result, the latter's health collapsed and he died in February 1882, with Clemens choosing not to attend the funeral.[30]

The story of Clemens's friendships, then, is of strong loyalties that lasted many years, but also of relationships that broke down and ended in enmity and (often) fierce recriminations. The many different places where Clemens and his family lived, and the range of his literary, lecturing, and business activities, meant, too, that his friendships were varied and geographically diverse. Leland Krauth's *Mark Twain & Company* (2003) charts some of Clemens's close relationships in the literary field, including those with Harte and Howells. But it would also be possible to group his friendships by way of place (Hannibal, Virginia City, San Francisco, Hartford, Elmira, New York, London, and Vienna, etc.); in terms of his business and professional life; or through his household, neighborhood, and domestic circumstances (so, for instance, his companion and biographer Albert Bigelow Paine was increasingly important to Clemens in the final years, from early 1906 onward).[31]

Clemens was also not without female friends, though by and large such friendships seem to have been family-centered during the time of his long marriage to Olivia. But his relationship with Mary Fairbanks—another *Quaker City* traveler who acted as a mentor to Clemens as he moved into a more cultivated social world—would last for most of the rest of his life (their last meeting was in February 1894).[32] And after Olivia's death, the friendships with Mary Rogers and Isabel Lyon were of particular significance.[33] But Clemens's closest and longest-lasting friendships were—as one would expect, given the conventions of the time—of the same-sex variety.

None of Clemens's other male friendships, however, shared the length and/or intensity of those on which I have chosen to focus. Moreover, two of these friendships began when Clemens was first making his professional way in the East. Not only are they revealing as their trajectories develop and change alongside, and in response to, Clemens's increasing celebrity. They are also suggestive of the social and economic factors in which friendships are usually strongly grounded—and to which I draw particular attention here. Though the Rogers friendship comes later, it matches the earlier two in its intensity and the closeness of the companionship it fostered. The fact, too, that it was initially built on financial grounds, and at one of the most stressful periods of Clemens's business life, gives it additional significance and interest.

There has been some work done on the individual friendships that I discuss, but nothing on the combination of the three. The friendship with Howells has had the most attention, though there has also been significant recent attention on the Clemens-Twichell friendship.[34] There is little written on the Rogers-Clemens relationship, probably—at least in part—because of the difficulty of accessing archive material on the Rogers side. It may be that concerns about his business methods and activities (and those of Standard Oil) have resulted in the destruction of much original material—evidently many of his "private business papers...were destroyed in the 1930's."[35] And if any of his papers do still exist, it is likely that they are largely inaccessible to scholars, in family hands.

But we are fortunate in having access to so many of the letters written by and to Clemens. Without such an invaluable set of resources, this book could not have been written.[36] The Clemens-Howells and the Clemens-Rogers letters are published.[37] The Clemens-Twichell letters are accessible in research libraries, but are as yet largely unpublished, though some of Clemens's part in the correspondence appears in other collections of his letters.[38] Information about these friendships is also scattered through the many biographies and encyclopedias devoted to Clemens and his work. Specific aspects of the relationships are also examined in specialist studies. So (for instance) the connection between Twichell and Clemens and the nature of their religious beliefs are explored in Harold K. Bush Jr.'s *Mark Twain and the Spiritual Crisis of His Age* (2007); Richard Lowry discusses Howells and Clemens and their parts in the professionalization of literature in the period in *"Littery Man": Mark Twain and Modern Authorship* (1996); while Rogers and Clemens's business links are examined in Peter Krass's *Ignorance, Confidence, and Filthy Rich Friends* (2007).[39] My references here are selective but suggest the types of material I have found useful in completing my own work.

This book has a number of intentions and is anchored in three main areas. In the first chapter, I focus on the general issue of male friendship. One core concern throughout the book will be to identify what made this particular set of friendships so important and enduring. As I begin, I explore the sociohistorical and ideological contexts that form the necessary ground for these friendships and introduce one of my main arguments concerning the framework of privilege and cultural power in which they need to be located. I also indicate something of changing paradigms of male friendship in the period (and of the marriages against which they must be measured), and the altered nature—and diminishment—of male intimacy that results. Other questions concerning the various orders and functions of male friendship, its emotional and psychological constituents, and the way it might relate to an increasing anxiety about male roles and status at the time, and especially in the American business world, will be considered as I continue. But the subject of male friendship in this period remains—despite the amount of work on masculinity as a whole—underexplored. I see this book then, to at least some degree, as exploratory and hope that it will encourage others to fill in many of the gaps I leave and to examine this whole subject more fully from other and related angles.

I follow my first chapter, which provides most of the theoretical base for the book, with a close examination of the three named friendships. In part, this work is biographical, comprising a study of the development of each friendship and its salient features. I use Clemens as my central pivot since he is the common factor in all three friendships, and the figure whose career and reputation is best known to a contemporary audience. But alongside this biographical focus, I also explore the larger cultural dynamic that helps to explain many of the determining features of each friendship, and its type and importance. A distinctive element of my project lies in the fact that these particular friendships bridge the space between the private and the public in fascinating ways. The roles of Clemens himself as popular author, celebrity, and (finally) national icon, of Twichell as Civil War veteran and Congregationalist minister and minor public figure, of Howells as literary editor and critic, writer and cultural commentator, and of Rogers as corporate executive, are themselves deeply suggestive in terms of any consideration of the overall cultural landscape of the period, and of the types of dialog taking place against that background.

These four men, then, variously represented key areas of cultural prestige of their time (religion, literature, and business). Their interactions at a private level accordingly connect to their roles and influence on a public stage. I consequently pair my overview of each relationship with a particular "case study," focusing on the way in which the personal dynamics of the friendship spill out into the larger public world. As I do so, I look to reveal something of the cultural tensions and changing social patterns and hierarchies of the time.[40] I vary this balance between the personal and biographical and the larger sociohistorical whole as it best suits my purpose. In terms of Clemens and Twichell's relationship, my case study focuses on religion. In Howells's case, it is his realist agenda that particularly interests me—one tied to his belief in social consensus, and the role of the writer as cultural guide and advocate of that consensus through what Alan Trachtenberg has described as "the authority and legitimacy of serious fiction as a serious enterprise."[41] I consider to what extent Clemens shared this vision and discuss (as part of my larger analysis) the way in which both writers looked to adapt to the new conditions of the market place, and take their place as professional writers within it. In the case of Clemens and Rogers's relationship, I focus on Clemens's own career in business (for he was a publisher as well as a writer) and on his failure during a period of severe economic depression. In describing how he hitched his financial destiny to Rogers, I explore something of the relations between literature, business, and the representation of masculinity at the time.[42] Throughout this book, I introduce and comment on Clemens's literary work where it is relevant to my larger argument.

I intend, then, that the detailed study and analysis of the particular friendships on which I focus, and the larger cultural contexts in which I position them, will further our knowledge of the individual relationships between these men, and their dynamics. But I also look thereby to add to our understanding of the nature of cultural change in this period of rapid modernization—as religion and literature (of so much cultural importance in mid-century America) looked to compete with, and accommodate themselves to, the rise of capitalist and business values in an incorporated America.

The final section of this book serves as a coda and may seem at first glance strange, given my main subject of male friendship. Here I explore these men's emotional lives in a rather different context—that of mourning, a form of behavior rooted in the private and domestic realm but with a larger cultural resonance. Three of these men (Rogers, Howells, and Clemens) had daughters who died young, and both Howells and Clemens—of whose reactions we know the most—were devastated by their losses. If much has been written on sentimentality in the period, there is still little written on the masculine expression of feeling as it relates to ways of coping with death. My aim here is both to fill something of this gap, but also to suggest that the grief of these men, and the form it took, serves as an implicit comment on the changing status of male friendship at the time. For they reflect a shift away both from sentimentalism and the same-sex intimacy that was one of its manifestations and toward, on the one hand, an increasing emphasis on private and more self-contained expressions of emotion, and on the other, the increasing importance of marriage and the nuclear family in men's lives at this time.

Overall, this particular combination of friendships—and the difference in status and value system associated with each man represented here—might seem an unlikely combination. But it is this very fact that makes the friendships so interesting. Their study will add, I hope, not just to our knowledge of the men themselves but to a wider understanding of American culture in this important period—and of at least some of the understandings, tensions, and compromises of which it was composed.

# 1

## Male Friendship and Post-Civil War America

On April 3, 1909, just a month and half before his death, Henry H. Rogers—accompanied by Samuel Clemens—went to Norfolk, Virginia, for the banquet to celebrate the opening of the Virginian Railway. This line, some four-hundred-and-fifty-miles long, had been built to carry high-quality bituminous coal from the mining areas of southwestern Virginia to port facilities in Hampton Roads (near Norfolk). It was, almost unbelievably, a project planned and realized by just two men—Rogers himself, in conjunction with civil engineer and coal-mining manager William Nelson Page. All the costs came from Rogers's private pocket or from capital that he personally had raised. Clemens's admiration for his friend was clear in the letter written to him on December 19, 1908: "You have carried that giant enterprise through as patiently and quietly and unostentatiously as a geologic period overlays a continent with a new crust—well, it's just great! That majestic achievement is the triumph of your life, and will be and remain your eulogy and your monument in the far by-and-bye."[1] Clemens's words here are a tribute from a man who made books to one who (in this case) made railroads. In comparing Rogers's handling of this large-scale industrial venture to some inevitable natural force, he conjures up both the romance of American business and the sense of "masculine" practicality, steadfastness, and potency to which it is linked.

I am, though, more interested in the speech Clemens made at the Norfolk banquet where he paid tribute to Rogers's "generous heart." Referring to the color of his friend's moustache and hair, he continued: "These are only emblematic of his character, and that is all. I say without exception, hair and all, he is the whitest man I have ever known."[2] Clemens's metaphoric play allows him to praise the quality of Rogers's character. But the last phrase also inevitably focuses attention on the status of their friendship—that of two white men, both of considerable prestige and influence in their contemporary American world. We must not forget, in other words, that the Clemens-Rogers friendship (together with the other friendships I explore in this book) belonged within a larger context of privilege and power. This was the case, despite the differences in professional and social circumstance, of all four men on whom I focus.

Much has been much written recently on masculinity in America in the nineteenth century and, as part of this, on changing attitudes to homosocial—and homosexual—relationships in the period. Much, too, has been written on the wider subject of gender roles, and the (often suspect) categorizations and divisions associated with them. My intention is pragmatic. I do not survey the whole field, a book-length task in itself. Instead, I keep in mind my main subject, the three male friendships under analysis, to use the work done on masculinity and gender roles in the period as it helps to contextualize and situate these relationships.[3] This necessarily means setting male sociality within a broader gender background, since (as Eve Kosofsy Sedgwick reminds us) "no element of [the] pattern" of the developing history of male friendship "can be understood outside of its relation to women and the gender system as a whole."[4] The particular topic of male friendship itself in this period (my book covers the years from 1868–1910) still remains surprisingly underexplored. This study, then, is something of a work-in-progress, a—sometimes tentative—starting point for further work.

Kosofsky Sedgwick reminds us that male friendship must be positioned within a larger gender frame of reference.[5] But gender is not the only issue at stake here. What appears at first glance to be something very private (the intimate connections between a few men) cannot be divorced from the public realm—the larger shape and development of American culture and society in the period. As Sarah Cole writes in her study of male friendship and British literature in the late Victorian period through to the First World War:

> Perhaps the biggest mistake one can make in conceptualizing friendship . . . is to assume that it is a private, voluntary relation, governed by personal sentiment and easy communion. It is not. Like any complex social relationship, friendship has its own conventions and institutional affinities (schools, universities, social clubs, as well as more rigidly arranged organizations from the Boy Scouts to the military platoon), and it is shot through with social meanings. The anodyne image of an uncomplicated relation—essentially outside of culture—should clearly be rejected. Like the family, against which it is often set as an alternative, friendship will be constructed in such a way as to reflect a culture's positions on sexuality, gender, hierarchy and power.[6]

As I proceed in this book, I look to explore some of these larger cultural meanings—in an American context and as they apply to Clemens's friendships. The professions of the four men about whom I write necessarily means that particular attention will be paid to the contexts of religion, literature, and business respectively.

The fact that Clemens, Twichell, Howells, and Rogers were all (white) men of considerable status in the (connected) social and professional communities to which they immediately belonged is crucial to a consideration of their friendships. In her important book on *National Manhood* (1998), Dana Nelson explores the relationship between whiteness and maleness in American history, showing how the two together came to act as guarantor of a larger shared "civic identity" or "national unity."[7] This unity depended on the concept of shared interests and symbiotically identified "white male exceptionality" and "white fraternity" with the larger interests of the nation itself.[8] Such an emphasis on a "national manhood" defined in these terms—according to the needs of a hegemonic white male community—came "at significant human cost" to this national manhood's "others—the white women, Indians, blacks, primitives, poor, foreigners, and savages through which white manhood defines and supplements itself."[9] As Nelson astutely also shows, though, this emphasis on the stake shared by white men in the larger civic whole masked a whole series of "uneven power relations" between these same men, in terms of class, economics, and professional interests.[10] This resulted in a crippling contradiction between the notion of "(equalizing) friendship" and divisive and "(hierarchizing) competition."[11]

Nelson's study covers ambitious and wide-ranging ground, while I write about just four men. But the sense of hierarchy and competition of which she speaks can still be identified here, if in much more limited form than in such larger groupings. Sarah Cole sees male friendship as inseparable from larger cultural questions of "sexuality, gender, hierarchy and power." The final two terms cover a lot of social ground, taking in such other categories as occupation, class, region and—especially significant in an American context—ethnicity and race. If the focus in this book is limited, it cannot be divorced from such larger informing backgrounds. Questions of hierarchy and of relative cultural authority are highly relevant to these three friendships though, in these cases, they tended not to have a disfiguring effect. This is because these men *all* held positions of privilege within the larger American community. Their professional and economic differences were, accordingly, less important than the values, opinions, and interests they held in common.[12] Indeed, their friendships and general sense of "easy communion" depended on a shared perception of social equality. Seemingly "uncomplicated" male relations are in fact riddled by determining factors of tradition, money, race, class, politics, religion and the like. (The fact that Rogers was *not* close friends with Howells, though he was with Clemens, may speak just of chance and opportunity, or of an unease on Howells's part—which Clemens did not feel—as the crossover between the worlds of business and of literature, and of different sets of political and social beliefs, took place.)

It may be instructive here to turn briefly to the subject of race, and to the effect—if friendship is "shot through with social meanings"—that racial difference had on intimate relationships in this male circle. I here step outside my immediate frame (the three main friendships of this book) to discuss the links between Clemens, Howells, Rogers, and Booker T. Washington, the conservative African American leader who, in the eyes of white America, was the main spokesperson for his race in these years.[13] The four main subjects of my study all had, or came to have, liberal credentials on racial issues.[14] Clemens personally helped fund one of Yale Law School's first African American students, explaining his actions with the words: "We have ground the manhood out of them [the African American], & the shame is ours, not theirs, & we should pay for it."[15] Little is known about his relationship with Booker T. Washington, but Washington did go several times to Clemens's New York City home and was a guest at the dinner held for Clemens by the Lotos Club (a literary and social club) on November 10, 1901.[16] Clemens also co-chaired the January 22, 1906, Tuskegee Silver Jubilee fundraiser at Carnegie Hall.[17] Howells, organizer of Clemens's 1910 memorial service, planned to have Washington as a speaker, to represent "a race which Clemens meant well by."[18] And he, too, appeared on the platform at a meeting Washington held for the benefit of his Tuskegee Institute endowment fund, at the concert hall of Madison Square Garden on December 4, 1899.[19]

It was Rogers, however, who had the strongest links with Washington. Washington wrote about Rogers shortly after his death, in the May 29, 1909, New York *Evening Post*. Describing him as "one of the best and greatest men I have ever met," he illustrated his generosity to the African American cause in the ten one-thousand-dollar bills Rogers had handed him for the Tuskegee Institute at their first meeting, and in his financial aid to a series of other industrial and small rural schools in the South.[20] At their last meeting, Rogers arranged for Washington to take a trip on the new Virginian Railroad, "for the purpose of studying the conditions of the colored people along the routes," and thus "devising some means by which he might assist them in their education and in the development of their agricultural life." Rogers's anti-racism spoke in other actions too. He invited Washington to travel on board his yacht, the *Kanawha*, at a time when such forms of interracial socializing were exceptional. He also employed "three or four bright young colored men who served as messengers" in his office.[21] (If these were menial roles, they nonetheless suggest Rogers's racial commitment.)

The concern for African American advancement by this small group of white men was unusual given the general racial attitudes of their time, and at first glance may seem to cut against Nelson's thesis. However, men of their color, social class, and region, and with their type of cultural authority, could well afford such a concern (given their own position in such hierarchies was guaranteed). And we remain aware that their relationships with Washington were necessarily marginalized by the fact of race, belonged to one side of other friendships with fellow and well-connected white men, and could not finally be divorced from wider, and slow-changing, structures of political and cultural power.[22] The conservative nature of

Washington's own racial politics also meant that no immediate challenge to the dominant white ruling class in America, or to the way that the economy and the social system was (racially) structured, was at stake in these men's support of his gradualist agenda.

All three men's relationship with Washington depended, moreover, on his exceptional status as an African American leader. Without that, it is extremely unlikely that such interracial fraternization would have occurred. We cannot know what exchanges took place as Washington met Clemens and his fellow Lotos Club members, but we can assume that differences in upbringing, background, cultural knowledge, and—most especially—in racial experience, put certain restraints on the type of relaxed social intercourse that might otherwise have occurred in all-white male company and among those of similar interests and social class. The larger history of American race relations inevitably formed the context for such occasions, together with the privilege accorded to "white male mutuality" in such a late-nineteenth-century historical space.[23]

On Rogers's death, Washington wrote that "I knew...[him] during that last fifteen years as well as I could know anyone."[24] But, if Washington depicts the relationship as an intimate one, his papers give little hint of any interaction that did not bear on the matter of African American progress, the political agenda that formed the backdrop to—and, one might suggest, the reason for—the friendship. This is not to deny that Rogers's friendship with Washington (or Howells's and Clemens's) had further dimensions or that the possibility of close interracial intimacy between men in the period did not exist. It is however to insist that the "institutional affinities" and "social meanings" of friendship at this time would inevitably be affected in significant ways by the fact of racial difference.[25]

We might approach this in quite another way to say that there are various types and intensities of male (and female) friendship possible and various arenas in which they work. Different orders of friendship exist, and any one friend is likely to fulfill different functions than another: something that would seem particularly true in Clemens's case. Friendships serve as a measure against which to check one's own ideas, to confirm (or to change) one's prejudices, and to reflect one's own particular interests and passions. Friendships can complement one's weaknesses, act as an ideological, psychological, or emotional support structure, and confirm one's sense of identity in a fast-changing and unpredictable world: for intimacy, Lauren Berlant writes, is—in part—"formed around threats to the image of the world it seeks to sustain."[26] Friendships can be based on nostalgia, an attitude toward or shared experiences in the past, and on new interests and challenges in the present. Friends, too, complement and compete with conventional family structures, offering emotional outlets and channels for expressive individualism, either in one-to-one relations or wider social groupings, which differ from a heterosexual domestic intimacy and other forms of family relationships.[27]

Friendships can then work in different ways and with different limits. Certainly though (and this harks back to Nelson), a man's position within his local and national community, and his status as it relates to larger forms of social organization and the value systems there encoded, necessarily affect the type, quality, and depth of his friendships. Friendship exists on a number of scales, all—to return to Cole's words—"shot through with social meanings." This is not to deny that friendships, sometimes very close ones, can be made between those whose backgrounds and social status are dissimilar. Such friendships can work for good reasons, from (for instance) shared ideological conviction or an emotional or intellectual attraction. But all friendships take place "inside culture" and are necessarily affected by their larger institutional and social context.

It does seem true that, in the case of Clemens and his closest friends, the links between them—in terms of social connections, ideological assumptions, domestic and professional backgrounds, and range of interests—were a crucial factor determining the strength and duration of the relationships. Again, I am reminded of Cole's comment: "What friendship appears to offer is a kind of infrastructure—practices, conventions, a language, a history—that imbues the often shaky relation between man and man with the sanctity of larger, more powerful and sustainable institutions."[28] The race, prestige, social position, and cultural authority of the four protagonists of this study are, then, a vital factor in analyzing the depth and nature of their intimacy.[29] I return to this crucial understanding in the final section of this chapter.

## II

Male intimacy and friendship cannot, however, just be seen in terms of a larger civic identity. It must also be measured against a gender background. E. Anthony Rotundo defines manhood as a "cultural invention," writing that "each culture constructs its own version of what men and women are—and ought to be." Friendships between men, then, must automatically position themselves within such gender conventions and expectations.[30] I here trace through some of the implications of this sense of relational difference, first in terms of the changing conception of male-to-male relationships emerging during the period, and then by placing male friendships of the time in the context of heterosexual intimacy.

Gender theorists, since Kosofsky Sedgwick's seminal work, have given considerable attention to male friendship and the relationship between the homosocial and the homosexual. The former can be defined as "the entire range of same-sex bonds," the latter as that "part of the homosocial continuum marked by genital sexuality."[31] This may at first glance seem to have little bearing on Clemens's—and/or his friends'—relationships. But I spend time on this subject because of the relevance such a connection, and distinction, has to changing patterns of male friendship within the period and to our ways of understanding them. It also, however, does in fact have some immediate bearing on the expressive nature of the men on whom I focus, and on the friendships I explore.

It is generally accepted that styles of male friendship in America changed as the nineteenth century progressed. In his valuable study of male friendship and literature in America in the eighteenth and early nineteenth centuries, Caleb Crain focuses on the importance of "sympathy" at that time, both as "a political as well as a psychological principle," and the form it took in an American context. "At the height of sympathy's reign," he writes, "American men could express emotions to each other with a fervor and openness that . . . would have to be consigned to sexual perversion a few generations later." It seems, though, that the cultural acceptance of such openness and tenderness, in most cases, stopped short of overt sexual expression, at least by the early nineteenth century. For—in contrast to a "Platonic" and selfless love of man for man—"actual . . . homosexuality was taboo in Victorian America."[32]

Such a taboo, though, took a very different form than it came to have toward the end of the century (and certainly by the mid-1880s and 1890s). Before that time, the line between homosocial and homosexual behavior was not so clearly marked, and "fond male friendship[s] [which] . . . from time to time . . . blossomed into something more intimate and intense" were, as Rotundo tells us, "common."[33] Bayard Taylor—the popular travel writer who also briefly served as a U.S. minister in Germany (and who was a friend of Clemens)—stood at the extreme end of this spectrum. He openly celebrated "'the other love' in mid-century America," feeling "no need to suppress the evidence of his intense male friendships and their physical expression in kisses and embraces." His friendships were, according to Robert K. Martin, still then seen as "part of the permissible discourse of the time"—presumably because of a certain blurring of the line between platonic and sexually active male friendship.[34] When homosexuality did occur, it was not seen—as it would be later—"as an individualized form of subjectivity" clearly contrary to (a normative) heterosexuality and marked off from it by means of "the electrified barrier of homophobia."[35] Rather it was seen as "something a variety of types might do as an aberration or under particular circumstances."[36] By the end of the century, however, and especially following the Labouchère Amendment, the Cleveland Street scandal (when, in 1889, the police raided a male brothel in London and found it to be patronized by members of the British aristocracy), and the Oscar Wilde trial in 1895, "the homosexual" became "increasingly recognised as a type of person with particular class and aesthetic affiliations," and became, too, subject to (virulent) homophobia.[37]

What has all this to do with the male friendships I examine? I would suggest that what we see here are friendships that—by the 1870s and 1880s—had largely moved away from the intimacy and intensity of the sentimental model. Such a move had partly to do with changing conceptions of manliness. Yacovone speaks of the "rejection of sentimentalized, genteel values" in Gilded Age America in favor of "the aggressive cult of masculinity."[38] This, in turn, relates to new workplace relationships that altered the structural conditions of male friendship not just in that environment but also at a wider and more general level.[39] Such changes, though, also had much to do with shifts in the parameters of the marriages that partly framed these friendships, and the expression of emotion and intimacy within such boundaries. The final sections of this chapter explore some of these developments in the contexts of male friendship in more detail. It is enough for now, however, to know that Clemens's friendships differed significantly in kind from the romantic "Soul...unto Soul" relationships of an earlier period.[40] Rather, they seem closer in kind to the patterns of present-day male friendship identified by Drury Sherrod—based more on companionship and commitment than on intimacy and disclosure.[41]

There is, nonetheless, evidence that three of these men were affected by, or aware of, a more fluid sense of gender roles that harked back to an earlier period and extended further along the homosocial continuum than would have been common by the century's end. This is expressed, however, (for the most part) outside the framework of the immediate sets of friendships traced in this book. Twichell, when still just twenty-two, signed up as a chaplain in the Civil War. During his army years, he quickly developed from a well-intentioned if narrow-minded young minister into an impressive and generous-spirited maturity. There is little that is unusual in his letters of the time in terms of the representation of his strong sense of comradeship and fellow-feeling with the officers and enlisted men who served alongside him. Occasionally, however, he describes feelings of emotional connection with, and intense affection for, young soldiers. His contemporaries would have judged these—according to the standards I have described above—entirely "normal," but (with our different sexual regime) they would now be associated with a homoerotic rhetoric of desire.

Thus Twichell writes to his father of his response to the death of one nineteen-year-old "fine looking young man": "I turned down the blanket from the face...and a throb moved by no stranger's heart swelled full and true to thy sweet memory Oh! My Friend...I feel a sob choking me as I write now, for I tell you, Father, this boy had a strange hold on me.... [T]he last time I saw him, when he could not talk much, he looked unutterable things as I stood and stroked the brown hair off his forehead." Similarly, he holds the head of a seventeen year old boy—"a handsome, black-eyed lad, full of fortitude" who has been shot in the leg—"in my lap and helped him grin and bear it" as his wounds are dressed. When the boy must be left behind at a field hospital during a retreat, Twichell reports: "I gave the little hero...a kiss of true love." And, after Gettysburg, he helps with the Confederate wounded, reporting: "There was one, a sweet handsome boy with beautiful deep eyes, with whom I fell in love.... One night I went to him, and was so touched by his nobleness that I stooped down and kissed him. The poor little fellow burst out crying."[42] The language of Twichell's Christian fraternal love is imbued here with the intense affection and emotional expressiveness that Crain associates with the antebellum world, with the sentimental and with "sympathy's reign." As such it would have caused no surprise to the father and stepmother to whom the letters were addressed.[43]

Similar forms of affection, on Twichell's part, spill over at times into the Clemens friendship. Here, his discourse can sometimes register quite another emotional key than that of his more restrained friend. Part of his June 8, 1878, letter—following Clemens's invitation to join him in Europe on the *Tramp Abroad* trip—reads: "I am to have my fill, or a big feed anyway, of *your company*—and under such circumstances! To walk with you, and talk with you, and sleep with you, and say my prayers with you, and see things with you, for weeks together,—why it's my dream of luxury. I can't tell you how it 'rises the cockles of my heart' to think of it. The fact is, Mark, I'm in love with you—but what's the use? I shall grow soft if I go on."[44] The reference to "growing soft" here constitutes Twichell's recognition of a certain "feminine" element in his sentimental outpouring (as opposed to a stiff "masculine" emotional reticence).[45] Clemens's own September 9 letter to Twichell, following the latter's departure from Europe for home, fully acknowledges the importance of their friendship. But his sentimental effusions are more muted, and quickly transposed from his person alone to the married couple of which he is a part:

Dear Old Joe—
    It is actually all over! I was so low-spirited at the station yesterday— & this morning when I woke, I couldn't seem to accept the dismal truth that you were really gone, & the pleasant tramping & talking at an end.

Clemens then talks of their sharing "a companionship which to me stands first after Livy's," before concluding: "Livy can't accept or endure the fact that you are gone. But you are—& we cannot get round it. So take our love with you—& bear it also over sea to Harmony [Joe's wife]—& God bless you both. Mark."[46]

Later letters from Twichell to Clemens are also characterized by the clergyman's use of an effusive romantic discourse. So, on August 26, 1881, a letter from his vacation in Keene Valley, New York, reads: "Dear old fellow, how I do love you and wish and wish and wish all manner of good to you." And on May 10, 1882, presumably responding to news of Clemens's (April to May) river trip gathering material for *Life on the Mississippi* (1883), he writes:

I have been suffering these three weeks past, hearing of your delights on the River, pangs closely, I fear, resembling those of jealousy. Your junketing with other fellows is to me, by turns, sweet . . . as those kisses Tennyson speaks of
    "By hopeless fancy feigned
    "Oh lips that are for others.
Well, my boy, may I never love you less, and I don't think I ever shall. . . .
Yours ever aff. Joe.[47]

Howells's correspondence with Clemens is less emotionally fulsome. But as John Crowley, in particular, has shown, the nature of some of his other same-sex friendships offers evidence of a man whose sexual and gender identity may have been less certain and more fluid than has generally been assumed.[48] Crowley describes the anxieties that shadowed Howells's expressions of masculinity in his younger years, and which spilled over into his literary life. So, his early literary passions "were expressed in fantasies of spellbound submission to a powerful [male] seducer." This "rhetoric of desire," however, coexisted "with a rhetoric of disgust, expressed in vividly excremental imagery," and directed (in Howells's own words) at "'bad' literature" and the "smear[ing]" effect it had on its reader.[49] This pattern of desire and disgust is repeated in the way Howells's own intense homosocial boyhood friendships—he would later acknowledge "the likelihood of *youthful* homoerotic attachments"—were countered by his repulsion concerning "the idea of same-sex genitality."[50]

Crowley's main interest, however, is in Howell's adult friendship with the poet and travel and memoir writer, Charles Warren Stoddard.[51] Stoddard was undoubtedly homosexual but the description, "undecided men," that Howells used to describe men of his type again speaks of a certain "cognitive vacuum" for middle-class Victorians as far as sexuality at "the erotic end of the homosocial spectrum" went. Crowley goes on to argue that such a sexual/gender identity was linked "not with viciousness or violence, but with childishness, as an infantile need, a mark of powerlessness . . . unlikely to provoke the virulent, accusatory projection that characterizes twentieth-century homophobia."[52] Indeed, this is how both Howells and Clemens tended to see Stoddard.[53]

Crowley charts the details of the Howells-Stoddard relationship to indicate that "there was a subtly erotic factor in their homosocial attachment." But he also shows how reticent Howells became at the point that Stoddard seemed about to cross "limits of candor" about his homosexuality. Howells's feelings, then, are again described in terms of that ambivalence earlier noted—a mixture of "wistful envy and compensatory contempt."[54] And he would later turn against Stoddard—once (Crowley claims) the latter had upset the terms of a relationship built (for Howells) on his own assumed "parental authority" over his friend's "infantile helplessness."[55]

In both Twichell's and Howells's cases, then, we see clear symptoms of a more fluid conception of homosociality than we might perhaps expect. Such signs, though, are repressed—or in Twichell's case, diluted—in favor of "the master narrative of conventional manliness."[56] Such a move coincided with altered conceptions of male friendship in postbellum America as a whole, and the increasing and inevitable acceptance (given the larger sociohistorical changes that were taking place) that such friendships be more "contained," both in the literal sense of day-to-day contact and in their emotional scope.

Clemens, too, fits something of the paradigm identified above. His case, however, is a more complicated one, and his acceptance of any type of fluid sexual/gender relations more limited. In "Rewriting the Gold Rush: Twain, Harte and Homosociality," Peter Stoneley focuses (in part) on the time Clemens spent in "gold rush" country early in his career and identifies a deep ambivalence in Clemens's representations of same-sex friendship, and indeed in his own gender performance. Stoneley examines written representations of the gold rush alongside biographical detail, and identifies a type of "fault-line" story, addressing "unresolved [gender] issues," common to the frontier mining setting. So humorist Dan De Quille, for instance, writing about his homemaking partnership with Clemens, adopts "the persona of a disappointed young wife" in his San Francisco *Golden Era* sketch, "No Head Nor Tail." Stoneley sees no evidence of homosexuality here, but rather a comic and "provocative image of inappropriate coupling." As—within the sketch—the idea of a partnership and of manly love collides with that of marriage, the hinge connecting (and separating) intense close male friendship and same-sex physical love is accordingly put in doubt.[57] Stories like this, Stoneley suggests, occur inevitably in a place and time where—in predominantly male communities—sexuality, gender role, and performance were often played out in unusual and disturbing ways.[58]

But Clemens, in his own self-representations, stepped well back from such fault-lines. Aware of the pull of affectionate and close male-to-male friendships, he nonetheless "emphasizes and re-emphasizes the distinct nature of manly relationship"—"the supposedly figurative love between men [rather than] the supposedly actual love between a man and a woman"—"compulsively remarking the borderline where it was closest to being effaced."[59] Thus when close homosocial intimacy is described, it is always to take a backward step from it. In *Roughing It* (1872), he depicts a form of utopian existence when (author and narrator) "Mark Twain" spends time at Lake Tahoe alone with a male companion. But he then brings the episode to an abrupt close with the destructive fire accidentally released.

Similarly, Clemens "does seem to use the gold rush to enter into the homoerotic celebration of manliness"—writing of "stalwart, muscular, dauntless young braves...erect, bright-eyed, quick-moving, strong-handed young giants...nothing feminine visible anywhere." He then, though, undercuts this impression by emphasizing the wasteful and destructive aspects of these men, their "avaricious" spoilation of the environment and their drunken and aggressive behavior.[60] Stoneley accordingly argues that the book "idealizes male-male partnership"—and one close to a type of marital intimacy—"in the allegorical recognition of its impossibility."[61] If Clemens, then, is attracted to forms of homosocial intimacy, he nonetheless "seems to want to modify and police the latitude of expression" (concerning the wider possibilities of male-male roles and relationships) to be found in others who wrote about this same gold-rush world.[62]

Stoneley builds his argument around an account of the Bret Harte-Clemens friendship and its vitriolic (on Clemens's part) collapse. He details the "partnership" they shared, working together and—even when they did not—sharing the same gold-rush material. And he explores the questions of "authority and gender" that emerge in this relationship, showing how, later in the century and after the Wilde case, Clemens represents Harte in his autobiographical writings by means of a discourse of homosexuality previously unavailable to him.[63] Stoneley suggests that Clemens, in so doing, sets up a contrast that "stresses his own Western, manly authenticity," and is thus able to "jettison his own former partner once and for all."[64] Describing Harte's "dainty self-complacencies," his "mincing" walk, dazzling neckties like "those splendid and luminous Brazilian butterflies" (and so on), Clemens stereotypes Harte in forms of self-expression that were—at that later point in time—seen as dangerously corrupt. In the process, he helped to contribute to that closing down of the more open and flexible model of same-sex relations previously available.[65]

Stoneley is astute, though, in pointing out the instability that marks Clemens's "statement of [hetero/homosexual] difference." He reminds us of the way Clemens himself played the dandy: with his sealskin hat and coat, when he first came back east from California; the white suits he wore compulsively in his later years and which matched "his obsessively washed aureole of white hair"; and the Oxford gown, set off in bright scarlet, that made him the center of attention whenever he wore it, even (and inappropriately) at his daughter Clara's wedding.[66] Despite such habits, Clemens's own heterosexual status remained unthreatened by such forms of display. As Stoneley comments, "he was able to manipulate the boundaries of convention in such a way that his deviancy would advertize his authority, not undermine it."[67] Clemens's attacks on Harte become, then, one way of confirming a masculine identity of his own that might otherwise be open to certain question.

My larger point here, though, is to identify the instability of the borderline between different kinds of sexual identity and gender performance at this time and the anxieties that could accompany it. All three of the men on whom I have focused (I omit Rogers for lack of information) show some attraction to the types of intimate and intense emotional and/or homoerotic impulses within same-sex friendship that are gradually waning during the period (and are radically redefined nearer the century's end). Clemens, however, would retreat early in his career from any representation of himself and of male friendship that strayed far from heterosexual norms. Similarly, if Twichell as a young man freely admitted the intensity of his feelings for handsome boy-soldiers, such an extreme of homosocial emotion was undoubtedly more contained in the different social contexts of his later life. He continued to use the language of intense male intimacy in correspondence, but his language was not accompanied (for any evidence we have) by equivalent forms of physical expression. In Howells, we see evidence of a capacity to experience male friendships of some emotional intensity and of a homoerotic nature. But, in adult life, it seems he was only prompted into such feelings in a relationship where the friend's "effeminized" status was obvious and his own male authority consequently went uncompromised—and where he could quickly step backward once any line that he considered inappropriate had been crossed.[68]

What we see overall, then, is something of a pattern. The possibilities and boundaries of male friendships narrow, and the intimacies and intensities common in eighteenth- and early-nineteenth-century male-male relationships are generally replaced (though not in every case) by more restrained forms of friendship. This change took on a particular charge toward the century's end, as homosexual relationships were redefined and re-evaluated (homophobically). The three sets of friendships I examine must be seen against this background. But they must also be seen in terms of a general change in patterns of heterosexual relationships and, most importantly, within the context of marriage.

## III

It is generally accepted that the impact of modernization (industrialization, urbanization, the emergence of a capitalist society) in the second half of the nineteenth-century—and especially, in America following the Civil War—had an inevitable and considerable impact upon gender relationships of all kinds. In a later chapter (on Clemens and Rogers) I explore some of the anxieties that came accordingly to affect the concept and construction of masculinity. The Rogers friendship, and the fictional narrative that seems indirectly to reflect on it, offers—for my larger narrative—the clearest expression of Clemens's identity within a business context and the way in which male friendship defined itself against that background.[69] In the final section of this present chapter, I give an initial, and rather different (though complementary), analysis of male friendship in the context of the working conditions of the time. I also give some attention in the later Clemens and Rogers chapter to the changing nature of the family life—and of heterosexual relationships—of the period, but here provide a fuller introduction to this subject. Such backgrounds provide the formative conditions for the three particular sets of friendship I explore.

In writing about Theodore Roosevelt's marriage, Peter Filene comments that:

> If the secret of men's marriages has all too often been adultery, the no-less-frequent secret has been dependency. . . . [T]his emphatic reliance on a woman . . . was the other side of manly independence, the emotional counterweight to the lonely demands of success. Out there in the world, the "true man" sought to be self-reliant, hardworking and brave, proving his worth through what Roosevelt called the "strenuous life." Against such odds, it is no wonder that a man—not only the one who was losing but equally the one who was winning—needed a home as a haven and a wife as comforter of his fears, tears, and other soft feelings. He depended on his other half to make him whole.[70]

There are a number of qualifications I would make to this statement, both as a general principle and in the cases of the particular men on whom I focus. First, on the general level, the outer world of manly success is not without its "soft" side.[71] Similarly, the home cannot be separated out from this public world as quite the "haven" here suggested.

This is not to say that Victorian men did not construct the meaning of "home" in such a way, for undoubtedly they did. So Susan K. Harris suggests that in nineteenth-century America, "a society panicked by the apparent dissolution of controls and boundaries of all kinds," the "family became a cultural symbol, an icon of order in a disorderly world."[72] The domestic sphere, though, also served as an inevitable mirror of the larger public world, in the values promulgated within its supposed confines. So T. Jackson Lears describes the home as the place where children were prepared for the larger competitive society they were soon to enter.[73] Sarah Cole makes a similar point but in a broadscale and telling way. She is writing about nineteenth-century British culture, but her words equally apply to the American context: "Certainly, private and public became central ordering tropes in nineteenth-century Britain, helping to configure the worlds according to a basic gendered division.... Yet, just as certainly, these were not monolithic spheres (male/female, public/private, world/home), nor was power located in an uncomplicated and totalizing way in one arena or the other."[74]

In the particular case of three of the men whose lives I (in part) explore, the notion of living "out there in the world" must be additionally qualified. Clemens and Howells were both businessmen, but the heart of their professional lives was in the books that they wrote. Consequently, in their cases, the worlds of work and of domesticity necessarily interleaved, with the majority of their writing taking place in home space or (sometimes) just on its margins. This was similarly true for Twichell, whose ministerial responsibilities were often conducted from a home base. This sharing of physical space—and the amount of time spent in it—undoubtedly had an effect on these men's marital roles and family relationships. Most other men of the time lived their lives under rather different conditions.

The day-to-day activities of these three men were, then, often strongly bound to their domestic base. Undoubtedly, and consequently, their dependence on the presence and support of their wives and families was more intense than may have been the case for those, like Rogers, who led more conventional business lives. But whatever the trajectory of the particular life, gender roles generally—always structured in dynamic relationship to the larger social whole—were subject to considerable adjustment in the period.

Marriage itself and the expectations that went with it were changing. Mary P. Ryan (in her case study of Oneida County, New York) describes a withdrawal—even before the Civil War—into "the private conjugal family as a way of mobilizing private resources for upward social mobility,"[75] while Margaret Marsh sees new models of "masculine domesticity" emerging after the Civil War, within "an ideal of marriage that emphasized companionship instead of either patriarchal rule or the ideology of domesticity."[76] Women, in this period, were increasingly self-conscious concerning the "significant roles" they had "to play in the shaping of society." So correspondingly "men began to enter the sphere assigned to women," playing a fuller part in the running of the household, in marriages that functioned on a more egalitarian basis.[77] In such marriages "the burdens of patriarchal authority and work-induced separation from family life" were (in theory) traded by the husband "for emotional closeness to their wives and the pleasures of spending time with their children as companions."[78]

Marsh is discussing the period leading right up to the First World War here. And at one point she refers to male leisure patterns organized around, or close to, the home as a contrast to those of "the great age of male fraternal orders"—a time she sees lasting to the nineteenth century's end.[79] The social world of which she speaks is also a specific one: middle class and suburban. There are, moreover, other versions of what marriage was like at the time, indicating a more ambivalent male response to its domestic world. Rotundo writes of the appeal of the men's clubs that Marsh mentions, seeing them as providing the "domestic advantages without the confining responsibility of home and hearth." He offers other late-Victorian constructions of the role of the wife, too, not in terms of shared emotional intimacy but as a "virtuous monitor," an over-idealized source of goodness and of moral and social restraint.[80]

Undoubtedly too, many Victorian middle- and upper-class men—anxious about an apparent debilitating "nervousness" that was linked to perceived dangers of over-civilization—identified with a "boy culture" that they imagined as unfettered by the "moral and physical confinements of [a female-coded] domesticity."[81] Sarah Cole writes, in words which again have a clear transatlantic resonance: "The late Victorians imagined and constructed multiple sites of flourishing male community, locations and languages dedicated to creating a sphere for intimate male ties, which worked in part as 'counter-discourses' to the leviathan of bourgeois respectability and to the sovereignty of a domestic ideal."[82] Rotundo expresses something of the same idea, but in more ambivalent terms: "there were men who cherished the freedom of male worlds even as they maintained a warm and lasting affection for their wives. This combination of love and separation was a common one in middle-class marriage—a kind of mid-point between alienation and intimacy."[83]

The critics I mention here are, by and large, discussing middle- and upper-class white manhood, and I allude to a fraction of the work on masculinity and family life in the period. But they do provide a useful context in which to consider Clemens's male friendships (with Rotundo's words proving particularly apposite). Clemens's profession means that he cannot be judged against a normative model, in terms both of class and working practice. But the fact that so much of his time was spent in the home and the knowledge we have of his relationship with Olivia mean both that we can define his marriage in companionate terms, and see his household role as one—in some considerable part—of masculine domesticity.

Howells wrote that Clemens's marriage to Olivia was "from the outside...one of the most perfect": "It was a greater part of him than the love of most men for their wives, and she merited all the worship he could give her, all the devotion, all the implicit obedience, by her surpassing force and beauty of character.... Clemens not only accepted her rule implicitly, but he rejoiced, he gloried in it."[84] If Howells's words shade into the "virtuous monitor" model described above—as Clemens's own words about Olivia also tended to do—it is clear that the marriage was based on an intense and (in the early years, at any rate) sexually charged intimacy.[85] A letter written by Clemens to Olivia on December 11–12, 1873, early in their marriage, while he was away in England to lecture, conveys something of this: "My own dear little darling.... [Y]our picture is before me (the same I have carried in my pocket so many many months) & I simply love it & I love you, Livy, my darling.... I do *love* you, Livy darling, & my last word is, (when I come) '*Expedition's* the word!'"[86]

Such evidence of the emotional closeness (and—it seems—the sexually expressive nature) of the marriage is supported by a larger domestic history. Clemens played a substantial and nurturing part in the life of his family. As far as work went, he was not as tied "to the time discipline associated with modernity" as most of his business associates.[87] The fact that he so often worked from home meant that (especially in the Hartford house) family and social life within the household often took priority over professional demands: "In the three seasons each year that he spent in Hartford, at least as much of his energy went into entertainment and family affairs as ever went into his books."[88] Kenneth R. Andrews claims that the Nook Farm community to which the Clemens's belonged was in fact engaged in a self-conscious attempt to shape domestic and family life along new and improved lines: "The everyday life of Nook Farm was lived less in the single family sphere than in the social area where families met on common ground.... Each of the Nook Farm families conceived of a fully-developed family experience at the heart of existence and devoted much energy to living up to this conception."[89]

Here, in other words, we see Clemens engaged in exactly the type of "masculine domesticity" that Marsh identifies, but in a more privileged context than that of the conventional middle-class world. While it is true that financial problems plagued many in the Hartford circle, including the Clemens family, the community was nonetheless generally affluent, with wives and husbands relieved of many of the normal household duties by servants. Clemens certainly had his faults as a husband and father.[90] His unpredictable temper in particular seems to have adversely affected his children. But his was certainly a marriage that was both companionate and family centered, and Victor Doyno gives strong evidence that Clemens was "extraordinarily devoted, perceptive and attentive" in his role both as a husband and as a father.[91]

Clemens undoubtedly had a closer engagement with his family than the majority of his male contemporaries. Andrews's description of his life at Nook Farm is again revealing: "As his family grew ... and particularly after his children were old enough to listen to stories, play charades, and act in private theatricals, [Clemens] gave much of his time and energy to their entertainment. Since he did not discipline himself in Hartford as he did on Quarry Farm [the Elmira family retreat] to write a large number of words each day, he was always available, when the children were not in the upstairs school-room, for play."[92] Andrews also suggests something of the role Clemens played in the larger Nook Farm community. He was a regular member and contributor to the Monday Evening Club—which met fortnightly, October to May, in the houses of its members to hear and present papers on matters of social and political interest.[93] Women were allowed to attend the club but only outside the meeting room, as silent listeners. Clemens was also involved in other group activities where women were less marginalized. He organized a Saturday Morning Club for the young women of the neighborhood, "for the formal purpose of cultural and social training." He also attended and read for the Browning Club, made up of Olivia's female friends. This met in the Clemens library to listen to and discuss Robert Browning's poetry.[94]

Despite all this family-based and local (but domestically oriented) activity, however, Rotundo's words about Victorian men cherishing "the freedom of male worlds even as they maintained a warm and lasting affection for their wives," and maintaining a balancing act "between alienation and intimacy," remain very much to the point in Clemens's case. His wife, Olivia, would often address him as "youth," acknowledging his (boyish) tendency to push against the more restraining aspects of the genteel respectability, "tender affection and moral suasion," of Victorian domesticity.[95] However much he loved his family, Clemens enjoyed plenty of time apart—either by himself (lecture and business trips) or in all-male company.[96] So, for instance (my examples are selective) he went to Bermuda with Twichell in May 1877 to gather material for a travel piece and to the Mississippi with James R. Osgood in April–May 1882 as he prepared to write *Life on the Mississippi*. Earlier (in 1874) he attempted a walk from Hartford to Boston with Twichell, the project's failure having little effect on the carousing that still followed (see chapter 2). Throughout his life, Clemens would frequently attend dinners and banquets in all-male company. He was also both a member and a guest (in Britain as well as America) at a significant number of the men's clubs so popular in the period. In such venues, an exclusively male membership could "talk, drink, smoke, read, eat, and play billiards and cards," and Clemens "could indulge himself in racy humor which he was not allowed as a family man or public writer."[97]

Such forms of separate male activity were normal in the period and need to be seen (in Clemens's case) against the background of a warm and sustaining family life. The same was true for Twichell, who enjoyed similar (if less frequent) bursts of male companionship. Twichell did recognize the issue of gender equality involved, when on June 8, 1878, he accepted Clemens's invitation to have Twichell join him (two months later) on his "tramp abroad" in Germany and Switzerland. Indeed, he wrote his answering letter on the very day his wife Harmony had given birth to their sixth child. But her response to his opportunity—conditioned, one assumes, by the then still-standard gender assumption that a woman's "only happiness lay in her husband and children"—has him quickly put aside any reservation, to grab his opportunity with both hands.[98] If the grammar of Twichell's letter is faulty, its meaning is clear: "...when I read your letter to [Harmony] widened her smile perceptibly and revived another degree in strength in a minute. She wouldn't think of her being left alone, which I flatter myself is rather rough on her, but only of the great chance opened to me, and said at once that nothing must prevent my going."[99] Both partners take more or less for granted that male adventure and self-expression take priority over what must have been quite tricky and exhausting domestic circumstance.

Clemens and Twichell, then, were typical in "cherishing the freedom of male worlds even as they maintained a warm and lasting affection for their wives." The spaces still clearly available for male socialization in the period (and especially the importance of clubs and fraternal societies) were in part a product of such needs. Their wives, moreover, seem to have accepted this situation with little question. However, marital relations were undergoing significant change—were becoming more intimate and emotionally fulfilling—at the same time as (male) domestic roles altered. As men's emotions centered increasingly on the family, and on the heterosexual relationship at its heart, so the importance and value of male friendships and the opportunities for their realization would both gradually narrow in their scope.

## IV

I have suggested how male friendship in the period needs to be measured against the background of altered historical patterns of intimacy between men and the changing nature of marriage and the domestic family circle. The move from a sentimental culture of the eighteenth and early nineteenth century to a more pragmatic and self-contained Gilded Age business culture—one major influence in such change—was by no means complete or thoroughgoing.[100] However, the nature of postbellum capitalism did, inevitably and strongly, affect men's relationships at this time. I conclude this chapter by identifying some of the ways in which this occurred.

In doing so, I return to my starting point to focus on the larger contexts of privilege and power in which male friendships are grounded. Peter Stoneley, in an important essay discussing Clemens's friendships, challenges any assumption that "the nature of friendship is automatic and unchanging, or that it is too casual or happenstance to bear much analysis."[101] He suggests that the beginnings of the three key friendships of Clemens's life imply their larger meaning:

When Twain and Howells met, Howells was an increasingly influential figure who had just given Twain a good review. When Twain and

Twichell met, Twichell was the Yale-educated parson who could ensure Twain's acceptance into the more exclusive circles of Hartford. When Twain and Rogers met, Twain was bankrupt and Rogers was a millionaire. I do not think there was a cynical motive on Twain's part in any of these relationships, but...the unexpected and playful aspects [of these friendships] were underpinned by a more mundane social logic.[102]

This analysis is convincing, and I will return to it later. It needs, however, to be contextualized within a wider framework of changing relations between men in an emergent and fast-expanding capitalist economy.

Commenting on the culture of boys and young men in nineteenth-century America, Rotundo identifies an "uneasy mixture of competition and camaraderie."[103] The same words can be applied to the relationship between men in the American business world of the later nineteenth century. In that case, the nature of the unease lay in the tension between an inherent interpersonal rivalry in, and the structuring hierarchies of, the capitalist system, and a belief in fraternal community and "the affective exchange of brotherhood" that nonetheless strongly persisted.[104] Such internal contradictions permeate (modern) American ideology as a whole, as a traditional belief in democratic equal opportunity meets the inbuilt limits of the economic and social system. But their existence can also be explained in the relays that join the individual male subject to—but also buffer him from—his larger institutional context.

In tracing the links between white manhood and civic identity, Dana Nelson refers to a "fraternal/national brotherhood" built on "the alibi of a unified national [white] manhood."[105] What appeared on the surface as (individual and national) interests held in common, in fact concealed deep divisions between male subjects—a product of "the forms and ideologies of capitalist social organisation."[106] Post-Civil War America was torn by large-scale social and industrial unrest, with class set against class. This was, in part, the result of rapid modernization. For "efficiencies" in American business practice, and the technologies that helped produce them, had a dramatic effect on the role of the individual worker, and on the status of all forms of labor: "Rapid industrialization, technological transformation, capital concentration, urbanization, and immigration—all of these created a new sense of an oppressively crowded, depersonalized, and often emasculated life. Manhood had meant autonomy and self-control but now fewer and fewer American men owned their shops, controlled their own labor, owned their own farms."[107]

These changing conditions affected the whole work force. I focus particularly on the white-collar worker, where class conflict was not the obviously divisive issue that it was further down the labor hierarchy. Capitalism depends on competition, a competition endorsed in postbellum America by Social Darwinism. This, together with the fast-changing nature of the economic and social landscape in a modernizing nation, led both to "opportunity" and to "anxiety": "Hierarchies of wealth, status, and power had not disappeared in the nineteenth-century United States, but were understood to be up for grabs, subject to change or even to constant redrawing. The resulting opportunity and anxiety...created a tension between the model of the free individual man and men's needs for certainty that a group existed in which to anchor male identity."[108] This tension between individual and group identity (or—put in slightly different terms—competition and conviviality) provides the wider context for any analysis of fraternal relationships in the period.

Dorothy Hammond and Alta Jablow argue that it is the "hunger for affiliation" that explains the ongoing "viability of the myth of friendship" in modern society: "The ideology of friendship—affection, loyalty, and trust—has never gone out of style.... Urbanization, and bureaucratization, social and geographical mobility, all may foster instrumental and expedient relationships, but they surely induce a sense of individual isolation.... The human need for enduring, emotionally satisfying relationships often remains unfulfilled."[109] The capitalist business model (as men "worked for wages, competing head to head") and the modernization process which brought it into being, fostered this sense of isolation: "in the new climate of competition (following the industrial revolution), intimate friendships began to give way to the more superficial ties of modern working men."[110] Such intimate male relationships were under even more pressure in the last decades of the nineteenth century, and it is then that Sarah Cole's reference to "the bleak interpersonal structures of modernity" first seems apt.[111] In theory, then, same-sex friendship is a democratic form of "equality" between men "based on non-hierarchic conventions and values" and an alternative to social stratifications elsewhere.[112] But, in practice, such an idealistic conception increasingly failed to fit the isolating realities of most men's lives in "the emerging world of a bureaucratized corporate capitalism."[113]

The social and economic hierarchies that were part and parcel of a working world predicated on intense competition did not, though, cancel out a continued emphasis on and belief in the value of friendship and companionship (even within that same working environment). There are a number of ways of explaining this apparent paradox. Lauren Berlant writes of the way that "the utopian, optimism-sustaining versions of intimacy meet the normative practices, fantasies, institutions, and ideologies that organize people's worlds," and defines our liberal society as "founded on the migration of intimacy expectations between the public and the domestic."[114] We should not, to put this more pragmatically, be surprised that men look to build close fraternal relations within and on the margins of their professional lives. For without the assumption that such friendships were both possible and sustaining, this (major) part of their existence would be pointless and empty. (The establishing of such fraternal relations must also in part have been a response to an increasing *female* presence in the workplace: that women accounted for 4.5 percent of stenographers and typists in 1870, 40 percent in 1880, and 63.6 percent in 1890, gives some idea of the rapid changes here occurring.)[115]

In the later chapter on Clemens, Rogers, and masculinity, I show how sentimentality (a quality associated with domesticity) "migrated" into the apparently "public" and business world of male transactions. Rotundo similarly shows that—if we would construct parameters for men's lives leading from the domestic, to spaces of male relaxation and leisure outside the home, to the workplace—the borders between the last two of these areas are extremely permeable.[116] Late-nineteenth-century male working life, then, constantly spilled beyond fixed professional limits—extending to those "informal talks" that "took place in train cars, on station platforms, in hotel lobbies; often...at formal social occasions." And this sense of a network of relays between individual working lives and their larger institutional frameworks can be further expanded:

> [T]he shared activity of middle-class men was not limited to the workplace. There was also a male world of play and relaxation, a sociable realm that was physically separate from the sites of business but still tightly connected to the life of the marketplace. This masculine recreational culture flourished in many settings.... By the last third of the century, this culture of play found new homes in restaurants and exclusive saloons, in fraternal lodges and elite men's clubs, and (for younger men) in the new athletic clubs that were also a part of the collective life of male youth.[117]

This, though, is where we return to the ideological and to Nelson's emphasis on the assumed existence of a "fraternal/national brotherhood" founded on "the alibi of a unified national [white] manhood." Nelson argues that the "anxieties generated in competitive economic relations between white men" were in fact "triangulated through and transferred onto "others"—"others" such as women, African Americans, Native Americans, and immigrants.[118] In this way—by constructing a sense of shared identity reliant on the competing presence of less powerful social and ethnic groups—"the (equalizing) *guarantees* of whiteness" acted to balance out the competitive and isolating effects of an emergent business culture.[119]

Nelson describes the proliferation of "fraternal space" at the century's end—from political parties to fraternal lodges to reform groups to professional organizations. Such "social spaces," she suggests, "offered themselves as a corrective to the abrasions of [the] workday, a haven where a man could be truly recognized apart from his competitive working role, could be rightly known in his individual particularity.[120] The problem, though, was (to recall Rotundo) that such fraternal spaces could not ultimately be divorced from the marketplace. Nelson astutely analyses the "patterned strategy" that consequently emerged:

> Men's social spaces came increasingly to rely on rituals to constitute the affective exchange of brotherhood, informally through a combination of..."verbal jousting"...with jokes and complaints about women that were the key activities at men's clubs and dinners, and

formally through fraternal orders' extraordinarily elaborate and explosively popular secret ceremonies and rites. But men's obsessive decoration of fraternal space with rituals of brotherhood barely papers over the fundamental inability of these havens to deliver what they promise. In a range of middle-class fraternal imaginings and practices, we find a patterned strategy. Men's rituals of friendship and brotherhood promise egalitarian emotional exchanges. But they depend on elaborate and hierarchical structures that merely symbolize such exchange. These sterilized symbolic spaces work, though, to help white men ward off having to confront fraternity's psychic and political abortiveness.[121]

Nelson argues, then, that we must see white male friendship in the period—and as it functioned in a modernized business context—as a bolster to the dominant social and political order. At the same time, though, the sense of imagined fraternity thereby produced was largely an illusion, and an illusion that masked the competitive and hierarchical nature of actual working relationships.[122]

To return to my main subject, the relationship between Clemens and his friends, and to summarize, is to make two main points. First, over this historical period (the 1870s to the 1900s) the forms of male friendship were in transition. Prior models of homosociality familiar in the eighteenth- and early-nineteenth-century American world were narrowing in their range—and dramatically so from the mid-1880s onward. This was the result of altered relations within the family and in the workplace and, accordingly, in modes of masculine behavior—the "independence and emotional austerity," for instance, deemed fitting to the male world of work.[123] But it was the impact of legal cases and of changes in the law that would consolidate such change. For if close affection and intimate relations between men noticeably diminished in the period, the homosexual scandals of the 1890s placed them under deep suspicion. The way the friendships examined here worked, and the nature of their limits, must be seen against such a background.

My second point relates specifically to the change in workplace relations in the period. Clemens's early adult working life belongs within the patterns identified above. He was a member of a typesetter's organization in his early years when he worked as a printer and was a freemason in the 1860s. However, his later friendships, by and large, were formed—as a result of the wealth, status, and/or social authority of the men concerned—at one remove from the more abrasive aspects of the socioeconomic world that I have described. Increasingly, and from as early as the 1870s, the clubs Clemens joined and the dinners and social occasions he attended were part of a world of privilege, a firm step away from the competitive pressures of working- and middle-class American life.[124] None of the men on whom I focus was in direct economic competition with any of their three fellows. All of them, however, were necessarily affected by the men's culture of their age, and all—excepting Twichell—had, in order to reach and retain their position of privilege, to compete in the market economy previously described. Their experiences and expectations of male friendships in part developed in this context.[125]

Susan K. Harris discusses Clemens's male friendships in terms of changing models of masculinity, as the "patrician" gave way to the "entrepreneurial."[126] She argues that Clemens and his friends rejected both paradigms, developing instead "sentimental...ties" outside of any business paradigm. Harris sees this as not atypical: like "many Victorian-American men," Clemens created "new affiliations based on friendship in the hope that affective ties would help usher in a different, and better, order" than that based on "purely business models."[127] Such a reading tends to position friendship outside the scan of the "social meanings" that in fact constitute it—as an utopian counterthrust to the history and ideology of the day. In line with the implications of Nelson's book, I (rather) would see the sentimental bound awkwardly together with the entrepreneurial within the one social and economic system, with such sentimental male friendships as a key aspect of that (male) order rather than offering some alternative to it.[128]

Perhaps, then, we can envisage a metaphoric ladder on which to position various types of male friendship, and in which work, wealth and/or status, and the conditioning larger sociopolitical environment all play their part. On one rung we have middle-class men caught between competition and fraternity, but identifying nonetheless as a group with the "nationally shared 'nature',", and interests, of "white manhood."[129] On a higher rung, we have more powerful men, whose wealth and/or status minimizes the element of personal competition between them.[130] Their friendships, consequently, can operate on a more playful level and in a more leisured context—and there may be a relationship between the two—than those lower down that ladder. Stoneley's description of the Clemens-Howells relationship as "vitally inconsequential...slightly out of the way of adult life" might be extended to all Clemens's friendships to suggest that these men's rituals of affective exchange stood to one side of—and were, to good degree, unaffected by—the power relations of the day-to-day business world.[131]

But this is not to say that these friendships stood beyond, or outside, the same set of ideological assumptions (about race, gender, and authority) that governed the relationships of working- and middle-class men. Stoneley writes on Clemens's fiction, and the Huck Finn-Tom Sawyer friendship, to say that "friendship is...represented in the willingness to forge a personal bond at the expense of a wider social bond." It is, however, that "social bond," "ultimately geared toward the will and needs of white manhood," that will finally prevail.[132] And if Clemens's friendships often worked themselves out "slightly out of the way of adult life" they must ultimately be measured in terms of their social grounding—the very respectability and success (in terms both of cash and/or status)—of those involved, and in the positions of all four men as figures of some authority and power in the larger fraternity of white male American citizens.

# 2

## Clemens and Twichell

I

J oseph Twichell was the popular and much-beloved pastor of Hartford's Asylum Hill Congregationalist Church for almost forty-seven years, from December 1865 to July 1912, and was one of Clemens's closest friends for almost as long. He was a pastor well-known for his good nature and his "muscular Christianity"—the combination, so popular in the period, of rugged manly quality with high religious principle.[1] The March 2, 1875, Hartford *Courant* report of "The Hartford Minister's Meeting," by Rev. William L. Gage, refers to "our 'glorious' brother Twichell, still profanely called Joe by those who know him best. That adjective and that pet name are at once the epitome and the eulogy of his character."[2] Such fondness, together with recognition of the wide range of his influence, forms a recurrent note in other public notes of praise. So, toward the other end of his career, in December 1905, the *Courant* similarly celebrates his fortieth anniversary in charge of his church: "How different he is from the traditional type of minister! Nobody stands in dread of him, everybody respects and loves him and to thousands he is still 'Joe' Twichell: he is approachable as one boy is to another.... Outside the pulpit and the parish he has taken a large place as a citizen, and he is one of the men of Hartford with a national reputation—a reputation as a most genial companion, a delightful wit, an eloquent speaker, and all the time a noble Christian gentleman."[3]

Joseph Hopkins Twichell was born on May 27, 1838, in the small Connecticut town of Southington Corners, into a family whose history traced back to the early years of settlement. He was the eldest son of Edward Twichell, a businessman and deacon (from 1851) of the local Congregationalist church. He was accordingly raised, in his own words, "in a community and a family in which religion and philanthropy were principal subjects of interest."[4] Twichell studied at Yale from 1855–59, and was briefly suspended for his part in an 1858 town-gown conflict in which a local fireman was killed. He

39

then entered Union Theological Seminary in New York to study for the ministry. But before his training was complete the Civil War broke out and he signed on as regimental chaplain of the Seventy-First New York Infantry (the "Second Excelsior"), serving a group of mainly Irish Catholic men, most of whom came from a very different social and religious background than his own: soldiers whom Kenneth Andrews later described as "the scourings of the pavement," and Twichell himself as "rough, wicked men."[5] But his own adaptable nature, and the shared and stressful circumstances of the war, helped bridge the gap between chaplain and serving men.[6] His three years' war service was undoubtedly a watershed in Twichell's personal development and, during this period, he was also to develop a close and (on the surface of things) unlikely friendship with Fr. Joseph O'Hagan, Jesuit chaplain in another regiment.

Twichell's period of enlistment finished on July 30, 1864, and he returned to Andover Seminary to complete formal preparation for the ministry. In December 1865, he became pastor of the new Asylum Hill Congregational Church in a wealthy area of Hartford, Connecticut. His marriage to (Julia) Harmony (Cushman) took place shortly before this, on November 1, 1865.[7] Horace Bushnell, whom Twichell—following a first meeting in 1858—had come to know during the war, recommended him for the Hartford pastorate. Bushnell was a controversial figure in Congregationalism, associated with the softening of the more rigid doctrinal tenets of the church. He emphasized, for example, individual moral growth inspired by both the nurturing family and the following of Christ's example, rather than traditional Calvinist beliefs of an "election" to grace.[8] His liberal and rational position suited Twichell, whose own religious teachings seem to have been predominantly concerned with individual strength of character—the need to act with moral integrity whatever the constraining circumstances—rather than with the fine details of theological debate. Twichell's Civil War experience in the company of men whose formal religious practice might have been lax but whose courage and selflessness he admired, undoubtedly prompted the emphasis on the actual practice of Christian manhood that marked his ministry.[9]

Clemens first met Twichell in October 1868 when visiting Hartford to work with Elisha Bliss, his publisher, on the printer's copy and illustrations for his first major book, *The Innocents Abroad*. The story has it that Clemens was taken to an evening reception held by a member of the Asylum Hill church and indiscreetly referred to the latter as the "Church of the Holy Speculators" as its minister stood close at hand. Mrs. Bliss then introduced the two men, saying that Twichell knew Clemens's work and wanted to meet him. As Clemens's early biographer, Albert Bigelow Paine, described it: "And so, in this casual fashion, he met the man who was presently to become his closest personal friend and counselor, and would remain so for more than forty years."[10]

Clemens's own past experience made him something of an oddity when he first entered this respectable eastern social world (where he would later establish his family home). His western and bohemian background and manner signaled his social difference from the more polished Hartford company he now kept. When Clemens first stayed in Hartford in January 1868 (to see Bliss), he stayed with John and Isabella Hooker—relatives of Henry Ward Beecher, one of the most famous (liberal) ministers in the country and a prior acquaintance of Clemens.[11] His comments during the visit suggest a mixed response to this genteel environment:

I have had a tip-top time, here [in Hartford], for a few days.... Puritans are mighty straight-laced, & they won't let me smoke in the parlor, but the Almighty don't make any better people.... I am the guest of Mr. Hooker's (Henry Ward Beecher's brother-in-law) family here for a few days, & I tell you I have to walk mighty straight. I desire to have the respect of this sterling old Puritan community, for their respect is well worth having—& so I don't dare to smoke after I go to bed, & in fact I don't dare to do *anything* that's comfortable and natural. It comes a little hard to lead such a sinless life.[12]

Clemens's background was the opposite of genteel, and in his California years he was well known for his drinking and for his unsettled lifestyle.[13] And in his early years back East, he was still far from conventional in mannerisms, dress, and attitude.

Clemens, then, was something of a loose and eccentric cannon in the formal and respectable Hartford world. This would always remain the case to some extent, but was particularly true in these early years. But Twichell, doubtless in part because of his Civil War experiences, responded positively to Clemens, able to see—one may suppose—something genuinely appealing beyond surface manner and appearance. The relationship, though, was not immediately an easy one from Twichell's perspective, or so the evidence of his April 22, 1910, obituary notice for his friend (published in the Hartford *Courant*) suggests. Recalling their first meetings, he wrote:

We were both young men, and the acquaintance so begun soon grew into a friendship which continued unbroken ever after, and went on strengthening with the flight of years. I cannot say that at that period we were wholly sympathetic in either thought or feeling. Our antecedent conditions and experience in life had been very different, and, in some ways, contrasted. But while originally attracted to him by the brightness of his mind, the incomparable charm of his talk, and his rare companionableness, I was not long in finding out that he had a big, warm and tender heart. He bore, indeed, marks of the rude society of the frontier and the mining-camp in which his youth was passed. He was eminently a man "with the bark on". He was compounded of elements strangely mixed,—in this and that respect to appearance contradictory. Exterior roughnesses he had; also, underneath them, exquisite refinements of taste and sentiment.[14]

Clemens himself seems not to have had any matching reservation, but rather to have seen Twichell as a sympathetic and kindred spirit in an otherwise alien social environment. His letter to Olivia, soon after the two men's first meeting, bubbles with enthusiasm: "Set a white stone—for I have made a friend. It is the Rev. J. H. Twichell. I have only known him a week, & yet . . . I could hardly find words strong enough to tell how much I *do* think of that man . . . He made me promise to spend Wednesday evening at his house. . . . I had a splendid time. . . . He is about my age—likes my favorite authors, too, just as you do."[15] And five months later, again writing to Olivia but this time about Twichell's concern for his spiritual welfare, Clemens again makes his liking for the minister absolutely clear: "Good fellow, Twichell is, & faithful & true—whole-hearted—magnificent. I love him."[16]

Any reservations Twichell might originally have had about Clemens receded as their lifelong friendship developed. Clemens's letter from London on January 19, 1897, in the period of distress that followed his daughter Susy's death, reveals something of his feelings for Twichell: "Do I want you to write to me? Indeed I do. . . . The others break my heart, but you will not. You have a something divine in you that is not in other men. You have the touch that heals, not lacerates. And you know the secret places of our hearts. . . . You have seen our whole voyage. . . . [Y]ou see us now, chartless, adrift—derelicts."[17] Twichell's *Journals*, on their part, are studded with references to "M. T. whom we had known and loved so long, and from whom we had received so many kindnesses and bounties," to "our beloved old friend Mark Twain," and to "dear Samuel L. Clemens."[18]

The note of condescension in Twichell's retrospect on their early friendship does, however, suggest the two men's difference in class and background. Clemens, despite his enthusiasm for Twichell, must have been aware of this. We might even read his representation of the cultural and linguistic clash between Scotty Briggs (the western "stalwart rough," with "flaming red flannel shirt, patent leather belt with spanner and revolver attached, . . . and pants stuffed into boot tops") and the minister ("a fragile, gentle, spirituel new fledgling from an Eastern theological seminary") in *Roughing It* (1872) as a sly and exaggerated reference on Clemens's part to the contrast between himself and this new friend.[19]

Twichell may never have been completely at ease with what he would call, in an 1878 letter to his wife Harmony, Clemens's "coarse spots."[20] But within a short time of their first 1868 meeting, Clemens's own social position had changed and the balance of power and authority in the friendship had altered significantly. By 1877, the date of the incident on which I now focus, Clemens was married and already something of a celebrity, and—settled in the impressive house he and Olivia had had built—was now an established, respected, and (generally) respectable member of the prestigious Hartford Nook Farm community.[21] And Twichell, by now a firm and close friend, was—in the realm of secular affairs at least—pretty much under his influence.

Clemens would rework the events of July 1877—which centered on Lizzy Wills, one of the family servants—into fiction later in his career, in "Wapping Alice."[22] Twichell, in real life, played the part that in the later tale Clemens gives to Rev. Thomas X.[23] I focus briefly on this narrative, and the incident on which it was based, to illustrate how the Clemens-Twichell friendship can be viewed within the context of shared class and economic interests (in accord with my comments on white masculinity in the previous chapter), and to suggest too something of the changing balance of the two men's relationship.

The facts of the original case were these. Clemens, vacationing with his family in Elmira over the summer of 1877, returned to Hartford to investigate the apparent entry of a thief into the Hartford house, indicated by the triggering of its burglar-alarm. After questioning the house servants, Clemens realized that one of them, an English girl called Lizzie Wills, had in fact been letting her lover, Willie Taylor, in and out of the house—and so setting off the alarm. Discovering that Wills was apparently pregnant but that Taylor did not intend to marry her, Clemens decided to intervene. He therefore set up an interview with the couple, with a plain-clothes detective in one room close at hand, and with Twichell in another. He then "persuaded" Taylor to marry Wills, and had his pastor friend immediately on hand to perform the ceremony. Calling in the other servants to celebrate with cake and wine, Clemens also gave the couple a hundred dollars to start their new life together. The ironic postscript to all this is that Wills had not been pregnant after all and may have been playing something of her own game as these proceedings took place.

The letters Clemens wrote to Olivia (who stayed in Elmira) make it clear that he enjoyed almost every moment of this episode. He likened himself to Simon Wheeler—detective-protagonist in a burlesque drama he was working on around this time—and wrote that: "I am judge, jury, & lawyer for both sides. Moreover, the Court of Appeals [Olivia] being in Elmira, I have a pretty swinging jurisdiction here; & it sets me up and makes me feel my oats. . . . [I]t chuckles me with comfort to be in this big authority for once." When Clemens found out Wills's circumstances, he was sympathetic: "I began to pity her, now, especially when she said she was lost irretrievably & her betrayer was manifestly never going to marry her." He then reported his plot to bring the couple together before him, and described (for Olivia's benefit) the sequence of events once this was achieved:

> I shake hands (with Taylor) with a lying cordiality. . . . [H]e talked of a "put-up job;" . . . I coaxed him, I argued, I pleaded. . . . I sprung a good joke on him. . . . Four times I worked him almost up to the point I wanted him. . . . [T]he fifth time he said, hesitatingly, "I—I believe I'll do it. . . . I am willing, though—"
>
> He never finished that sentence. I rang three bells (& *instantly* enter George and Mary [other servants])!; I snatched the door leading to Mother's bath-room open & said "the Rev. Mr. Twichell will come in.—here is the license"—(which I had procured in the afternoon.)
>
> Enter Joe & marries them, in presence of witnesses—this bridegroom murmuring a moment later, "But it was a put-up job." . . .
>
> Enter George with champagne & glasses, places his waiter first before Lizz & says, "Champagne if you please, *Mrs. Taylor*." Whereat, general jollity. . . .

Do you see my plan? The man in the library was a detective in plain clothes. If persuasion had failed with Mr. Taylor, my purpose was to lock the door & say "You either leave this room a married man or you leave it with an officer, & charged with being in this house at midnight in March with a dishonest intent—take your choice."[24]

Twichell's journal version of this episode was similar but, to do him justice, he did manifest some unease about Clemens's tactics and thus (implicitly) the benevolent authoritarianism, and social and moral condescension, that they signaled. Telling more or less the same story as Clemens, he was, however, more cautious, and noted that Clemens's suspicion that "the [supposed] burglar was the lover of ... Lizzie" was in fact probably unwarranted. Twichell represented the climax of the drama as follows: "I was placed in a chamber adjoining the study where Mark took his position.... Mark, by reasoning and expostulation ... finally persuaded the fellow to say "yes". I was called in straightway and the business finished on the spot. I never had performed the marriage service with such mingled feelings. I felt great sympathy for the bride and groom and gave them the best counsel I could."[25] He then did go on to say that "things really took a cheerful tone" with the wedding party and the giving of the check. But Clemens's later recollection that Joe "gave me his tearful blessing for my good deed" may nonetheless indicate a partial version of what was, on Twichell's part, a much more ambivalent response.[26]

Twichell appears to have found himself caught up in the momentum of events here as Clemens indulged the circus side of his nature. But the conjunction of concerns about property ownership (the initial fear of burglary), the preservation of conventional moral standards (following Wills's apparent promiscuity), and the taking of responsibility for the lives of a lower social class, do suggest how we might consider the two men's close relationship within a broader ideological context. Their actions are predicated on the restoration of a disrupted social order. All ends up back in its proper place when, with all suspicion of "burglary" excised, the errant couple are wed (though dismissed from the household) and apparently happy: "Lizzy cried through the service & the prayer, & then her husband put his arm about her neck & kissed her & shed a tear & said 'Don't cry.'"[27] Clemens exercises his social authority as a wealthy and respectable householder and employer, backed up by representatives of the law and the clergy. The rest of his staff then implicitly validate the positive outcome of his intervention as they join in the wedding celebration, acting as witness to their employer's generosity as he seals the ceremony and bestows his blessing on the couple together with that hundred dollars cash.

One cannot help but recall Tom Sawyer's later fictional actions here in paying Jim off at the end of *Huckleberry Finn* and, as in that case, any reader of this story will have questions going through her or his mind as it proceeds. What is the couple's future now Wills has been dismissed from employment? What is their response to these events (the only voice

Clemens reports directly is Taylor's, with his accusation of a "put-up job")? And what are the prospects of a marriage made under such circumstances? Whatever the answers to these questions, Twichell's "mingled feelings" are well justified. But Clemens is clearly on something of a roll here. Caught up in the excitement of the moment, he plots and directs the action like a protagonist in one of his more facile melodramas. It is his status and social position, however, that enables him to do this without any restraint placed upon him.

When Clemens, much later, converts the incident into fictional form in "Wapping Alice," he adds twists to the narrative. He presents the story within a frame, as told to the first person narrator by "Jackson," the descendant of southern planters and owner of an "old plantation mansion." It may be significant that Clemens should—at this later stage—use one of the prime examples of patriarchal authority and class privilege in American history to provide a fictional backdrop for his own real-life tale.[28] While Clemens used many of the original factual occurrences in his story, he completely changes its emphasis by revealing from the start that "Alice . . . had a secret. It was this: she was not a woman at all, but a *man*"—and one with so much "ingenuity" that "he was able to masquerade as a girl seven months and a half under all our eyes and never awake in us doubt or suspicion."[29]

Jackson admits to "[m]y native appetite for doing things in a theatrical way."[30] He also completely misreads the actions of the unemployed Swedish joiner (who loosely plays Taylor's role) and is blind to Alice's true identity. Thus Clemens does raise questions here about what one can really know about the motives and being of any other. It may just be that, as he writes this narrative and in part rewrites history as he does so, he is remembering his former actions with something less than the certainty and pleasure that marked them at the time.

But there is one final element to this story that brings us back to the Clemens-Twichell relationship—though this time it mainly involves Harmony, Twichell's wife. Twichell's son recalls how, when the Clemenses left Hartford: "[T]here were hard feelings left behind with some people who had'nt [*sic*] gotten along with Mark Twain. Around 1900 (I think) . . . some people tried to smooth over these sores by inviting Mark Twain back to Hartford to talk to a women's organization." He then describes his parents going to fetch Clemens and spending the night at his Riverdale house (though this location is followed by a question mark). After dinner there, Clemens read to them from the story he was then "trying to write" about "the domestic that claimed she was with child and came to Mrs. Clemens." Despite the misleading reference to Olivia, this seems to refer to the "Wapping Alice" narrative. And this impression is reinforced as the memory continues:

> While MT read my mother became disgusted and her mouth became set very hard. This caused my father to laugh heartily. The more my father laughed the more disgusted my mother became. MT thought

my father's laughter was excited simply by the story, which was not the case.

Well, when MT came to Hartford the next day to talk to the women's club my mother was invited to the meeting. She came home ... and marched straight into the house and, without taking her hat off, marched straight upstairs to dad's study and walked in without knocking. She was mad right through. I could not hear what went on, but at one point dad started to laugh, but he quickly choked [it] off.... MT had read that domestic story to the Hartford women's club and they had been perfectly horrified! So was mother![31]

Differences in class and status had, then, been an issue of some fascination for Clemens and Twichell from early in their friendship. And if Twichell originally saw—and continued to see—Clemens as something of a "rough diamond," it is clear he quickly became enamored by the man himself, and pleased (and proud) to play the satellite to his huge celebrity.[32] He seems, too, to have completely accepted Clemens's status as a wealthy and deserving member of the Nook Farm community, and was willing (with whatever degree of reluctance) to back up his domestic and social authority in the Lizzie Wills case.

The apparent response of Harmony and her fellow women to Clemens's performance of his "domestic story" tells us that—for others—Clemens remained (and especially without his wife's presence) on the margins of this cultured and conservative Hartford world, despite all his success. He remained unpredictable and capable of unexpected actions that transgressed the codes of many of those around him, and never quite seems to have received from the others in this narrow but exclusive social circle the warm acceptance he got from Twichell. Twichell's wife, Harmony, clearly had her reservations about Clemens, however rarely they surfaced. The letter of April 24, 1901, that Clemens writes (from New York) to Twichell, might well be revealing in this general context: "It is curious that Hartford has not found out that we live in New York; you and three others have rung our doorbell in the last half year, but I call no others to mind."[33] Despite his undoubted social prestige and the status which his celebrity gave him, there remained times and places where Clemens apparently still struggled for full acceptance in genteel mixed company. Male-only relationships were a quite different matter.

II

The Lizzie Wills narrative illustrates (and despite the caveat above) the social authority that Clemens's family circumstances, wealth, and celebrity gave him, and the moral and ideological assumptions that—on this occasion—then followed. Whatever Twichell's own discomfort, he used his pastoral role to support his more impetuous but persuasive friend. In the "Wapping Alice" story, we see a small illustration too of the way that Clemens used the friendship with Twichell to his own professional literary ends. Indeed, a particular aspect of their friendship lies in Clemens's frequent representations of Twichell (or a fictional version of him) in his writings. He seems to have found him, for whatever reason, more suitable for such literary usage than any other person close to him. So, annoyed at the newspaper coverage of his financing of Twichell to join him in Europe on the *Tramp Abroad* trip, Clemens writes to Charles Dudley Warner: "It isn't any harm for Joe to take a trip at my expense if I invite him.... I bullyrag Joe into coming over here,—perfectly aware that nineteen-twentieths of the *pecuniary* profit & advantage are on my side, to say nothing of the social advantage,—& by jings, one would imagine, from the newspapers[,] that *Joe* is the party receiving a favor. I could live a whole year in Europe out of the clear cash I have made out of Joe Twichell."[34]

One of the lesser known examples of Clemens's adapting his dealings with Twichell to his own literary ends is in the "Profane Hostler" story— retold by Clemens both in the manuscript version of *Life on the Mississippi* and in the manuscript of *Innocents Adrift* (a narrative mainly based on his European travels in the early 1890s).[35] This was based on an incident quite early in their friendship when, in November 1874, Clemens and Twichell set out to walk from Hartford to Boston. Walking was one of the best-loved activities of the two men who, in Clemens's Hartford days, made regular pedestrian excursions to Bartlett's Tower (on Talcott Mountain, about eight miles from Hartford), talking nineteen to the dozen on their way. So, for instance, Twichell's journal entry for October 26, 1874, reads, "With M. T. to Bloomfield by rail, thence afoot to the Tower, and back afoot to his house to dine at 6 1/2 o'clock. Splendid exercise and lots of pleasant talk." And an entry for October 2, 1875 reads, "Walked to the Tower and back with M. T.—a long full feast of talk."[36]

It was in November 1874 that the two men set out on their well-publicized hundred-mile trek to Boston, engaging in mock competition with the great long-distance walker of the time, Edward Payson Weston: "They would show their independence of the cars, and notify Mr. Weston, the great walkist, that he must look to his laurels."[37] The whole venture turned out to be something of a farce as, after some twenty-eight miles, Clemens was crippled by a stiff knee ("it was as though I had wooden legs with pains in them") and the men completed their journey first by horse and cart, and then by rail.[38] Clemens—always a sharp self-publicist— immediately made comic capital of the project's failure, telegraphing James Redpath (the Boston lecture agent) from Webster, Massachusetts: "We have made thirty-five miles in less than five days. This demonstrates the thing can be done. Shall now finish by rail. Did you have any bets on us?"[39]

The press had a great deal of fun with this whole episode. Clemens's celebrity was already such as to ensure considerable newspaper coverage. One report, giving the context for the walk, suggests something of the flavor of Clemens and Twichell's relationship during such activities:

The Innocents Abroad–Mark Twain, accompanied by a clerical attendant or chaplain in ordinary, started at eight o'clock this morning to start to walk from Hartford "to Boston in twenty-four hours—or more." . . . It has long been the custom of these two gentlemen to take walks of about ten miles in the vicinity of Hartford for the purpose of enjoying a social chat and exchanging views on nothing in particular and everything in general, the result of which, to use Mark Twain's own words, is, that Mr. Twichell sometimes gains ideas from his companion which he embodies in his sermons, and Mark Twain obtains information from his pastor which he works up into comical and humorous stories, and makes note of every joke which unconsciously falls from the clerical lips.[40]

Twichell clearly thoroughly enjoyed the venture. Howells greeted them in Boston by laying on a party in their honor, with Twichell noting in his journal: "got back to Young's [his and Clemens's Boston hotel] at 1 o'clock [a.m.] and went joyfully to bed." Clemens, in response, hosted a supper for Howells, Thomas Bailey Aldrich, James Osgood, and others, and again Twichell comments with obvious pleasure: "a rare good time which I enjoyed to the full. Heard lots of bright good talk. Mark called on me to ask a blessing which I was glad of." Describing their journey home, Twichell would then write: "9 o'clock train to Hartford, after, on some accounts the most pleasant experience of my life. There has been no end of talk in the papers about our 'tour.'"[41]

The "profane hostler" incident took place on this journey as Clemens and Twichell looked for accommodation after Clemens's knee gave out. Clemens—and this may stand as something of a paradigm in terms of his use of biographical material—takes the incident and embroiders it for comic effect, in this case at a much later stage of his writing career. Twichell is the straight man in the sketch he writes, with the hostler's crude vernacular and ignorance of the minister's profession forming its comic base. Similar types of exchange (involving others' ignorance of Twichell's status) became something of a running joke between the two men, feeding into exactly the kind of humor—as different social worlds and forms of discourse clash—that suited Clemens's particular writing talents.

In his journal entries of the time, Twichell does not make much of the incident, though he does show an appreciation of the hostler's eccentricities and does give a name to Clemens's consequent literary activity: "Put up at a low tavern [at Westford] but the best that was to be had. . . . Saw some characters [here], . . . notably a sublimely profane hostler whom you couldn't joggle with any sort of mild remark without bringing down upon yourself a perfect avalanche of oaths,—and the poor drunkard who recommended to Mark the use of "Karosene" for his lame knees, he—the recommender—haveing [sic] often, he said, proved its virtue as antidote to the stiffness produced by lying out nights in cold weather, drunk."[42] The whole incident obviously tickled Clemens's literary fancy. Twichell's appreciation of the humor of the situation is replaced in Clemens's much longer version, however, by a construction of his minister friend as a fastidious and genteel figure, both uncomfortable and embarrassed in the face of such vulgar behavior. Perhaps this transformation hints at some buried critical impulse on Clemens's part toward Twichell's cultivated eastern background, or perhaps the author's comedy of extreme contrasts depends for its effect on such a characterization.

Clemens starts this section of *Innocents Adrift* by discussing the "over-free speech of American men in situations and in presences not strictly suitable for its exercise" and reports that: "I was witness of a notable case of this sort, myself, the time that I walked to Boston with a purist & got entertained a couple of hours by the hostler of a village inn with a tranquil and innocent flow of profane and indelicate talk.... The man had ... no thought of offending; he was using his natural speech, ... was doing his honest best, in his simple, untaught way, to entertain us—& with me he was succeeding. But my friend, who was a clergyman, was not thankful, and not happy."[43] The narrator describes how, though, it was the clergyman who had started the "hostler's amazing mill ... by asking questions." He tells how "I was miserably tired, mentally and physically exhausted" and "steeped in melancholy" after the twenty-eight mile walk just completed, and the skinned heels ("every step was torture") that resulted. "I was dying for a chance to rest," he continues, "& that little coop of a bar-room ... was a vision of paradise in my eyes.. .. I sank limp & lifeless into a chair ... desiring nothing but to be left alone":

> But the dominie was an old campaigner; he had been a chaplain all through the war, & had breathed the smoke of a hundred battles. Twenty-eight miles?— that was nothing to him ... he was as fresh as ever. I hated him for it, although I loved him so.... I knew his infirmity—he *must* talk, or die. He asked the hostler a question—about horses.... Horses was the right subject. It went to the hostler's heart; it electrified him, melted him.... What a smooth & glib and loving talker he was, & how wonderfully & wastefully his freshet of sparkling profanity and obscenity streamed forth! I knew that the dominie was aghast, but I was in paradise ... my miseries were all gone, & all my depression.... I was dying the happiest of all deaths, suffocation by joy. In half an hour I was as tired as ever, again, & had cried until I had no more tears left, yet still the killing show went on.

Finally, and two hours later, the dominie has a "sudden idea" and takes an envelope from his pocket, leaves it on the counter, and moves away as if he has forgotten it. The hostler goes and studies it and then:

> [H]e burst out with a welcoming & reverent enthusiasm, saying— "A preacher! Hellfire! & I've let you sit on that old crippled chair all this time, like a —— muttonhead as I *always* was!" ... [And, giving the dominie his own chair, he] snuggled up to him ... & fairly snowed him under with profanities and indecencies of entirely new &

stupendous patterns; & the whole burden of it was his admiration of the clergy . . . & his honest & humble reverence for their great office!

The narrator then comments that "I believe it was the most heart-satisfying evening I have ever spent, & there has never been a time when I would not have walked twenty-eight miles—or twenty-eight thousand, for that matter—to have it repeated."[44]

Clemens would use his friend—described as "the Reverend . . . a good man, one of the best of men, although a clergyman," in "Some Rambling Notes of an Idle Excursion"—as literary material on other occasions too.[45] "The Reverend" plays a relatively small role in "Some Rambling Notes," but is the source of one good joke. When "Mark Twain" steps ashore in Bermuda to find it free of pestering hack men and the like, he says "it was like being in heaven." The follow-up to this is immediate: "The Reverend rebukingly and rather pointedly advised me to make the most of it, then."[46] And his friend's presence provides the author with the opportunity for comic dialog concerning Bermuda's more unexpected sights:

> One night after I had gone to bed, the Reverend came into my room carrying something, and asked, "Is this your boot?" I said it was, and he said he had met a spider going off with it. Next morning he stated that just at dawn the same spider raised his window and was coming in to get a shirt, but saw him and fled.
> I enquired, "Did he get the shirt?"
> "No."
> "How did you know it was a shirt he was after?"
> "I could see it in his eye."[47]

Clemens makes double use of Twichell in this text, as he is also the model for the Rev. Mr. Peters, shipboard talking-companion to Captain "Hurricane" Jones (a stand-in for Ned Wakeman).[48] He would also figure— fleetingly—as "The Rev. Mr.——," in Clemens's 1876 short story "A Literary Nightmare" ("Punch, Brothers, Punch").

Twichell is better known, though, for his key part in the later travel narrative, A Tramp Abroad (1880), in the character of "Mr. Harris," the travelling companion of the "Mark Twain" narrator-protagonist, and his "agent."[49] Russell Banks points to the multiple roles "Harris" plays in the book as "the narrator's foil, fool, goad, guide, and all-purpose straight man . . . Sancho to his Quixote."[50] Though introduced on the opening page of the book, "Harris" plays little part in its opening sections and only begins to feature strongly in chapter eleven. His role, from that point on, varies. He acts as unwitting victim to the narrator's comic fool in the extended sequence in chapter thirteen when "Mark Twain" undergoes "exquisite suffering" as he lies awake listening to the sounds of a mouse "gnawing the wood-work" in their German hotel room, and presently hurls "a shoe at random, and with a vicious vigor. It struck the wall over Harris's head and fell down on him; I had not imagined I could throw so far. It woke Harris, and I was glad of it until I found he was not angry; then I was sorry." The scene then continues to its climactic comic end as the narrator decides to dress in the dark and quit the room, starts to "paw gently around and rake the floor" attempting to find a missing sock, loses all sense of direction, and finally (after considerable comic byplay) knocks a water pitcher to the floor. This disturbance wakes Harris again—"Harris shouted 'murder,' and 'thieves,' and finished with 'I'm absolutely drowned'"—and also wakes the whole household too.[51]

Harris is the straight man here, but on later occasions he joins "Mark Twain" in their twin personae as comic innocents abroad. An example of this is when the two men express their desire to see a sunrise on the summit of the Rigi in Switzerland. Waking on their first morning at the mountaintop hotel, they cocoon themselves in red blankets, make their way to the platform at the summit only to realize that they have overslept, and that it is the sunset they are watching:

We had missed the *morning* horn-blow [the evening one had woken them] and slept all day. This was stupefying. Harris said,—
"Look here, the sun isn't the spectacle,—its *us*,—stacked up here on top of this gallows, in these idiotic blankets, and two hundred and fifty well dressed men and women down here gawking up at us. . . . They seem to be laughing their ribs loose."[52]

Harris is most strongly delineated in *A Tramp Abroad* in the Swiss sections of the text (and the various walks and climbs made there), and his presence undoubtedly brings additional vitality to the book—just as Mr. Brown, and then "the boys," do in previous travel narratives. But James Leonard is right when he suggests that the use of "Harris" never quite works as well as it might: Clemens's "high regard for Twichell perhaps caused him to treat Harris, Twichell's fictional stand-in, so gently that Harris's comic potential is not thoroughly mined."[53] The crucial effect, though, that Twichell's presence on the trip had on Clemens's writing of a book with which he particularly struggled is clear in the March 16, 1880, letter to his friend:

My dear "Harris—" [these words are crossed through]
No, I mean
My Dear Joe—Just imagine it, for a moment: I was collecting material in Europe during 14 months for a book, & now that the thing is printed, I find that you, who were with me only a month & a half . . . are in *actual presence* (not imaginary) in 440 of the 531 pages the book contains! Hang it, if you had staid at home it would have taken me 14 *years* to get the material. You have saved me an intolerable whole world of hated labour, & I'll not forget it, my boy.[54]

Twichell, on other occasions, would serve as a different sort of prompt to Clemens's literary work. It was on one of their Talcott Mountain walks, for example, that Twichell encouraged him to write up the tales of his early river days (in the "Old Times on the Mississippi" *Atlantic Monthly* series).

## III

The Hartford *Courant*'s celebration of Twichell's fortieth anniversary at the Asylum Hill Church refers to his role "outside the pulpit and the parish." Noting the "large place" he has taken as a citizen, it observes that "he is one of the men of Hartford with a national reputation." Given that, today, hardly anyone has heard of Twichell while everyone has heard of Clemens, I comment briefly here on the relative status of the two friends.

To read Twichell's journal selectively for the years between 1895 to 1900—when perhaps his influence was at its peak—is to gather something of the range of his activities both within and outside the church. In October 1895, he addressed the Triennial National Congregational Council on "Civil and Religious Liberty, 275 years from Plymouth Rock." Twichell here celebrated the 1639 Connecticut Constitution ("that memorable free Connecticut constitution, which was an echo pure and clear and strong of the political note struck nineteen years before in the cabin of the 'Mayflower'") that, for him, was such a vital stage in the development of American democracy. He also here urged an ecumenical agenda—a need to strive for Christian unity, a "vivid yearning sentiment of catholicity"—quite exceptional for his church and for the period. In the spring to early summer period of 1896, Twichell noted that the previous summer (while on their usual family vacation in Keene Valley in the Adirondacks) he had been asked to write a biographical article on Mark Twain. He had "reluctantly consented to undertake it" (reluctantly, probably, as he never found such tasks easy and was not a natural writer):

> H. [Harmony] thought that it due to M. T. whom we had known and loved so long, and from whom we had received so many kindnesses and bounties, that I should,—especially as he had fallen into financial troubles and had a special present claim on us for anything that might be construed as an office of friendship.
>
> I did the best I could, but wished much that I might have done better.[55]

The essay, "Mark Twain," came out in the May 1896 issue of *Harper's New Monthly Magazine* (817–27).

In June 1896, Twichell gave an address at Yale, at the dedication of the statue of President Woolsey (Yale's tenth president, 1846–71).[56] Twichell brought a note of controversy to the celebration as he describes in his journal: "I was just going upon the platform . . . when Dr. Newman Smyth told me that the graduating class were, that afternoon, to plant an ivy taken from the grave of Gen. R. E. Lee, the Confederate chief. I disliked the thing so much that I could not forbear an open protest against it.... I interjected a few words accordingly in which I said that Lee was, though a good man, 'the historic representative of an infamous cause.'"[57] In a period of reunionist sentiment (as America looked to heal regional tensions), Twichell could not put his own war experiences, and the deaths of those who served with him, behind him. Throughout the century, he would take an active part in Union army reunions.[58]

In April 1898, Twichell was in Washington "for a little respite, and to see what was to be seen of the final stages there of the procedure leading up to war with Spain." Despite the unofficial nature of his visit, he met with John Addison Porter, the President's secretary, who "told me that in his judgment (which presumably was the President's judgment) had Congress left the affair in the President's hands, Cuba might have been delivered without war." In December, he attended a meeting of the Yale Corporation and gave an address on "The Soldier Puritan." And in the following October (1899), again at Yale, it fell to Twichell "as the senior member of the Corporation" to perform "the office of inducting the new incumbent," Arthur Hadley, as the new President of the University. He returned to New Haven on the twentieth of November, "to assist in welcoming, on a visit to Yale, Gov. Theodore Roosevelt of New York, one of the most shining heroes of the day."[59] Two days later Twichell was in New York with Harmony, speaking at a dinner of the Society of Mayflower Descendants. In May 1900, he went "by special train ... to the Annual Meeting of the Third Corps Union at Gettysburg—of which I was elected president." In October, he attended daughter Harmony's graduation at the Hartford Hospital Training School for Nurses, and gave an address there.

This gives a brief window on Twichell's public life, though at a time when Clemens no longer lived close by (in Hartford). There were other strings to his public career too: for instance, his earlier work on behalf of the Chinese educational mission in Hartford, and his involvement in the Atlanta University African-American educational project.[60] And during the 1884 presidential elections, Twichell took (unusually for him) a public stance that was of some political risk. Acting against the grain of his affluent and solidly Republican community, he spoke out publicly—alongside Clemens—against James G. Blaine, whose Congressional record marked him for both men as corrupt (his nativist activity no doubt contributed to their dislike).[61] While Clemens voted with the Mugwumps— Republicans who, in these circumstances, supported the Democrat Grover Cleveland—Twichell voted for the prohibition candidate, John St. John. There is some dispute as to how far Twichell's actions (and a Cleveland victory) alienated him from his community, but he wrote at the time that "the displeasure which my political action in regard of Mr. Blaine excited among my friends and parishioners was considerable," while Clemens, in his later autobiographical dictations, reported that "his congregation 'soured on him.'"[62]

It is noticeable that Clemens (until the last decade of his life) rarely commented on Twichell's public role, other than in making generally innocuous remarks about his preaching. Occasionally he read a Twichell sermon on a topic with national relevance and responded favorably. So on the occasion of Henry Ward Beecher's death, Clemens wrote praising his "noble sermon.... It is great & fine; & worthy of its majestic subject. You struck twelve."[63] Similarly, this time in the context of an 1889 Twichell speech (on Thomas Hooker to the Connecticut Historical Society), he praised his "great & admirable performance."[64] And even when Twichell did lead the way (prompted by Yung Wing) on an issue of wider social and cultural moment, the fate of the Chinese educational mission, it was Clemens who arranged the meeting with ex-President Grant they both attended, and Grant himself who (at least in Clemens's account) rather left Twichell metaphorically standing as he swiftly grasped the situation and went on to act effectively on that understanding.[65]

By and large, then, the *Courant*'s reference to Twichell's "national reputation" may be something of an exaggeration. Certainly Twichell was well-known in Connecticut and even (to lesser degree) in New York. His interest and expertise was generally limited, though, to church affairs, local religious and constitutional history, his strong attachment to Yale and membership in its ruling Corporation, and to army matters and connections dating from his Civil War days. Occasionally, such army affairs did have relevance to larger postbellum concerns. Thus throughout his life Twichell would publicly defend the actions of his Commanding Officer, General Daniel Sickles, at the battle of Gettysburg—where he moved his troops without orders and, in the eyes of some, thus compromised the Union position.[66] Twichell was also in some demand in the region as an after-dinner speaker, and had a minor reputation for various literary pieces (on Clemens, Charles Dudley Warner, Harriet Beecher Stowe) and for his 1891 book on John Winthrop.[67] His work on the Chinese educational mission and for Atlanta University did have connections to the national political scene, but the part Twichell played was a minor one at that level.

There was indeed never any doubt in the eyes of both Clemens and Twichell—certainly from the Clemens's earliest Hartford years—which one of the two was the more important in terms of celebrity, public reputation and influence. And we might see here a reflection of larger lines of cultural authority. As the church gradually faded in its influence, the power of the popular press and an increasing emphasis on the cult of personality meant that Clemens, his opinions and his wit, were never far from the nation's public attention. At the same time, Twichell—perhaps finding it difficult to retain his own sense of spiritual vocation in the increasingly liberal religious context of these post-war years—never seemed quite secure in the authority that we might expect his faith and his ministerial status to have given him. On occasion, indeed, he seemed plagued by doubts about his role. So, as the new year of 1880 came in, he wrote in his journal: "As for me, I confess my many, many sins and my deep unworthiness—also my unprofitableness as a servant of Christ in the ministry. May the year now opening witness in me . . . a new devotion to and efficiency in my work."[68] Similarly, when he read Mary Cheney's biography of Horace Bushnell, he noted: "It has given me ... a fresh instigation to try and struggle out of my low estate and reach some high ground. I am convicted of sin, sin, sin, and emptiness. ... Oh, Lord, must I live on to the end in this poverty?"[69] In the flyleaf of the journal covering Clemens and Twichell's last trip away together to Bermuda in 1907, Twichell wrote—upside down (as was his practice with his more confidential thoughts)—some additional notes. One reads: "MT 1907 [—] If you have enjoyed your fame I have enjoyed my obscurity."[70] This statement may allude to the public recognition of the two men on holiday, but it is also suggests a larger cultural truth.

## IV

Twichell's friendship with Clemens functioned in terms both of larger family relationships and one-to-one fraternal interaction. The two families apparently got on very well together, though—as Steve Courtney implies—Harmony's friendship with Olivia may well have been restricted by the domestic circumstance of Harmony's "difficult life, which combined pastoral service with the direction of a busy household and the raising of nine children."[71] And, within the Nook Farm community, much mutual entertaining took place, especially at the Clemenses' house. On some of these occasions just Joe Twichell would attend, but even when this was the case it was in the context of the larger gathering of the Clemens family and their friends, rather than in the more contained sphere of his and Clemens's male intimacy.

Twichell's *Journals* have many references to such activities in the Clemenses' Hartford years. Many of these events included both visiting celebrities and members of the local community. A few examples—scattered over the period—will suffice, though they give little impression of the intensity of social relationships in this community on an almost day-to-day basis:

To M. T.'s to dinner with H[armony]. The special occasion was the presence of W. D. Howells the author, who came to town two days since to lecture. We heard the lecture on Gibbon, and the next morning I attended an extra meeting of the (Girls) Sat. morning club at M. T's where Mr. Howells talked most charmingly about Venice. ... W. D. H is the most pleasing personally of all the literary folk I have met. He seems to be a downright and simple *good* man. [December 14, 1877] H. and I dine at M. Ts where we met Mr. Geo P. Lathrop, Hawthornes [*sic*] son-in-law, and Mrs. H. B. Stowe—a delightful evening—especially in the pleasure of hearing Mrs. Stowe talk. She was in the mood for it, and struck a reminiscent strain having much to say of the old anti slavery days. We were conscious of a great reverence toward her. [November 17, 1882]

H. and I went to M. T.'s in the P. M. to meet Matthew Arnold, his wife and daughter, at tea.—a great pleasure.... Mr. Arnold, in particular, was a gentler, more sympathetic person than his writings would lead some people to expect. [November 15, 1883]

Clemens's tendency to take center stage at such social events—perhaps a response to the expectations of his guests—comes across strongly in these journal entries. Thus on New Year's Eve 1876–77 at the Charles Dudley Warners': "At 12 o'clock, after much pleasant talk and storytelling (M. T. was at his best), we sang together 'Nearer My God, to Thee,' and I led the company in prayer, all uniting at the close in the Lords [sic] Prayer." And—at a February 3, 1882, dinner "at M. T.'s with a company of gentlemen, invited to meet Mr Frechette the poet laureate of Canada"—Twichell comments that "M. T. *never was* so funny as this time. The perfect art of a certain kind of storytelling will die with him."[72]

If these were some of the more formal social occasions in which the families participated, a good degree of informal coming and going also occurred. Such activity could spill over into other (and more professional) areas. So, on October 1, 1888, Twichell tells how Clemens, just returned from his summer vacation, came over and, catching "us dining in the kitchen," asked "if we had a room to spare him as a hiding place he could use while finishing a book he is writing" (presumably *A Connecticut Yankee*). Twichell writes that their house was in some disorder, with "carpenters and painters still infesting it and adding their racket to the natural Twichell tumult," but that they were happy for Clemens to use it as a "literary retreat," which he accordingly did.[73]

What comes over clearly is how much kindness and affection the two families had for one another, particularly where their respective children were concerned. When Twichell was asked to accompany a church member, Mr. Case, and his party to Europe in 1882 (as it happened, soon after Harmony had given birth to another child, Sarah Dunham Twichell), he reported on "an offer from our most-beloved friend Mrs S. L. Clemens (Mrs. Mark Twain) to bear the cost of [daughter] Julia's going... with me"—an offer then gladly accepted.[74] As Twichell's children grew up, Clemens showed a continuing concern for their welfare. So when Harmony Twichell—who had been working (since 1901) under considerable pressure, in terms of hours, conditions, and numbers of patients, for the District Nursing Service of Chicago—decided to come back home, Clemens (in one of his more conservative modes) wrote: "I am so glad young Harmony is out of those Chicago slums. I was always cordially glad to have her ease the pains of those unnecessary people, but it distressed me to have her trying to delay their dissolution."[75]

Similarly, when Clemens heard of Joseph Hooker Twichell's football injury at Yale—he was unconscious for several days—he was quick both to send Twichell a telegram ("Is the report true that one of your boys is hurt, answer paid") and then to express his concern in letter form.[76] He also, evidently, wrote a "handsome letter of introduction" when David

Twichell, a newly qualified doctor, went to Saranac Lake to work in Dr. Edward L. Trudeau's new tuberculosis sanatorium there.[77] Equally, Twichell's relationship with the Clemens children, and their affection for him, is indicated by Clara's letter of September 26, 1909, when she asks him if he can "keep a secret for just ten days? So secret that not even the cat hears a breath of it?"—as she reveals her planned wedding and asks him "to come and marry us." Both the opening and closing of the letter ("My dearest Uncle Joe . . . I couldn't get married without you.—Yours devotedly—") speak clearly of the deep warmth between them.[78]

The two men's friendship had a number of different dimensions outside this family context. They attended many events together which were male-dominated (and usually men-only) occasions—Yale Glee Club concerts, meetings of the Monday Evening Club, single-sex dinners ("Dined at M. Ts. with a company of gentlemen to meet Stanley the African explorer"), a banquet at Delmonico's on April 8, 1889, (in honor of "A. G. Spaulding and his party of American base-ball players who have made a tour of the world"), meetings of the Kinsmen and the like.[79] The two also accompanied each other on activities connected with their professional lives. So when Twichell went to lecture on his South American travels at the local "Insane Asylum," he reports that Clemens "went with me to study the audience."[80] And when Clemens went to lecture to the cadets at West Point, Twichell went along too ("[Clemens] said he would go, if I would; not otherwise").[81] I focus here primarily, though, on the leisure activities that just the two men shared.

Twichell was a great outdoorsman. The family holidays were usually spent in the Adirondacks (Keene Valley) for one to two months in the summer, and it was here that he best relaxed with his family: "Oh, my, how good it seems to get a flannel shirt on, and stretch out on the veranda, novel in hand, pipe in mouth, a big cool mountain up against the sky yonder, and six clear weeks of unalloyed indolence ahead. To lie thus at sweet lawful leisure . . . —what bliss it is!"[82] Twichell also sampled such "mountain and wilderness delights" elsewhere.[83] So—in the summer of 1875—he went salmon fishing in Canada (as the guest of Dean Sage, another of his life-long friends), returning ". . . enthusiastic in his praise of this most magnificent sport that fishermen are ever privileged to enjoy."[84] Clemens had no liking at all for fishing, revealing an unusual sensitivity to the victims of such pursuits. Twichell must have suggested (late on in their lives) that his friend take up the sport, for Clemens wrote him, with a typical barb in the tail, on August 28, 1901: "You would teach *me* fishing? Go to—you make me shudder. I haven't caught a fish—for 'sport'—in 42 years. I'd rather lose a finger-joint, than see the poor devil struggle. Why? I don't get any real satisfaction—that is, any lasting satisfaction—out of seeing a *man* in pain. Except the missionary the other day."[85]

But Clemens and Twichell enjoyed doing most things together, many of a physically active nature. They took pleasure in travelling abroad in one another's company (two Bermuda visits and the *Tramp Abroad* trip); in the walks they went on, especially in the local Hartford area; and in a number of other outdoor leisure pursuits. Twichell's diaries for the trips abroad are relatively skimpy and tell us little that we do not know from Clemens's published work. He notes a "long charming walk" on the first Bermuda stay.[86] On the 1878 Europe trip, he records floating down the Neckar in a small boat ("Blistered my hands rowing but it made me feel young").[87] He also gives details of the two impressively long walks he took alone, Clemens "being rheumatic," in the Swiss Alps: twenty-five-and-a-half miles and thirty-two miles, on August 17 and 19, 1878, respectively.[88]

The pleasure Twichell took travelling in Clemens's company is clear in a journal note made on their second Bermuda visit (with Isabel Lyon, from the second to the ninth of January 1907): "The weather was perfect every day; the company altogether delightful, M. T. being in excellent spirits all the while. . . . We took several long drives, and a lovely sail in the waters about Hamilton, delighting ourselves on the soft balmy air, and in viewing again the scenes that had enchanted us thirty years before."[89] In his travel diaries, recording their stay at the Princess Hotel, Twichell adds a telling detail: "Miss Lyon did everything. M and I like two children in her charge."[90] In her own diaries, Isabel Lyon herself indicated that the overall picture of the trip may not have been quite as rosy as Twichell imagined— that, as he had aged, so he had become (to his longtime friend) the more irritating:

> Mr. Twichell tires him beyond words—so that the King [Clemens] almost loses patience . . .
> The King . . . is so gentle & gay—when Mr. Twichell doesn't make him too nervous . . . .
> The King & Mr. Twichell walked up & down, but it wasn't comforting companionship for the King as Mr. T. is so deaf & can only hear when he is shouted at.[91]

As Hartford neighbors, and clearly close friends in those much earlier years, the two men did other things together too—and without such strains. They attended "a grand baseball match between the 'Hartfords' and the 'Bostons'" on May 18, 1875. (Clemens lost his umbrella at the game, and made it the excuse for a little self-publicizing humor.[92]) Twichell was quick to take up the new activity of cycling. On May 19, 1884, he wrote in his journal: "Today I had advanced far enough in the art of the wheel to begin using the new 'machine' which is to be my own, having hitherto taken lessons on one furnished by the Bicycle Mfg. Co. It has been a rather rough experience till now, but I am over the worst at last and begin to see possibilities of pleasure in this modern way of locomotion." Two weeks later, Clemens had been drawn into the new venture, but clearly with less than one hundred percent success: "June 3 & 4th On the morning of these two days M. T. and I were up at about 5 o'clock for bicycle exercise in the fresh and cool of the day. . . . The experiment on the whole was not satisfactory."[93]

Twichell and Clemens's relationship was based on a number of assumptions, and by a humorous intimacy on each side. Twichell took considerable pleasure in his role as "Mark Twain's pastor," and found himself accordingly something of a minor celebrity, especially on his visits to the United Kingdom. He tended to take rather a proprietary attitude to Clemens at times, often asking him to sign autographs for his own friends and correspondents. It was this type of intervention that led to their one major falling out, when Clemens sent him details of a "history game" he had invented (with his children's assistance) up in Elmira.[94] Twichell replied that "I'm going to let Charlie [Hopkins Clark, *Courant* editor] print part of [your letter],—that part about English History—and I'm going to do it before you will have time to prevent me; so don't fret a minute." Clemens was absolutely furious, since he planned to release the game as a commercial enterprise and did not want the details made public. At the top of Twichell's letter (which he evidently forwarded to family or close friends), he wrote: "I send this to beg that at least *you* folks will avoid this damned fool's example. I shall never thoroughly like him again. SLC."[95] Twichell played the innocent and never gave Clemens much of an apology ("it was a good sin I committed"), and Clemens gradually put the incident behind him.[96]

Clemens, on his part, enjoyed pushing Twichell to his limits, especially in matters of a sexual or smutty nature. It clearly entertained him to target his clergyman friend when he wanted to write in this mode—and it seems Twichell was quite broad-minded enough to enjoy such exchanges. Thus, famously, Clemens wrote *1601: Conversation As It Was by the Social Fireside in the Time of the Tudors* in summer 1876 with Twichell mainly in mind, and—once back in Hartford—read it to him and gave him the manuscript.[97] In this parody of Elizabethan discourse and manners, the elaborate forms of speech of the period are contrasted with an indelicate subject matter—sex, masturbation, farting, and so on. And on other occasions, too, his correspondence with Twichell would lead in similar risqué directions. So, in a June 10, 1879, letter from Paris about writer and critic Hjalmar Boyesen, he looses a series of double-entendres: "Boyesen called on Renan & Victor Hugo, also, & had a good time with both of those old cocks, but I didn't go—my French ain't limber enough. I *can* build up pretty stately French sentences, but the producing of an erection of this sort is not my best hold—I make it too hard & stiff—& so tall that only a seaman could climb it...."[98] In a June 28, 1888, letter, he takes up the subject of women's periods—arguing that if men were thus affected, they would use them to much better advantage than women for occasions they wished to avoid: "January 1. Gentlemen: I am sorry to be obliged to say that my monthlies having come upon me last night, etc."[99] There are other letters too of similar type.

## V

Novelist Russell Banks (married to Twichell's great-granddaughter) comments on the Twain-Twichell friendship and the *Tramp Abroad* trip, and particularly on the escape from domestic bonds it brought the minister. He describes Twichell as: "a man as likely as Clemens was to long for escape from the confines of Hartford respectability and High Victorian family life, which surely must have felt stifling at times to both men. It's an old male dodge... leaving the women, children, and servants behind and lighting out for the territory with his best male friend."[100] Such a (temporary) move beyond the scan of genteel and feminine authority is also indicated in Clemens's sharing of off-color jokes. For on the "old cocks" page of the letter described above, he notes that: "This page is private to Joe. Mum!" While in the second (June 1888) letter, he adds: "I shall not tell Livy I have written, because she would want to know what it was I wrote."

Such moves to male "territory" are, though, occasional—and seen, moreover, very much as marginal to the main and serious business of life. They do recall, however, other allusions to similar "escapes." So Twichell describes Clemens as acting "just like a boy," "shouting in the wildest ecstasy" at Kandersteg (on the *Tramp Abroad* European visit) as he chased beside driftwood cast on "a torrent tumbling down the gorge."[101] And he would himself refer to times spent with Clemens as the recovery of a boy's world. Writing to Clemens about the 1877 Bermuda trip, he rejoices in the "happy four days we spent ashore—how innocent and mirthful! I was more like a boy in my feelings than I remember being for many a year."[102] While the conclusion to the letter in which he responds to the news that he is to join Clemens in Europe in 1878—"Good night. Imagine me turning handsprings as I make my exit"—again implies a return to a Tom Sawyer-like realm of boy's play.[103]

Twichell's reference to Clemens "junketing with other fellows" on the May 1882 Mississippi River trip catches something of their own sense of companionship—letting their respective hair down in a man-to-man relationship at one remove from the normal workaday world. Clemens, too, would take special pleasure in the ludicrous scrapes in which Twichell was occasionally involved. So, on one occasion, Twichell went to visit two "fluttery old ladies," and—while he was waiting to see them—his back started itching. To relieve it, he picked up a long ivory paperweight and pushed it down inside his collar, but only for it to break off at the handle. One of the elderly sisters had then to help retrieve the fragments.[104] On hearing of this episode, Clemens wrote: "It is delicious, delicious! It couldn't have happened to anybody but you."[105] On another occasion, also to Clemens's amusement, Harmony bought her husband a tonic (also a type of dye) to remedy hair loss. Twichell failed to read the instructions properly and when he next spoke from his pulpit, it was with "strangely dyed hair."[106]

These details may seem irrelevant, merely amusing footnotes to the two men's relationship. But I am reminded again here of what Peter Stoneley says about the "juvenile quality" of Twain's friendship with Howells—and its quality of being "slightly out of the way of adult life."[107] Exactly the same seems true for much of the Clemens-Twichell relationship. Their enjoyment of leisure activities together and the shared boyishness that

characterized them, and their sometime delight in the slippage of bourgeois respectability either in sexual innuendo or in forms of ludicrous
behavior, provide an ongoing playful—but *marginal*—element to the
"more mundane social logic" underlying their bonds.[108]

The friendship, then, worked first and foremost in terms of the social
benefits it brought to both men. So Twichell helped—early on—to bolster
Clemens's position as he looked to marry into Olivia's respectable, eastern,
and moneyed family and as he (and his new wife) became members of one
of the most conservative and cultured communities in the country. He
then reaped his own social reward as Clemens's own celebrity and cultural
standing grew.[109]

Twichell was—as a Civil War (Union) veteran, Congregationalist minister to this exclusive Hartford community, and member of the Yale Corporation—the very epitome of American respectability and conservatism,
even as we take his 1884 rebellion against the Republican Party into
account. Harold K. Bush speaks of him as "a major figure in Gilded Age
civil religion." He is referring here to the late-nineteenth-century link
between religious belief and political thought—and the way in which the
providentialism associated with the former became joined to the idea of
American historical destiny itself. Twichell's role as the "outspoken disci-
ple" of this civil religion is suggested by his part as main orator at the
Hartford 1876 centennial celebrations, and the fact that he "frequently
spoke or led prayers at other major and minor events commemorating
America throughout New England and New York State."[110] So, speaking (for example) of the "bright side" of the Civil War at the May 1865
meeting of the American Tract Society, he elided church and country in
saying that: "The strong days of the country had come, the strong days of
the Church were not far off; and he hoped the days were near when those
noble soldiers would advance the banner of the Church as they did the flag
of the country."[111] There is but a short step from here to his support for
Theodore Roosevelt and the missionary activity and imperialist ventures
at the century's end—support that helped to lead to an ideological rupture
with Clemens in their later years. (See chapter 3 for more on this.)

The two men, though, managed to retain their warm friendship despite
this. Clemens's 1907 reference to Twichell as "my oldest friend—and
dearest enemy on occasions" perfectly sums up its contradictory nature.[112] Twichell was always conservative, and it suited Clemens earlier
in his life to have such a friend, and to share many of his values. But
Twichell's conservatism stiffened as Clemens himself gradually became
more and more critical both of conventional religious assumptions and of
the actions abroad of his country and its representatives. In the later years
of his life, Clemens—while still enjoying the status and privilege that his
celebrity and his money brought with them—would distance himself considerably from many of the hegemonic values that Twichell continued to
represent. But if such a distancing was accompanied by something of a
retreat from the immediate forms of their friendship, the bonds between
them remained both affectionate and strong. (Katy Leary said that "[a]s

long as either Mr. Clemens or Mr. Twichell lived they were really close friends."[113]) With the family's financial problems, Susy's death and Olivia's long-term illness, Clemens pulled down many of the shutters and depended on his family for his main support. And when he did socialize it tended to be with Henry Rogers and his family rather than back in Hartford—a place more or less off-limits to him once Susy had died there. When Olivia then died in her turn, Clemens was increasingly thrown in on himself. As Twichell wrote at the time, "All who knew [the Clemenses], and the manner of their life together, are saying, 'How will he ever do without her? With what pitiful dismay he is now saying it, poor fellow, to himself, can be only imagined.'"[114] On Jean Clemens's death, late in 1909, Twichell wrote of his own family's response: "we were all oppressed in spirit by the thought of desolate M. T. in his lonely house" (in Redding, Connecticut).[115]

But even in these last years, the two men did still see one another. Twichell, for instance, was there to meet the remaining family in New York when, after Olivia's death, they came back from Italy with her body. He then went with them up to Elmira ("Going and coming...I had much talk with M. T. of former fondly remembered years").[116] And he visited Clemens during the latter's final New York residency of 1904–8. Their relationship, though, was mainly continued though their written correspondence. And whatever Clemens's feelings about his opinions, Twichell remained very special in the former's life, as the 1897 ("something divine in you") letter quoted earlier in this chapter suggests. When Twichell died in 1918, Howells would particularly comment on the depth of Clemens's affection for him: "... when [Clemens] spoke of 'Joe' Twichell, the famous author's face assumed a wonderfully affectionate aspect, and he showed in every word that he loved the simple, manly, unassuming clergyman who had been his friend for so many years."[117]

Unlike Clemens, Twichell himself did tend in his own later years to introduce a negative note to the picture he gave of his friend (remember the obituary he wrote with its reference to Clemens's nature and its "elements strangely mixed"). It may be that the outbursts of Clemens's last years, whatever the equanimity Twichell usually showed on the surface, were just too much for his good-hearted Christian nature to easily take. Despite this, though, the friendship was clearly of huge importance in the lives of both men. On Clemens's side, it helped to sustain him in some of his darkest hours, while the picture of Twichell, desolated by his own wife's death in 1910, reading over and over again "Uncle Mark's letter written when Aunt Livy died," suggests some kind of final reciprocity in the exchange.[118]

# 3

## Clemens, Twichell, and Religion

By birth and by marriage [Clemens] was of the Calvinistic faith which bowed the neck of most Americans in the early eighteen-seventies . . . and then began to break of its own impossibility and to substitute the prevailing scientific agnosticism. His personal unreligion went far back in his early life. The faith he had been taught in his childhood passed with his childhood, but it held against his reason and remained in his affection long after it had ceased in his conviction, and until his church-going became a meaningless form. Then when he turned from the form the heroic woman who had no life apart from his could only say, "Well, if he must be lost, I do not wish to be saved," and their Christianity ceased to be a creed and remained a life. . . . [T]he doubt that has always haunted [Clemens] hardens into denial and effects itself at last in such an allegory as *The Mysterious Stranger*, who bedevils a world without reason and without pity.
  —William Dean Howells, *Harper's Magazine* (March 1918).

I

ᴛ he Clemens-Twichell friendship lasted from 1868 to 1910. In that period the belief systems and authority of American Protestant religion changed dramatically. A general move took place away from the lingering effects of a Calvinist heritage, while the more liberal forms of religion that replaced it were challenged by an increasing secularism and agnosticism and a diminishing belief in an ethnocentric, anthropocentric, and geocentric version of the Deity.[1] Such a transition was the result of new scientific formulations of the universe (especially Darwin's) and a response, too, to rapid social change. But a host of other factors also played their part.[2]

Twichell's part in Clemens's life has been recognized, but the lifelong influence of their friendship on the latter's "religious" sense is still relatively fresh ground. Clearly, pastors like Twichell retained much of their prestige and power at this time, even as the theological underpinnings of their faith shifted—and their congregations remained sizeable and strong. But we do see a renegotiation of cultural authority taking place as religion lost ground as a central organizing principle in the lives of many Americans, and as pastors and their churches became marginal rather than central in a nation increasingly fixed on the business of making a living rather than on future salvation. I am of course generalizing here. But I would nonetheless suggest that in Clemens's relation with Twichell, and his gradual disengagement from Twichell's church, his belief system, and his political views, we see paradigmatic signs of a larger social process. Religion increasingly struggled to retain its position and force in a nation where the answers to the questions Clemens put in his "The Revised Catechism" (1871) ran as follows:

What is the chief end of man?
A. To get rich.
In what way?
A. Dishonestly if we can; honestly if we must.
Who is God, the one only and true?
A. Money is God. Gold and greenbacks and stock—father, son, and the ghost of the same—three persons in one: these are the true and only God, mighty and supreme; and William Tweed is his prophet.[3]

Clemens's attitude to religion was complex and often contradictory. Stanley Brodwin traces in some detail "his virtually lifelong engagement with the religious ethos of his culture, his personal struggles with theology and with the way theological belief shaped a humanity ultimately (and justifiably) 'damned.'"[4] This engagement illustrates Clemens's increasing skepticism about orthodox Christian belief, but a skepticism fueled by "a kind of controlled spiritual and moral rage," basically theological in character.[5] Clemens's relationship with Twichell does not contradict such a reading. It does, however, conveniently divide into three clear stages, which may helpfully illustrate the larger patterns of Clemens's thinking and beliefs.[6]

Clemens's courtship, and the role Twichell played in his life at the time, shows him at his most pious, seriously engaging with the task of spiritual reformation necessary to the successful fulfilment of his relationship with Olivia, his wife-to-be. The Hartford years following close on that marriage have him living a relatively conventional life as a member of a close, wealthy, and church-going community, regularly attending religious services and giving considerable support to Twichell's Asylum Hill church. There is, at this stage, little sign of that earlier strong spiritual commitment. There is, however, the sense of a man who, whatever his inward feelings and conflicts, is happy to play a part supporting a local church that made no stern doctrinal demands and expected little in the way of formal requirements from those who attended it. What is perhaps surprising is just how extensive and committed a role Clemens played in this church community.

Finally, in the years following Clemens's departure from Hartford, his relationship with Twichell takes on—at least in terms of their exchanges about human nature and religious belief—a somewhat predictable shape. Twichell tries, as he puts it, to take Clemens's "pessimist tricks with my optimist trumps."[7] With his firm Christian principles, he plays the role of gentle and temperate respondent to his friend's often savage and irritable, but always deeply felt, outbursts. Predictably such exchanges ended in stalemate, though the role the minister played in deflecting the full public force of Clemens's more intemperate outbursts was recognized by both men. Apparently a world apart in terms of religious sentiments, there are however moments—and especially at the time of Twichell's wife's death—when Twichell seems to briefly come close to sharing his friend's attitudes. Their two positions are not always dissimilar in their view of the world but rather in their response to it. I look here both to provide a type of "thick description" of the religious dimension of their relationship and to further flesh out our knowledge of their friendship.

## II

Twichell's identity was first and foremost defined as a clergyman. Clemens did not always have much time for the clergy and enjoyed making jokes at their expense.[8] In Twichell's case, at least in the early years of their friendship, these remained harmless ones. So he reports in his Journal entry of December 30, 1875: "M. T. being sick with an attack of *dysentery* sends me the following":

> Religious Conundrum suggested by my present disease.
> *Question:* If a Congress of Presbyterians is a PRESBY*tery*, what is a Congress of dissenters?
> *Answer:* A DYSentery.[9]

Clemens's reputation on first coming first east was as something of a wild and dissolute man. It is generally recognized now, though, that his anarchic humor and satiric attacks on genteel authority were never more than just one side of a more ambivalent whole.[10] Leah Strong (Twichell's first biographer) describes Clemens's early relationship with him as follows:

> Twichell and Twain, very different in background and beliefs, found something in each other which each quickly liked. That Twain could overlook the parts of Twichell's theology with which he might disagree does not seem improbable, because Joe was a good companion, active, athletic. . . . That Twichell could accept Twain with his roughnesses, as well as his unorthodox beliefs, is only slightly more difficult to understand.[11]

While I would not disagree with her analysis, it may over-emphasize Twichell's own commitment to theological orthodoxy—at least, when it came to discussing religious matters with his more secular-minded friends. It may also downplay the extent to which Clemens *was*, at least early on, attracted to the religious aspects of his friend's life, and willing to give serious commitment to them.[12]

It seems clear that the time when Twichell's religious influence was most strongly felt by Clemens was in the fifteen-month period from their first meeting until the marriage to Olivia (February 2, 1870). To have any chance of winning the latter's hand, Clemens needed to turn over a moral new leaf. He had first (famously) come across his wife-to-be through the "ivory miniature" carried by her brother, Charley, fellow passenger and friend on the *Quaker City* expedition. He first met her in New York, where over the Christmas and New Year period, 1867–68, he seems to have seen her on a number of occasions.[13] When he visited Elmira, and the Langdon family home, in the August of 1868 he appears to have fallen fully and "precipitously in love with [her]."[14] It was, though, evident both to Clemens and to everyone else around him that, if he were to succeed in his courtship of this delicate young woman from a wealthy and respectable northern liberal family, he would have considerably to mend his former ways. For, as Susan K. Harris says, he had previously "been a wild young man, a fact he readily admitted" with a history of various forms of what, to the Langdons, could only be called loose behavior.[15]

Twichell, at this point, provided an important sounding-board to Clemens and a source of spiritual advice. Olivia and her family were of pious disposition. Thus Clemens's new friendship, and Twichell's moral influence, came at a propitious time in his own changing personal life. David, Twichell's son, in his memoranda on his mother's death in 1910, kept notes of his father's words at that time. He includes the following passage: "Dad in bed about Uncle Mark:—'The first time he came to family prayers at our house, he went into the hall crying aloud.'"[16] The religious atmosphere of the Twichell household, then, clearly affected Clemens deeply as he looked to personal reform. And in his letters to Olivia and her family at the time, we see him reflecting on his past and engaging with the Langdons on their own religious terms as he attempts to assure them both of his own better qualities and the thoroughgoing nature of his character change. So, in a letter to Olivia, he meditates openly on his previous "sowing the wild oats" and how his attitude to that early behavior has now changed:

> No, Livy, I yield in the matter of sowing the wild oats. I have thought it over—& I have also talked it over with Twichell the other night, & I fear me I have been in the wrong. Twichell says, "Don't *sow* wild oats, but *burn* them." I was *right*, as far as I went—for I only thought of sowing them being the surest way to make the future man a steady, reliable, *wise* man, thoroughly fitted for this life, equal to its emergencies, & triple-armed against its wiles & frauds & follies. But there is a deeper question—whether it be advisable or justifiable to trample the laws of God under foot at *any* time in our lives? I had not considered that. Through your higher wisdom I now & then catch glimpses of my own shallowness, my idol, my darling. God keep you always free from

taint of my misshapen, narrow, worldly fancies—& keep me always pliant to your sweet influence. You must lead, till the films are cleansed from my eyes & I see the light. Thenceforward we will journey hand-in-hand. Hand in hand till we emerge from the twilight of Time into the fadeless lustre of Eternity.[17]

This is not, to say the least, the kind of voice or discourse we would normally expect from Clemens, and it would be easy to accuse him of hypocrisy. But this would be too harsh a judgment. He was a many-sided and paradoxical man, and as he looked "to rise to [Olivia's] level—to reform his rough habits, overcome his religious skepticism, and adopt a more conventional, self-consciously Christian way of life," he undoubtedly cast himself fully into that particular part. As Smith and Bucci sum up: "He may well have been working a deception about his own character and beliefs—but it is impossible to read [the] letters [of this period] without realizing that if he was, he was not aware of it at the time."[18]

As the letter above suggests, Twichell was clearly a crucial figure of support to Clemens as he embarked on his reform program and simultaneously conducted his dialog with, and courtship of, Olivia. In an earlier letter to her (addressed as "My Honored Sister"), he writes that "I pray as one who prays with words, against a firm-set mountain of sin.... Mr. Twichell has confidence that I shall succeed, & says that I will be a most useful man in the world then."[19] Clemens moved very quickly in pressing his case: as he wrote to Olivia's father, "I am not hurrying my love—it is my love that is hurrying *me*."[20] By the end of November his success in doing so had resulted in an unofficial engagement. As Clemens wrote to Twichell exultantly:

My Dear J. H.
   Sound the loud timbrel!—& let yourself out to your most prodigious capacity,—for I have fought the good fight & lo! I have won!...[I]f ...I prove that I have done nothing criminal or particularly shameful in the past, & establish a good character in the future & *settle down*, I may take the sun out of their domestic firmament, the angel out of their fireside heaven....I am so happy I want to scalp somebody....I walk in the clouds again. I bow my reverent head—thy blessing![21]

The contradictions of discourse here, in the final move from violent western vernacular to religious piety, are entirely appropriate to Clemens's own self-divisions.

Twichell's response to this news is equally revealing, and also marked by mixed forms of discourse. He congratulates Clemens in a jovial way, gently satirizing the nature of the particular ministerial language expected of his profession before then substituting it with a more vigorous and immediate colloquial response: "Receive my benediction, Mark.... I breathe it toward you—that particular doxologic & hallelujah formula thereof which I use on occasions which but for the sake of propriety I should celebrate by a smiting of my thigh...& three cheers with a tiger!" The last phrases suggest something of the heartiness and warm and immediate good-fellowship that undoubtedly marked their relationship.[22] There follows a passage in which the minister's sense of pastoral responsibility is more clearly evident: "I don't care very much about your past, but I do care very much about your future. I hope & expect, that it will be...nobly lived...ending with the dear life eternal which our Savior gives for repentance & faith.... And while you are in the mood of gratitude...begin with genuine diligence to pray for & seek that peace in believing in Jesus Christ....Be assured, my friend, I have not forgotten you in my secret hours with God, & I shall not." Clemens then comments, as he reports the words to Livy: "It is just like him—the gorgeous, whole-souled fellow! What splendid nights we had together!—& how gently & how tenderly he taught the religion that is all in all to him. And shall be to me, likewise, I hope & pray."[23]

I do not need to labor my point. Twichell played the role of confidant and religious prompter and advisor to Clemens during the courtship and Clemens obviously took his lead very seriously, while still remaining aware of his own spiritual weaknesses.[24] The letters to Olivia that follow show his continuing to record the reliance he placed on Twichell in this period and his own stumbling move toward moral and religious improvement. So, five days after the letter just quoted, he again writes, this time concerning a three-hour late-night conversation with the minister when:

> We had talked a great deal about you, of course; & we had also held a long & earnest conversation upon the subject of religion. I told him, Livy, what was the truth—that although I had been praying...since about the middle of September, & here latterly day by day & earnestly, I feared I had not made as much progress as I ought to have done—& that *now* I began clearly to comprehend that one *must* seek Jesus for himself alone, & uninfluenced by selfish motives....And Livy, that most excellent friend told me *clearly* and *concisely* HOW to seek the better life....And at last, in the midst of the solemn night, he prayed fervently for my conversion, & that your love & mine might grow until it was made *perfect* love by the approving spirit of God—& that hand in hand & with hearts throbbing in unison we might compass that only worthy journey of life whose latest steps ushered the wayfarer into the home of eternal peace.[25]

The letters to Olivia and Twichell that follow mine a similar vein, and Clemens's relationship with Olivia reached a successful climax with their official engagement and marriage. Twichell assisted Thomas K. Beecher, pastor of the Elmira Congregational Church, at the marriage ceremony held in the Langdon home on February 2, 1870. He and his wife also visited Clemens and Olivia five days later at their new house in Buffalo (a gift from Mr. Langdon). The closeness of the relationship, and its extension on a family level, is suggested by the joint vacation planned in the Adirondacks in the August of that same year—though Clemens eventually pulled out of this due to his father-in-law's illness and Olivia's pregnancy.[26]

III

Whatever the level of Clemens's own self-deception in this courtship period, his commitment to Christian orthodoxy, and to Twichell's influence as a spiritual guide, were considerable. The next stage in the relationship between the two men (and their families) effectively starts with the Clemens family's move to Hartford in late September 1871. During his engagement, Clemens had looked to acquire a share in the Hartford *Courant* but had been unsuccessful in his overtures.[27] Both the desire to live in Hartford and to become a regular member of Twichell's congregation had figured in this plan. So Clemens wrote to Olivia on February 15, 1869: "I told [Twichell] we meant to live a useful, unostentatious & earnest religious life, & that I should unite with the church as soon as I was settled; & that both of us, on these accounts, would prefer the quiet, moral atmosphere of Hartford.... I wanted him to understand that what we want is a *home* ...."[28] The couple had first settled in Buffalo after the marriage, Clemens working as co-owner and co-editor of the *Express*, but—after a series of "catastrophes and near-catastrophes"—he and Olivia decided to leave just over a year later.[29] The move to Hartford would instigate the most settled and, for the most part, happy period in the family life, with the building of the home on Farmington Avenue in 1873–74 and residence there till 1891.[30]

Until Kenneth R. Andrews published *Nook Farm: Mark Twain's Hartford Circle* (1950), it was generally held that Clemens had completely retreated from religious commitment after the early period of his marriage. Clemens's biographer, Albert Bigelow Paine, had undue influence here in suggesting the parting of Clemens and Twichell's religious ways, in his report of a conversation between them during the *Tramp Abroad* trip of 1878. He quotes Clemens as follows: "Joe,... I'm going to make a confession. I don't believe in your religion at all. I've been living a lie right straight along whenever I pretended to. For a moment, sometimes, I have been almost a believer, but it immediately drifts away from me again. I don't believe one word of your Bible was inspired by God...." Paine continues: "So the personal side of religious discussion closed between them, and was never afterward reopened."[31]

It is difficult, though, to take this recollection as the crystal truth, as both Andrews and Courtney suggest.[32] One of Twichell's own letters to his wife, Harmony, written during the same trip, carries no such sense of rupture— at least, at that particular stage of their expedition. It does, though, suggest that both men were fully aware of Clemens's failings on the spiritual and moral front. But this is a significant letter in more than one respect, as it contains some of Twichell's most considered judgments on his friend's character:

Mark and I had a good talk after dinner this evening on religion. A good talk, I say: he got to speaking of himself in a way that gave me a chance to declare gospel truth to him. "Romola" [George Eliot's 1863 novel] started it. Mark observed that he had been seeing himself as in a looking glass in the skilful uncovering of the working of motives which characterizes the book. And presently he said "There's nothing that makes me hate myself so, and feel so mean as to have Livy praise me and express a good opinion of me, when I know all the while that I am a humbug, and no such person as she takes me to be." He said this very heartily and I sympathized with him, dear, and told him that I knew just how it was, having experienced the same humiliation from a like cause myself. And so we got onto the subject of character and the state of the heart, and the application of Christ's gospel to the wants of a sinful man.

People don't know Mark's best side. I am more persuaded of it than ever.... Would that the grace might touch him with power and lead him into larger views of things spiritual than he has ever yet seen!! He is exceedingly considerate toward me in regard of everything, or most things, where he apprehends that my religious feelings are concerned [Twichell then gives an example regarding Clemens's cancellation of plans to travel on a Sunday].... And when we kneel down together at night to pray, it always seems to bring the spirit of gentleness upon him, and he is very likely to be affectionate after it. After all, coarse as he is in streaks, he is a genuinely loveable fellow. As to the whiskey, most of the time he doesn't take any, and drinks no more wine and beer than I should, if I indulged, as I feel I might without sin. Anybody here would call him temperate. Really I am enjoying him exceedingly and take delight in being with him.[33]

Twichell's much later remark to his son, following Harmony's death, suggests that the pattern of their relationship, at least when they were away together, changed little over the years: "When he and I have been off together and sleeping in the same room, Uncle Mark always knelt with me in the evening when I prayed for the families and in the morning repeated the Lord's prayer for me. When it was time for our prayer he would say, 'Come on Joe.'"[34] The extended story Twichell's journals tell is rather different, too, than the one Paine would suggest. Clemens never formally joined Twichell's church (perhaps as he and Olivia were already members of Thomas K. Beecher's Park Church in Elmira) and his religious beliefs were decidedly less than orthodox. But, along with Olivia, he regularly attended that church, played a regular part in its activities, and supported it financially—sometimes raising funds by performing on its behalf—during the period in which they lived in Hartford. Indeed, he rented a family pew at Asylum Hill right up to 1891.[35] I give a number of examples of such activity, dating both before and after the supposed 1878 incident. Early in the Hartford years, even before the Farmington Avenue house was built, Clemens's distinctive presence in Twichell's church had been publicly noted. The "Correspondence" of the Springfield Union of December 20, 1872, contains a first-person report from Hartford: "Invited by a friend, I attended last Sabbath, one of Hartford's 'model churches.'" The writer describes the congregation there, including "a delegation of Chinese,"

Rose Terry (the regionalist writer) and Charles Dudley Warner (editor of the *Courant* and soon to coauthor *The Gilded Age* with Clemens), then continues: "Directly behind [Warner] appears a man, dressed in furs, with a rather awkward, hesitating manner, as if he wasn't sure where his pew was located; his locks were rather curly over a somewhat low forehead, but, after all, he was one concerning whom a stranger would say, as I did, "Who is that?" and the answer would be "Why, don't you know? Mark Twain? . . . He resides on the hill, in a cottage leased of Mrs Isabella Hooker, the famous woman suffragist."[36] From then on, evidence of Clemens's participation in church-related affairs during the Hartford years is relatively abundant.

On at least two occasions, Clemens supported Twichell's work on behalf of the Hartford City Mission, run by Father Hawley. Clemens advertises the first of the lectures given on behalf of this cause in the Hartford *Evening Post* of January 28, 1873. He writes here of Hawley's work and the help needed that "vigorous winter" on behalf of "women & children—women broken down by illness & lack of food, & children who are too young to help themselves" (and, Clemens is careful to specify, *not* "in behalf of able-bodied tramps who are too lazy to work").[37] His statement that "several of us have conceived the idea that we might raise a thousand dollars . . . through the medium of a lecture" fails to mention that it was a plea by Twichell from his pulpit on January 26 that had prompted this response from some "prominent citizens" of the Hartford community.[38] A further Clemens lecture on Hawley's behalf followed in 1875. Twichell had, the previous year, visited Peru with fellow Hartford resident and Chinese educational and welfare worker, Yung Wing, to look into the conditions of the Chinese workforce there.[39] He himself initially planned to give a public lecture on this subject, but then withdrew: "I was to lecture for Father Hawley on Peru, and M. T. was to introduce me. But when it came to the 'scratch' I backed out and got M. T. to stand in my place." Twichell describes the event itself, a little dismissively given the circumstances, in his March 5 journal entry: "M. T. lectured in the Opera House for the City Poor. $1200.—H [Harmony] and I sat in the box with Livy. The subject was 'Nevada'—a pretty fair performance for a *lecture*, but not at all equal to what he commonly does in private talk."[40]

Clemens regularly supported Twichell's church. His celebrity must have made his participation in its fundraising activities very welcome. And his support was generally of the type that allowed him to tap into his humorous talents. So Twichell pasted in his journal the May 12, 1875, report from the Hartford *Courant* of the "spelling match" that had taken place the previous evening at the Asylum Hill church. Clemens's "preliminary remarks" to the match itself are quoted at some length:

The temperance crusade swept the land some time ago—that is, that vast portion of the land where it was needed—but it skipped Hartford. Now comes this new spelling epidemic, and this time *we* are stricken. So I suppose we needed the affliction. *I* don't say we needed it;

for I don't see any use in spelling a word right—and never did. I mean I don't see any use in having a uniform and arbitrary way of spelling words. We might as well make all clothes alike and cook all dishes alike. Sameness is tiresome; variety is pleasing. I have a correspondent whose letters are always a refreshment to me, there is such a breezy unfettered originality about his orthography. He always spells Kow with a large K. Now that is just as good as to spell it with a small one. It is better. It gives the imagination a broader field, a wider scope. It suggests to the mind a grand, vague, impressive new kind of a cow. Superb effects can be produced by variegated spelling.

A full account of the match is then given (with a description of the prize donated by Clemens himself, a "nosegay painted on a slate surface"): "Altogether the match proved very amusing," runs the report, "the Rev. Dr. Burton, Mr. Twichell and Mr. Clemens especially enlivening the exercises by occasional comments."[41] Twichell's parish scrapbook also contains a notice of a "Concert and Readings by the Park Church Quintette and 'Mark Twain' at the chapel of the Asylum Hill Congregation'l Church" scheduled for May 31, 1876.[42]

Casual journal entries by Twichell recording (June 13, 1875) that "M.T. and W. D. H[owells] walked home from Church with me," and (November 5, 1876) that "After evening service went over with H. to M. T.'s and had a very pleasant hour with Bret Harte (who had been at morning service)," confirm that Clemens and his guests regularly attended the Asylum Hill church.[43] This was clearly a community where church-going, and the values that accompanied it, were the norm—and Clemens was apparently happy be part of it, and to toe its (liberal) line regarding beliefs and rituals. That Twichell can write to Clemens, "Next week *Friday* night...I want you at the Chapel. Do you hear?"[44] suggests that he can easily make such a demand without it being taken as anything other than a matter of course.

On February 16, 1881, Twichell again asks, "Dear Mark, Will you read for us—and for me in particular—in the Chapel next week Friday evening, Feb. 25th?? It will be for you a preparation for West Point [where Clemens was to give a reading], and for our good folks a service that will be much appreciated." Clemens replies—"Dear Joe replies: All right, I'll do your lecture-humbug for you the 25th. Keep it quiet, you know; no printer's ink. The way we did it before was right."[45] On a trip to Europe in the summer of 1882, Twichell and his daughter Julia visited Chester Cathedral.[46] Talking to a local clergyman, Twichell expressed his particular interest in the old crypt, "coming as we did from a country that had nothing old in it": "To which he responded that we had some things that England didnt [*sic*] have. 'I take one of your magazines' he said, 'and *there's* Mark Twain.' Mr Case [who had funded Twichell to lead his party] looked at me, and quietly remarked 'Why, he is a near neighbor of mine; and this gentleman (pointing to me) is his minister.' And Julie put in 'and at our house we call him Uncle Mark.'"[47] This sequence of evidence makes it clear that Clemens had close affiliation to the Asylum Hill church. Twichell, in Strong's words, "often adopted the attitude of pastor toward parishioner in the relationship with Twain, and Mark Twain seems to have accepted this attitude completely."[48]

Two more examples of this relationship will suffice. On July 17, 1883, Twichell writes Clemens about a Mr. J. M. Allen, one of the church deacons, who had recently met ex-President Hayes at a social event. Hayes had asked Allen if he knew Clemens, and Allen replied, "A little . . . but not as well as I wish I did. I *see* him often. He goes to our church."[49] Indeed, in May 1888, Clemens played a lead part in a reception held by Twichell's parishioners to celebrate the minister's fiftieth birthday. The *Courant* reported the event as follows:

> Mr. S. L. Clemens, who followed [Dr. Gallaudet], said that he supposed he had been called partly because he was a considerable portion of the congregation. He stood as an evidence of what Mr. Twichell had been able to construct. . . . We all feel alike, continued Mr. Clemens, about the limitless degree of affection expressed in the paper read by Mr. Morris and hope it will be kept up so long as Mr. Twichell continues to do so well. Mr. Clemens then related an absurd incident which occurred in Switzerland, showing how great an influence Mr. Twichell had exerted upon him during their sojourn together in that country, and closed by reading the following poem which, he said reminded him so strongly of his pastor.

The poem, partly transcribed below, is St. George Tucker's "Days of My Youth." Charting the fading of energies that comes with age, it also looks forward, in a suitably pious way, to the coming years:

> Joys of my age,
> In true wisdom delight:
> Eyes of my age,
> Be religion your light.
> Thoughts of my age,
> Dread ye not the cold sod;
> Hopes of my age,
> Be ye fixed on your God.[50]

If the poem seems more suitable for an older man than Twichell, it nonetheless suited the spirit and tone of the occasion. Clemens seems to have found the right balance between humor and tribute without stealing the occasion from those around him (something of a tendency for him). Here, despite his celebrity, he takes his place among others in the church community and very much speaks as one of them. Twichell's value to his congregation can be measured by its generosity toward him at this event, when, as previously mentioned, his parishioners presented him with a gift of the deeds of his house and additional money to enlarge and improve the property.[51]

Clemens attended church on a regular basis and played a relatively conspicuous part in its affairs. But we get little sense in the above detail whether this was something he mainly saw as a social obligation in such a respectable community, and which he was, additionally, pleased to do as one of Twichell's closest friends, or whether genuine religious commitment lay beneath such actions. Kenneth Andrews's verdict seems as close as we will get to the truth: that Clemens "had rejected Christianity . . . ruled out all theology, and the supernatural that it attempted to interpret, but he was not contemptuous of Christianity as a basis for an equitable society and not at all at odds with his community's regard for personal and public morality."[52] The odd comment attributed to Clemens, taken with whatever pinch of salt, certainly suggests his church-going was less than fully devout. The Twichell Family Scrapbooks, for instance, contain a May 1906 article pasted from *Human Life: A Magazine of Today*, discussing the two men's relationship in some detail:

> Mr. Twichell, who himself possesses so broad a sympathy and so pervading a kindliness that he can understand almost any sort of nature and tolerate almost any kind of vagary, had, perhaps, a more complex understanding of Mark Twain's somewhat complex nature than any other man in Hartford—than any other person in Hartford except Mr. Clemens's wife. . . . [The article goes on to describe a compliment Clemens once paid Twichell]. . . . At the conclusion of the morning service he waited at the door for the preacher, and, taking him to one side, said:— "I mean no offence, but I am obliged to tell you that the preaching this morning has been of a kind that I can spare. I go to church to pursue my own train of thought. But to-day I couldn't do it. You have interfered with me. You have forced me to attend to you—and I have lost me a whole half hour. I beg that it might not occur again."[53]

There is, though, no reason why we should put Clemens's actions, and the belief system on which they rested, under too close a scrutiny. After all, it was doubtless the liberal nature of religious practice in Hartford that made the Asylum Hill church so comfortable to him.[54] Twichell himself, though, does seem to have felt a certain anxiety and sense of failure of responsibility concerning his friend's religious state: "I'll try to be a better minister than ever to you, Mark, i.e. I'll try to *be* one, which I often fear I haven't been at all. I've got the affection any how, whatever else is wanting."[55] As far as Clemens was concerned, however, Twichell's status as "my pastor" went unquestioned. At least, this is the term he was still using to describe him as late as 1898.[56]

## IV

Paine's suggestion of a spiritual rupture between Clemens and Twichell in 1878, then, appears misleading and one-dimensional. The Hartford life that followed shows Clemens's continued close relationship with the minister and his church. It is obvious that, very soon after his marriage, Clemens's religious skepticism returned.[57] But the nature of contemporary Hartford Congregationalist religious practice meant that no break from the church, its services and its social rituals was necessary—Christianity could be lived out within that community as a way of life rather than as a strictly followed creed, to recall Howells's initial quote.[58] It was only later, as his attitudes toward the conventional structures of Christian belief became increasingly ironic and angry, that a definite rupture occurred. This roughly coincided with his effective departure from the Hartford community in 1891 and the changes in fortune that followed: both his increasing business difficulties (climaxing in the 1894 Webster & Co. bankruptcy) and domestic tragedies (the death of Susy in 1896 and of Olivia in 1904).[59] His attitude toward religious belief, and indeed toward human nature itself, became increasingly mordant in these later years.[60] He did continue, right to the end of his life, to engage in religious debate and dialog with Twichell but that debate came to take something of a fixed and formulaic quality, with Twichell acting as the positive counterpoint to Clemens's pretty thunderous nay-saying.

Indeed, both men came to recognize the somewhat ritualistic quality of their exchanges. Twichell would chide Clemens about his misanthropy in a semi-jocular manner: "Mark, the way you throw your rotten eggs at the human race doth greatly arride me. We preachers are extensively accused of vilifying human nature, as you are aware; but I must own that for enthusiasm of misanthropy you beat us out of sight."[61]Clemens, in return, would admit his need to release his darkest thoughts and views, with Twichell as their foremost recipient. This seems to have been done primarily as a type of necessary release mechanism, but Clemens must always have known that Twichell would provide at least some counterbalancing response. So, on June 24, 1905, he launched a vituperative attack on Theodore Roosevelt's "[w]hitewash & slumgullion" in a letter to Twichell, noting in particular the gap between the president's rhetoric and his actions: "Joe, even the jelly McKinley was a man, compared with this kitten that masquerades in a lion's skin." A (long) tirade against Roosevelt continues until near the end of the letter when Clemens breaks off to say: "I have written you to-day, not to do you a service, but to do myself one. There was bile in me. I had to empty it, or lose my day tomorrow. If I tried to empty it into the North American Review—oh, well, I couldn't afford the risk. . . . I *have* to work my bile off, whenever it gets to where I can't stand it. . . . I have used you as an equilibrium-restorer more than once in my time, & shall continue, I guess . . . ."[62]

As I suggest earlier, by this point Clemens and Twichell had moved pretty far apart in terms of their political and religious opinions—especially on missionary activity abroad, on imperialism, and on Roosevelt. Twichell grew up in an atmosphere of revivalism and, even before the Civil War, would describe his envy of the missionary graduates from his own Union Theological Seminary who had chosen to spread the Gospel abroad.

After his war experiences, he settled quickly into the pastorate of Asylum Hill Church but would often refer to his (and Harmony's) own desire to enter missionary life in the late 1860s.[63] And in later life his passion for missionaries seems to have been as fresh as it was early on.[64] As far as imperialism goes, Twichell was an Anglophile, and believed firmly in the popular philosophy of John Fiske, whose view was that the Anglo-Saxon nations, and particularly the Protestants, were destined to bring light to the rest of the world. He did not seem to have a great deal of problem with American dominance in, say, the Philippines, or British dominance in India and the rest of the empire. In other words, Twichell displayed a conventional though intelligent conservatism. His affection for Roosevelt was strictly along traditional Republican lines. He had the standard view of him as a manly, athletic figure, hero of San Juan Hill, who made the nation strong and extended its reach overseas but also had a reformer's zeal against the trusts.

But despite their political, social, and moral differences, and the fierceness of some of Clemens's verbal assaults, the two men continued—at the wider level—both to tolerate and remain affectionate toward each other. So Twichell responded to Clemens's June 24, 1905, letter on July 3 as follows: "All right, Mark; go ahead. I give you free leave to syphon out to me all such secretions whenever they accumulate to the pitch of discomfort. . . . 'Tis an old saying that 'some mens [sic ] oaths are more worshipful than some mens [sic ] prayers.' The *motive* of your automatic curses is, I allow, pure, though the *object* of them might, in my opinion, be more judiciously selected. But I will not argue that point with you."[65]

Twichell gently deflects Clemens's "bile" here, while crediting the moral impulse that drives it. In the last decade of his life, Clemens would rail to Twichell at a variety of targets, and, as he did so, managed to beat most others—both in his ridicule and in his pessimism—out of sight. He denounced western missionary activity in China, using comedy (see note 85, chapter 2) but also anger ("the Chinese . . . have been villainously dealt with by the sceptered thieves of Europe") as his medium.[66] Imperialism, too, and especially the Philippines venture, was high on Clemens's list of moral targets, with the attack here becoming personal as Twichell is chided for his conservative role: "This nation is like all the others that have been-spewed upon the earth—ready to shout for any cause that will tickle its vanity or fill its pockets. . . . *I* can't understand it! You are a public guide & teacher, Joe, & are under a heavy responsibility to men, young & old; if you teach your people—as you teach me—to hide their opinions when they believe the flag is being abused and dishonored, lest the utterance do them & a publisher a damage, how do you answer for it to your conscience?"[67]

Clemens lashes out in all directions in these years, by now challenging those progressive and providentialist versions of history in which the majority of his contemporaries, and certainly Twichell, believed. He saw "civilization" as bringing some progress ("better than *real* savagery"), but judged its overall gains unimpressive: "My idea of our civilization is that it is a shabby poor thing and full of cruelties, vanities, arrogancies, meannesses, and hypocrisies. As for the word, I hate the sound of it, for it conveys a lie; and as for the thing itself, I wish it was in hell, where it belongs."[68] Twichell acted for Clemens as sounding board and escape valve for such verbal assaults, often a more personal, spontaneous, and intemperate version of his public writings of the time. If Clemens saw Twichell as an "equilibrium restorer," there were clearly many issues where this just could not happen, so great was his sense of anger, injustice, and ironic contempt for all he saw around him.

We see more generally in this correspondence Clemens trying out ideas, attitudes, and language that frequently resurface in his more formal written works. So the part of him that would move from bleak satire and deterministic pessimism to solipsism (a step away from reality, using the imagination to extinguish it and refashion it as a fiction) is given expression in a letter to Twichell of July 28, 1904, shortly after Olivia's death. Here, Clemens gives an early version of the ending of *No.44, The Mysterious Stranger* (published posthumously) in expressing his sense of dislocation and estrangement:

Dear Joe:
"How life & the world—the past & the future—are looking"—to me? (A *part* of each day—or night) as they have been looking to me the past 7 years: as being NON-EXISTENT. That is, that there is *nothing*. That there is no God & no universe; that there is only empty space, & in it a lost & homeless & wandering & companionless & indestructible *thought*. And that I am that thought. And God, & the Universe, & Time, & Life, & Death, & Joy & Sorrow and Pain only a grotesque & brutal *dream*, evolved from the frantic imagination of that insane Thought.[69]

Twichell recognized a fundamentally Calvinist mentality underpinning much of his friend's anger: "your milk is ... pretty sour it seems to me, old fellow. Really you are getting quite orthodox on the doctrine of Total Human Depravity anyway. And as a Protestant (in the original, literal sense) you surely hold the belt."[70] For Clemens now saw human nature as both corrupt and predetermined. "The largest bulk of the human race," he lectured Twichell, is composed of "the fools, the idiots, the pudd'nheads."[71] Twichell would recall, in the public meeting held in Clemens's memory at Carnegie Hall that: "He once broke out in a letter I had from him: 'Oh, this infernal Human Race! I wish I had it in the Ark again—with an auger.'"[72] Clemens himself would cancel two lines in one letter to Twichell, where he refers to humankind as "that noble race which was made out of the excrement of the angels."[73]

Clemens, however, added a postscript to follow the deleted comment above: "That erasure was an ungentle slur at the human race. Ungentle, and unfair. I retract it. I wish I could learn to remember that it is unjust and dishonorable to put blame upon the human race for any of its acts." Something of Clemens's inconsistencies surface here. For his view of man as a creature to be denounced for his cruelties and corruption clashes with a mechanical determinism—fully enunciated in *What is Man?* (1906)—that undermines as a meaningful category both the concept of the self and the moral agency it may possess. So the same letter to Twichell continues: "For [the human race] did not make itself, it did not make its nature, it is merely a machine... moved wholly by outside influences... a helpless & irresponsible coffee-mill ground by the hand of God." This must have been just one of that type of "abominable heresies, of which you are now sporting quite a menagerie" to which Twichell was constantly responding.[74] He was, though, perceptive enough to notice the different direction in which Clemens's versions of humankind were taking him. For at the Carnegie Hall Memorial Service he insisted: "[Mark] had.... the keenest appreciation of the ignoble side of human nature, and was wont, on occasion...,to rail at the human race accordingly.... [H]e was not a cynic. The theory of character, as determined absolutely by the conditions to which the individual is subject, with the deduction of man's total moral irresponsibility which some of us had heard him maintain long before he came out with it [was] so inconsistent with those impeachments of mankind that have been referred to...."[75]

In these late years, Twichell hardly seems to have faltered in his friendship for Clemens.[76] Despite the severity of Clemens's critiques of conventional religious belief and the assumptions on which they rested, he continued to respond in a calmly good-humored and unflustered way to such barbs. While aware of the more eccentric sides of human nature, he would reject his friend's more damning and contemptuous responses to it. He wrote Clemens on January 25, 1904, about an old woman of Hartford who had "made arrangements with [a local undertaker] for her funeral in every detail, bearers and everything," and her consequent annoyance as those bearers gradually died themselves: "The last time she came on that errand [to tell the undertaker of such a death], she... grumbled 'If this sort of thing goes [on], there will be *nobody* to attend my funeral!' as if all her anticipated enjoyment of the occasion was in danger of being destroyed." Twichell then comments: "Human Nature! I don't think so ill of it as you do, Mark, but it is, indeed, a queer affair, in spots."[77]

Twichell certainly did not dismiss Clemens's words and opinions out of hand and was not always so relentlessly upbeat as my chapter thus far may suggest. Indeed, we might see him, in some ways, as peculiarly twinned with Clemens, the Angelo to his Luigi (see *Those Extraordinary Twins*)—sharing some of his thoughts and feelings but, as a result of his foundational religious faith, usually able to respond in a quite opposite manner. He, too, clearly had his moments of religious doubt. Replying to Clemens's "there is no God & no universe" letter, he is sensitive to his friend's distress and admits to having responded similarly to life's seeming lack of meaningful logic. But he then sets his conventional Christian response against Clemens's skeptical one and looks to fix the latter's eyes on what he continues to see as the more positive side of things, rather than validating his despair:

I can't wonder . . . that with the light of your life gone out you sit dazed in the dark seeing no meaning or reason in anything, the Universe appearing to you only a confusion of unintelligible phantasmagoria. But it makes my heart ache for you, old fellow. I wish I was with you. . . . For I am not ignorant of the thoughts you are thinking. They have visited me too. I, indeed, *believe*, that behind the riddle there is a Hidden and Awful Wisdom; that for one tempest-tost [sic] on these wide weltering seas there is an Anchorage, that for the mortal spirit there is practicable victory over the world with all its baffling mysteries.

Of course I do, or I wouldn't be a Christian minister. But I am not going to preach to you. . . . I would, though, as I say, like mightily to be at your side just now. Maybe, Mark, we would kneel together once in a while, as we have done in times past. Really, it seems to me, that is the posture for a man *to* take in the midst of these unfathomable realities. I do hope that you have some company to your taste. . . . I fancy you more or less solitary . . . .

As for yourself, Mark, in some ways [the past few years] have been how splendidly prosperous and successful! . . . How marvellous [your career] has been! . . . Do hold yourself to think on your more than royal fortune and lift up your head.[78]

However, Clemens may have received this (and one suspects there may have been more than one ironic shake of that very head here), Twichell writes in obvious concern and good faith, desperately unhappy on his old friend's behalf.

Twichell's own wife, Harmony, died on the night of Clemens's New York funeral service. This was completely unexpected, with Twichell urgently summoned back to Hartford by his son, receiving his message just before the service began. The blow was such that even his Christian confidence seemed to have briefly wavered. The note in his son's memoranda following the death is suggestive here: "In bed with Dad,—He said that once Uncle Mark said to him, 'Now, Joe, if it had been left to you and seriously, would you have started the human race . . . .'" Twichell was obviously devastated, and read over and over the letter his friend had sent him when Olivia died.[79] But even in this desolation he was able to keep faith: "Dad getting out of bed Wednesday morning,—'I may as well get up, Dave, and face life, with God's help. We have many, many blessings to be thankful for.'"[80]

Right to the end of their friendship, with Clemens's own death, Twichell remained—due to the nature of his profession and his own religious belief—the yea-sayer to Clemens's nays. The "optimist trumps" he would play in their exchanges ranged from his expressions of belief in a Christian providentialism (the August 17, 1904, letter), to his progressive and evolutionary stance towards human affairs as a whole:

I do not despair of the Republic, or of the Human Race, for that matter. Dig down in history anywhere you like five hundred years . . .

and then go down on your knees and ask forgiveness for being such a dog-goned pessimist at the opening of the twentieth Century. At the same time felicitate me on its being...given to me to see...that the coming in this world in a steady progress from age to age is the kingdom of God—of righteousness. Yes, sir; the signs preponderantly of a brief millenium point that way; they surely do....Climb out of your hole, Mark; get up where you can see a distance; drop your cussing and shout Glory...The *war* isn't ended yet, nor will be for more milleniums. But the parsons are winners, I tell you.[81]

Clemens, of course, was not convinced and his letter to Twichell the following day starts with the words:

Dear Joe,—I have a Pudd'nhead maxim:
"When a man is a pessimist before 48 he knows too much; if he is an optimist after it, he knows too little."

He then goes on to talk of *What Is Man?* the book that "[f]or seven years I have suppressed" and "which my conscience tells me I ought to publish." As he answers Twichell's points about human progress, he gets entirely into his stride:

Well, the 19th century made progress...colossal progress. In what? Materialities....But the addition to righteousness? Is that discoverable? I think not....All Europe and all America are feverishly scrambling for money....Money-lust...has rotted these nations; it has made them hard, sordid, ungentle, dishonest, oppressive....If there has been any progress toward righteousness since the early days of Creation—which...I am obliged to doubt—I think we must confine it to ten per cent of the populations of Christendom, (but leaving Russia, Spain and South America entirely out.) This gives us 320,000,000 to draw the ten per cent from. That is to say, 32,000,000 have advanced toward righteousness and the Kingdom of God since the "ages and ages" have been flying along, the Deity sitting up there admiring. Well, you see it leaves 1,200,000,000 out of the race. They stand where they have always stood; there has been no change.

N. B. No charge for these informations. Do come down soon, Joe. With love, Mark.[82]

That last touch is typical of Clemens. By giving both sides of his long, long friendship with Twichell and the various forms it took, we can see both the real warmth of that personal relationship, but also the deep difference that came to exist in their theological positions and worldviews. Twichell (and the conventional Christianity he represented) stood in dialogic relationship to much of Clemens's later writings about God and the human race; as the optimistic voice that, by then, Clemens felt bound to refute. Earlier in life, the two men's outlooks were more compatible.

Twichell played an important spiritual role for Clemens in the period just before his marriage. And Clemens accepted his authority as local minister in the (happy) Nook Farm years that followed, whatever the exact nature of his own religious beliefs. Given the explosive ruptures that marked many of Clemens's relationships, and the particular diverging philosophies of these two men, the enduring nature of the friendship is remarkable, a tribute to the tolerance and emotional warmth of which they both, on different occasions and in their different ways, were so capable.

Having said that however, Clemens's later move away from Twichell in terms both of politics and religion was tinged with frustration for his friend's solid predictability and (by that point in his life) defense of the status quo. His liberal and rational religious viewpoint—one which insisted "on the dignity rather than on the depravity of man"—increasingly failed to fit Clemens's increasingly mordant vision, and the larger historical circumstance of a Western world caught up in imperialist disputes and drifting toward the catastrophe of the First World War.[83] Liberal Protestant religion was influential in the early 1900s (as it still remains) but in terms of the cultural dialog then occurring, its power had considerably waned.[84] This was in part the result of rapid intellectual and sociohistorical change and of increasing secularization. But it was also due to the fact that the type of guidance—especially in the world of public affairs—previously given from the pulpit was now often found elsewhere. The churches accordingly increasingly struggled to retain both congregation numbers and loyalties. The manner in which Clemens rather left Twichell behind as a determining influence on his life and thought was thus indicative both of their differing personal visions as time passed but also of a larger American reality where the church and its ministers no longer quite had the influence they once had.

# 4

## "My Dear 'Owells"
### Clemens and Howells

I

In a 1908 letter, Howells refers to Clemens's recent move to Redding, Connecticut, and to a reading he was to do at the local library, with the words, "I thought you went to Redding to get rid of Mark Twain."[1] For Joe Twichell, Clemens was always "Mark Twain," an indication perhaps that the latter's celebrity provided an element in their friendship that was never really put to one side.[2] Howells—who usually addressed his letters to "Dear Clemens" or "My Dear Clemens"—seemed more aware of the private man behind the nom de plume. But he also knew that there was a shifting relationship between the various parts of the Clemens/Mark Twain identity, and that the two could not finally be separated out.[3]

It is Howells's and Clemens's social identities, however—their community and cultural status and shared professional concerns—which (I argue here) provided the vital glue to their strong and long-lasting friendship, and shaped its expressive parameters. Howells's latest biographers, Susan Goodman and Carl Dawson, suggest an almost Siamese connection between the two men. Though they link this in part to Clemens's and Howells's problematic relationships with their respective brothers, Orion and (the mentally infirm) Henry, this was mainly the product of wider similarities: "Each man must have felt that he had found a missing brother... Physically unlike, especially in later life—Howells balding, short, and stocky; Twain tall, wild-eyed, and feathery-browed—they shared professional, social and financial aspirations that made them almost Janus-like halves of the same person."[4] This last set of connections, in particular, cemented the mutual bond between them.

The Clemens-Howells relationship has had more attention paid to it than any of the other Clemens friendships examined in this book. Howells's own memoir, *My Mark Twain* (1910), has been followed more recently by Kenneth E. Eble's *Old Clemens and W. D. H.* (1985) and Louis

J. Budd's "W. D. Howells and Mark Twain Judge Each Other 'Aright'" (2006).[5] Leland Krauth has a chapter, "Creating Humor: Mark Twain & William Dean Howells," in his *Mark Twain & Company* (2003), though his main interest is in the two authors' literary relations and their similar use of the comic form.[6] Perhaps the best and fullest short account of the friendship, however, is in Susan Goodman and Carl Dawson's *William Dean Howells* (2005). Here the authors break off their otherwise linear and chronological biographical account of Howells's life to give an overview of "His Mark Twain, from 1869."[7] My own work builds on these sources (among others).

The most revealing portrait of the relationship between the two men, though, is provided by the two-volume *Mark Twain-Howells Letters* (1960). In a January 1882 letter to Clemens, Howells speculates on literary fame, and concludes: "I wonder how long you will last, confound you? Sometimes I think we others shall be remembered merely as your friends and correspondents."[8] While this overstates what has in fact happened (indeed, critical interest in Howells's work is undergoing something of a revival), their particular correspondence certainly deserves the attention and praise it has received. Howells wrote that "Letters are shorter autobiographies, and perhaps contain more truth than the long ones."[9] And the letters that passed between the two men tell us a great deal about both their lives, thoughts and emotions. So Leland Krauth writes:

> The best record of that friendship is forty-one years of correspondence—wonderful letters full of information, plans, criticisms, affection, and fun—letters that range from cockamamie schemes to cool-headed calculations, from tender reflections to angry condemnations, from contrived performances to spontaneous revelations. If Howells was a genteel writer, given to an occasional flight of subversive play, and Twain a free-flying humorist, given to treading moral ground, each man grasped the full nature of the other. For whatever was secret or concealed or just hard to discern in their published works is quite visible in their personal letters.[10]

Howells's biographers judge similarly: "the openness and intensity of the Twain-Howells correspondence testify to an extraordinary friendship." They see it as possibly "the most important of their collaborations" in a relationship that was "collaborative... in both small and large ways."[11] I refer to these letters, when and where appropriate, throughout the present chapter.

The various collaborations between Clemens and Howells (including this correspondence) followed—to slightly alter the phrase from Peter Stoneley earlier introduced—a mundane social and professional logic. They helped both men build and/or solidify their places in the elite social worlds through which they moved, and as they looked to extend their success and influence within them. Both men were, then, of considerable practical use to one another as they pursued their lives and their careers.[12]

Clemens first met Howells in 1869. He went to the offices of the *Atlantic Monthly*, where Howells was assistant editor, to thank him for his generous review of *The Innocents Abroad*. In that piece, Howells had judged Clemens against his fellow California humorists (the context in which he was then seen) to call him, "in an entirely different way from all the others, quite worthy of the company of the best."[13] Remembering their meeting in *My Mark Twain*, Howells draws immediate attention to their different approach to the conventional eastern proprieties, contrasting his own conservatism with Clemens's transgressive presence. Appropriately, he first uses a literary figure to describe this difference, contrasting the freedom of Clemens's "graphic touch" with his own "fainter pencil." Clemens's flamboyant dress on that first encounter had prompted the metaphor, his wearing of "a sealskin coat, with the fur out, in the satisfaction of a caprice, or the love of strong effect which he was apt to indulge through life."[14]

Howells's focus is of some relevance in terms of their fuller relationship. For—as we trace the then life-long trajectory of their friendship—we will find that it was Howells who (perhaps surprisingly) would be the more transgressive in terms of the more substantial matter of social and political viewpoint. But, in *both* men's cases, we can identify an adherence to the social proprieties and the dominant values of their period that runs alongside—and ultimately reins in—any more radical urge and gesture. Howells adopts the perspective of his employer, the *Atlantic* editor James T. Fields, in describing Clemens on that first meeting as "an original who was not to be brought to any Bostonian book..."[15] The tension between social convention and iconoclasm was in fact (and in the long run) one that characterized both men—and despite Howells's self-representation here. This, though, was the moment that (in Camfield's words) "began a friendship that served the professional, intellectual and social interests of both," even despite the fact that "only for a brief time near the end of Clemens's life when he lived in New York City did the two [actually] live near enough to spend much time together."[16]

After that first meeting, Howells's "recollections of Clemens," as he writes in *My Mark Twain*, had "a gap...of a year or two." He remembered the relationship resuming at a Boston lunch given by Ralph Keeler, Clemens's friend from the California years.[17] On this occasion, Howells famously recalled Bret Harte "putting his hand on Clemens's sealskin shoulder, and sputtering out, 'This is the dream of his life,'" in recognition of the place he was now taking in Boston literary circles. If the date for this event was as Fischer and Frank suggest (November 2, 1871), then Howells would by then have been editor of the *Atlantic*—he had formally accepted the position the previous July—and his influence in the literary world the more considerable.[18]

Goodman and Dawson suggest something more of the close similarities between Clemens and Howells. Born within eighteen months of each other, and raised in near-frontier towns, "both men married Eastern women higher on the social scale than they themselves." They also give other reasons for Howells's attraction to Clemens: "In Twain, who sympathized with his ambitions and admired his writing, who was a doting father, supported his extended family, and rescued a feckless brother, Howells found a validation of his [own life] choices."[19] Their relationship would also soon become two-way rather than the one-way traffic it first was (with Howells as Clemens's literary superior) as it served to reinforce and further the professional interests and careers of both the men. Thus "from about 1875 to the mid-1890s," both could be judged in "roughly equal [terms] as working writers if prestige, productivity, readership, and versatility are somehow computed together."[20] I give more detail on the relationship's literary and professional context in the following chapter. At this point, I focus on the usefulness of each man to the other as they pursued their careers.

## II

Howells's biographers are partly right to challenge the traditional view of the Clemens-Howells relationship, when they argue that "to call Twain the genius and Howells the skilled critic or literary broker misses the point."[21] There was, though, some element of this quality to their friendship, especially in its early years. Much of the material to which I refer here is familiar so I will not labor my points. Howells, in his role both as *Atlantic* editor and as one who had gained the earlier status and authority in the eastern literary world, undoubtedly helped both to build Clemens's own literary reputation, and to provide him with an extraordinary amount of help in editing and proofreading his books for publication. He reviewed Clemens's books regularly, often on the latter's prompting, and was always generous—sometimes perhaps too generous—in his critical responses.[22] But Howells often did catch what was important about Clemens's work, and was tireless in promoting him even in the face of the critical coolness of many of his Boston literary peers (for, as he put it, "Clemens seemed not to hit the favor of our community of scribes and scholars, as Bret Harte had done," when Harte too had come from the West).[23] And his comment on Clemens's use of the autobiographical persona still bears repeating for its insight into the latter's literary talent and tactics: "The personal books . . . have not only the charm of the essay's inconsequent and desultory method, in which invention, fact, reflection, and philosophy wander after one another in any following that happens, but they are of an immediate and most informal hospitality which admits you at once to the author's confidence, and makes you frankly welcome not only to his thought but to his way of thinking."[24]

Howells, though, served Clemens as more than this—acting throughout his writing career as adviser, promoter, and careful critic. Clemens wrote to him about his problems with *A Tramp Abroad*, saying: "Give me your plain, square advice, for I propose to follow it."[25] And when Howells gave that advice—here and elsewhere, and often in specific matters both of style and of plot detail, Clemens usually followed it almost automatically and usually to the letter. So, too, Howells proofread for a number of Clemens's books, including *Huckleberry Finn* and *A Connecticut Yankee*. In the latter case, Clemens more or less dumped the job on him, though with some humor: "I've *got* to get you to read the book . . . I have stood between you & this sorrow with a steadfastness which there is none but me to admire . . . But you will not have to take it at a bite. I will spread it thin, & leave resting-spells all along." Howells responded with his normal generous graciousness: "You know it will be purely a pleasure to me to read your proofs."[26]

For Clemens, Howells was an editor, a promoter, an appreciative reader and a generous reviewer.[27] He encouraged Clemens to write for the *Atlantic*, thus presenting his work to a wider and more respectable audience. He advised him on the choice of content for *The Stolen White Elephant, Etc.* (1882).[28] And he praised him on his work, at times with a metaphoric power to match the material at hand: "The piece about the Mississippi is capital—it almost made the water in our ice-pitcher muddy as I read it."[29] His tact, too, was extraordinary, especially as he managed the difficult task of telling Clemens—usually so quick to take offence—when his work just was not up to scratch.[30]

As I suggest above, however, this was not just a one-way exchange for, as Goodman and Dawson note, Clemens "certainly . . . saw Howells as an equal: a humorist, critic and novelist unmatched among American writers."[31] It may be that both men tended to over-praise the other and (usually) to pull their critical punches. But the importance of their mutual sense of appreciative support more than cancelled out any adverse side effects this brought.[32] Howells would write to Clemens that, "your foundations are struck so deep that you will catch the sunshine of immortal years, and bask in the same light as Cervantes and Shakespeare."[33] And Clemens would respond exactly in kind: "Possibly you will not be a fully accepted classic until you have been dead a hundred years,—it is the fate of the Shakspeares [*sic* ] & of all genuine prophets . . . In that day *I* shall still be in the Cyclopedias, too,—thus: 'Mark Twain; history & occupation unknown—but he was personally acquainted with Howells.' There—I could sing your praises all day, & feel & believe every bit of it."[34]

The sense of mutual appreciation runs throughout the correspondence. For Howells, *Tom Sawyer* is "altogether the best boy's story I ever read . . . The adventures are enchanting. I wish *I* had been on that island."[35] *A Connecticut Yankee* is "a mighty great book, and it makes my heart burn and melt."[36] While *Following the Equator* is "enormously good."[37] "You are my shadow of a great rock in a weary land, more than any other writer," he wrote Clemens in 1899.[38] Howells would, though, chide Clemens about his failure to return such an engagement: "I have a feeling that you don't read me as much as you ought."[39] And the one critical piece Clemens wrote on his friend, the essay "William Dean Howells" (published in *Harper's Monthly* in July 1906) is oddly limited in scope—his judgment that Howells is "without his peer in the English-writing world" based on technical quality rather than on any thematic consideration.[40] Despite this, in his letters to Howells, Clemens could not have praised his work more warmly.[41] Referring to *The Lady of the Aroostook* (1879), then running in the *Atlantic*, he wrote: "If your literature has not struck perfection now we are not able to see what is lacking."[42] Later he commented on the serial version of *A Woman's Reason* (1883): "We have all read your two opening numbers in the Century, and consider them almost beyond praise."[43] Again, while reading the serialized version of *Indian Summer* (1886), he wrote: "You are really my only author; I am restricted to you; I wouldn't give a damn for the rest."[44] Similar high praise is scattered throughout the correspondence.

Such a repeated pattern whereby the writing of the one is then endorsed (privately or publicly, or both) by the other—along with the accompanying tendency to hyperbole—is unsurprising. For each man, committed in his own different way to literary success and public recognition, "had a stake in the career of the other," and gave support whenever that was possible.[45] Both, moreover, shared—as I show in the next chapter—a concern regarding the role and status of the writer in a postbellum America subject to rapid and extreme social and cultural change. The solid basis for the friendship, then, lay in their joint professional and social agenda—committed to wealth, prestige, professional success, and even cultural authority, in their America. But the friendship equally depended on the shared knowledge that such authority—in both their different cases—always lacked stability, and involved something of a delicate balancing act. Both men were serious writers in terms of the judgments they would make on their American (and larger) world.[46] Their position, as such, was necessarily in some ways a marginal one—accepted by society, and gaining a living from its consumption of what they produced, but acting at the same time as its conscience, as types of outsider checking and critiquing its values and beliefs. Such a two-way process involved costs and compromises. Louis J. Budd has just the right phrase to describe the friendship when he says that: "Crucially, Howells and Twain did not try to rearrange each other."[47] They led different lives, shared some friends but not others, and had different value systems. But ultimately each understood the pressures of the other's social and professional role, and served as support and sharer in such circumstances.

Clemens and Howells's drive for professional and financial success is nowhere clearer than in their collaborative literary work. Both men were always aware that a writer's career, in what was a newly professionalizing context, was a risky business. And both men, through early and mid-careers, had financial worries of one kind and another.[48] It is then the less surprising to hear Howells sounding so much like Clemens (who always had his eye on the main financial chance) as he considered a number of their projects together. In 1882, the two men were working on a long-planned project, the *Colonel Sellers as a Scientist* play, and on December 9, 1883, Howells wrote about it to Edmund Gosse: "Entre nous—I have just finisht [*sic* ] writing a play with Mark Twain, from which I hope big money. It seems to me now at least very droll. We have the notion of doing half a dozen, with always the same character for protagonist, whom we wish to make the American mask—like Pantalone for Venice, Stenteretto for Florence, etc."[49] An earlier Howells letter (October 17, 1882) about the same production—but here under its previous title of "Orme's Motor"—refers to "the great American comedy... which is to enrich us both 'beyond the dreams of avarice.'"[50]

The two men were full of similar schemes. So, writing on March 18, 1882, to John Hay, Howells described how he had "seen a great deal of Mark Twain" and how each had confessed to a lack of "literary ambition" (as "the years had tamed us") but: "before we went to bed we had planned a play, a lecturing tour, a book of travel and a library of humor. In fact, [Clemens] has life enough in him for ten generations, but his moods are now all colossal, and they seem to be mostly in the direction of co-operative literature."[51] To read through the two men's correspondence is to find, for example, Clemens suggesting that Howells "tackle" a play based on *Tom Sawyer* "in the odd hours of your vacation."[52] Another idea is for Howells "helping to put" Clemens's brother Orion—"a field which grows richer & richer the more he manures it with each new top-dressing of religion or other guano," according to Clemens—"into drama."[53] Howells himself tried to interest Clemens in a syndicate novel in 1900—and Howells (but not Clemens) agreed to take part in another such scheme, to result in the 1908 book, *The Whole Family, A Novel by Twelve Authors*, launched by the editor of *Harper's Bazaar*.[54] Howells, also—in the only one of all the joint plans which reached any kind of proper fruition—played some part in helping Clemens put together the anthology *Mark Twain's Library of American Humor*, published by Webster & Co., in 1888 (though Charles H. Clark, the Hartford *Courant* editor who also helped prepare the book, did by far the most work on it). Even this not very successful project, though, rather limped along and, despite the occasional effort by Howells to keep it on proper track, took some seven years to complete.[55]

The fact that so little resulted from so much planned activity is significant. Though both men undoubtedly saw potential profit in their collaborations, these projects were subsidiary to their main sources of income and so took inevitable second place in their professional minds. Both men, however, came to rather revel in their ineptitude as far as any joint work of this type was involved, as something that cemented rather than undermined the friendship. Howells made a jokey reference to their becoming "beautiful old [men]" if they would attempt it jointly, since: "We can do anything together."[56] But most of the things they in fact jointly planned—from attempting to travel to the 1876 Concord Centennial celebrations to the *Colonel Sellers as a Scientist* project—were failures. Such sources of immediate frustration, however, became afterward (sometimes quickly, sometimes slowly) a matter of some relish.[57] So when Howells dropped out of a proposed Mississippi River trip that Clemens was to take as he worked on his *Life on the Mississippi* book, leaving publisher James Osgood as Clemens's companion, he wrote of the spoiling of the arrangements, that "this last affair shows that *when there is no outside interference, we cannot fail to fail.*—I am sorry that Osgood is with you on this

Mississippi trip; I foresee that it will be a contemptible half-success instead of the illustrious and colossal failure *we* could have made it."[58]

The *Colonel Sellers as a Scientist* collaboration was something of a debacle, and with little comic side to it at all at the time. Basically Howells lost faith in the project: "It *is* a lunatic whom we've pictured and while a lunatic in *one* act might amuse, I'm afraid that in three he would simply bore." Accordingly, he left Clemens—very much at the last minute—to step out of the contractual arrangements that had been made, to the financial cost of both men.[59] Unusually for Clemens, his clear annoyance at Howells's shilly-shallying dissipated into good humor even as he wrote to complain of his friend's "folly."[60] And he was quick to fully forgive him: "you've done your full share of suffering, & I give you absolution. But don't you turn *again*—lay quiet."[61] From then on the episode seems to have been consigned to the "illustrious failures" category alongside the two men's other blunders.

## III

The pattern of the Clemens-Howells relationship is a familiar one in Clemens's friendships, rooted as they usually were around shared mutual interests in terms of career, the sustaining of the family, of public celebrity, and of social status. When all was running relatively smoothly in such terms, so the joy and the good humor in the friendship could be freely released and enjoyed (as a type of unnecessary but very welcome bonus once such success and stability was assured). So the two men could make jokes about the inept failures of friendship's interaction in the knowledge that they *were* just jokes, with no doubts at all cast on their real abilities, talents, and worth. So, too, Howells and Clemens celebrate their friendship in terms of its indulgent, and even subversive, quality, but knowing that this could be encouraged and allowed exactly because of the respectability and social and professional status that each held secure.

This can be seen in the way their friendship fitted its fuller domestic and social context. In the early years of the relationship, Clemens and Howells tended to stay over at each other's houses—the easiest way of managing the Boston-Hartford distance. The Clemens's architect-designed house was both ornate and extravagant, and Olivia and her husband were generous hosts. Howells was more appreciative of the hospitality than of the house itself, writing his father on March 14, 1875: "We had a really charming visit [to Hartford], not marred by anything. The Clemenses are whole-souled hosts, with inextinguishable money, and a palace of a house, to which, by the way[,] I really prefer ours."[62]

We get a good impression of the luxury of the Clemens lifestyle in Hartford, as opposed to the Howells's evidently more modest and restrained domestic circumstance, in the reactions of seven-year-old John Howells, who accompanied his father on a March 1876 visit. Again writing to his father, Howells tells how: "I took John with me, and as his mother had prepared his mind for the splendors of the Twain mansion, he came to everything with most exalted fairy-palace expectations. He found some red soap in the bathroom. 'Why, they've even got their soap painted!' says he; and the next morning when he found the black-serving-man getting ready for breakfast, he came and woke me. 'Better get up, papa. The *slave* is setting the table.' I suppose he thought Clemens could have that darkey's head off whenever he liked."[63] One way in which the Clemens and the Howells households were similar was in their lack of permanent roots. Henry James called Howells "the most peripatetic man" he knew.[64] The Clemenses too (with the Hartford years as the exception) made frequent moves from one house to the next, and from America to Europe and back again.

It is very clear, though, that whether Howells visited Clemens or vice-versa, the two men got on like a house on fire.[65] I give selective examples. After Howells had stayed over at the Clemenses on June 12–13, 1875, Clemens would write him that, "O, the visit was just jolly! It couldn't be improved on." While Howells reported to his father that he had had "a beaming visit . . . and did a month's laughing."[66] Clemens then writes of the "royal good time" he and Olivia had on the latter's first visit to the Howells house in the autumn of 1875.[67] And when Clemens lectured in Boston in November 1876, spending much of his time at the Howellses' house, Howells wrote to him afterwards, saying that: "Your visit was a perfect ovation for us: we *never* enjoy anything so much as those visits of yours. The smoke and the Scotch and the late hours almost kill us; but we look each other in the eyes when [you] are gone, and say what a glorious time it was, and air the library, and begin sleeping and dieting, and longing to have you back again."[68]

The two men, "kindred spirits with contrary temperaments," strongly appreciated each other.[69] Clemens, typically, targeted his friend with pretend abuse, describing him for instance as "a blamed old sodden-headed conservative," and—in an invented scenario—as "a stumpy little gray man with furtive ways & an evil face."[70] He initialed a photo of the gloomy-faced and long-bearded Sultan of Turkey, "W. D. H," sending it to Thomas Bailey Aldrich with accompanying witty commentary.[71] Howells too enjoyed the joke. Clemens was, for Howells, "the most amusing talker I know: his humor is incessant, and he is genuinely witty."[72] But he also valued Clemens's generosity and absolute truthfulness—writing him that: "You always rather bewildered me by your veracity."[73] And he appreciated what he called Clemens's "exquisite compassion," especially at the time of his daughter's death: "I remember that in a black hour of my own when I was called down to see him, as he thought from sleep, he said . . . 'Oh, did I wake you, did I *wake* you?' Nothing more, but the look, the voice, were everything; and while I live they cannot pass from my sense."[74]

But it was the talk and the fun in their relationship that were its conspicuous features, and ones that remained strong. For this was a relationship, unlike that between Clemens and Twichell, that seemed to suffer little, if any, diminishment even as time passed. In 1902, the two families summered in Maine, just forty minutes apart, and Howells later recalled that "we saw each other often . . . [W]e used to sit at a corner of the veranda farthest away from Mrs. Clemens's window, where we could read our manuscripts to each other, and tell our stories, and laugh our hearts out without disturbing her."[75] In April 1903, Howells would write to Charles Eliot Norton (the only other man with whom he was as close) that despite the changes brought about by Olivia's increasingly serious illness, there was still, "when [Clemens] can break away, almost the best talk in the world . . . left in him."[76] Both men recognized the passing of time, and a sense both of age and of nostalgia increasingly entered their correspondence: "we *are* a pair of old derelicts drifting around, now, with some of our passengers gone & the sunniness of others in . . . eclipse."[77] But even after Olivia's death, and at the very end of Clemens's life, the men could still take a boyish delight in each other's company. So Howells writes of a visit to Stormfield: "Every morning before I dressed I heard him sounding my name through the house for the fun of it and I know for the fondness; and if I looked out of my door, there he was in his long nightgown swaying up and down the corridor, and wagging his great white head like a boy that leaves his bed and comes out in the hope of frolic with some one."[78] This is one of the passages Peter Stoneley quotes when he speaks of the "boyish element" in their friendship—Clemens's tendency to act as a type of Huck Finn, and "for the brief periods that they spent together, [to push] Howells into raft-like, vagabond existence."[79]

That boyishness connects too with the way both men represent themselves in their marital relationships—as held in check by their sense of the social proprieties associated with upper-middle-class life and the institution that most fully upheld it, and as continually "catching it" for their own failures to meet such standards.[80] As Kenneth Eble puts it, "Mark Twain and Howells were, in some aspects of their personal friendship, captives swapping tales of their captivity." He then quotes Dixon Wecter on how both men "enjoyed fabricating . . . a similar hen-pecked role. It was their private little joke . . . , and it was good for a laugh precisely on the score of its improbability."[81] As Howells himself suggested, it is tricky to judge a marriage from the outside—and let alone when one is writing a century and more after its occurrence. But, in his memoir, *My Mark Twain*, he nonetheless represents Clemens's and Olivia's relationship as a particularly strong and sustaining one.

His own marriage to Elinor, though, does not seem to have been completely fulfilling to either party, even if, as Goodman and Dawson suggest, he "could not . . . imagine life without the woman he described as half himself and whose loyalty he never doubted."[82] The evidence for this is based on Howells's letters and on his other writings. His biographers quote from his 1888 novel, *April Hopes* —"If he had been different, she would not have asked him to be frank and open; if she had been different, he might have been frank and open"—with the implied assumption of an autobiographical resonance. And in an 1897 interview, Howells would himself say that "[a]s things are, marriage is very haphazard . . . The belief that there is destiny in it—that there is only one person in the world you could truly love will not hold water."[83] If we can interpret this statement as part and parcel of his commonsense campaign against sentimentalism, he and Elinor do not, nevertheless, seem to have shared any intense intimacy. While John Fiske would describe Elinor in 1871 as "very pretty and charming, vivacious and amusing as always," it is her ongoing health problems—and Howells's skeptical attitude toward them—that sound the dominant note in his own letters.[84]

Both Olivia Clemens and Elinor Howells suffered periods of invalidism, but Elinor's affected the tenor of her marriage more fundamentally and systematically than in Olivia's case. Physically frail—a family letter of 1873 has Howells writing that "Elinor sticks to her old *stylish* weight of 82 pounds. Anything beyond that is not lady-like"—her health was always an issue in their joint lives.[85] In March 1875, Howells would write to his father that "Elinor commonly has a break-down at this time of year, which we hope to avert by going into different air."[86] In 1889, he is writing to Clemens that: "My wife is not well, nor likely to be well all winter."[87] By early 1892, she was evidently "virtually confined to the [Howells] apartment by her long-standing nervous condition."[88] In a 1904 letter to S. Weir Mitchell—whose earlier treatment of Howells's daughter Winny seems to have been pretty much disastrous—he refers to the ending of Elinor's important role in his literary life, in writing that: "[she] used to edit my things before her wonderful electrically critical nerves gave way."[89]

The double-edged, and ironically detached, quality that some of Howells's remarks seem to carry, comes more plainly into view when in 1880 he writes to Clemens that: "Ever since your letter to Mrs. Howells came, I have been wanting to tell you how wonderfully good that comparison of her to a Leyden-jar was. She never *does* quite go to pieces, but it always looks like a thing that might happen."[90] Similarly, in 1898, he refers to Elinor as "debilitating round, as usual."[91] There are also other comments to Clemens about marital incompatibility that, if they remain at a level of generality, may have a self-reflexive element to them. So in the same letter as that quoted immediately above, he wrote that, "Disunion seems to keep people together politically as well as matrimonially."[92] And on August 1, 1906, he reported: "We have been worrying through a summer of suffering from the East wind for my wife. This gale, which I like to let soak my bones to the marrow with its delicious chill and damp, shrivels her up, and she has to hurry indoors and make a fire. Why are people so mismated? This error will never be put right till men marry men. But then there will be no children to appreciate their writings."[93] Howells was clearly fully committed to his marriage, and when Elinor died in 1910, he wrote to his brother Joe that "I suppose [her] death has broken my life in two."[94] But the evidence points to a lack of complete emotional fulfilment within it.[95]

Undoubtedly, however, and despite this, for both Clemens and Howells the maintaining of a certain accepted way of life, based around marriage and the family, respectability and social position, was a primary end. The playfulness within the friendship is that of a "safe microsphere," at one step apart from such responsibilities and priorities.[96] Thus both men can joke about the domestic tyranny of their wives, and their own failures to perform their husbandly role competently and effectively as exactly such a playful release, secure in the knowledge that they *were* good husbands, fulfilling their responsibilities both as prominent citizens and as domestic patriarchs and providers. In Clemens's case such feelings would sometimes be compromised, in the longer term by his own financial mismanagement and bad luck, in the shorter by moments of inappropriate behavior, including (at a public level) the apparent social disaster of the 1877 Whittier birthday speech. But the paradigm still for the most part holds true.

So, in the correspondence, it is the Clemens and Howells wives who wear the trousers, and who are represented by their husbands in ways that counter a real-life genteel and respectable reality. Clemens starts one early letter, "Consound my cats—as Mrs. Clemens says when roused to ferocity."[97] He later writes of his wife's annoyance at missing the "delightful time" he has shared with Howells and Elinor in Boston: "Mrs. Clemens gets upon the verge of swearing & goes tearing around in an unseemly fury."[98] Howells constructs Elinor as an equally fierce presence, writing when he hears of George W. Cable falling ill (with the mumps) in the Clemens house: "What is the matter with Cable? If you had got sick in our house, Mrs. Howells would have killed *me*. She would have killed *you*, *any* way."[99]

In early 1875 Clemens writes to Elinor about the Howells family photo sent to him and his wife: "I can perceive, in the group, that Mr. Howells is feeling as I so often feel, viz: 'Well no doubt I *am* in the wrong, though I do not know where or how or why—but anyway it will be safest to look meek, & walk circumspectly for a while, & not *discuss* the thing.' And you look exactly as Mrs. Clemens does just after she has said, 'Indeed I do not *wonder* that you can frame no reply: for you know only too well that your conduct admits of no excuse, palliation or argument—*none!'*"[100] And when Clemens and Howells were planning a trip to New Orleans together, Howells represented Elinor as the disciplinary presence standing in their way: "And speaking of Mrs. Howells brings me to New Orleans,— or rather it doesn't."[101] There is more than a touch of the Tom Sawyer in the assumption of such roles and identities.

Elsewhere the two men would play on a more general domestic incompetence. Clemens tells an involved story of how, at three in the morning and in dealing with the cat mistakenly shut up in the conservatory, he makes all the wrong decisions. Opening doors and disabling the burglar alarms, he leaves the whole house potentially at the mercy of burglars: "Language wasn't capable of conveying [Mrs. C.'s] disgust. But the sense of what she said, was, . . . '[i]f you had Mr. Howells to help you, I should have admired [your actions] but not been astonished, because I should know that *together* you would be equal to it; but how you managed to contrive such a stately blunder all by yourself, is what I cannot understand.'"[102] Such "routine patter" between the two men becomes, then, a comic way of confirming an opposite reality—their general domestic stability and success, and their wives' reliance on, and trust in, them within the marital relationship.[103]

IV

The different friendships I explore in this book did not, of course, exist in a vacuum. And not only must we see them against the background of family relationships but also within a larger context of male group companionship. So, as Budd says in the case of Clemens and Howells, both men "brought along" to their individual relationship "a thickening social circle."[104] As this book illustrates, one-to-one male friendships work in a number of different ways and on a number of different levels, and the same is true of larger male groupings. So the mutual support, literary companionship and social sustenance which generally prevailed within the Clemens-Howells coterie could cover over extreme differences between its members, not least in terms of their political opinions. Clemens's fondness for, and relaxed intimacy with, Thomas Bailey Aldrich—also a good friend of Howells's—can be glimpsed in the October 26, 1906, letter he sent him (with Clemens now a widower): "It is with mighty pleasure that I record the fact that you will spend Nov. 9th & 10th (& as many days as thereafter as you can spare), under this roof. We will gather some more stags together & eat, drink & get drunk, understanding that on some happy tomorrow we die & are likely to be damned. I am very glad you are coming, old man."[105] Aldrich was, however, at the opposite (right-wing) end of the political spectrum from Howells—and probably some considerable distance from Clemens too—as his May 14, 1892, letter to George Woodberry (then Professor of Comparative Literature at Columbia) indicates:

I . . . wrote a misanthropic poem called "Unguarded Gates" . . . in which I mildly protest against America becoming the cess-pool of Europe. I'm much too late, however. I looked in on anarchist meeting the other night . . . and heard such things spoken by our "feller citizens" as made my cheeks burn. These brutes are the spawn and natural result of the French revolution; they don't want any government at all, they "want the earth" (like a man in a balloon) and chaos . . . I believe in America for the Americans; I believe in the widest freedom and the narrowest license, and I hold that jailbirds, professional murderers, amateur lepers . . . , and human gorillas generally should be closely questioned at our gate. Or the "sifting" that was done of old will have to be done over again.[106]

My point here is not so much to draw attention to Aldrich's extremism but to the fact that it did not appear to affect the sense of community and friendship with his literary fellows.[107] Their shared membership of a certain class and type (cultured men of prestige and importance in their America) provided, it seems, a bond able to sideline even acute divergences of political viewpoints.

This takes me, in turn, to Clemens and Howells, and to their politics, philosophical outlook, and changing views both of the national and international scenes around them. Again, I would suggest that their joint membership of the (white) social establishment provides the crucial framework for any such exploration. Both men mounted serious challenges to what we might call hegemonic values and assumptions: those by and large shared by the nation as a whole and by those who directed its affairs. But both men—literary practitioners positioned, in this respect, on the margins of the world of public affairs—never stretched the boundaries of what they could acceptably do and say too far. Neither man ever ruptured his connection with other members of what we might call (on the broadest of levels) an American ruling class or ceded his status and privilege as a member of that group, though Howells, on one occasion, came very close to doing so.

I am not accusing either man of hypocrisy here, and that must be made absolutely clear. I am saying, rather, that each man followed his conscience, protested at the inequities and political injustices he saw around him, and developed personal philosophies that departed considerably from the cultural norm. As *artists*, however, whose voices carried some weight in the larger American cultural conversation, neither man ever escaped the inbuilt contradiction of their position—critical of (some of) their country's values yet necessarily working within the conventional limits of public expression; looking to change American public opinion and policy but dependent on that same public for their continued celebrity and professional success. Both Clemens and Howells trod a narrow line. In critiquing aspects of American political life, each man undoubtedly compromised his public reputation to some degree. But such criticism was contained within certain boundaries, by the need to consider their own best interests as well as by the limited nature of their voices and power of their influence. Howells (famously) wrote to his father in 1890 about the "way of thinking" the Clemens and Howells families shared: "we are theoretical socialists, and practical aristocrats. But it is a comfort to be right theoretically, and to be ashamed of one's self practically."[108] This sense of being caught between the two poles of radical opinion and practical concession, critical words and comfortable living, affected both men throughout their careers.

Howells, though, pushed the limits of acceptable opinion in matters of public affairs and policy further than Clemens. In the 1870s, he was a Republican supporter and the 1876 biographer of successful presidential candidate (and relative on his wife's side), Rutherford B. Hayes. But even at this time Howells showed unease with the way the fast-changing social and industrial landscape was shaping the larger American world, writing to his father in April 1873: "By the way, do you think that farmer's rebellion against the railroads will spread into Ohio? I'm glad of any union amongst them, for I hope it may lead to some sort of communism and society which is the only thing that can save them from becoming mere peasants."[109] When Clemens jumped Republican ship to become a Mugwump in 1884, Howells would remain loyal to Blaine.[110] But in making his choice, Howells would still express a certain disaffection for the behavior of both the main political parties of the time: "Politician for politician, self-seeker for self-seeker, I prefer a Republican to a Democrat."[111]

By the late 1880s, Howells was increasingly concerned over the influence of capitalism in the period and the nature of its political supports. He had accordingly largely withdrawn from close party affiliation, taking instead what Goodman and Dawson call a "metapolitical view" of his country's affairs.[112] In an 1888 piece on Matthew Arnold, he would note his anxieties about the changes in the American way of life: "the relations of capital and labor in our free democracy are about as full of violence as those in any European monarchy; we have wasted the public lands which we won largely by force and fraud, and we are the prey of many vast and corrupting monopolies."[113] And in the same year, he would famously write to Henry James: "after fifty years of optimistic content with 'civilization' and its ability to come out all right in the end, I now abhor it, and feel that it is coming out all wrong in the end, unless it bases itself anew on a real equality." He then adds—in an earlier version of the "practical aristocrats" reference—"Meantime, I wear a fur-lined overcoat, and live in all the luxury my money can buy."[114]

The particular events that had triggered such feelings were those following the supposed "Haymarket Riot" in Chicago of May 4, 1886. This story, and its impact on Howells, is well known so I keep my account brief.[115] During an ongoing wave of strikes and labor organizing (in support of an eight-hour working day), an anarchist group arranged a meeting in the Chicago Haymarket. When police acted to break up the crowd (in actuality already well on the way to dispersing) a bomb was thrown by an unknown person, killing one policeman. The police then reacted, with six more policemen and a number of demonstrators losing their lives and with many wounded. A number of anarchists were consequently arrested, eight of whom went on trial in July and August 1887. The trial was a legal farce, the men—mostly immigrant workers—in effect being condemned for the nature of their beliefs, with all defendants found guilty of murder, and with seven condemned to death. Four men were hanged on November 11, 1887. The other three were eventually pardoned six years later.

Howells was horrified by the proceedings and (following the trial) took a "practical" part in supporting the anarchist cause—or rather, for this was the point for him, the cause of American justice. His activity was in accord with his professional calling, writing both a private letter urging clemency to the governor of Illinois and a public letter to the New York *Tribune*. The latter, published five days before the hangings, spoke strongly against "punishing [men] because of their frantic opinions for a crime which they were not shown to have committed."[116] A second letter, written the day after the condemned men's deaths, was either unsent or went unpublished.[117] Howells showed considerable bravery here in a public action that flew directly in the face of majority opinion.

Howells was strongly influenced by Tolstoy's Christian socialist beliefs when he first came across them in 1886. He was later similarly affected by the radical Danish-American socialist Laurence Gronlund, whose anti-capitalist *Cooperative Commonwealth* (1884) was a blend of German socialism and Christian idealism. Such influences, which figure heavily in his fictions and especially *A Hazard of New Fortunes* (1890) and *A Traveler from Altruria* (1894), suggest Howells's more usual step beyond the direct political arena to a position where he looked to his fiction and magazine work to guide his readers, and his country, toward the development of a more active, humane, and inclusive social conscience. He was, however, very aware of the limited scope of his influence: "One is so limp and helpless in the presence of the injustice which underlies society."[118] From the point of his involvement with the Chicago anarchists, however, his attitude toward American capitalism, and the political system that supported it, hardened. He would write to Clemens on December 29, 1889 (still in the wake of the Haymarket events), "there is no longer an American Republic, but an aristocracy-loving oligarchy in place of it."[119] In 1896, a temporary commitment to the Populist Party ended when its energies were focused on a free-silver agenda, with Howells again—in his own words—"rather left stranded, politically."[120] Later in the same year, and following McKinley's victory, he wrote that "[t]here is no longer a Republican party except in name. It is the party of industrial slavery."[121] And in December 1897 he would write Charles Norton from New York, following his return to the U.S. after a winter in Europe, that "we are not yet fully repatriated, in our tastes and feelings. It is so ugly it *hurts*, whichever way I turn."[122]

Howells would continue to comment publicly on the American life around him. His biographers note the "astounding range of topics" in his Editor's "Easy Chair" columns for *Harper's Monthly* from December 1900: among them pieces on capital punishment, women's voting rights, the federal income tax, subsidies for farmers, and on topics such as drugs and guns, and the cinema.[123] His main politically related activity, however, was in opposing—from the turn of the century on—American entanglements abroad. He was strongly against the 1898 Spanish-American war: "Poor men will pay for it with their blood and money, and the wicked fortunes will begin to flourish up from the horrors of the battle fields."[124] A later letter of that year (July 31, 1898) to Henry James reads: "Our war for humanity has unmasked itself as a war for coaling stations, and we are going to keep our booty to punish Spain for putting us to the trouble of using violence in robbing her."[125] A member of the Anti-Imperialist League, first set up in response to American activity in the Philippines, he showed his dislike of similar ventures by other nations in his refusal to have anything to do with Winston Churchill's Boer War lecture, "The War in South Africa as I Saw It," which was held in New York on December 12, 1900.[126]

Howells, then, did play an active—and at times radical—role as commentator in his country's affairs, but usually from a relatively detached perspective. As a writer and intellectual, he stood outside politics, looking to influence the larger public where he could, but aware that both his livelihood and any power his voice might have actually *depended* on what we would now call his establishment position, as the foremost and most respected man of letters in the country.[127] He remained, despite this, clearly a man of conscience, and did on occasion foreground views that were both unpopular and (in the public mind) "anti-American," despite their possible adverse consequences.

Clemens joined Howells in his anti-imperialist stance, and indeed took a more visible role than his friend, as Vice President of the Anti-Imperialist League from 1901 to his death. One of his series of powerful essays on the topic, "To the Person Sitting in the Darkness" (1901), was published in the *North American Review* at Howells's prompting. Clemens also showed the more astute political mentality of the two men in agreeing to give an introduction to the Churchill New York lecture, but in then using the occasion to critique both British and American foreign policy.[128] In the August 1901 "Easy Chair," Howells referred apparently to Clemens as one sharing his own acute unease with America's internal development, and as speaking "darkly of a dying republic, and of a nascent monarchy or oligarchy."[129]

Despite the anti-imperialist activity of Clemens's late years, however, the two men differed considerably in their political positions and general world views. Goodman and Dawson suggest how the early friendship, when the two men's critical impulses about their social surroundings were in balance with their sense of optimism and strong good humor, changed over time. "It might be said that their fun fed their fury until life interceded—Howells growing more pointedly political from the 1880s and Twain more misanthropic."[130] Leland Krauth, too, identifies what appear to be the clear differences between the two men, saying that "just as Howells's satiric outbursts in their correspondence tended to focus on specific civic arrangements—the economic order, class cleavage, and the principles underpinning these—... Twain concerned himself more broadly with the nature of human nature and the construction of life itself."[131] While Howells's vision was social and political—what a "just society" would be—Clemens's was (to use Kenneth Eble's words) "basically astronomical." Eble explains further: "In Mark Twain's misanthropic moods, the purposeless of humans striving extended to the universe." Seeing our world in terms of this larger cosmic whole, he denied "any purpose posed by man residing in the earth's tiny speck...."[132] But this (as Eble indicates) represented just one element in a more complex whole. For Clemens would always swerve in his view of the world from this type of (often blackly humorous) cosmic relativism to reformist urge or bleak deterministic passivity.

Clemens did, then, concern himself with politics too, but he was usually positioned some way from Howells on such matters. In 1880, Howells describes Clemens (together with Charles Dudley Warner) as "hot Republicans."[133] While Budd says that though Clemens "doubtlessly... did his share of rearranging the world and listened benignly to Howells" utopian wishes or his...Bellamyite Nationalism...[his] political-social dissent never reached the faintest pink of socialism."[134] There are no letters extant between Clemens and Howells between August 1887 and the end of March 1888—so we do not know to what extent (if at all) they discussed the Haymarket trial. But Clemens did not apparently share Howells's impassioned views. Howells saw Clemens as a friend of labor, writing in *My Mark Twain* that—excepting the time of the "[g]reat coal strike in Pennsylvania" (1902)—"he seemed to know that whatever wrongs the working-man committed work was always in the right."[135] But this seems wishful thinking. Clemens did write Howells in 1899 of his support for "laborers' rights &...trade unions & strikes."[136] But his attitude to working men's militancy and to the role of labor as it affected business efficiency (and we must remember his owner's stake in Webster & Co. here) was equivocal at best.[137] Like Howells, Clemens would—as time went on—withdraw from a party politics he increasingly distrusted, but their political and social vision remained very different. Kenneth Eble sees the friendship (in line with my own analysis) first and foremost in terms of the two men's class and social position—in the fact that they were not too "far apart...in number of tangible ways—wealth, public recognition, literary reputation." The "continuing common interests" clustered around such factors could, in both the short and the long run, enable them, then, always to put personal friendship above sociopolitical difference.[138]

Howells wrote of Clemens that "something of the life joke makes itself felt in all the sad sense of creation's irony."[139] And there is some evidence that, if "in [his] ample flesh [Howells] leaned consistently forward against Twain's pessimistic tirades," he did come to share something of his friend's later vision of the world.[140] By 1899 humankind had become, for Clemens, "an April-fool joke, played by a malicious Creator with nothing better to waste his time upon."[141] Howells would occasionally reveal similar feelings, though usually without quite his friend's comic edge. So, in a June 14, 1891, letter to his father, he modulates from a (qualified) positive sense of social vision to one of naturalistic futility: "The whole of life seems unreal and unfair; but what I try to teach the children is to be ready for the change that *must* come in terms of truth and justice...Sometimes, however, the whole affair goes to pieces in my apprehension, and I feel as if I had no more authority to judge myself or to try and do this or that, than any other expression of the Infinite Life,—say a tree, or a field of wheat, or a horse."[142] Similarly, Howells introduces a note of relativism, and one where the notion of human sense making is cast in some doubt, in a April 26, 1903, letter to Charles E. Norton—one in which Clemens's influence seems palpable. Speaking of his own work, he writes: "I am not sorry for having wrought in common, crude material so much; that is the right American stuff; and perhaps hereafter, when my din is done, if anyone is curious to know what that noise was it will be found to have proceeded from a small insect which was scraping about on the surface of our life and trying to get into its meaning for the sake of the other insects larger or smaller."[143]

Howells, though, generally took things more phlegmatically than did Clemens. While his friend railed against life and its blows, Howells accepted and bent to them. Thus on the death of his wife Elinor, he writes at times in a mode similar to Clemens, but veers away from the type of angry conclusions his friend would often have reached:

> My life is a succession of shocks...I do not know whether I believe that we shall meet again; [Elinor] had totally renounced any such hope with regard to [daughter] Winny; and I cannot affirm anything. What I am sure of is that it will all be arranged without consulting me, as my birth was, and her death. I feel that we are in the power of an awful force, but whether of fatherly love, I could not honestly say anything. I submit, and we must all submit...I go about bewildered and incredulous. Yet we were old people, and the blow was to be expected by one or the other through the logic of our common life on this mad planet.[144]

## V

I end this chapter by returning to the Clemens-Howells letters, the best primary source for any commentary on their friendship. Howells, reviewing Paine's *The Letters of Mark Twain* (1918), wrote that their author "tells himself" in his letters "more explicitly and directly than in all his other work."[145] But—and this is a more general issue and one that concerns all the correspondence used in this book—letters sent from one person to another are a form of self-representation in which the revealing of the author's thoughts and feelings is always tempered by self-censorings, by the particular version of selfhood chosen for display, and by the nature of the relationship with the particular correspondent.[146] It is generally agreed that the Clemens-Howells *Letters* provide a full and sometimes moving testament to a very close friendship. But we should keep in mind that Howells would write in 1890 to author and illustrator Howard Pyle that, "I wish we could meet, and talk again. *Letters are not my natural expression, though literature is* " (my emphasis).[147] We should remember, too, Howells's comment in *My Mark Twain* —though in a different interpersonal context—on the way Clemens looked and smiled at people (and we can presume that this included Howells himself) "with a sort of remote absence; you were all there for him, but he was not all there for you."[148]

What I am hesitantly (but crucially) suggesting here—and I revert here to my larger commentary on male friendship in the period—is some changing quality to such relationships in the postbellum years: some retaining of privacy, the putting forth of a face to meet an immediate and particular set of needs, a sense of self-protection that we do not find to the same extent in the letters of close friend to friend in an earlier time. This may have been the natural corollary of an increasingly modernized and fragmented society, where family intimacy, business relationships, and other friendships were increasingly compartmentalized—this despite any connections and continuities between them. But there was also a concern in the period with the whole question of identity, a challenging of notions of fixed and essential selfhood. It was increasingly recognized— and especially by literary artists—that subjectivity was fluid and multi-form, adjusted its shape to suit its circumstances.[149]

By this time, then, it would appear that it was becoming increasingly difficult for a male intimacy to function that carried with it any full sense of the removal of the barriers between one man and another, or of self engaging with self in an unreservedly expressive way.[150] In *My Mark Twain*, Howells speaks of coming away "hollow," like "those locust-shells which you find sticking to the bark of trees at the end of summer," after the intensity of the nonstop talk with Clemens during visits to the Hartford house.[151] The image of intact outer casing and depleted inner substance here might be linked to other representations of the relationship between outward appearance and inner reality in Howells's writing, and to his awareness of the mutability of subjectivity. So in a letter to publisher Frederick Duneka, regarding the advertising of *Through the Eye of a Needle* (1907), he writes: "will you please use the last and best photo . . . I have had taken . . . which falsely represents me as bland, benevolent and blameless, with a mouth in which butter would not melt."[152]

Though Howells is joking here, he shows his awareness of the gap between the outward impression of the subject—in this case as he himself wishes it advertised—and a deeper version of selfhood. But Howells would also query the notion of a stable interior sense of identity beneath any metaphoric or assumed shell. In a 1902 letter to Thomas Bailey Aldrich, he talks of losing "the young, sure grip of myself," now replaced by "this dreamy fumbling about my own identity." He continues: "Once I thought that I meant something by everything I did; but now I don't know."[153] Clemens, too, as many of his writings illustrate, shared Howells's fascina-tion with "the riddles of the self," and his questions over "what makes an identity uniquely himself or herself."[154] Forrest Robinson speaks of Clem-ens's own identity as "so unformed and free-floating that it provided no anchor from which various roles and masks might be perceived to depart. Because it had no centre, his sense of self was vague, almost boundless."[155] Clemens and Howells's relationship was, then, close—probably as close as two men could get, given the times in which they lived, the physical distance that usually separated them, and their different domestic and business concerns. But we should beware of seeing in their friendship, or their correspondence, a full representation of either man. Howells's 1907 letter to Norton, in which he talks about another friendship—with Thomas Bailey Aldrich (after the latter's death)—is paradigmatic here. He starts by suggesting the limited nature of the friendship: "I miss Aldrich out of the world rather than out of my world. We were for more than half our lives companions . . . but we were never close intimates." But it is the following passage I would emphasize: "With whom is one really and truly intimate? I am pretty frank, and I seem to say myself out to more than one, now and again, but only in this sort to one, and that sort to another."[156] Howells's recognizes here that we reveal different facets of the self to different friends and correspondents, depending on our needs and circumstances: that "real and true" intimacy had become problematic in the modern American culture in which he lived.

# 5

## Clemens, Howells, and Realism

In this chapter, I discuss the literary connections between Clemens and Howells. I explore the commitment of both writers to a mode—realism—that became increasingly dominant in the post-Civil War period in America, and that developed as a cultural response to the rapidly changing social and economic conditions of the time. I connect this form of writing—one particularly difficult to pin down to a single and satisfactory definition—to the changing status of the literary artist, and his (in this case) desire both fully to engage with the fast-modernizing, and increasingly commercial, world around him and to play a significant cultural role within that context.

If the friendships examined in the book span the three major fields of religion, literature, and business, the story that this chapter ultimately tells is of the failure of the literary artist quite to find the larger social function that Howells, at any rate, envisaged, and of the fissures that appeared within the realist aesthetic and philosophy as it looked to represent a world that finally escaped its grasp: "'America is so big and the life here has so many sides,' [Howells] would tell an interviewer in 1898, that no writer could synthesize it."[1] Howells and Clemens were different types of writers and approached the question of realism in different ways. I suggest here, however, that Clemens was influenced by Howells's theories, just as Howells learnt from Clemens's novelistic practice. Both writers looked to adjust to a newly professionalized working environment, and to understand and represent their surrounding world, and—in doing so—they stand alongside, and act as a paradigm for, other leading writers of their times.

Finally, however, in an American world in which, to quote George Santayana, the gap between "Will" and "Intellect" (or civilization and "culture") was stretching ever wider, they had—as literary artists—to accept both certain limits and a good degree of marginalization in the face of the "aggressive enterprise," "invention and industry," which composed the world of "practical affairs."[2] We might recall here Howells's 1903 comment that Clemens "takes things intensely hard, and America is too much for him." More than this, though, if the writer's ability to take his place in the capitalist world surrounding him was always a struggle (which Clemens in fact managed much better than most), both these men found themselves at an increasing remove from the dominant values and attitudes of the time—a belief in a successfully realized sense of personal autonomy and agency and a confidence in the American social and political system with which (and even despite the serious economic problems of the time) it still went hand and glove. Both Clemens and Howells tasted considerable success and held their own—though Clemens only with Rogers's assistance—as business-men. Clemens too, was able to reach the large-scale public audience of which Howells could only dream. But as this chapter reveals, as artists and in their literary works, both men's visions came to be pervaded by doubts and uncertainties.[3] Both were increasingly skeptical about their ability to define the "reality" they saw around them or to depict the recent history of their country in any positive sense. Both too found it increasingly difficult to endorse a sense of the individual subject as the shaper of his or her environment rather than as being shaped by its influence.

## II

Brander Matthews reviewed *Adventures of Huckleberry Finn* enthusiasti-cally in 1886. He noted that "There is scarcely a character... who does not impress the reader at once as true to life. ... Mr. Clemens draws from life, and yet lifts his work from the domain of the photograph to the region of art."[4] He particularly praised "the skill with which the character of Huck Finn is maintained": "We see everything through his eyes—and they are his eyes, and not a pair of Mark Twain's spectacles. And the comments on what he sees are his comments... not speeches put into his mouth by the author. One of the most artistic things in the book... is the sober self-restraint with which Mr. Clemens lets Huck Finn set down, without any comment at all, scenes which would have afforded the ordinary writer matter for endless moral and political and sociological disquisition."[5]

William Dean Howells is the writer most closely identified with the development of American realism in the 1880s and early 1890s. Critics who have explored the Clemens-Howells connection have rightly noticed "the absence of this term from [Clemens's own] critical vocabulary," an absence that appears to have "the force of a deliberate avoidance" given the campaign then being waged by his "closest literary friend."[6] They have also identified the awkwardness of the fit between Clemens's fiction and Howells's realist theory, that Clemens's writings paradoxically "under-mined realism even while serving to define it."[7] I explore such paradoxes as I proceed. But Matthews's response to *Huckleberry Finn* clearly suggests a relationship between Howells's theory and Clemens's fictional practice, and also how Howells's thinking permeated the critical assumptions of his contemporaries.

For Matthews echoes Howells's own praise for (other) realist texts. Most obviously we are reminded of the latter's dislike of authorial intrusions, like those of a Trollope, "so warped from a wholesome ideal as . . . to stand about in his scene, talking it over with his hands in his pockets, interrupting the action, and spoiling the illusion in which alone the truth of art resides."[8] The distinction Matthews makes between photography and art in Clemens parallels that Howells draws between science and art in Zola (and between "mapping" and "picturing" elsewhere): "[Zola] fancied himself working like a scientist who has collected a vast number of specimens. . . . But the fact is, he was always working like an artist, [building up] every suggestion of experience and observation . . . into a structure of fiction. . . ."[9] Matthews praises the way Clemens lets us "see [Huck] from the inside," and his use of Huck's first person voice: "the comments of an ignorant, superstitious, sharp, healthy boy."[10] He does not, though, go on to make the further step we might expect and explicitly comment on the use of the vernacular. It was Howells himself who would associate "the use of dialect" with "the impulse to get the whole of American life into our fiction" and would celebrate its value in one of his best-known assertions of realist tenets.[11] Though Howells is generalizing here, he might have been writing with *Huckleberry Finn* in mind: "But let fiction cease to lie about life; let it portray men and women as they are, actuated by the motives and the passions in the measure we all know; let it leave off painting dolls and working them by springs and wires . . . ; let it speak the dialect, the language that most Americans know—the language of unaffected people everywhere . . . ."[12]

Clemens's best-known novel can, then, certainly be read in a realist context. More generally, too, it would seem perverse not to class Clemens in the American realist ranks. He "took up arms in the ongoing battle between romance and realism, joining passionately—indeed good-humoredly—in what . . . [his] friend and sponsor, William Dean Howells, called 'banging the babes of romance about.'"[13] "Romance" here had a wide range of connotations, conflating high cultural form (that practiced by a previous generation of American writers), genteel sentimentalism, and sensationalist popular fiction. Clemens attacks the sentimental from the start of his career, and quite independently of Howells.[14] That he did so is to indicate the extent and range of the realist impulse during the period. As David Shi says, "[a] realistic outlook seeped into every corner and crevice of intellectual and artistic life during the second half of the nineteenth century. . . . Realists of all sorts . . . muscled their way onto center stage of American culture and brusquely pushed aside the genteel timidities, romantic excesses, and transcendental idealism then governing affairs of the mind."[15]

As Clemens's career progressed and his close friendship with Howells developed, he could hardly have avoided being influenced in some way by the latter's realist campaign.[16] So, when Clemens wrote about literature he judged it according to the same stylistic criteria as Howells: the need for an "accurate, unromanticized observation of life and nature . . . [and an] insistence on precise description, authentic action and dialogue."[17] Clemens's attacks on Cooper are notorious, and Edwin Cady calls "Fenimore Cooper's Literary Offences," "a major critique in the mode of negative realism."[18] Less well known are "A Cure for the Blues" and "The Curious Book Complete," published as twinned texts in *Merry Tales* (1892). Clemens here anticipates the Cooper essays and establishes the aesthetic and representational failures of the genteel romance as his critical target.

*The Enemy Conquered; or, Love Triumphant* ("The Curious Book Complete") is a direct reprinting of a short 1845 pamphlet romance by S. Watson Royston—though Clemens changes the authorial name to G. Ragsdale McClintock. Clemens had first come across the text in 1884 when George Washington Cable was recovering from illness at his home, and both men were much tickled by the sentimental and inflated nature of its language and the resulting unintentional humor. "A Cure for the Blues," placed immediately before this reprinting, is Clemens's critical assault on the story and shows him taking considerable delight in targeting its high-flown rhetoric, illogical plotting, and generic determinants. He focuses especially on the author's style, which "nobody can imitate . . . not even an idiot," the "jingling jumble of fine words [that] seemed to mean something; but it is useless . . . to try to divine what it was."[19] So the alliterative simile "like the topmost topaz of an ancient tower" has, he says, not "a ray of sense in it, or meaning to it." Clemens describes the names of McClintock's fictional characters as ones that "fantastically fit his lunatics," and draws particular attention to that of the heroine, Ambulinia Valeer, which "can hardly be matched in fiction."[20] He pillories, too, the inconsistencies and absurdities of the plot. So when Elfonzo and Ambulinia, the two lovers, hide among the orchestra to avoid being seen together at a village show, Clemens comments: "This does not seem to be good art. . . . [O]ne cannot conceal a girl in an orchestra without everybody taking notice of it."[21]

Clemens's belief in a realist aesthetic underpins and motivates this essay, and the later more vehement attacks on Cooper. Howells described realism's aim as "to picture the daily life in the most exact terms possible."[22] Henry James praised Howells's own writing for its "art of imparting a palpitating interest to common things and unheroic lives," adding that "truth of representation . . . can be achieved only so long as it is in our power to test and measure it."[23] Clemens critiques *The Enemy Conquered* for its complete divergence from just such principles: "The reader must not imagine he is to find in it . . . purity of style . . . , truth to nature, clearness of statement, humanly possible situations, humanly possible people, fluent narrative, connected sequence of events—. . . or logic, or sense. No; the rich, deep, beguiling charm of the book lies in the total and miraculous *absence* from it of all these qualities."[24]

Clemens's literary principles and practices, then, certainly share a number of key elements with the larger realist movement. And the critics who have written about his major novels have regularly also consigned them to this category. Brook Thomas calls Clemens "one of the most important practitioners of realism," speaks of *Huckleberry Finn* as the work that established him as a realist, and praises his "active presentation of reality" (his word "active" has a particular force here) in *Pudd'nhead Wilson*.[25] Richard Brodhead calls *Huckleberry Finn* one of the "classic texts" of American realism.[26] Michael Davitt Bell defines Hank Morgan, in *A Connecticut Yankee*, as "a fictional embodiment of the 'realist.' "[27] Eric Sundquist then complicates things by describing the same novel as a "visionary wor[k] of nineteenth-century realism."[28]

But this verdict is far from unanimous. Sarah Daugherty, taking her lead from James Cox and Alfred Habegger, says that Clemens is "no realist."[29] Phillip Barrish, writing about Howells's major protagonists, speaks of "the clear-eyedness that they bring to hard realities" (such as the urban poverty and the violence of the streetcar strike in *A Hazard of New Fortunes* ).[30] This serves to remind us of the lack of any direct representation of contemporary America and its social problems—a vital component in Howells's own realist art—in the three Clemens novels just mentioned. *A Connecticut Yankee* is a fantasy. Everyday reality is turned upside down, within its pages, by the introduction of another and obviously *unreal* scenario: an alternative and different world set against Hank Morgan's (and Clemens's) everyday America. *Pudd'nhead Wilson*—particularly if considered with its twin text, *Those Extraordinary Twins*—veers from farce to tragedy and, with its flattened characters and strongly determining circumstances, seems as close to allegory as anything else.

Critics are extraordinarily divided as to Clemens's relation to realism, and make all kinds of twists and turns as they look to position him. David Shi calls him "a truant member" of the "realistic 'school,'" "an idiosyncratic fellow traveler to his friends among the professing realists."[31] Lee Clark Mitchell seems to lose his way as he refers to literary careers (Clemens's among them) that "resist classification" when they had "otherwise seemed straightforwardly realist."[32] Things do not get much easier when we turn to those who write explicitly on the Howells-Clemens connection. Richard Lowry says that Howells wielded a "profound influence" on Clemens. Acknowledging their significant differences, he nonetheless suggests that Howells uses his critical writings about Clemens to identify him, in a "remarkable" way, with his own agenda. Thus he manages to make Clemens "*his*, a realist who, despite—indeed, perhaps because of—his mass appeal, wielded a moral authority over the democratic masses who nourished his vision."[33] Louis J. Budd says just the opposite. He quotes passages from *My Mark Twain*, which refer to its eponymous subject as "[a]t heart . . . romantic" and as one working in an "essentially histrionic" mode. Budd then continues: "Howells unavoidably realized how far Twain's fiction differed from, and for some readers, worked against the mode of novels he was developing . . . ." He does, though, also quote Howells's response to *Tom Sawyer* as "realistic in the highest degree, . . . [giving] incomparably the best picture of life in that region as yet known to fiction."[34]

The fissure that arises here may have something to do with the fact that in 1910 Howells was reevaluating his earlier critical opinions, but there is more to it than this. I can, indeed, find ways of agreeing with both judgments. Even as realism was being used as a rallying cry for post-Civil War writers and artists it remained a somewhat indeterminate and elastic concept, and one that came to contain a number of different and sometimes incompatible meanings (aesthetic, ethical, social, and ideological). Amy Kaplan indicates something of this when she refers to realism as "an anxious and contradictory mode."[35] Realism, she suggests (and even Howells's own), "can be examined as a multifaceted and unfinished debate re-enacted in the arena of each novel and essay...[r]ather than as a monolithic and fully formed theory."[36]

As I stir these already-muddied definitional waters, one further issue needs to be raised: the relationship of realism to the literary movements from which it supposedly departs. For there are always problems in periodizing literature and imposing generic categories upon it. Richard Brodhead usefully reminds us "how illusory the separation is that we erect between pre-Civil War and postwar American authors."[37] He carefully charts how Howells was powerfully influenced by Hawthorne, his apparent polar (romantic) opposite, who was "strongly present to Howells in the making of his novels." Indeed, he argues that Howells's whole realist project ("trying to formulate a contemporary social ethic and to enforce its reign within his culture") is in part undermined by a skepticism that pervades the fictions that he writes. "This skepticism," Brodhead concludes, "is Hawthorne's legacy to Howells."[38]

Taking Clemens as his subject, Leland Krauth similarly illustrates how, despite the biting quality of his attacks on "the romantic in its various forms," he was—and remained—deeply indebted to sentimentalism.[39] The use of the "sentimental in order to drive home a moral point," he rightly argues, is "a fundamental gesture in his writing." Clemens's "shared... outlook" with an earlier generation of "sentimentalists" explains why Krauth can then describe *Huckleberry Finn* as "often as sentimental as it is realistic."[40] Philip Fisher lists the distinguishing traits of the Sentimental Novel (his capitalization), at its most influential as a cultural form in the pre-1860 period and epitomized by Stowe's *Uncle Tom's Cabin*: "The extended central scenes of dying and deathbeds, mourning and loss, the rhetorical treatment of the central theme of suffering, the creation of the prisoner as the central character, the themes of imprisonment, the violation of selfhood, power relations in the intimate and familiar territory, freedom, the centrality of the family, and the definition of the power of literary representation in terms of tears."[41] To read this account of the "sentimental procedure" is to realize the affinities between Clemens and his literary predecessors. There is further work to be done on the way he adapts, subverts, and departs from such procedures. But Clemens is certainly highly aware of this arsenal of sentimental effects and uses them— sometimes with ironic intent, sometimes (in Emily Dickinson's word) "aslant," but sometimes in all seriousness—throughout his writing career. Fisher himself recognizes this, speaking of him as one of a series of writers whose "works...preserved the core of sentimental technique even in the process of adapting it to later conditions or obscuring it beneath a veil of toughness, elegance, or self-irony."[42]


## III

All I have just said threatens, at first glance, to reduce the term realism to meaninglessness. And a number of recent critics have chosen to follow such a lead, either avoiding the term completely or bypassing some of the generic distinctions (between realism and naturalism, for example) previously current. Realism is, however, still a useful and a valid generic category. I proceed to investigate some of its various connotations as I now explore the connections between Clemens and Howells, and the differences between them.

Before I go further, but as a step in that direction, I briefly return to *Huckleberry Finn* to show how it both fits, and fails to fit, the realist category, depending on the particular criteria applied. Realism as an aesthetic makes a claim to transparency, appears to offer a clear window outward onto the solid world it represents. June Howard describes this in terms of a "privileged relationship to [the] assumed extratextual world, invoking an ability to embody 'reality'... as constitutive of the genre itself."[43] Thus Clemens uses Huck, his first person narrator, to provide a seemingly direct depiction of the immediate world through which he moves.

Clemens, indeed, out-realists Howells in his use of this first-person vernacular voice. Phillip Barrish analyses a complicated dynamic in *The Rise of Silas Lapham* by which the crude tastes and values of Lapham and his daughter Irene are subordinated to the more cultivated taste of Tom and Penelope. But that cultivated taste is defined by its appreciation of Lapham and Irene's "vernacular" qualities. In other words, for Howells, an "alignment *with* the simple and the natural always precludes any preferential taste *for* the simple or natural."[44] Such a discrepancy is considerably diminished in Clemens's more genuinely democratic art.[45] Clemens relies *only* on Huck's voice and viewpoint to take us "transparently" through to a solidly framed historical context, the small town antebellum Old Southwest and river life on the Mississippi. It is this regional and historical reality we are asked to take for granted, together with the range of social practices, racial distinctions, and cultural codes that compose it. Such an assumption, and the details that reinforce it, provide the realistic glue holding the whole novel in place.

One (other) definition of realism is in social and ethical terms: the relationship between the human subject and her or his surrounding environment, and the moral potential of that subject. At this time, prior romantic beliefs in the authority and autonomy of the sovereign self were no longer easily tenable. Realist texts looked accordingly to firmly embed their protagonists in their larger social context, and focused on such areas as dress, manners, occupations, community practices, and connections as ways of doing this. The closeness of the connection between the individual and the material details and social practices of everyday life lay at the very core of the genre (when defined within this framework). Despite the increasing pressure of environment on character in the post-Civil War American world, though, realist authors assumed the essential wholeness and coherence of the human subject. Indeed the genre is commonly described in terms of the *balance* it represents between the individual and his or her social world, the ability of that individual to act as a free moral agent despite the increasing complications and determining networks of that larger environment. Thus Lee Clark Mitchell loosely groups Clemens, James, and Howells as realists, identifying a shared key concern in the fact that "they all presented characters as 'subjective selves' who possessed clear capacities for restraint and responsibility.... Realist authors enforced a moral perspective on narrative action, a perspective involving the same considerations of intention and responsibility we habitually project on each other (and onto fictional characters as well)."[46]

*Huckleberry Finn* works as a realist text according to such criteria. Huck can accordingly be seen as a unified subject, a sympathetic and free-speaking—in the sense, at any rate, that he speaks the text—young boy, making his way through a difficult world but responding to it with a clear-seeing and pragmatic eye. The fabric of the antebellum southwestern world provides the backdrop against which Huck's negotiations with the established social order occur. Huck's decision to choose hell rather than allow Jim back into Miss Watson's hands is for many critics the climax of the book, and can be read—in realist terms—as an act of individual moral responsibility that counters the determining tendencies of the larger social environment. This reading of the novel, when taken alongside my earlier comments about Brander Matthews's review of it, clearly explains why so many commentators have read the novel as a realist text.

But there are other ways of approaching the book that problematize that reading. If we focus on plot rather than point of view, for example, Clemens's one-time idea of having Huck visit a circus and then escaping on an elephant might alert us that any reading of the book in terms of Howells's "fidelity to experience and probability of motive" may be tricky. Such random incidents as the boarding of the *Walter Scott*, the hiding of gold in Peter Wilks's coffin, and the shenanigans of the "evasion" routine, indicate—especially when combined with the book's insistent strain of burlesque—its failure to conform to such realist criteria. At another level, the possibility of escaping social determinants in independent moral action (Huck's decision) is deeply undermined by Miss Watson's prior actions (Jim has already, in fact, been freed), by the negative quality of Huck's choice, and by his consequent position as Tom Sawyer's minion.[47] The very idea of the intending and coherent subject is, moreover, questioned by the extent to which Huck's own language and thought are inevitable products of his larger society, and by the textual play on disguise and identity slippage that necessarily subverts any notion of fixed selfhood. Finally, and in a quite different way, the mythic and symbolic structures that permeate the novel, and its (remaining) debt to a romantic tradition of unfettered individualism, once more counter its realist status. So Jane Tompkins sees the novel as defying easy categorization: *"The [sic] Adventures of Huckleberry Finn* has for a long time stood as a benchmark of American literary realism, praised for its brilliant use of local dialects and its faithfulness to the texture of ordinary life. Twain himself is famous for his scoffing attacks on the escapism of sentimental and romantic fiction. But...the events of *Huckleberry Finn* enact a dream of freedom and autonomy that goes beyond the bounds of the wildest romance."[48]

I am happy here, though, to revert to my earlier position. Realism is not a coherent and unified genre. Some aspects of Clemens's novel undoubtedly fit its criteria, while others do not. Tensions and ambiguities stretch the text in a number of generic directions. Daniel Borus usefully sums up such instabilities in his more general comment:

> The realists...violated their theoretical premises as often as they observed them. Fidelity to everyday life and to probability of motive were easier to theorize about than to realize. The classic texts of American realism boast more than their share of intruding narrators, improbabilities and coincidences, and cataclysmic or heightened moments of life deployed as plot devices. In addition to these textual qualities often associated with romanticism, realism also pointed ahead to modernism with the use of subjective narration, a stress on the fragmented self, and forays into symbolism and impressionism, all of which contradicted the realist dictum of an anchored reality."[49]

## IV

Recent studies of realism have introduced another factor to an already-complicated field by focusing on the changing relationship between literature and the marketplace in the period, and the stresses and accommodations that resulted. Howells and Clemens adjusted in their different ways to market demands, and looked to define their cultural roles accordingly. As they did so, similarities, but also some highly significant differences, appeared between them.

Richard Lowry introduces his discussion of the two writers in the context of the complicated relationship between culture and capital at the time.[50] Most commentators on the period stress the extraordinary rapidity of the modernization process, "the bewildering social transformations of industrial capitalism" and its related effects.[51] Realist writers saw one of their main tasks to be the use of modern scientific techniques, with their "stress on observation and exactness," to produce "a living map of the new society."[52] One of a whole new range of experts—sociologists, city planners, business managers and the like—"the literary novelist...emerged...as an expert in a field of knowledge described loosely as 'real life,' which he...mapped with assiduous care both to material and to ideological detail."[53]

Gender role was a significant issue in this self-conception. Unlike an earlier generation of American writers, the male realist writer saw his role in terms of masculine authority, central rather than marginal to the business of the nation. Thus Brodhead compares Howells with Hawthorne. "In sharp contrast with early Hawthorne, 'for a good many years, the obscurest man of letters in America,' Howells became a somebody" when he became an editor for the *Atlantic Monthly* in 1866.[54] This recognized "authority in the literary sphere" was just a prelude, though, to the part he then figured for himself in the larger social and cultural whole.

The relationship between the realist writer and business took another, and more immediate, form. Such factors as the greater organization of markets and distribution systems, the more efficient production and more attractive presentation of books, and—most especially—the increasing size of the reading public and developing needs of a new "mobile society," led to what Daniel Borus calls the rise of a "literature industry" by 1900.[55] As book markets grew, so fiction especially flourished, and "the boundaries that separated literature from business, nineteenth-century tastes from twentieth-century practices" started to collapse.[56] Writers measured their success in terms of financial profit. So Howells, acutely aware of the literary market and its demands, kept careful check on the revenue his various literary activities brought in.[57] Clemens "pursued the business of authorship" with, if anything, even more enthusiasm.[58] His writing habits, when they needed to be, were rigorously disciplined and he was literally aware—when in "business" mode—of the worth of every word he wrote. His professionalism was "essential to his sense of masculinity," as was the rhetoric he used, that of "the literary entrepreneur who cornered markets and waged military marketing campaigns."[59] (As we will see in the next chapter, this sense of masculinity would be diminished by his business misfortunes.)

Clemens wrote for the *Atlantic* magazine that Howells edited, largely as a result of his friend's encouragements. But the two men differed widely in the type of work they produced and in their readership. It is here that Howells's particular conception of the relation between the realist writer and a newly available and potentially vast audience ran into problems.[60] Howells believed in "the authority and legitimacy of serious fiction as a serious enterprise" and the beneficial social effects thereby produced.[61] The realist novel, mapping this new society, had—in his view—a moral and educative purpose, providing its readers with a secular "guide to life in the late nineteenth century": "In a modern society afflicted by isolation and atomization, the mass-circulated novel held out the promise of a new common currency that would promote a new unity. . . . The goal of this new discourse was to provoke in readers a new sense of their commonality both as readers and as citizens and to stimulate an active participation in social life."[62]

There were a number of problems with this agenda, and they became increasingly obvious as time passed. These had to do both with the nature of Howells's audience and with the larger social and historical context he engaged. The issues are interrelated but I focus on the former at this point. The serious cultural product Howells looked to sell (fiction as a guide to life) was *not* one that suited a heterogeneous mass market, and he realized this. His "cultural program to make [one] type of literature preeminent" was mainly directed at the middle and upper classes.[63] For, like it or not (and Howells did not), he knew that "the common people do not hear [the man of letters] gladly or hear him at all."[64] The American reading public was hugely fragmented, and the "common people" tended not to read serious fiction but rather dime novels, cheap magazines, and sentimental and sensationalist fictions. Too many of his target audience, too, shared a taste for such "adventure and romance."[65] Howells waged literary war against such "injurious" stuff, condemning it as "the emptiest dissipation," a form of "opium-eating" that "drugged the brain and [left] the reader 'weaker and crazier for the debauch.'"[66] But the battle was lost almost before it had begun, for as Borus puts it: "Invariably the novels that flooded the market were standardised, deficient in craftsmanship, and lacking in serious purpose. As realists surveyed the results of the literary marketplace, they saw an incessant demand for instant gratification rather than enlightenment, and a fiction that justified itself as a relief from boredom."[67] Howells's vehement attacks on such popular forms were a measure of his "sense of calamity" that his own version of literary taste and function was not widely shared.[68] Literary art, for him, had the status of "special communication." For too many of his intended readers it was mere "merchandise."[69] His sense of a realist mission, and of his own central cultural role in pursuing it, consequently fell further and further apart as the century advanced.

It might seem difficult to connect this version of literature with Clemens, except to recognize the two men's shared sense of professionalism in the literary marketplace. But Clemens did share aspects of Howells's thinking. In the 1880s Howells was still strongly waging his battle against the harmful nature of sentimental and dime fiction, and Clemens's "A Curious Experience" (1881) endorsed much the same message about poor reading habits. For the story effectively dramatizes the "deepest, most unsettling fears" of Howells and other "respectable critics"—"that for the young readers of such sensational and fantastic fiction, the line between fiction and real life might indeed be entirely obliterated."[70]

"A Curious Experience" is a lengthy narrative that works as a type of hoax. The story concerns young Robert Wicklow, a drummer boy who enlists on the Union side at Fort Trumbull, Connecticut, during the Civil War. His mysterious activities and the letters he writes eventually lead his commanding officer (the main teller of this tale) to judge him a Confederate spy. Both the life of the Fort and of the local community are disrupted as this occurs. Finally, though, this narrative of mystery, betrayal, and rebellion turns out to lack all substance, a product of Wicklow's invention alone: "It turned out that [the boy] was a ravenous devourer of dime novels and sensation-story papers—therefore, dark mysteries and gaudy heroisms were just in his line. Then he had read newspaper reports of the stealthy goings and comings of rebel spies in our midst, and of their lurid purposes . . . till his imagination was all aflame on that subject. . . . Ah, he lived in a gorgeous, mysterious, romantic world during those few stirring days, and I think it was *real* to him, and that he enjoyed it clear down to the bottom of his heart."[71] The only thing to fear, then, has been a boy's imagination and his bad reading practices. That Clemens seems here directly to dramatize Howells's warnings about "sensation-story" fiction may not be surprising, given the closeness of their friendship. His critique is, moreover, in line with repeated attacks, from a realist perspective, on fraudulent sentimentality and romance throughout his work. Nonetheless, to have one of America's best-known humorists critiquing popular forms of entertainment, and their injurious appeal, does have something slightly odd about it.[72] I discuss this further in due course.

"About Play-Acting" (1898), a later Clemens essay, is also relevant here. In this piece, Clemens indicates his acceptance of Howells's view that the writer has a "higher function" than that of mere entertainer, and that serious fiction could act as an educative tool, with "a certain kind of authority in and over culture."[73] Indeed many of Clemens's *nonfictional* pieces were undoubtedly spurred by the same belief. Neither the form nor the setting of the "remarkable" Austrian play Clemens has seen in Vienna (*The Master of Palmyra* by Adolf von Wilbrandt) is "realistic" in terms of Howells's "vigorous insistence that realism directly confront the moral and material problems of society."[74] But its main theme certainly conformed to Clemens's own developing view of reality, showing "what a silly, poor thing human life is; how childish its ambitions, how ridiculous its pomps, how trivial its dignities...how wearisome and monotonous its repetition of its stupid history through the ages."[75] As I (awkwardly) use the words "realistic" and "reality" in different ways, we get something both of the ambiguities and instabilities of the term and of the reason for Howells's own growing dissatisfaction with aspects of his original limited premise.

It is not, though, the metaphysics of von Wilbrandt's play that solely interested Clemens. For he used his essay to comment generally on a lack of seriousness in the American theater, and criticized its audience accordingly:

> You are trying to make yourself believe that life is a comedy, that its sole business is fun....America...neglect[s] what is possibly the most effective of all the...disseminators of high literary taste and lofty emotion—the tragic stage. To leave that powerful agency out is to haul the culture-wagon with a crippled team....What *has* come over us English-speaking people?...Comedy keeps the heart sweet; but we all know that there is wholesome refreshment for both mind and heart in an occasional climb among the pomps of the intellectual snow-summits built by Shakespeare and those others. Do I seem to be preaching? It is out of my line: I only do it because the rest of the clergy seem to be on vacation.[76]

This plea for "high literary taste and lofty emotion" and its benefits for a wide audience—who at present see the theater (and analogously the novel) as a source only of "fun"—accords more or less exactly with Howells's conception of the role and function of a serious, yet widely influential, art.

Clemens does here seem (considerably) influenced by Howells's realist program. But at this point, we should remember his very different place in that literary marketplace for which both men wrote. Clemens was a humorist whose appeal included the mass audience that had so little time for Howells and his reservations about fiction that "aims merely to entertain."[77] Clemens, as is well known, had a highly ambiguous attitude to his own comic art. He remarked on his first book, *The Jumping Frog of Calaveras County, and Other Sketches*, that "I don't know that it would instruct youth much, but it would make them laugh."[78] But elsewhere, and commonly, he would insist exactly on that "preaching" he half-mocks above: the "deep seriousness" that he saw as "an absolutely essential part of any real humorist's native equipment."[79] His work veered between playful relativism, the straightforwardly ludicrous, and the clearly serious and moralistic, sometimes with all such elements contained within a single text. Famously, he told Andrew Lang around 1890 that he wrote not "to help cultivate the cultivated classes [but] always hunted for bigger game, the masses . . . the Belly and the Members. , . . [T]he cultured classes . . . could go to the theater and the opera, they had no use for me and the melodeon."[80] In his various moves between "genteel culture" and populist entertainment, instruction and amusement, a reliance on—and the burlesque of—popular forms, there lie a series of ongoing and irreconcilable tensions at the root of Clemens's artistic identity.

Clemens, then, sympathized to some degree with Howells's notion of realism as a cultural force and endorsed it in some of his work. But his own comic art was multidimensional in kind and could not be contained by his friend's narrow definitions. Clemens had no need to reconcile his contradictory feelings about the relationship of art to the mass market. Nor, as a corollary, did he need to commit himself to a particular cultural program—to find a common ground of value that could provide a basis for the responsible exercise of American citizenship (though this was undoubtedly sometimes his intention). Clemens marketed his literary merchandise with great success across class lines. His serious essays rode on the back of a massive popularity, established through his fiction, travel writing, and lecturing and confirmed by his celebrity. He may have had some sympathy with Howells's desire to offer the readers of his fiction a guide to life in turbulent and changing times, but neither the latter's artistic methods nor his (initial) ideological certainty suited him.

The realist novel would, for Howells, "be anchored in its own place and time, accord psychologically mimetic attention to the customs and actions of common people, and rely on observation and a 'neutral' dramatic method of narration."[81] Clemens made use, as he needed, of fantasy, adventure, sentiment, romance, the tall tale, burlesque, and farce (amongst other modes) in his work, and never directly addressed the problems of his own time in his major novels. Howells looked, often unsuccessfully as it happens, to reconcile social differences in his work.

Clemens's fiction was more likely to accept social fragmentation and inequality and personal alienation as the unalterable "realities" of American late-nineteenth-century life. It is now accepted that, in *Huckleberry Finn*, *Connecticut Yankee*, and *Pudd'nhead Wilson*, Clemens *was* addressing immediate social concerns (race and Reconstruction, modernization and its effects, class difference, concerns about masculinity, personal agency, law) but in a highly indirect way. The seriousness and contemporary relevance of such issues are generally thickly disguised by the genres and settings he uses, and by his comic forms. For, ultimately, his cultural identity and success relied on his humor, and not on his increasingly bleak view of human nature and of American life at the century's end.

Howells described the attraction of the "unthinking multitude" to the kind of writing he calls "melodrama, impossible fiction, and the trapeze" and accepts that the "highly cultivated person" too will occasionally revert to such "barbarian" moments.[82] Clemens played his melodeon for anyone who cared to listen and did not establish the same kind of cultural hierarchies and boundaries as Howells—or, at least, not in any consistent way. In chapter twenty-two of *Huckleberry Finn*, Huck enjoys a "bully circus," with clowns and with lady horseriders "dressed in clothes...just littered with diamonds" (though with no mentioned trapeze), immediately after Colonel Sherburn has killed Boggs. Clemens takes us from an entirely "serious" incident, and one that implicitly harshly critiques the inhumanity and violence at the heart of the Southern social system both before and after the Civil War, to the enjoyable entertainment of the circus with whatever gaudy misrepresentations of reality (those diamonds) it contains.[83] This move might stand as a metaphor for Clemens's art. Sympathetic to Howellsian realism and sharing some of its aspects, his work extends far beyond its relatively narrow limits.


## V

Realism, to summarize, is a flexible term, and one that can be approached in a number of ways—in terms, for instance, of aesthetic practice, cultural role, and ideological belief. Any analysis of the genre must recognize too the slipperiness of the boundaries between realism and its bordering literary movements.[84] Howells is the single figure round whom all the various strands of late-nineteenth-century American realism cohere, but Clemens was sympathetic to aspects of his program. Howells does seem to have had a direct influence on Clemens, though some of the latter's realist practices were developed independently.

Eric Sundquist writes that "no one strategy of 'realism' seemed adequate to portray the effects of capitalism across the spectrum of American life."[85] Phillip Barrish comments similarly that "what comes to count as most real" in the texts produced in this period "not only changes from literary work to literary work but also shifts within individual works."[86] His phrase, "what...count[s] as most real," draws attention to the way that "reality"—as it is represented in a text—is always already mediated, produced by the particular social position of the writer, her or his motivating values and beliefs, and particular angle of vision. The indeterminacy of such definitions does not, however, reduce the term to meaninglessness. Realism attacks sentimental forms. It emerges from—and measures and reflects—the rapid and dramatic changes in American social conditions in the years following the Civil War. It is informed by a particular conception of the subject and her or his capacity for moral action. And it is identified by a set of formal and stylistic practices that aim towards the type of transparency lacking both in romance (with its conspicuous use of allegory and symbol) and in modernism (with its explicit attention toward the shaping hand of the artist). Though such descriptive boundaries may be crossed and muddied within and between individual texts, this does give us a base from which to work.

My comments on the way "reality" is textually produced lead to one further strand of my argument in terms of the Clemens-Howells relationship. I have indicated something of the narrowness of Howells's conception of realism, and Clemens's move beyond such limits. I now expand on this to show how Howells's *changing* view of reality affected his novelistic practice. Following Daugherty, I suggest that there are clear signs that Howells realized the limitations of his earlier position, and that it may indeed—and unexpectedly, given traditional readings of the two men's relationship—have been Clemens who (to some degree at least) "liberated Howells from his own most restrictive canons."[87]

The contradiction and flaw at the heart of Howells's realist credo lies within his statement that "every true realist...is careful of every fact, and feels himself bound to...indicate its meaning."[88] For it is the relation between fact and meaning that haunts and finally explodes his whole project. Facts, Howells rightly implies, cannot speak for themselves. But as soon as larger meanings are indicated, so the ideological preconceptions of the artist necessarily distort any conception of "the real." To put this slightly differently, Howells saw the realist as a type of scientist, who through his "precision of vision accurately and objectively observes the world, records its facts, and draws out clearly their ramifications. Such a 'science' of composition would simply capture the fact of the world and present it."[89] But—returning to the early distinction between mapping and picturing, photography and imaginative art—he also saw the realist writer as performing a "shaping function," using his "designing...intelligence" to arrange and order the materials of the text.[90] That designing intelligence, though, necessarily *re*-presented (represented) reality in a *subjective* and ideologically loaded way.

The first stage of Howells's realist career was to falter as the particular shaping vision he brought to his fiction failed to match the unfolding facts of late-nineteenth-century history. As he lost confidence in the possibility of objectively recording the version of "America" in which he believed, so he modified his earlier realist practice. The first part of this argument is now a standard critical reading. Howells, at the heyday of his realist campaign, had a particular view of his contemporary American world. Anxious about the troubling social problems of the time, he nonetheless believed that they could be contained. Realist fiction would represent different classes and types of Americans to each other and in doing so would "create 'solidarity'" (a key word for Howells), "pave a common ground between diverse social groups through the recognition of the essential likeness of individuals in all social classes."[91] The ideological agenda of his realist art was to shape the reality he represented to emphasize what all Americans shared, rather than the countervailing sense of fragmentation and division—while yet recognizing those divisions within his texts. The novel form itself, with its orderly and coherent plot, thus mirrored the solid orderliness that cohered, in this vision, in "reality" itself.[92] Howells, then, "envisaged realism as a strategy for containing social difference and controlling social conflict within a cohesive common ground."[93]

From an early point, however, this never quite worked. Howells's anxieties concerning the shape and direction of contemporary society were never fully resolved either in his mind or within his fictions. There are all kinds of "gaps and rifts" that unbalance and disrupt the desired sense of coherence and ordered resolution in his novels. His use of "contrived devices" and "arbitrary plotting" give the lie to the well-balanced "picture" of American social reality he looked to represent.[94] Howells was faced with two problems, neither of which his realist program could resolve. The first was the fact that actual and developing social conditions denied his vision of any shared common ground, for "intense and often violent class conflicts" were in fact producing "fragmented and competing social realities."[95] The other (to return to my previous argument) concerned markets and audiences. A fracturing of the literary marketplace, an increasingly marked gap between high and mass culture and between serious novels and forms of popular entertainment, looked to reduce Howells's own literary aim, to provide serious social and moral instruction for a significant part of the national audience, to ruins.[96]

Howells would, in his 1894 novel *A Traveler from Altruria*, turn away from realism and, ironically, back to romance as he looked to expose "the social indifference, corruption, and cruelty at the heart of the American class system."[97] But we can see a series of shifts occurring before that point. He increasingly lost confidence in his ability artistically to contain the fracturings in American social life and to link individual moral perception and action to the larger social ground (both foundation stones of his realist beliefs). And, as a corollary to this, a growing sense of subjective instability and relativistic uncertainty came to trouble his fiction. Howells continued to work within a realist mode in terms of topic and setting. The sense of social engagement and dialog at its heart remained central to his attempt to address questions of how American life worked and what its meanings might be. There are indications, however, that as the beliefs that initially underpinned his fiction gradually eroded, so his use of the genre became—to significant degree—inhabited by doubts and hesitations. I use the work of three recent critics as the most economical way of (selectively) charting some of these changes. I then return to Clemens, to bring him finally back into the frame of my argument.

Amy Kaplan shows how "the elaborate balancing act" of Howells's realism starts to collapse in *A Hazard of New Fortunes* (1890).[98] Lindau, the German socialist, views America as a class battleground and thus a disunited country: "der *iss* no Ameriga anymore!"[99] He thus gives a voice to what Kaplan calls "the centrifugal force of realism," and, despite the ways in which his voice is undermined and Lindau himself necessarily killed off, his message cannot be completely cast aside.[100] Similarly in the last stages of the novel, despite Howells's shift from "background" (the violence and the social division of the New York streetcar strike) to "foreground" (the social intercourse between his main characters), he cannot altogether bypass "the abyss of conflict and fragmentation" his text has revealed.[101] The final problems in closing the novel—Kaplan speaks of its combination of "too many different finite and limited conclusions"—again suggest how Howells's realist needs for "picture" and "form" are being stretched to their very limit.[102] He does find ways to combat such disruptions, but the fissures in his earlier conception of realism are clear.[103]

Phillip Barrish continues to see Howells in realist terms, but his reading of the genre here takes a particularly negative and ironical turn in its focus on the *separation* of the subject from the larger social whole. Barrish concentrates on realism's "intellectual orientation towards various sorts of negativity."[104] He shows how, in the late 1880s and 1890s, Howells focuses on "the intractabilities, impossibilities and ironies" that "cluster around America's socioeconomic system," and illustrates the penetrating and clear-eyed look his protagonists now bring to the "hard realities," "the irreducible complexities . . . of America's social problems."[105] There is, for Howells, no longer the possibility of finding "common ground" between members of different social classes. Indeed, an "inescapable *lack of transparency*" (my emphasis) means that they necessarily see each other through "distorting lenses of one sort or another."[106] America's "bottom-line 'real'" "now becomes "a taste for contingency." Barrish uses the work of Richard Rorty to explain further: "all facets of a given culture, from language to widely accepted social practices to a specific individual's deepest commitments, are *contingent*. That is, they are produced by multiple factors of history and chance and hence cannot be legitimately grounded either in universal nature, in the supernatural realm (God), or in abstractions such as absolute justice."[107] Intellectual distinction becomes accordingly, for Howells, the ability to empathize with members of other social groups but also to recognize "the unfixable brokenness of both self and world." A series of internal and external factors will always block the Basil Marches of this world (the liberal middle-class character who is most like Howells himself) from "effective action." Laughter has a special place in this reading of the world, as "a bodily index of . . . balance and perspective," the sign of an awareness both of self and world and of the impossibility of matching vision to action.[108]

What we see here is a gradual move away from that confident sense of a solid and shared reality conveyed in Howells's earlier fictions and critical work. Sarah Daugherty further explores this loss of "grounding" in the later Howells with her analysis (complementing Barrish) of his growing uncertainties over his realist program and the humanism that sustained it. She suggests that "his lingering hope for a moral order based on shared values" gives way before a sense of "psychological and verbal instability," an abandonment of a "faith in objective truth," and a substitution of the "belief in a common reality" by an acceptance of "the play of differences."[109] This runs alongside a developing recognition of the instability of selfhood and the collapse of confidence in the unified and morally responsible subject as the very source of meaning and action. She illustrates this changing conception of the subject by referring to an astonishing passage in *A Boy's Town* (1890) where Howells talks of the instability of a boy's identity and the way that when he gets to be a man: "He may turn out to be like an onion . . . nothing but hulls, that you keep pulling off, one after another, till you think you have got down to the heart, at last, and then you have got down to nothing."[110] Daugherty never quite develops her argument as fully as she might, and it is open to challenge just how far the instabilities and uncertainties she identifies affect Howells's later literary works taken as a whole. Nonetheless, her indications of the changes in Howells's vision, his increasing skepticism and development of a sense of relativistic uncertainty, are significant.

How, then, does this relate to Clemens? Howells's darkening vision was undoubtedly a result of increasing evidence of unbridgeable social divisions in his America, and of his personal crisis following the 1886 Haymarket Riot and its aftermath. The changes in his work identified above, though, suggest noticeable parallels with Clemens's artistic practice. Given Howells's close engagement with his friend's work, it is reasonable to suggest an influence here, or at the very least, two writers working on parallel track.[111]

Clemens (in *Huckleberry Finn* and *Pudd'nhead Wilson*) is more concerned with race than class. But Brook Thomas's reading of the latter novel is pertinent: "Pudd'nhead's triumph . . . signals the formation of a larger community of fools, Northern and Southern, who united after the war by collectively selling down the river blacks' efforts to integrate into the national community."[112] Both novels can be read in terms of a disguised message: that Clemens too is effectively saying "der iss no Ameriga anymore!" We can interpret *Connecticut Yankee* similarly, though here issues of labor, class, and region replace that of race. Clemens, however, is more skeptical whether there ever *was* such a unified America as Howells implies. And, within *Pudd'nhead Wilson* at least, he makes little attempt to combat the grim quality of his vision.[113] Conflict and fragmentation were always central facets of Clemens's vision. *Huckleberry Finn* is composed of a whole range of types and levels of social languages, fiercely battling it out for authority (even despite Huck's overall narrative control). White is ranged against black, father against son, class against class, and neighbor against neighbor in this fictional world. *Connecticut Yankee* ends with the Battle of the Sand Belt. The possibility of finding "a moral order based on shared values," or a form to mirror the solid orderliness of the larger sociohistorical world, looks in that novel to be a very bad joke indeed.

Barrish's description of the sense of contingency, too, could almost be written with Huck Finn in mind. In his clear-eyed way, Huck adopts a series of necessary social roles but "keeps those . . . roles from sticking," retains "a space of emptiness" that enables a distance from, and a "reflective self consciousness" about, the world through which he moves.[114] Again, Barrish's comments on laughter as an index of "balance and perspective" as a complex and irony-filled world is engaged fit Clemens's art exactly.

Clemens's undermining of the notion of the unified subject and of secure identity is clear throughout his writing career. In *Pudd'nhead Wilson*, the only way of telling Tom and Valet apart is through their fingerprints. When, in chapter five of the novel, Tom comes back from Yale to have his "fancy Eastern graces" mocked by "the old deformed negro bell-ringer," we see an old black man imitating his young white (social) superior. This young white man though is a fraud, is in fact a young "black" man— the "real" Valet, but that Valet who ironically is not black at all—imitating a young white man (the "real" Tom). The "real" young white man now in turn is placed in a role where he imitates his "black" counterpart. If my word "imitate" implies an intention that is in some part absent, this sequence still indicates the spiraling dizziness that tends to inhabit concepts of distinct identity in Clemens's work.

Clemens's fictions are marked from the first by relativistic uncertainty and the play of differences. And as he continued writing such a sense of pervasive instability, the lack of any reliable ground for the finding of any fixed or final "truth," would only increase. One has only has to think of his late fictional meditations on telling—or failing to tell—dream from reality, or of *Three Thousand Years Among the Microbes*, where human life is miniaturized and parodied in the microbic universe represented. The failure of objective certainty, and the indeterminacy that results from that failure, is illustrated in *Connecticut Yankee* in the story of the prisoner viewing the world through an arrow slit, and the limited (and false) perspective given by that single frame.

My conclusions are tentative, and there is more work to be done here. But Howells and Clemens did apparently come to share elements of a similar view of the world and of man's place in it. Clemens, though, developed his vision early, and followed it into much darker spaces than his friend. From the first, too, Clemens conveyed his views of what "reality" was through the play of a number of literary forms. Indeed it was only by *retreating* from any transparent representation of immediate reality that these views *could* be conveyed. Clemens acknowledged his own difficulties with the traditional realist novel when he wrote to Howells in late 1899: "Ah, if I could look into the insides of people as you do, & put it on paper, & invent things for them to do & say, & tell *how* they said it, I could write a fine & readable book now. . . ."[115] Rather, he used any literary tactic at his disposal to convey his desired message: fantasy in *Connecticut Yankee*; an extraordinary mixture of defamiliarizing effects in *No. 44, The Mysterious*

*Stranger*—with its boisterous jokester who takes human time and history and reverses and rearranges them, replays conversations backwards, and throws the difference between dream and reality, self and world in utter doubt. Howells, for the most part, remained much more committed to the conventional "realist" model.[116] Finally, though, Clemens's example may have shown him that to move beyond such realist practices—"objectively observ[ing] the world, record[ing] its facts, and draw[ing] out clearly their ramifications"—did not necessarily mean a lack of engagement with contemporary social problems and concerns: indeed, quite the opposite. One of Clemens's great strengths as a writer is the way he always resists easy categorization, stretches our literary definitions to their limits. This is true of his relation to realism. While his work certainly shares a number of key realist attributes, it also escapes the boundaries of the genre at almost every turn. As this happens, he suggests the problematic relationship between the writer and his larger culture in the period, the difficulty both he and Howells found in connecting with their contemporary (capitalist, racist, and socially divided) world.

# 6

## Clemens, Manhood, the Rogers Friendship, and "Which Was the Dream?"

I wish to retain your services, sir; and it is my intention to raise your salary. Let us get back on the financial platform, now, and do another tour. It is much better than literature. Literature is well enough, as a time-passer, and for the improvement and general elevation and purification of mankind, but it has no practical value.

—S. L. Clemens to H. H. Rogers, January 24, 1899, in Lewis Leary, ed., *Mark Twain's Correspondence with Henry Huttleston Rogers*, 386.

I

In 1893 Samuel Clemens was in trouble. The country was in severe economic depression and his business interests were in crisis. Work on the Paige typesetting machine, in which he had sunk massive amounts of money over a twelve-year period, was at a halt. His role as investor in, and promoter for, the venture would shortly be revealed as the "catastrophic gamble" it was.[1] Clemens's publishing business, Charles Webster & Co., was on the rocks, to founder completely the following year. At one of his lowest ebbs, he wrote to his Webster business partner, Fred J. Hall, in mid-year: "I am terribly tired of business. I am by nature and disposition unfitted for it and I want to get out of it. . . . Do your best for me, for I do not sleep, these nights, for visions of the poor-house."[2]

Hall, himself "worried half to death" by business conditions, could not help.[3] Nothing, moreover, could be done to save either the typesetter or Webster & Co. from failure. But, in autumn 1893, Clemens reported that Dr. Clarence Rice "had ventured to speak to a rich friend of his who was an admirer of mine about our straits."[4] He was referring here to the powerful figure of Henry Huttleston Rogers—"Hell Hound" Rogers, vice president of the Standard Oil Company. The friendship Rogers and Clemens consequently formed would grow increasingly close and lasted through to Rogers's death in May 1909.

The time and skill Rogers gave to Clemens meant he survived the "wreckage" of his businesses and eventually regained prosperity.[5] Rogers's masterstroke when Webster & Co. foundered was to transfer the copyrights of Clemens's books to his wife Olivia, as the company's "preferred creditor."[6] The complex negotiations he then conducted, and contracts he steered through, with Harper's and The American Publishing Company were highly advantageous to the Clemenses and helped further to secure their financial future. In March 1898, the newspapers announced Clemens's clearing of the Webster & Co. bankruptcy debts, and the family's financial worries were effectively over.

In February 1899, Clemens wrote to Rogers from Vienna, commenting on the investments made on his behalf: "Why, it is just splendid! I have nothing to do but sit around and watch you set the hen [a pun on Rogers's first name] and hatch out those big broods and make my living for me. Don't you wish you had somebody to do the same for you?—a magician who can turn steel and copper and Brooklyn gas into gold. I mean to raise your wages again—I begin to feel that I can afford it."[7] The extent and effect of Rogers's stock market interventions seemed sheer wizardry to Clemens.[8] Here, though, in a typical reverse move, Clemens both acknowledges his friend's authority in the realm of speculative finance, but comically puts himself in the superior role, the boss to Rogers's wage employee.

My intention here is not to retell this familiar part of the Rogers-Clemens narrative, but to explore representations of manhood at the turn of the nineteenth century within the framework of their correspondence and friendship (and in terms of the relationship of writer to corporate businessman). I conclude by linking my discussion to the way manhood is depicted in one of Clemens's late texts, "Which Was the Dream?" The chapter complements my opening chapter both in its references to the larger context of recent work on late-nineteenth-century gender relations in America and in its return to some of the motifs there identified. There has been considerable debate on whether a "crisis" in masculinity occurred in this period. If the current consensus is that the term "crisis" is misleading, "middle-class men" do, nonetheless, "seem to have been unusually interested in—even obsessed with—manhood" at this time.[9] This can be put down to a large number of factors including severe economic depression and the threat it posed to the ideology of self-made manhood; fears of effeminacy, overcivilization and "neurasthenia" in a culture where physical inactivity and mental effort had apparently replaced a reliance on, and admiration for, the muscular male body; and anxieties about the advance and effect of the women's movement.[10]

As suggested earlier, any straightforward reading of gender role in the period has been complicated by recent critical work undermining notions of clearly limited "separate spheres" of male and female activity and influence. Amy Kaplan, for example, in her groundbreaking *The Anarchy of Empire in the Making of U.S. Culture* (2002) explores representations of domesticity and female subjectivity in the 1850s to show how they "contributed to and were enabled by narratives of nation and empire building"—how "the female realm of domesticity and the male arena of Manifest Destiny were not separate spheres at all but were intimately linked."[11] As I later show, a similar relationship connects the "male" world of business in the later nineteenth century to the supposedly "female" realm of sentiment. I do not, however, completely abandon the notion of separate spheres, for to do so runs flat in the face of commonly accepted belief.[12] So Mark C. Carnes makes a convincing case for the determining influence of "the gender bifurcation of middle-class life" in his study of fraternal organizations and ritualistic behavior in the American Victorian world. Members of "male secret orders," he shows, "repeatedly practiced rituals that effaced the religious values and emotional ties associated with women."[13]

I am treading on slippery ground here. Critical work on constructions of manliness in the period is still very much an ongoing project, and we should remember the multiform rather than homogenous nature of the term. So Bederman reminds us that "[a]ttempting to define manhood as a coherent set of prescriptive ideals, traits, or sex roles obscures the complexities and contradictions of any historical moment." Carnes and Griffen comment more simply that "constructions of masculinity vary in different contexts within the same culture."[14] Moreover, writing on the subject tends to be class and race oriented, with particular emphasis on middle- and working-class white manhood.

Clemens and Rogers make an exceptional and interesting pairing who do not fit normal class categories. Both were, in different ways, self-made men with backgrounds in printing, steamboat piloting, mining, and journalism (Clemens) and grocery, railroading, and oil refining (Rogers) respectively. At the time of their friendship, Rogers was "one of the most ruthless businessmen and financial speculators in the country."[15] As such, he fitted one common model of successful masculinity—to "find adventure and get rich at the same time by becoming a robber baron."[16] As a best-selling author and celebrity, Clemens's social and cultural status was also unusual. Because of his chosen career, his gender positioning was—as I have earlier suggested (and will here show)—considerably more complex than Rogers's.

To immediately suggest something of that complexity, I would see Clemens as an early example of the pattern of "masculine domesticity" identified by Margaret Marsh among the suburban middle class in the period.[17] Clemens was neither suburban nor middle class, but his work took place outside the boundaries of conventional business practice, based in the home and within a family context. Accordingly, the changes in Victorian family life Marsh identifies—an increase in "companionate marriages" and the father's "involve[ment] in the internal workings of the household" (especially in parenting)—applied, in Clemens's case, from the earliest days of his marriage.[18] Whatever the family use of servants and governesses, however much his attraction to the rituals of male friendships outside the home, and despite his satiric depreciation (in the loosely autobiographical McWilliams stories) of his own domestic role, undoubtedly Clemens spent far more time in the family setting than the vast majority of his male contemporaries, time that he genuinely enjoyed.

Any generalization outward from the Clemens-Rogers friendship to other class, business, or status groups, then, is tricky. But there are connections to be made. In their relationship the worlds of literature and business intersect, and we gain insight into life near the top—even despite the Clemens's financial problems—of the Victorian status hierarchy (I return to this crucial fact of shared social position in my next chapter). And the two male identities on display, although exceptional in many ways, cannot be read in a vacuum. Constructions of masculinity may vary in a culture but undoubtedly they also share considerable common ground.

## II

> Through letter writing the individual unfolded himself in his subjectivity...[The letter is] a conversation with one's self addressed to another person. (Jürgen Habermas)[19]—Quoted in Scott A. Sandage, "The Gaze of Success: Failed Men and the Sentimental Marketplace, 1873–1893," in Mary Chapman and Glenn Hendler, eds., *Sentimental Men: Masculinity and the Politics of Affect in American Culture*

Letters are essentially social, a way of building understanding and mutuality. But, as Habermas suggests, they can also provide a form of self-assessment and self-enquiry, carried out before others. Thus Clemens's use of images of natural disaster, as he reflects on his financial collapse and the circumstances that caused it, is of some significance. Scott Sandage, writing on the distinctive genre of "begging letters" sent to the rich and successful in the 1870s to 1890s (a period of common business failure), speaks of the writers' need to "reconstruct masculine identity in the wake of failure—a foreclosure at once economic and psychological."[20] The letters from Clemens to Rogers are not begging letters. Despite the (hierarchical) relationship of economic dependency involved, the correspondence is conducted on equal terms. For Clemens's literary status and celebrity matched Rogers's business success and reputation. The notion of psychological, as well as economic, foreclosure is nonetheless relevant.

Clemens writes about his financial collapse and Rogers's role as rescuer using a series of different metaphors. News of another failure, under test conditions, of the Paige machine, hits Clemens "like a thunderclap."[21] A following letter changes metaphorical direction in its suggestion of a drowning at sea: "I shall always remember what you have done for me...I am 59 years old; yet I never had a friend before who put out a hand and tried to pull me ashore when he found me in deep waters."[22] Later, there is still another figurative shift when Clemens talks of having "been through the fire."[23] I do not wish to make too much of these few images, but would suggest that in his "conversation with himself" and with Rogers, Clemens tends to shift the reasons for his own business failure to "natural" disaster, and thus to unavoidable circumstance. We see similar tendencies, though with different emphasis, elsewhere. Clemens does at times recognize his own failings. He admits that "I am to blame" for putting the Paige machine on exhibition before it was properly ready, and would refer to his own "leather-headed business snarls."[24] But, as he retrospectively assesses his life, Clemens reclaims something of his own business manhood by placing the reasons for failure outside the self. His vehement attacks on previous business partners are part of this pattern. So, for instance, Elisha and Frank Bliss (of the American Publishing Company) are accused of having "robbed me for a quarter of a century."[25]

A more obvious reclamation of manhood occurs with Clemens's 1898 clearance of his bankruptcy debts. Gail Bederman discusses the "remaking" of manhood in America between 1880 and 1910, and sees an ideology of "manliness" replaced by one of "masculinity." "Manliness" depended on the business ethos of the self-made man and signified "strong, manly 'character,'" a sense of male authority emphasising the "honor, high-mindedness, and strength stemming from [a] powerful self-mastery" (the repression of "masculine passions"). It existed within a larger context where "honesty, probity and family life" served as the bedrock of male economic and cultural identity.[26] As changes in the capitalist system occurred, with the multiple bankruptcies that followed a recurrent cycle of economic depression, so this ideology faltered. The emphasis on "masculinity" replacing it occurred, Bederman suggests, as "[m]any men tried to revitalize manhood by celebrating all things male." The popularity of fraternal organizations, the stress on physical virility, athleticism, and martial values, and attacks on "excessive femininity"—and a consequent valorization of activities and attitudes previously associated with working-class manhood—were all part of this revised order of male identity.[27] "Manliness," then, was "synonymous with 'honorable, highminded'" and consisted of "all the worthy, moral attributes which the Victorian middle class admired in a man." "Masculinity" was a much more flexible signifier, attached not to the "'highest conceptions' of manhood" but to "any characteristics, good or bad, that all men had" (like masculine occupations and physical abilities).[28]

The border between these two concepts of male identity might be more porous than Bederman suggests, but Clemens's actions as he recovered from the Webster & Co. bankruptcy can be seen in terms of the notion of "manliness" represented here. The decision to pay off the Webster creditors could have been sidestepped. Clemens presented his refusal to do so as a marker of personal integrity, of "honor [as] a harder master than the law." He described his planned world lecture tour in terms of "the imperious moral necessity of paying these debts... accumulated on the faith of my name." And he asked the firm's creditors to "trust to my honor" that the outstanding portion of their claims would be paid.[29]

If it is the discourse of "manliness" Clemens uses here, his creditors (and other interested commentators) responded in kind, once recompense had been made. One letter sent to Rogers's office in early December 1897 speaks of appreciating Clemens's "manliness no less than his incomparable humor."[30] Another creditor refers to Clemens's "sterling integrity" in clearing the debts, noting how exceptional in the writer's entire "business experience" this was.[31] The London *Daily News* reported (in March 1898) on Clemens's final clearing of these debts as "a fine example of the very chivalry of probity... rank[ing] with the historic case of Walter Scott."[32] This last comparison suggests, again, that the standards of manhood Clemens chose to meet may have been outmoded in the turn-of-the-century business world. There are, however, plenty of signs of continuing anxiety about his male identity even despite his "manly" behavior in this particular respect.

### III

> You and I are a team: you are the most useful man I know, and I am the most ornamental.
>
> *Mark Twain's Correspondence with Henry Huttleston Rogers*

The opposition Clemens constructs here between the businessman and the artist, usefulness and ornamentation, is common in turn-of-the-century America. I have previously referred to Santayana's well-known essay, "The Genteel Tradition in American Philosophy" (1911) and his identification of a schizophrenic divide in the American sensibility between civilization and culture. He describes the world of "practical affairs" (business, technology, and science) as separated from that of "culture" (art, education, religion). This gap is, moreover, defined in gendered terms: "The American Will... is the sphere of the American man; the [American Intellect], at least predominantly, of the American woman." The realm of high culture has, here, become "slightly becalmed... float[ing] gently in the backwater," disconnected from the vital creativity and masculinity of the American business world.[33] Santayana, in part, excepts Clemens from his critique. And the latter's own acceptance of the "ornamental" label is, to a degree, comic self-denigration. The correspondence with Rogers shows the gap between commerce and art, business and sentiment, masculine assertiveness and feminized dependency, to be far more porous and unstable than his words would initially suggest.

Clemens was, from the first, formed in a different mould from many of his literary peers. I have suggested in my last chapter how this period saw "the triumph of business relations in the creation of literature" and, accordingly, the emergence of "a new type of writer... attuned to the financial possibilities of writing."[34] Clemens was just such a writer, and "pursued the business of authorship" in the mass market with decided vigor.[35] His writing habits were rigorously disciplined and he was literally aware of the worth of every word he wrote. A December 1903 letter to Rogers is typical in this respect: "I shipped [Harper's] a brief [article] a few days ago; 2,000 words exactly—I had them counted, word by word. Due, $600–30 cents a word."[36] He "aggressively sued anyone he thought was breaching his copyright" and helped in the campaign that would result in the 1909 revised copyright law.[37] His insistent literary professionalism was "essential to his sense of masculinity"—acted as the very marker of his manhood in the marketplace.[38] He never really filled the ornamental role proposed to Rogers.

I suggested previously, however, just how difficult literary men as Clemens and Howells found it to find their place in the world of the market-place—and in terms of the national values and assumptions reflected there. And, in more immediate business terms, Clemens's authority as a professional writer was greatly compromised just at the time the relation with Rogers began. The marketing of his work was inseparable from the publishing company he ran (Webster & Co.). And his stake in Webster's could not, in turn, be divorced from the money sunk into his other main business interest, the Paige compositor. Thus the financial problems Rogers looked to address affected every area of his professional (and private) life. Sandage's comment on the relationship between masculine identity and economic and psychological foreclosure is very much to the point here.

To read the Clemens-Rogers correspondence is to become aware of the extraordinary delegation of responsibility from one to the other. No wonder Clemens writes that "it troubles me to put so many loads on your generous shoulders; and it troubles Mrs. Clemens, too. She thinks I ride you too hard...."[39] Clemens would, much later, describe the demands of the Webster creditors, "bent on devouring every pound of flesh in sight and picking the bones afterward," as if—in a rare image for him—the integrity of his own male body was at stake.[40] It was Rogers who protected him, handling the Webster collapse and sorting out the Paige business as far as it could be sorted out. He negotiated the new contracts with Harper's and the American Publishing Company in a time-consuming and extended process, lasting from 1895 right through to 1906.[41] Rogers also managed the placing and the sale of many of Clemens's shorter writings, besides making the (previously mentioned) stock-market investments on his behalf.[42]

Rogers commonly represents his actions on his friend's behalf in terms of an assertive masculinity: "Walter Bliss [of the American Publishing Co.] and I had a very plain talk... I think I *forced* him to the position of saying that he would be willing to surrender all of the old books to Harper & Bros. for the uniform edition... I believe that the American Publishing Co. can be *whipped into line*..."[43] Clemens, of course, continues to get involved in all these various business matters, worrying, calculating, in frequent dialog with Rogers, and others, about them. In essence, though, he was mostly reduced (if that is the right term given Clemens's major talents) to being a writer and a lecturer. He describes himself as having to "work like a slave" as he prepares his world lecture tour.[44] And a contemporary periodical, *The Chap-Book*, reports him as a "pathetically flaccid and groveling figure" as he responds (in its view) inappropriately to his business losses.[45] If there is only a hint of it here, it seems likely that his reversals, and new dependency on Rogers, carried with them a sense of depleted masculinity. The fact that his wife, Olivia, had (on March 9, 1894), as part of a maneuver by Rogers to protect the family interests, been assigned all Clemens's property, including his book copyrights and his Paige-machine holdings, must have supplemented this feeling. "The $30,000 Bequest" (1904) describes gender role reversal, with Saladin Foster, the main male character, given the "curious and unsexing...pet name" of Sally, while his wife Electra (Aleck) is portrayed as the "calculating business-woman" of the family.[46] Clemens's anxieties concerning his own male identity, his awareness of his past dependency on his wife's inherited money, and the transfer of his own property into her name, may all be reflected here.

## IV

Revered Doctor:
I knew you many years ago, before you got piety and the balance of your vices, and I suppose you may have a remembrance of me because of my distinction as an evangelist.
 —Rogers to Clemens, December 18, 1908, Leary, *Mark Twain's Correspondence with Henry Huttleston Rogers*

I have suggested that Clemens's "manliness" may have been upheld to some degree in the Webster bankruptcy dealings, but that his larger sense of male identity was nonetheless unavoidably damaged. I have argued, too, that in his dealings with Rogers throughout this period, it was Rogers whose tough assertiveness and business vigor acted on his dependent friend's behalf. But the Clemens-Rogers relationship was predicated on a basis of equality. And in the details of the friendship, as well as in Clemens's humorous construction of it, we find the two men have more shared qualities than we might expect. Any reading of the friendship in terms of strong financier and anxiety-ridden dependent is only a partial representation of a more complex truth.

Twinning is a constant motif in Clemens's writing, and he and Rogers were, in certain ways, twinned figures. Despite his history and apparent determination to say "Farewell—a long farewell—to *business*! I will *never* touch it again!" Clemens would never quite let go of his image of himself— rather in the Rogers mould—as a venture capitalist and businessman.[47] He never left his own business dealings completely in Rogers's hands. Asking Rogers to check a letter written to one of the Webster creditors, George Barrow, Clemens writes that, "The idea of it is to let him know that I have dropped back to a cold business basis with him and am not having any more sentimental bellyaches on his account."[48] (I return to this business/sentiment binary later.) Discussing various publishing matters and the rates he is determined to get for his work, Clemens talks of "my backbone [being] stiffened in several ways."[49] Whatever his anxieties and failures, Clemens brings a sporadic sense of confident and assertive masculinity to his business dealings.

His letters to Rogers from Austria (where he lived for an extended period in the late 1890s) reinforce this self-belief, at times extravagantly. Writing of a textile-design machine in which he intends to invest, Clemens represents himself in a vigorous outdoors metaphor, as having "landed a big fish to-day."[50] Having then spent three hours putting questions to the machine's inventor and his banker/backer, he continues in similar vein, though with a final bow in the direction of past failure: "I was ashamed to question him as if he were on trial in a court, but it had to be done, (and I had to imitate you, the Master of the art,) and he [the banker] said he didn't mind it. Said I could get my living as a financier if authorship should fail me—a very nice compliment and quite true, too, though you probably don't believe it."[51] What is perhaps most extraordinary here is not the resurgence of Clemens's confidence in his own business abilities (for there always would be a touch of the Tom Sawyer/Colonel Sellers about him), but rather Rogers's indulgence of him. Even while Clemens seems aware of his own hyperbole, he presents investment in the machine as a great opportunity and gives Rogers a list of instructions to follow and of details to check through.[52] Rogers did then go some way to comply with his requests, however much he must have been aware of the fool's errand he was probably running.

Clemens then, to some degree, re-establishes joint ground with Rogers as he again pursues investment and business interests.[53] So in their correspondence he humorously blurs the boundaries between their roles and identities and comically distorts the nature of their relationship. Writing to Rogers about the Federal Steel stock purchased on his behalf, he assumes the role of junior business partner, using the mask of naïveté to narrow their professional distance and to humorously establish himself as Rogers's near equal: "It just occurs to me: am I a Vice President, or a Director in the Steel Company, or only a General Manager? And what do I get? What is the wages? ... Do you think I had better go on with literature for a while, or begin to run the Company *now*? You know more than I do about these things. Tell me."[54]

The gap between Rogers and Clemens also narrows in a different way, as the form of their friendship alters over time. Clemens, at the start of their relationship, "jump[s] at" Rogers's offer to take on all his "business bothers" to concentrate on his main career as writer and humorist.[55] As the friendship develops and Rogers (quite clearly) relaxes into it, so his own sense of humor is increasingly evident. A series of shared private jokes scatter the later correspondence.[56] And in 1902, Rogers, in cahoots with his friend, assumed the role of Clemens's father-in-law in writing to a New Zealander who had asked Clemens for a message for his church literary society: "Mr. Clemence [*sic* ] has been in good health until recently, but a trip to the West Indies with a party of riotous gentlemen [a reference to a trip in March on Rogers's boat, the *Kanawha* ] has laid him low, and we are quite doubtful as to his recovery. He has lost his sense of humor entirely, and is now writing on metaphysical and religious subjects. His latest, and to my mind his best production is in the form of a sermon which has been published in the 'Christian Pulpit.' His text is 'Why will ye doubting stand?'..."[57] When Clemens adds to the end of his July 13, 1905, letter to Rogers, "Jessus [*sic* ]! but I had a narrow escape. Suppose you had gone into humor instead of oil—where would I be?" he is of course joking.[58] But the positioning of the two men on each side of the business-humor divide is certainly less rigid than commonly assumed.

In Rogers's company, Clemens took part in a predominantly male-oriented social world, with their shared delight in billiards, in poker playing, in boisterous male company (especially on the *Kanawha* trips), and in attending boxing and billiard matches.[59] And the relationship expressed itself through a particular type of jocular masculinity—a pleasure in badinage, off-color humor, and attitudes and forms of expression taboo to the "domestic, female world."[60] So Clemens tells Rogers his anecdote about the deaf Mary Stover and the "small fart."[61] And Rogers refers to the "drunkenness, profanity and sodomy" promised by a transatlantic voyage in each other's company.[62]

In the very last years of the relationship, its early pattern—with the forceful Rogers propping up the anxiously dependent Clemens—had quite changed.[63] Rogers's age and the intense pressure of his job combined to make him into more of a wreck than Clemens had been a decade earlier. Certainly, in the early stages of the friendship, it was Clemens who was at the point of collapse.[64] But in 1904, under enormous pressure from anti-trust cases, it is Rogers who drops his normal guarded manner to admit freely to his (now) old friend the pressure he is under. On January 8 he writes of "everything seem[ing] to pile on so I have but little time to think of anything but care and worry." Four days later he refers to being "about fagged out again," and soon "to go on the rack again" in a Boston court.[65] In July, he is "but a shadow of my old self," as the Boston trial continues.[66] His sudden death on May 19, 1909, followed soon after the opening of the Virginian Railway, a favored business project in which he suffered heavy losses. Unlike Clemens's earlier case, these did not bankrupt him. They did, however, wipe out half his personal fortune.[67]

Any reading that would put Rogers and Clemens at opposite ends of a spectrum of male strength and weakness, then, collapses once a full overview of the relationship occurs. Each man's sense of gender identity finds its complement in the other in the symbiotic quality of their relationship and the shared nature of their leisure pursuits. Clemens's anxieties about his own manhood seem accordingly to fade from view as the friendship continues. Rogers's 1904 crisis and sense of paralysis—and the Virginian Railroad problems that were to follow—indicate that he was not immune from the pressures on manhood that Clemens, in his different way, had previously felt.[68] Even here, surprisingly, their status as twinned figures is confirmed.

Figure 1.   Clemens and Twichell. February 1905, 21 5th Avenue, New York. Photograph by Jean Clemens. Courtesy of the Mark Twain Project, Bancroft Library, University of California, Berkeley.

Figure 2.   Joseph Hopkins Twichell. February 1905, 21 5th Avenue, New York. Photograph by Jean Clemens. Courtesy of the Mark Twain Project, Bancroft Library, University of California, Berkeley.

Figure 3.   Twichell and his family on vacation in the Adirondacks.
Courtesy of the Yale Collection of American Literature in the Beinecke
Rare Book and Manuscript Library, Yale University, New Haven,
Connecticut.

Figure 4.   Clemens and Twichell on SS Bermudian (1907 Bermuda Visit).
Photograph by Isabel Lyon. Courtesy of the Mark Twain Project, Bancroft
Library, University of California, Berkeley.

Figure 5.   Section of group photograph with Howells and Clemens center, farewell party for Howells before leaving for Italy, given by Colonel Harvey (of Harper's) in late 1907. By permission of the Houghton Library, Harvard University, call number *90 M–19 (f).

Figure 6.   Clemens and Howells outside Stormfield. 1908. Photograph by Isabel Lyon. Courtesy of the Mark Twain Project, Bancroft Library, University of California, Berkeley.

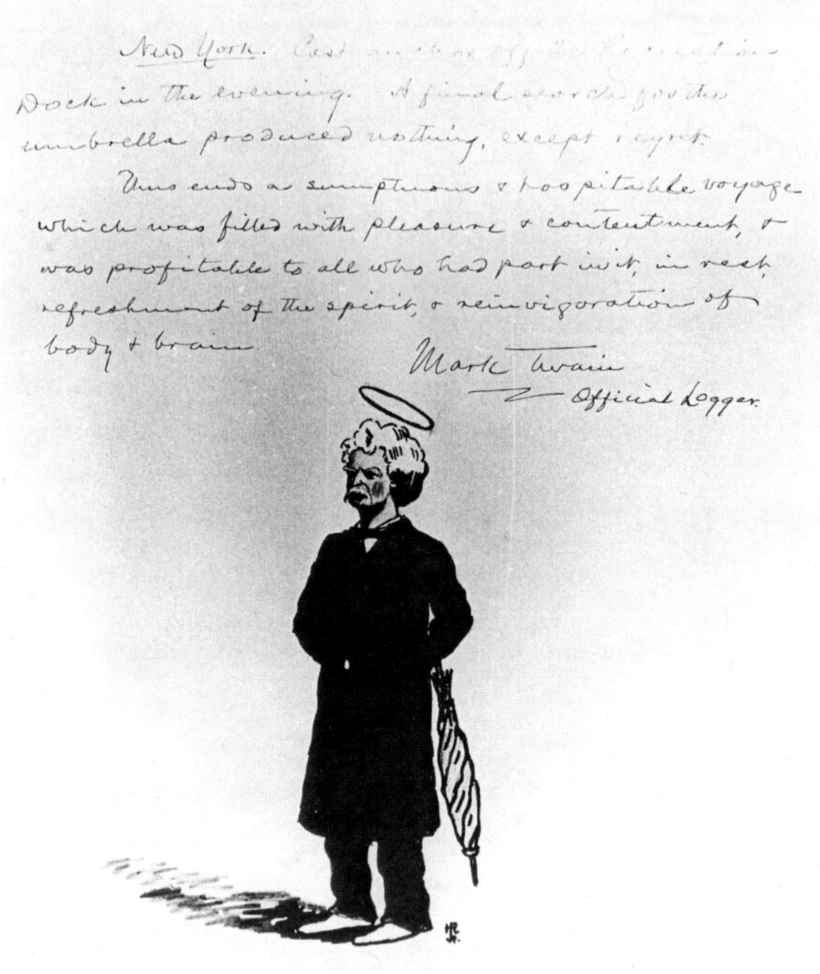

New York. Cast anchor off the recreation
Dock in the evening. A final search for the
umbrella produced nothing, except regret.

Thus ends a sumptuous & hospitable voyage
which was filled with pleasure & contentment, &
was profitable to all who had part in it, in rest,
refreshment of the spirit, & reinvigoration of
body & brain

                              Mark Twain
                                  — Official Logger.

Figure 7. Clemens, drawn by Harry Rogers, in the Ship's Log of Henry H. Roger's Steam Yacht, the *Kanawha*, 1901. Peter Salm collection, courtesy of his family.

Figure 8.   Clemens, Henry H. Rogers, Elizabeth Wallace, Mary Allen
Peck, Isabel Lyon and one other. 1908 Bermuda. Courtesy of the Mark
Twain Project, Bancroft Library, University of California, Berkeley.

Figure 9.   Clemens and Mrs. Emilie Rogers in carriage. 1908 Bermuda.
Photograph by Isabel Lyon. Courtesy of the Mark Twain Project, Bancroft
Library, University of California, Berkeley.

Figure 10.   Clemens and Rogers. 1908, Princess Hotel, Bermuda.
Photograph by Isabel Lyon. Courtesy of the Mark Twain Project, Bancroft
Library, University of California, Berkeley.

Figure 11.   Clemens and Rogers. 1908, Princess Hotel, Bermuda.
Photograph by Isabel Lyon. Courtesy of the Mark Twain Project, Bancroft
Library, University of California, Berkeley.

Figure 12.   Clemens and Rogers at sea, 1908. Courtesy of the Mark Twain
Project, Bancroft Library, University of California, Berkeley.

Figure 13.  Clemens and Harry Rogers in automobile. Photograph by
Nathan Lazarnick. Courtesy of George Eastman House, Rochester, New
York.

V

> I note what you say about helping me with your heart and head and
> pocket...
> —*Mark Twain's Correspondence with Henry Huttleston Rogers*,
> Clemens to Rogers, January 29, 1895

In studies of late-nineteenth-century American culture, business and sentiment are traditionally opposed. "Sentiment" is associated with the domestic and the womanly and seen to belong outside the male domain of work. This was true in the period itself too, so when Clemens writes to Rogers about his Plasmon investment he stresses the tough-mindedness of his fellow syndicate members: "rich business men, and not sentimental."[69] Heart and head, in other words, were not normally seen as compatible where "business" was at stake.[70]

But recent criticism has shown this view, and its related tendency to see American society of the time through rigid gender binaries, as one-dimensional. Sentiment did, despite prevailing myths, have its place in business. The gap between Clemens's words and his own common practice suggests both his, and his culture's, ambivalence about the relationship of the two spheres. Susan K. Harris puts the Rogers friendship in the context of other "business mentors" to show how much, in fact, Clemens relied on sentiment and emotional affinity "rather than on legal or contractual relations." She sees this, in turn, as a marker of a wider dissatisfaction with business relationships in the period and a more general desire to develop new models of male interaction.[71] I rather see such "affective ties" as part and parcel of the larger pattern of male relationships at the time—part of a complex and ongoing move between business and friendship and between contractual and non-contractual forms of bonding.

But this is not to say that all men combined sentiment with business. Rogers—perhaps because of the exceptional power and authority vested in him—normally did not. Clemens was a celebrity when Rogers took an interest in his troubles, and Rogers himself gained in various ways from their exchange.[72] Whatever their different motives, though, and the larger cultural conclusions that may be drawn, business and deep sentiment do conspicuously run together in the two men's relationship. A bond of mutual and affectionate esteem quickly developed between them as Rogers helped put Clemens back on his economic feet. Thus, in February 1894, Clemens comments to Olivia on his refusal (on behalf of Webster & Co.) to publish a book attacking Standard Oil:

> I *wanted* to say—
> "The only man *I* care for in the world; the only man I would give a *damn*
> for; the only man who is lavishing his sweat and blood to save me and
> mine from starvation and shame, is [referring back to the rejected book]
> a Standard Oil fiend. If you know me, you know whether I want the book
> or not."[73]

The sentimental regard Clemens and Rogers had for each other is evident in much already said. The warm esteem in which they came to hold one another is clear in both their language and expressed emotion. Clemens writes Rogers, "You have been to me the best friend that ever a man had."[74] He tells his daughter Clara (after he has referred to other members of the Rogers family), "as for old Henry himself, he is the finest they make."[75] Rogers is less forthcoming but his August 14, 1902, telegram to Clemens, when Olivia was seriously ill, clearly indicates his (and his wife's) feelings: "we are both desirous of serving you if we can Dont [sic] fail to command us because we are to be classed among your warmest friends."[76]

The close attachment between the two men is perhaps best expressed in the intimate jocularity of the letters, the clear pleasure in their talk of sharing one another's company, and in Clemens's obvious fondness for time spent with Rogers's family. This is particularly true of the later years of the friendship.[77] Both men begin their correspondence by addressing their letters formally ("Dear Mr. Rogers"/"Dear Mr. Clemens"), though Rogers soon moves to "My dear Clemens" or "My dear Mr. Clemens." In 1905 the pattern changes. From then we see an increasing intimacy as Clemens addresses Rogers, at different times, as "Dear H. H.," "Dear Uncle Henry," and "Dear Admiral." This is matched on Rogers's part by his "Dear Parson" and "Revered Doctor" (after Clemens's Oxford Degree award). A letter from Mrs. Rogers, following her husband's stroke, ends with the words, "Mr Rogers says he would like to see 'Old Mark.'"[78] Clemens was devastated when he learnt of his friend's death from Clara at Grand Central Station, when on his way from his Connecticut home to see Rogers. His words, according to the *New York Times*, were: "This is terrible, terrible, and I cannot talk about it...I am inexpressibly shocked and grieved. I do not know just where I will go..."[79] The (unpublished) tribute to Rogers, written prior to that death, finished with the words: "He is not only the best friend I have ever had, but is the best man I have known."[80] The exceptional nature of their case, and Rogers's own normal business dealings, preclude the drawing of too many wider cultural conclusions here. But the fact that this friendship did, for Clemens at any rate, conform to a larger pattern, suggests that standard readings of the gulf separating male business relations and sentiment in the period are not always necessarily reliable.

## VI

"The loss is total."
My God, the words went through me like a bullet...I was dumb, I could not find my voice.
—"Which Was the Dream?" (unpublished during Clemens's lifetime), in Twain, *Collected Tales, Sketches, Speeches, & Essays, 1891–1910*

Clemens had the stuffing knocked out of him by the Webster & Co. bankruptcy and the Paige-typesetter failure. The death of his daughter Susy in August 1896, and of his wife Olivia in June 1904, further diminished him. He writes to Rogers about *Following the Equator* (1896) on December 21, 1897, that the well-received book had not "exposed" his real condition, for: "All the heart I had was in Susy's grave and the Webster debts."[81] The earlier images of wreckage and natural disaster associated with Clemens's financial collapse recur with the "thunder-stroke" of Olivia's death when, as he says, "I lost the life of my life."[82] Clemens became, to large extent, economically dependent on Rogers when his business interests went belly-up. But he seems always have to been dependent on Olivia's authority in the domestic realm—even when she is ill, he describes her as "remain[ing] what she always was: boss" to the rest of the family's "weaklings."[83] In summary, there is clear evidence of the shakiness of Clemens's sense of male authority in this period, both in business and domestically, whatever his various attempts—in his letters, his activities, and his relationships—then to shore it up.

In this chapter's final section, I briefly comment on the implications of this sense of diminished male selfhood for Clemens's fiction, focusing on the unfinished "Which Was the Dream?" (1897). This type of interpretative move is not new. John Cooley, for instance, notes how "[d]uring his last fifteen years as a writer his male characters, regardless of age or intentions, are . . . characterised by ineptitude and cowardliness."[84] However, study of the representation of male identity in Clemens's writing is still at a relatively early stage and there remains significant work to be done in the area.

What is immediately noticeable is the way in which turn-of-the-century anxieties about American manhood suffuse Clemens's late work. They provide the context for the representation of Thomas X in "Which Was the Dream?" Scott Sandage identifies a need to "reconstruct masculine identity" for those who suffered the "engulfing anonymity" accompanying business failure in the period.[85] The fact that Clemens's protagonist is partially anonymous is itself significant in this narrative of diminished identity and business loss. And gender identity is foregrounded as an issue early in the text when Tom recalls his small-town Kentucky boyhood. His own class background—he is from a "quality" family—and the consequent need to wear shoes even as spring commences, leaves him open to gender-inflected ridicule: "All the common boys had been barefoot for as much as a week already, and were beginning to mock at us for 'Miss Nancys,' and make fun of us for being under our mother's thumbs and obliged to be unmanly and take care of our health like girls."[86] Eleven-year-old Tom is already at this point marked out both for his potential failure to act in a manly way, but then for his avoidance of that charge as he swiftly escapes matriarchal surveillance to go "barefoot; the first 'quality' boy in the town to be 'out.'"[87] The context for this information, though, is significant, for Tom is describing the start of his relationship with five-year-old Alice, eventually to become his wife. The swing between boyhood self-assertion and family romance here reminds us of Anthony Rotundo's account of nineteenth-century boyhood, that "dialogue in actions between the values of the two spheres" (home and a boyhood "alternate world") that shape nineteenth-century male identity.[88]

Tom engages this dialog successfully to become, as an adult, the very epitome of forceful masculinity. A West Point graduate, and famous for his "conspicuous" and "distinguished" service as a young soldier in the Mexican War, Tom becomes not just "the boy General" but also the youngest ever elected U. S. Senator. His military success brings huge public acclaim: his village welcomes him accordingly with "a rain of rockets, and glare of Greek fire, and storm of cannon-blasts, and crash of bands and huzzahs." His political career, too, flourishes. He would have been President were it not for his young age (which Constitutionally bars him from the office).[89] Tom's robust performance perfectly reflects the manly military ideal so strongly valued at the century's end.[90]

But Tom's success on the public stage is matched in the domestic sphere. At the narrative's start he is a father with two daughters (born in 1846 and 1849), deeply content in a Victorian companionate family. He is wedded to his wife in the fullest sense: "We two were one. For all functions but the physical, one heart would have answered for us both."[91] And he plays a central role in the lives and development of his small children, both playful companion and inventive storyteller to them.[92] He is no stern paterfamilias, but a more modern model of nurturing and companionable fatherhood for whom "the concepts of masculine domesticity and 'manliness' were...more complementary than antithetical."[93] The perfect fit between public and private realms is implied at the start of the narrative, where Tom and Alice look forward to hosting five hundred of Washington's top servicemen and diplomats in their "costly and beautiful" home, for a performance of their daughter Bessie's play, as part of the build-up to her eighth birthday.[94]

The one slightly jarring note in Tom's story of manly republican success is the fact that his wealth is inherited, a matter of luck rather than self-earned. Clemens uses clearly self-reflexive detail when Tom reveals that "it was [his wife's] wealth that made this choice life possible"—for it is funded by coal (the source of Olivia Clemens's wealth, inherited from the Langdon family business).[95] This resource is discovered on Alice's father's land immediately after his death. We have a hint here that masculine authority and independence are not fully secure. Unpredictable circumstance then kicks in more immediately with one of those complete narrative upsets so common in Clemens's late work, as the family home is extensively damaged by fire. Natural disasters, as we have seen, constantly figured for Clemens as signs of the vulnerability of his own sense of manhood.[96]

Male identity cannot exist in a vacuum. In Clemens's own case, literary and business success, property, and financial status all buttressed secure selfhood. "Which Was the Dream?" starts to take on a stronger autobiographical hue as Tom's consciousness, and the apparently secure manhood it represents, fail.[97] The burning down of the house acts as the preliminary correlative of this collapse. Tom may be a great soldier (for

Clemens, read writer) but he is ignorant in matters of business: "I knew nothing of business and had an aversion for it." Depending strongly on sentiment, he relies on an old friend, Jeff Sedgewick, to run his affairs for him with full power of attorney. Moreover, Jeff has practiced Tom's writing style so that their signatures—"genuine" and "imitation"—are indistinguishable.[98] Fulton, one of the bankers investigating Tom's affairs, sums up Tom's consequent dependency: "As I understand it, sir, you . . . a man of the world, a general of the army, a statesman, a grown person, put yourself, body and soul, together with your wife's whole property and your own, unreservedly into the hands of a man . . . empowering him to originate and write letters for you in your own hand-writing, sign and endorse your name upon checks, notes, contracts, in your own hand, and speculate in anything he pleased, with the family's money—and all without even your casual supervision of what he was doing, or enquiry into it? Am I right?"[99]

There are several things to note here. Clemens is writing in the wake of the Webster & Co. bankruptcy, and we cannot forget that. He is certainly aware that men he judged on the basis of sentiment as well as business had, to his mind, let him down. His own culpability in business matters is, however, fictionally excised, given Tom's complete lack of participation in this realm. Tom's identity and agency is swallowed up in, and jeopardized by, Jeff's actions. His autograph, the very sign of individual difference and stamp of selfhood, is invalidated by Jeff's skilful copy.[100] Jeff's financial machinations, carried out under the supposed authority of Tom's name and signature, are motivated by resentment and malevolence. For Tom has failed to recognize, as his wife has, that Jeff is "bad to the marrow."[101] Tom's believes that his money is invested in a Californian gold mine (the "Golden Fleece") but this is a fraud. Resonances of Clemens's own involvement with the Paige machine—his own particular golden fleece—are clear here.

However, this passage hints at subconscious anxieties about Clemens's present dependency on Rogers as much as it, in part, offers refracted commentary on his past financial collapse. The similarities between Jeff and Rogers are too close to ignore. Rogers had power of attorney for Clemens, invested his money and made contracts for him. Their relationship, too, depended on a sentimental model. Clemens trusted Rogers and knew that his financial and business affairs could not be in better hands. Nevertheless, deep and continuing anxieties about the status of his own male identity in the light of his financial dependency subliminally surface here.[102]

The story must not, though, just be read autobiographically, for it has a wider cultural relevance than this. Clemens writes a counter-narrative to hegemonic tales of tough masculinity and imperial adventure in the period, and his doubts about male authority and autonomy represent the more anxious side of the late Victorian mind. For "Which Was the Dream?" is about breakdown and the collapse of male identity. Tom, like many in the period in which Clemens writes, is financially ruined in a business world with no immediate room for sentiment (as Simmons, another banker, says: "This is not a time for womanish sentimentalities"). His reputation is in shreds, his "word" worthless.[103] He finds himself in the role of passive victim, all manly and masculine authority and self-possession obliterated. The markers of traditional American manhood—fiscal soundness, social responsibility, paternal protectiveness—are one by one stripped from him here.[104]

The final stage of the narrative occurs in a further loss of self-mastery as—after springing at Fulton, the banker who accuses him of forgery—Tom suffers complete breakdown. Following his act, he "remember[s] no more" until waking up eighteen months later in a log cabin with rude furnishings in a town called "Hell's Delight," California.[105] Tom, all signs of his former status lost, and wearing jeans and an army shirt, is now known as Edward Jacobs.[106] His girls are barefoot and in linsey-woolsey frocks. His wife starts to recount their story since their ruin, but the narrative is unfinished. The title and structure of the story fits a larger pattern in Clemens's late works where the very fabric of reality is in question: where uncertainty reigns over which life is the dream and which the reality, and the nature of the connection between them.

My continued focus, though, is on the theme of manhood. Home and career are, as I have shown, by no means distinct in terms of Tom X's construction of male identity. But by the end of the narrative, his easy negotiations of the public and domestic world have been halted, and normative gender roles are completely awry. The man of the family is recovering from breakdown, at home, poorly dressed and supine, "stretched upon a bed." His wife, meantime, has (in terms of their Washington life at least) assumed the role of breadwinner.[107] A log cabin and its rough-hewed interior may have "primitive connotations," but there is no renewal of masculine power implied here.[108] Rather, the constriction of the narrative to a cabin interior on the edge of a small Californian town implies historical regression and convalescence, with the home as the only center of meaningful activity, and the manly role and authority in firm abeyance.

The fact that this narrative is one of a number of "dream manuscripts" may itself be significant in the light of William James's dismissive reference to "the nervous sentimentalist and dreamer...who never does a concrete manly deed."[109] Thus Clemens's fictional move to dream worlds and incomplete narratives may be a further sign of his anxieties about male role and agency. His work in a sentimental mode ("A Dog's Tale," 1903, and "A Horse's Tale," 1905, come particularly to mind) may be another. Where Clemens does write a dream narrative that can be interpreted in terms of extravagant masculine adventure ("The Great Dark," 1898), any confidence in that masculinity is undermined by the generic and ontological uncertainties that define the text. Clemens's writing is never single-dimensional and the concerns I identify form one element in a much larger intertextual whole.[110] Nevertheless, his anxieties about male identity circle outward from his correspondence to his fictional works, and intersect in resonant manner with the larger cultural preoccupations of his time.

# 7

## Clemens and Rogers
### "Both Members of This Club"

**Henry H. Rogers (Deceased)**
**Occupation: capitalist**
**Born:** Fairhaven, Massachusetts
> one of large stockholders and v.p. and dir. Standard Oil Co.; pres. and dir. Amalgamated Copper Co., Nat. Transit Co., Nat. Fuel Gas Co., N.Y. Transit Co., Richmond Light & R.R. Co.; v. p. and trustee Anaconda Copper Mining Co.; v.p. and dir. Brooklyn Union Gas Co., United Metals Selling Co.; trustee Mut. Life Ins. Co. of N.Y.; dir. U.S. Steel Corp., Atchison, Topeka & Santa Fe R.R. Co., Chicago, Milwaukee & St. Paul Ry. Co., Union Pacific R.R. Co., etc. Has made many gifts to his native town, including a library, town hall, sch., ch., etc. Home: Fairhaven, Mass.

**Death**
Died 1909.

> —*Who Was Who in America*, vol. 1 (1897–1942).

[William] Laffan must be prospering greatly, now, and will need a large house, and will want to rent his present one to a capitalist of high character; and so I am going to write him and let him know that I am approachable.

> —Clemens to Rogers, February 19, 1899, in Lewis Leary, ed., *Mark Twain's Correspondence with Henry Huttleston Rogers*

I wonder what it is you've got your financial eye on now—for I guessed from a remark you made that you are watching another combination. Don't leave me out; I want to be in, with the other capitalists.

> —Clemens to Rogers September 3, 1899, in Lewis Leary, ed., *Mark Twain's Correspondence with Henry Huttleston Rogers*

I

oth *Members of This Club*, George Bellows's famous 1909 painting, was originally titled *A Nigger and a White Man*. Set in Tom Sharkey's Athletic Club on Broadway it featured the African American boxer Joe Gans apparently about to defeat his (bloodied) white opponent. The immediate ringside members of the crowd are depicted, in an expressionistic manner, as "grotesque caricatures roaring approval of the bloodshed."[1] The two titles of the work point in a number of directions, drawing attention both to the gap between the performers themselves and to the particular nature of the "club" of which boxers and their audience are a part—and the different types of club to which it might be contrasted and compared.

The continued defining facts (at that time) of racial difference, and demeaning prejudice shown to African Americans whatever their talent, are implied in both titles Bellows gave his work. The second and final one is, though, more subtle in this respect. For as Marianne Doezema explains, at a time when public prizefighting was illegal (due to past corrupt practices in the sport), the painting's title "made reference to the device of charging 'memberships' to circumvent the law against public prizefights but also underscored the issue of race. The title becomes a dark satire of the fact that by virtue of transforming sports arenas into 'clubs,' favored membership status was conferred on a black fighter [only for the duration of the bout] as well as a white, at the same fraternal society and at the same time. Few contemporary organizations would have condoned or tolerated such an occurrence under ordinary circumstances."[2]

The white audience of Bellows's painting, also club members, are painted in nonrealistic manner but appear to be from a lower-class background. Robert Haywood writes that the "fights staged . . . at Sharkeys" at this time "lured unfashionable men into its dark, illicit space,"[3] while Doezema refers to the painting in terms of "Bellows's nightmarish experience in the urban underworld."[4] We should not forget, however, the ambiguous public attitude to boxing at that time. For "at the turn of the twentieth century, there was an unsuccessful attempt to clearly differentiate between 'boxing' and 'prizefighting.'" "Boxing" was seen as a "'pure' and gentlemanly sport"—and one associated with virility and masculinity, providing some answer to contemporary anxieties about a perceived sense of enfeebled overcivilization. "Prizefighting" was viewed more simply, as combat between corrupted, money-hungry barbarians. So Theodore Roosevelt attempted to distinguish boxing as healthy and manly while condemning prizefighting as 'simply brutal and degrading' and debased by gamblers."[5] Such mixed attitudes to the sport as a whole meant that boxing took place at a number of venues, some more respectable than others, and that "[g]amblers and longshoremen were increasingly joined at ringside by middle- and upper-class gentlemen, who were indulging their taste for raucous amusements and their curiosity about urban low-life." Audiences, even at Sharkey's, 'crossed class lines.'[6]

It is the activities that drew Clemens and Rogers together as intimate chums that leads me to refer to Bellows's image.[7] Gregg Camfield writes that "[p]ersonally, [Rogers] was, like Clemens, charismatic, a fine raconteur, and devoted to smoking, billiards, cards, and profanity. When his friendship with Clemens began in 1893, he pulled Clemens into his social sphere, entertaining Clemens on his yacht or at his New York or Fairhaven homes. The Rogers circle, in some respects, returned Clemens to the kind of masculine world of business and sporting events in which Clemens began his literary career before he married Olivia Langdon."[8] Fred Kaplan endorses such a reading of the two men's friendship. Rogers's "love of hearty male companionship," he writes, was "as great as Twain's—for dining, jokes, billiards, cards, off-color stories, humorous teasing, and yachting excursions."[9]

Clemens may have been a much more conspicuous and publicly gregarious figure than Rogers. Both men, however, moved in the same upper echelons of American society. Rogers, Lewis Leary says, was "a good companion" to Clemens "on every occasion, at a boxing match, a horse show, the opera, at billiards, or just for an evening of talk."[10] When the two men went to Chicago in December 1893 to inspect Paige Typesetter affairs at close hand it was in the private railcar of Frank Thompson, president of the Pennsylvania Railroad, and in some luxury: "The colored waiter knew his business, and the colored cook was a finished artist. Breakfasts: coffee with real cream; beefsteaks, sausage, bacon, chops, eggs in various ways, potatoes in various— yes, and quite wonderful baked potatoes, and hot as fire. Dinners—all manner of things, including canvas-back duck, apollinaris, claret, champagne, etc."[11] While when they watched the heats of the America's Cup yacht race off Sandy Hook in early October 1901, it was from the deck of Rogers's 227-foot *Kanawha*, "the fastest cruising steam yacht in American waters."[12]

Both men, too, literally were the members of the same club—one very different from the (mainly) working-class Sharkey's—the Lotos Club, a literary club founded in March 1870 and with a varied membership of journalists, scholars, artists, historians, novelists, college presidents and the like. Clemens, an early member (1873), called it the "ace of clubs," and was guest of honor at a dinner there on November 10, 1900 (with Rogers sitting with him on the main table), to celebrate his return to America after a long period of expatriation.[13] Rogers himself would become a club member in 1895: "In the member register, in which all candidates for membership are inscribed, his occupation is listed as 'Gentleman'; his address is East 57th Street (no house number); and his proposer and seconder were, respectively, Walter R. Benjamin and Frank R. Lawrence. Lawrence was the president of the Club at the time."[14] Benjamin was the brother of William Everts Benjamin, husband of Rogers's eldest daughter.

Such New York clubs—as Camfield comments—generally "traded on exclusivity, and while they invited entertainers like Twain, often granting them free memberships, they primarily served to keep the well-to-do in regular contact with one another."[15] Clemens was undoubtedly more of a clubman than was Rogers. The Players Club (motto, from *As You Like It*,

"I like this place. And willingly could waste my time in it") was one of his most frequent haunts, and the place where he would generally stay when he returned to New York from Europe during the Paige Compositor and Webster & Co. crises. Clarence Rice, Clemens's doctor and his initial link to Rogers, suggests something of the hectic quality of Clemens's "bachelor" existence in New York. He reports how Clemens was "good enough to take me with him to numerous dinners, public banquets, to his lectures, to athletic exhibitions, and, several times, to prizefights."[16] He also indicates something of Clemens's sociable nature, and its costs, when he describes his time at the Players:

> I suppose, he slept at our house when he got tired of the Players.... All of the club, and they were all his friends, wanted to pass the time of day with him and hear him talk—and in the evening to ask him to have a hot Scotch with them.... I am sure he didn't want to repeat hot, hot drink too many times, but, in his kindly, simple way, accepted drink after drink, rather than displease his friend the host. I don't know how many he ever drank in an evening, but I do know that I never saw him affected by alcohol—except that it made him a little more talkative.... Don't get the idea that he was an habitual drinker. He was not.... At his own home and at Mr. Roger's [sic] house I don't recall that he ever took more than one drink.[17]

Clemens, as Rice suggests, seems to have liked boxing, and the attending of fights was one of the various activities he shared with Rogers. Indeed both men featured in a scene with some similarity to that Bellows represents—though in a more upmarket venue—when on Saturday, December 30, 1893, they went (with Rice) to the New York Athletic Club to see Frank Craig, the "Harlem Coffee Cooler," defeat the white boxer, Joe Ellingsworth, by a knockout in the seventh.[18] The following January 27, the two men—again with Rice along—went to a boxing exhibition featuring heavyweight champion "Gentleman Jim" Corbett at Madison Square Garden (Rogers had bought a box). The next day Clemens described the event in a letter to Olivia:

> There was a vast multitude of people in the brilliant place. Stanford White came along presently & invited me to go to the World-Champion's dressing room, which I was very glad to do. Corbett has a fine face and is modest and diffident, besides being the most perfectly & beautifully constructed human animal in the world. I said:
> "You have whipped Mitchell, & maybe you will whip [Peter 'Black Prince'] Jackson in June—but you are not done, then. You will have to tackle me."
> He answered, so gravely that one might easily have thought him in earnest—
> "No—I am not going to meet you in the ring. It is not fair or right to require it. You might chance to knock me out, by no merit of your own, but by a purely accidental blow; & then my reputation would be

gone and you would have a double one. You have got fame enough and you ought not to want to take mine away from me." ...

There were lots of little boxing matches, to entertain the crowd: then at last Corbett appeared in the ring, & the 8,000 people present went mad with enthusiasm ....

Corbett boxed 3 rounds with the middle-weight Australian champion— oh, beautiful to see!—then the show was over and we struggled out through a perfect wash of humanity.

Clemens went on to a musical evening, with a "wonderful Hungarian Band," told two stories to the assembled group, and joined in the dancing: "By half past 4 I had danced all those people down—& yet was not tired; merely breathless. I was in bed at 5, & asleep in ten minutes. Up at 9 and presently at work on this letter to you."[19]

We can then—to a degree at least—map something of the Clemens-Rogers friendship, and the social form it took, in terms of the paradigm suggested by Bellows's painting. The "club" to which Clemens and Rogers belonged (Clemens in part because of Rogers's financial support) was that of privileged white America, with lower-class or less affluent citizens gaining temporary entry as entertainers, or in the necessary service-industry support, or (sometimes)—taking the poorer seats—as the remainder of the audience where a public event was involved.[20] Occasionally the members of this (unofficial) fraternity would "slum" it, themselves entering lower-class spaces and communities for purposes of entertainment. The role of the African American in such contexts would generally be either that of sporting performer, or—as in the case of the private railcar on Clemens and Rogers's Chicago trip—as cooks, waiters, and other functionaries.

Clemens and Rogers both worked on behalf of African American advancement, and certainly Clemens's writings and public statements validate Shelley Fisher Fishkin's claim that he was "a writer ... profoundly engaged by the conundrum of racism" in his America and one who was highly aware of "the toll racism takes."[21] However, at the same time and as a member of the club of white gentlemanly privilege I have described, he would occasionally slip into exactly the kind of discourse of racial denigration that was the period's norm rather than its exception—and among the cultural elite as well as lower-class groups. Such forms of discourse were not only used in the case of African Americans but toward other minority groups too. So Robert Collyer—the minister who performed the marriage ceremony between Mai Rogers (Henry H. Rogers's daughter) and William Coe in June 1900—would write to Clemens in November 1905, withdrawing from a particular scheme because "I think the whole thing is on the get rich quick basis and suspect there are jews "pushing behind.'"[22]

As I have argued earlier, even where crude racial and ethnic stereotypes were explicitly employed, they seem not to have disturbed fellow group members, but were accepted rather as the sounding of common prejudices and opinions that (if extreme) could be harmlessly contained within the upper-class social whole. So in his correspondence with Rogers, on his

round-the-world lecture tour, Clemens would write of the village of Cur-
epipe in Mauritius: "The population of the island is guessed at 360,000.
French 20,000; English 8,000; the rest is made up of East Indians, creoles,
niggers, and mongrels."[23] And in "Winter-end Excursion to the Sutherd,"
the log Clemens kept of the *Kanawha* 's three-and-a-half-week trip to Palm
Beach, Miami, Nassau, Havana, Key West, Havana, Santiago de Cuba,
Rum Cay, Charleston, and Norfolk, in March to April of 1902, he spoke of
the "pest of small niggers swarm[ing] continually after the carriages" in
Nassau, continuing: "The population is black, with a mere sprinkle of
whites; the only prosperous industry is the begetting of more niggers; the
only other industry, the sponge-fishery. Of the new crop of niggers the
Commodore [Rogers] was offered two for fifteen dollars by their dam. This
does not pay for seed." The population of Key West is then described as
composed of "Niggers, mulattoes, whites, Spaniards, Cubans & other
human wreckage." And, on a visit to a Havana cigar-factory—noting how
"the nigger licks...the end of a cigar-wrapper [when it] does not fasten
properly"—Clemens added: "Some day there will be a new disease among
the wealthy & the noble & the doctors will not know whence it came."[24] We
see another side of Clemens here in his (unsurprising) tendency to echo
the racist language and assumptions that were shared by most of the
wealthy upper classes of his American time.

## II

As I have suggested earlier, during the years from 1893 onward, Rogers
and his family became increasingly important in Clemens's life. Very little
has been written about the relationship either with Rogers or his family.
Clemens's own accounts of the friendship are given in the *Autobiography*
and in his 1902 "A Tribute to Henry H. Rogers" (unpublished in either
man's lifetime). The Clemens-Rogers letters (1969) provide the best source
of information about the relationship and are notable for the volume and
intensity of the correspondence (often concerning business matters).[25]
Two short books giving Clemens's correspondence with the larger Rogers
family have also been published. *Mark Twain's Letters to Mary* (1961) is
Lewis Leary's account of Clemens's relationship with Rogers's daughter-
in-law—wife of his son, Harry—built around the available letters, while
*Mark Twain's Letters to the Rogers's Family* (1970), edited by Earl Dias,
includes letters to other family members. Dias, a resident of Rogers's
hometown of Fairhaven, also wrote the one specific account of the Clemens-Rogers relationship that has appeared, *Mark Twain and Henry Huttleston Rogers: An Odd Couple* (1984).[26] I have previously mentioned Peter
Krass's *Ignorance, Confidence, and Filthy Rich Friends* (2007), which describes the business relationship between the two men. The major biographers (including Albert Bigelow Paine, Justin Kaplan, Andrew Hoffman,
Fred Kaplan, and Ron Powers) all, too, have sections on the friendship—of
which Justin Kaplan and Fred Kaplan's accounts are particularly useful.[27]

This relatively thin coverage may at first appear surprising. It may be explained, however, by the difficulty of finding out anything much about Rogers excepting information readily available in the general history of the period. His private and business papers appear to have been systematically suppressed, destroyed, or kept in private hands. Rogers, though, (as detailed previously) meant a great deal to Clemens. If Clemens would write from Vienna to Laurence Hutton, New York drama critic and Princeton lecturer, that "It is friends that make life—localities & languages have nothing to do with the matter," then it was Rogers who certainly helped make his.[28] In a 1904 autobiographical dictation, Clemens noted that "For eleven years [Rogers] has been my closest and most valuable friend."[29] Later, on December 27, 1909, he wrote to Rogers's daughter Mai (Mrs. William Coe) just after his own daughter Jean's death, that "[i]t wrung my heart to lose Jean, who was so dear to me...; but I know my nature, & I knew I should soon be happy again, & not mourning any more, but only absorbed in remembering how beautiful her character was & how fine—how exquisitely fine—the very finest I have ever known except her mother's and your father's."[30]

Rogers's larger family, too, became central to Clemens's later life. He appears, first of all, to have very much taken to Harry, Rogers's son—"the storage battery" or "the Electric Spark" as his "Uncle Sammy" called him—who was fourteen when his father first became involved in Clemens's affairs.[31] After Harry got married in November 1900, Clemens developed an affectionate and light-hearted relationship with his wife Mary, whom he called my "dear pal and incomparable niece."[32] Clemens it seems was always attracted to vivacious youth, and particularly vivacious female youth.[33] As Lewis Leary comments, "He sought companionship, especially young companionship which in its innocence and vigor recalled happier days."[34]

Leary writes that Mary "was playmate, conspirator, and he called her his niece but she was a surrogate daughter besides."[35] There does seem to be some truth to this last comment. Clemens's relationship with Clara, the elder of his two remaining daughters (after Susy's and wife Olivia's deaths) was an uneasy one. He had mixed feelings about her singing career and seems generally not quite to have "connected" with her—Howells wrote revealingly to his daughter Mildred on March 15, 1907, that "Clara seems to be having a real success, and [Clemens] seems *for the first time* proud of her" (my emphasis).[36] In the *Letters to Mary* he represents Clara as something of a sternly restrictive presence in terms of their family life together: "I went Sabbath-breaking to Broughton's, and beat him five games out of seven [at billiards, probably]. Clara tried to stop me from going on such an errand.... The fact is, I have to lead a life of chicane and deception with this end of the family...."[37] Youngest daughter Jean's silence, "melancholy moods," and serious and ongoing illness (epilepsy), meant that her presence, too, was rarely a comforting one.[38]

In fact, the Rogers family seem to have become something of a surrogate family for Clemens during his final years. Fred Kaplan says exactly that: "Gradually, the Rogers family ... were becoming Twain's family also;

it was the only household that he went to as if he were a welcome relative."[39] When he lived in New York after Olivia's death ("It was always lonesome . . . in New York," he would write later to Emilie, Rogers's second wife), Rogers would often drop in on Clemens just to pass the time with him.[40] Clemens, too, was always welcome at the Rogers's Fairhaven home and became a frequent guest there. After his move to Redding in June 1908, he travelled little, but "[w]hen he did go occasionally to New York, he stayed with or dined with the Rogers family."[41] Clemens made this arrangement the subject for his usual jokes—writing of one proposed trip, he asks, " . . . am I going to find eatables, drinkables and lodging at your tavern at reduced rates?"[42] But it is clear that he could come and go with Rogers and his wife more or less as he pleased. The larger family—the Broughtons, Coes, and Benjamins—became close to him too. Clemens shared the Rogers's family events and corresponded with them, played billiards with Urban Broughton (married to Cara, Rogers's second daughter), and received visits from various family members up in Redding.

It was the relationship with Rogers, though, that held this larger network together. The friendship was characterized by a bluff good humor, the use of a register of language beyond conventional (and female-coded) genteel boundaries, and the mutual exchange of light-hearted insults. Clemens set up a playful routine based on his supposedly kleptomaniac tendencies after staying with the family, writing to Mrs. (Emilie) Rogers:

> In packing my things in your house yesterday morning I inadvertently put in some articles that was laying around, I thinking about theollogy and not noticing. . . . Two books, Mr. Rogers brown slippers and a ham. I thought it was ourn it looks like one we used to have. I am very sorry it happened but it shant occur again and don't you worry He will temper the wind to the shorn lammb and I will send some of the things back anyway if there is some that wont keep.
> Yores in Jesus
> SLC[43]

This letter was obviously meant for Rogers's eyes, but Clemens perhaps sails close to the wind here—given the letter is addressed to his wife—in his parody of an untutored religious discourse (oddly reminiscent of Flannery O"Connor's fiction). Rogers replied in kind: "First, before I forget it, let me remind you that I shall want the trunk and the things you took away from my house, as soon as possible. I learn that, instead of taking old things, you took my best. Mrs. Rogers is at the White Mountains and I am going to Fairhaven this afternoon. I hope you will not be there."[44] There is just a touch of the Huck Finn here, as Clemens projects himself, using a written language over which he pretends not to have the proper grammatical control, as absent-mindedly "lifting" Rogers's ham. This is, of course, just a passing joke, but to represent himself as both unlearned and a thief in fact serves as a reminder of Clemens's real social status—as a member of an elite and sophisticated social world where such suggestions *can* only be taken as jocular.

This brief exchange is symptomatic, too, of the larger relationship between the two men and of Clemens's other important male friendships—summoning up a world at one remove from business concerns and the pressures of everyday life and based on the type of "vitally inconsequential" and playful interaction earlier identified. I am reminded here of Miss Lyon's account of Clemens's return from an August 1906 cruise on the *Kanawha*, "gay and jolly and darling; and full of his yachting trip to Bar Harbor and Mrs. Harry [Rogers], and the joy of living. Sly, he was: and like a boy fresh from his wild oats."[45]

The equation of Clemens's male friendships with a reversion to boyhood freedom and irresponsibility—and marking a type of space apart, "an approved alternative sociality that re-enabled men to take up their usual rights and obligations"—has become a repeated motif in this book.[46] In this case, however, with Clemens's life in its final decade, financially secure, his wife dead, and coddled by Miss Lyon, he had begun to put those usual obligations completely aside—or rather, felt that they no longer existed.[47] Such a feeling took final form in August 1908, when he wrote to Howells from Stormfield that, "I have retired from New York for good, I have retired from labor for good, I have discharged my stenographer, & have entered upon a holiday whose other end is in the cemetery."[48]

Another example of the playful quality to the Rogers friendship—in this case, before his wife Olivia's death—can be seen in the logs Clemens wrote of the (1901 and 1902) *Kanawha* yachting expeditions. The first—an August 1901 excursion to Maine, New Brunswick, and Nova Scotia—was taken with the Rogers family (Henry, the Harry Rogers, the Coes, the Benjamins), but with various others either starting the journey, or coming on board as it continued. These included Colonel Augustus Paine (a New York businessman), Dr. Rice, Rev. Collyer and Rev. Minot Savage, and ex-speaker of the House of Representatives, Thomas B. Reed. Both logs are lightweight pieces and no doubt meant only for the amusement of the participants. In the first, Clemens characterizes the "garrison," as he names the group, as untrustworthy and even criminally inclined: "Sailed to Booth's Bay & lay there all night. The garrison remained on board, by request of the police."[49] Jokes about items going missing take on a surrealistic flavor with Clemens's note following an expedition ashore in Yarmouth (Nova Scotia): "The authorities visited the yacht in the evening and said an anvil had been missed. Mr. Rogers paid for the anvil."[50] Much of the humor in the log, though, circles around the poker games: "Judge Cohen came over from another yacht.... He was invited by the Combine to play poker—apparently as a courtesy.... Mr. Rogers lent him clothes to go home in."[51]

The second log (1902) is rather more of a travelog. This time the yacht's company was all male: Rogers, Clemens, Reed, Paine, Rice, Laurence Hutton, and New York Congressman Wallace T. Foote. And Clemens does reveal his anti-imperialist sentiments here when he writes of "the American flag . . . waving its sarcasms to the breeze" in Havana.[52] Poker is again, though, the main prompt for humor: "Paine & Reed played poker, & Reed won 23 pots *in succession*. This without prayer or other unfair advantage. Paine won not a single pot during the conflict—Reed got the first & the last, & all between; then Paine jumped the game & went below to replenish his vocabulary."[53] The log ends with a celebratory note about the time away, but with a comic squib tied to its tail: "A most delightful month, & everybody in the gang physically & mentally the better for it. Morally—...."[54] Again this is a little reminiscent of Huck and Jim on the raft (or perhaps, more accurately, of "Mark Twain" and Mr. Harris on their raft on the Neckar in *A Tramp Abroad* ) in its conjuring up of a stress-free and companionable time-out from day-to-day existence.

But what is particularly noticeable is the type of men that surrounded Clemens. Travelling on a luxury yacht as the guest of one of America's most powerful figures, he was mixing with other members of the WASP hierarchy: businessmen, politicians, and ministers. In his *Autobiography*, Clemens tells the story of Joe Twichell (who met Rogers through Clemens) coming on board the *Kanawha* to watch an America's Cup race, and how Twichell put the "worldings" Rogers had also invited at total ease in his clerical company by his anecdotal ability and uninhibited manner of speech. (The story Twichell recounted about his Civil War days ended with a teamster in his brigade saying, "Mr. Twichell, do you take me for a God damned papist?"). Clemens uses this incident to illustrate Twichell's "wide catholicity of feeling and conduct," adding, "and I was able to furnish something in this line myself."[55] There are only narrow boundaries here between "catholicity of feeling and conduct" and the enjoyment of the company of those with power and wealth, and a tacit—and even (as I shall show) overt—approval and support of this group's values and actions: support that can be seen as socially and ideologically questionable. In his relation with Rogers, Clemens would sometimes end up crossing this last line.

III

[B]y 1906, four years before his death,...[there ran] the serious suggestion that...Mark Twain had outlived not his fame but the identity that had made him famous. The stage-coach and the river boat, symbols of the Western Mark Twain, had become the motor-car and the steam yacht, symbols of the plutocracy. He had shed his negligence about what he wore and was now, in his highly individual way, even something of a fashion plate. Sometimes he wore what Howells called "that society emblem," a silk hat. He lived on Fifth Avenue, rented a summer house at Tuxedo Park. He was to be seen in the company of Henry Rogers and other moguls at Palm Beach and Bermuda. His friendship with Rogers had continued to deepen—"I am his principal intimate and that is my idea of him." Stretched out on the sofa in Rogers" private office in the Standard Oil Building, smoking or reading while Rogers conducted his daily affairs, Clemens was completely at home and completely trusted.

He was now a family friend as well: he had dedicated *Following the Equator* to Rogers" son, Harry; ... and almost day and night for the rest of his life he played billiards ... on a luxurious table given him as a Christmas present by Rogers" wife. He was Andrew Carnegie's crony and dinner companion, the recipient and consumer of Carnegie's private-stock Scotch.... To each other they were "Saint Mark and Saint Andrew."

"Money lust has always existed," Clemens could say to Twichell, "but not in the history of the world was it ever a craze, a madness, until your time and mine." But the moralist and the people's author had also become the pet and the peer of the moguls, and on a personal plane he was loyal to them in return.

— Justin Kaplan, *Mr. Clemens and Mark Twain*

Justin Kaplan gets Clemens generally about right here.[56] I would, however, query that 1906 date, since long before this time Clemens had enjoyed the company to be found in the particular unofficial "club" of the powerful and very rich and had reveled in being "in, with the other capitalists."

This is not to say that Clemens abandoned his political and social conscience, for he did not. His work on behalf of the Anti-Imperialist League, for example, and his public criticism of the activity of the Rev. William Ament in China on behalf of the American Board of Commissioners for Foreign Missions (in "To the Person Sitting in Darkness," 1901) give clear evidence of his counter-hegemonic position on such matters. And, if it might be argued that it was easy enough for him to attack American policies abroad while remaining silent on matters closer to home, this too would be to do him an injustice. The "Sitting in Darkness" essay, indeed, began with a recognition of social problems on home soil: "The purpose of this article is not to describe the terrible offences against humanity committed in the name of Politics in some of the most notorious East Side districts. *They could not be described, even verbally*."[57] In a speech made in the same year Clemens would indict Tammany (the Tammany Hall Democrats in New York) for "monopoly of office; monopoly of the public feed trough; monopoly of the blackmail derivable from protected gambling hells, protected prostitution houses, protected professional seducers of country girls for the New York prostitution market, and all that."[58]

Earlier, in 1892, Clemens had explicitly criticized robber baron Jay Gould, when he died at fifty-six years old (and worth seventy-two million dollars): "Jay Gould was the mightiest disaster which has ever befallen this country. The people had *desired* money before his day, but *he* taught them to fall down and worship it."[59] But Gould was only a Rogers of a slightly earlier breed and without some of the latter's obfuscating talents in terms of his stock market and business dealings. And Clemens himself had been happy to approach Gould when he needed investors in the Paige typesetter.[60]

There were then a number of different—and paradoxical—subject positions that Clemens assumed in these years (indeed, this had always been true of him). That he continued to enjoy the three such different friendships outlined in this book is also some measure of this fact. I have suggested in my earlier chapter on Clemens and Howells how the two men's roles as respected, and (in Clemens's case, by this point in time) respectable, literary artists meant that their criticisms of, and sense of alienation from, their larger society went hand-in-glove with their own acceptance by that society and a general conformity to its principles and values. We can see, however, that by the last decade of Clemens's life, and symbolized in the close friendship with Rogers, his ironic distance from an American business culture had lessened, for he shared and enjoyed the company of Rogers and others like him with little apparent sense of self-compromise.

Clemens had—from early in his career—always enjoyed the company of those who possessed social authority and prestige. He felt at ease with both Rogers's family and friends and was especially reliant on them in the years following his wife's death. But he moved in other types of (socially select) circles, too. In the summer of 1906 he stayed in Dublin, New Hampshire, and wrote to Mary Rogers:

> This is a very remarkable society here and you would like it and feel at home in it. Professor Pumpelly [geologist] and wife, learned people; Mr. Secretary Hitchcock, the best man in the Roosevelt cabinet, I think; several Yale and Harvard professors; two historians—Hart and Henderson; Wm. Cabot, explorer of the Great Lone Land [north-western Canada]; Handyside Cabot and wife—music and art; Joe Smith, artist and playwright; George Brush, artist of high repute and an able and interesting talker; Abbott Thayer, capable artist and dis-coverer of Nature's real color-scheme [Thayer wrote on protective coloration in nature]; Colton Greene, author—and so on.[61]

Clemens himself, perhaps inevitably, took on coloration—in terms of values and ways of thinking—from the society in which he moved. And he became in these years, with so much time spent in Rogers's close company and friendship, something of a defender of capitalist business values. If Justin Kaplan speaks of the freedom with which Clemens made use of Roger's New York private office, later biographer Fred Kaplan expands:

> He was welcome...at Rogers' eleventh-floor Standard Oil office on lower Broadway, where Rogers' much-valued executive secretary, Katherine Harrison, made him comfortable whether Rogers was there or not. Reclining on a sofa between the back of Rogers" desk and the windows commanding the harbor, he amused himself by reading, watching Rogers at work, and looking out at the magnificent view.... Upstairs, in the executive dining room, he dined with men of power, the arrangement, he boasted, providing him with privileges in the best club in town, infinitely better than the Lotos Club or the Players.[62]

Clemens, we have seen in the previous chapter, would joke about his status as a corporate executive, sharing places in his imagination with Rogers himself. And we have seen too how he took full advantage of what we would now call Rogers's insider trading. He did, though, pay for his membership in this new "club" in the public support he then gave his host. Clemens seems to have convinced himself that the Company his friend ran—like the friend himself—was free from moral censure. So when he writes about Standard Oil in the *Autobiography*, it is from a favorable perspective. Describing an occasion when "[t]he Standard Oil declared one of its customary fury-breeding 40- or 50-per-cent dividends on its $100,000,000 capital, and the storm broke out, as usual," he continues: "To the unposted public a 40- or 50-per-cent dividend could mean only one thing—the giant Trust was squeezing an utterly and wickedly unfair profit out of the helpless people; whereas in truth the giant Trust was not doing anything of the kind, but was getting only 5 or 6 per cent on the money actually invested in its business, which was eight or ten times a hundred millions."[63] Elsewhere, he used the fact that Standard Oil employees had—over a forty-five year period—never been on strike, as evidence that the Company "chiefs cannot be altogether bad."[64]

Clemens also stepped in on Standard Oil's behalf when Rogers wrote him a carefully worded letter on December 26, 1901—one of the very few where Rogers asks Clemens for *anything*—indicating that Clemens could be of some service in ensuring that Ida M. Tarbell gave a balanced representation of Standard Oil in the history of the company she was then writing for *McClure's Magazine*. Clemens suggested Tarbell should contact Rogers personally before writing her piece, and she and Rogers subsequently met at the latter's house in New York for "frank" discussion.[65] In an action that was more publicly revealing, Clemens appeared on May 20, 1908, with Rogers before a group of magazine publishers at the Aldine Club in New York to support the two John D. Rockefellers, senior and junior (who were also present), in a response to the public's increasing disenchantment with Standard Oil's rapacious business practices. Though the occasion was arranged to publicize the charity foundation the Rockefellers had established for medical research, the real agenda here was as part of a strategy for "the public rehabilitation of John D. Rockefeller, Sr."[66]

There is a gap, then, between Clemens's various writings and remarks prompted by his concern for social justice and anxieties concerning the effects of capitalist expansion in America and his own private (and sometimes) public behavior—the bonds he formed with men like Rogers (in particular) and Carnegie, and the status, luxury, and pleasure that such friendships brought with them, especially in his final years. Olivia's death, and the loss of her moral influence, may possibly also have made some degree of difference here.[67] Perhaps, too, Clemens believed that the powerful men with whom he mixed saw their wealth as bringing social responsibility with it. And if it is easy in retrospect to demonize the "robber barons," we should also remember that they were subject to the forces of history—and the incredibly rapid processes of industrial and economic transformation in these years—as well as its agents, and that their final influence was not simply malign.[68]

Rogers was clearly a likeable, generous, and witty man to those whom he saw (in whatever way) as on a parity with him, or to those for whom he felt a sense of social obligation.[69] As we have seen he gave whole-hearted support, personally and financially, to Booker T. Washington and his Tuskegee Institute project. He also helped fund Helen Keller's education, with Clemens responsible for bringing her case to his attention.[70] He gave massively, too, to his home town of Fairhaven (just over the water from New Bedford), building its lavish public library, town hall, high school, and (Unitarian) church, draining land for a public park, and investing "a million dollars in a tack-factory...with intent to supply employment to every man or woman, or boy or girl, in Fairhaven who desired work."[71] But such benevolence was of course only one part of the larger picture. In the 1906 exposé *Frenzied Finance*, Thomas Lawson portrayed the other side of Rogers in hyperbolic manner: "Once [this remarkable man] passes under the baleful influence of 'The Machine,' however, he becomes a relentless, ravenous creature, pitiless as a shark, knowing no law of God or man in the execution of his purpose. Between him and coveted dollars may come no kindly, humane influence—all are thrust aside, their claims disregarded, in ministering to this strange, cannibalistic money-hunger, which, in truth, grows by what it feeds on."[72] And Standard Oil itself was synonymous in the period with price-fixing, autocratic and rapacious business practice, and political chicanery. So Ron Powers describes Rogers as "a perfect avatar of the 1890s. With Rockefeller, Andrew Carnegie, J. P. Morgan, and a few others, he bestrode a decade that hurled the United States from the populist creativity of raw postwar industrialism...and toward a brutally efficient top-down organization of capital, and capital assets, and human assets."[73]

We should remember too that if Andrew Carnegie (Clemens's "St. Andrew") was, in theory, a pacifist and a member alongside Clemens of the Anti-Imperialist League, he also made large amounts of money armoring ships in the period from 1898 onward and looked to defraud the Navy department by the use of defective plating in the process.[74] And if Carnegie, too, was a philanthropist (to the tune of some 350 million dollars) and professed himself the friend of labor and the defender of trade-union rights, he nonetheless "worked his men [at the Homestead steel works] every day of the year except Christmas and the Fourth of July," and imposed a twelve hour workday and a seven day working week on them. His tacit support of intransigent and confrontational actions during the 1892 strike, moreover, caused both considerable bloodshed and the wiping out of union power in the steel industry for a generation.[75]

Clemens chose not to see, or at least not to comment, on such contradictions and injustices. Loyalty to his friends, and his sharing of their world of wealth and privilege, seem to have pretty much blunted aspects of his social conscience in these years. As Ron Powers writes: "[A]s far as Clemens was concerned, Rogers's dark side did not exist....[In 1902], at a tribute to the industrialist, he told the guests, "He is not only the best friend I have ever had, but is the best man I have known." If William Dean Howells was listening somewhere, he kept his reaction to himself."[76] In his friendship with Rogers, the closest one of his last years, we see Clemens fully integrated in the "club" of wealthy white men whose status and mutual attraction was guaranteed by their wealth and cultural power. Indeed the friendship appears in many ways dependent on just these factors. Earl Dias tells the story of Clemens being approached by a "haughty, Whaling City dowager" while walking in nearby New Bedford during one of his Fairhaven visits:

"'Mr. Clemens,' she began, 'how can you be so friendly with Mr. Rogers—a man whose money is tainted?'
Clemens responded immediately, with eyes blazing, 'Right, Madame! 'T'aint yours and 't'aint mine'"![77]

The anger here (if Dias can be trusted on the incident), but certainly the fact that Clemens converts that 'taint' into a punning joke is a sign of his tendency in these last years to put questions of principle to one side in the environment of luxury, good living, and general bonhomie in which he had become immured.

# Coda
## Friendship's Limits: Fathers and Daughters

W riting about Clemens and his three close male friendships, I have been aware of one subject that affected (in one way or another) all these men's lives, but which does not form an easy or immediate fit with my overall topic. This is—and I concentrate on Clemens and Howells here, and to lesser extent, Rogers—the emotional pain these men had in common in each having to face the deaths of young daughters.[1] I include this material at this point to bring a different perspective on these men into play, one that helps illustrate the lessening in intensity in close male friendships in these years as nuclear family relationships became more and more emotionally consuming. Winifred, Howells's eldest child, "misdiagnosed and mistreated" by her doctor S. Weir Mitchell, died after a debilitating long-term illness in 1889, at the age of twenty-five.[2] Millicent Gifford Rogers, Henry H. Rogers's third daughter, died in 1890 of heart failure when she was seventeen. Susy, Clemens's oldest daughter and favorite child, died in 1896 at the age of twenty-four of cerebrospinal meningitis. Jean, his youngest, died on Christmas Eve 1909 (just under four months before Clemens's own death), aged twenty-nine, apparently during an epileptic seizure while taking her morning bath. It must have been unusual for three families—in this group of four—to be so affected.[3] Infant death rates were still high in these years. In the 1890 census 242,163 deaths were recorded in the "Registration States." Of these, 59,563 were for infants under one year old, and 85,652 for those under five. But only 6,571 deaths were recorded among those in the fifteen-to-twenty-year-old age group, with 9,997 among the twenty to twenty-fives. (To give some idea of individual state figures, the Connecticut equivalents were 14,470; 2,951; 4,294; 431; and 658 respectively.)[4]

As a prelude to discussion of these deaths, some comment is necessary on the status of father-daughter relationships among the professional classes and the well-to-do in the period. If the men on whom I focus are in any way representative of this group, it would seem that fathers faced some difficulty in allowing their daughters to separate out from the family and to lead an independent life. The evidence for this is relatively thin but it is nonetheless persuasive. Twichell was "struck into dumb amazement" by the 1891 engagement of daughter Julia (then aged twenty-two)."[5] He would shortly write to Clemens:

> We are omnipresently conscious of the shadow of [Judy's approaching marriage]... It stalks, a ghost, amongst us from morn to eve.
>    Mark, I feel *bad*, by turns downright ugly. But I try not to show it. The young man is well enough—... which is only a mitigation; it does not cure the disease... "Hello, Howard" I exclaim, with counterfeit cordiality, when he appears; and then I give his hand a scr-e-e-unch that sends a spasm across his confounded grin; and wish I could twist it off him...
>    I wish the obsequies were over. I wish they had eloped. Are you keeping a suitable watch on your girls? They are in danger. Do have out your pickets against those foreigners![6]

Similarly, Twichell described the 1904 engagement of daughter Louise—then in her mid-twenties—to a New York attorney as a "severe domestic jolt." Hall (the fiancé), he continues, "is a nice enough fellow, but [the engagement] takes us rather unprepared."[7] Such signs of over-protection, of a desire to keep the family unit static and undisturbed, can similarly be glimpsed in a 1907 letter that Clarence Rice sent to Clemens: "Did you know that Marjory was engaged to a Boston young man we like very much and they expect to be married in November. I wish it all could be postponed for several years."[8]

Clemens's own relationship with his three daughters was undoubtedly problematic. This issue has been touched on in some of the main biographical works (see especially Andrew Hoffman's *Inventing Mark Twain*, Karen Lystra's *Dangerous Intimacy*, and Linda Morris's *Gender Play in Mark Twain*) and, though much still remains to be told of it, I keep my commentary brief.[9] It is clear that when Susy Clemens left the family at eighteen in 1890 to go to college, the family—and especially her father—found the parting extremely hard. Clemens, Hoffman writes, "had difficulty separating from Susy—Livy swore that [he] would take any excuse to go to Bryn Mawr, even just to bring Susy her laundry."[10]

As she settled into Bryn Mawr, Susy began an intimate friendship with classmate Louise Brownell, the intensity of which can be judged from Susy's letters ("...I feel so near you today precious beautiful Louise! I take you in my arms. I kiss your lips, your eyes, your throat. I am your own own Olivia").[11] Hoffman confidently talks of Susy's "homoerotic desires," and of Brownell as "her lover," but we should be wary of pinning twentieth-century assumptions to nineteenth-century emotional lives.[12] Whatever the status of the relationship, though, it does seem as though its effects caused Clemens and his wife to look to bring Susy back within the protection of the close family circle.

The claustrophobic and repressive aspects of this move, and its effects on Susy's outlook at the time, are suggested in a letter she wrote to Clara, also from Florence but earlier in that same year of 1893. (Clara—then based in Berlin—was another problem child for Clemens, who struggled both with her desire for independence and her ambition to pursue a career in music.[13]) Writing of Clara's plan to rejoin the family at the Villa Viviani, rather than remaining in Berlin (where she was studying), Susy writes:

I assure you you would be *wretched* here coming straight from Berlin...I really cannot bear to have you make the experiment for I feel *sure* you would be so *unhappy*. Of course I can only judge from *my* experience. I am contented here much of the time and satisfied but with me it is different for entre nous I have rather given up expecting much real happiness constructed as I am and all. But you have your music, your work, your talent and your natural good luck; so why should you come here when you might as well stay in a gayer freer place? Clara, my *dear* Clara, be careful what you do! You know how you will be fretted here by the family discipline... You seem to *forget* the life of the Villa Viviani. What *are* you thinking of?[14]

Such details are indicative of the fact that young women of this time (if we can take these cases as typical) found themselves very much between a rock and a hard place. Looking to express their identities in a culture where the rights of women and the realizing of their full potential were increasingly a pressing issue, they were nonetheless still bound by Victorian conventions, with few clear and obvious avenues open for vocational fulfilment, and "protected" by anxious parents who valued domesticity and the closeness of the family as tokens of safety and stability in the face of disorienting social change. It is little wonder then that we see in the lives of the daughters of such families signs of the pressures that they were under.

So Twichell repeatedly comments on the health of his daughter Sally—writing to Clemens, for instance, in January 1904, that "Sally is up [at Saranac Lake] now...taking a rest-cure for a nervous debility into which she had fallen."[15] Susy, Clemens's eldest daughter, was (Hoffman tells us) "thin and nervous" and "rarely ate full meals."[16] Clara Clemens, in the period of her mother's final illness and death, veered from practical strength (taking over the running of the household) to complete emotional and psychological collapse, eventually retreating to "the isolation of a rest cure in a private New York sanitarium."[17] Jean's epilepsy made her, the meanwhile, and throughout her adult life, more or less completely dependent on parental care and authority.[18]

Winifred Howells had perhaps the hardest time of all these daughters. Following in her father's footsteps as a writer (her poetry received some contemporary recognition), but of an intensely serious, melancholic, and introverted temperament, she suffered—certainly from the age of sixteen onward (1880)—from long-term debilitating illness.[19] Despite rest cures and other treatments by a series of doctors, she became more-or-less a permanent invalid. The process of this illness, and the way it "oversha-dowed" the family's life, can be traced through Howells's letters.[20] I give a handful of examples. On August 6, 1881, he writes to Thomas Bailey Aldrich, "Winny is doomed to an indefinite season in bed, that being the uncertain cure of the nervous prostration from which she is suffering."[21] In September 1887, a letter to John W. De Forest notes that: "about the 20th, we shall go to Dansville, where there's a Sanitorium; I want to see if my oldest girl, who's been suffering from nervous prostration for five or six years can get any help in it."[22] In February 1889, he tells Edward Gosse that "Our poor Winny is a wreck of health and youth—sick for years yet to come, I'm afraid."[23] In fact, she died just six days later, on March 2, 1889. Weigh-ing (at the time) only fifty-nine pounds, she had been put in the care of the famous women's doctor, S. Weir Mitchell. His dubious medical practices, as they are now judged, took the form—in her case—of the force-feeding of "rich and fatty foods" together with "vigorous exercise," and may well have been responsible for the heart failure of which she apparently died.[24]

I return to Howells's response to Winny's death shortly, but first briefly mention Henry H. Rogers. The cases described above indicate the pro-blems that daughters could face in middle-to-upper-class Victorian fa-milies, and the types of nervous prostration, emotional anxiety, and physical debilitation that were their by-product. They suggest, too, the problems these daughters had in carving out any independent life for themselves. Such pressures and problems seemed to increase where (as in Clemens's and Howells's cases) the fathers were both famous and socially prominent. Little information is available concerning Rogers's relationship with his daughters. But there is evidence that—in the case of Mary H. Rogers (Mai)—the powerful authority Rogers wielded in the business world was also brought into play to protect (what he saw as) his daughter's best interests. Mai—when still a teenager—eloped with, and married, a Joseph Cooper Mott. The bare facts of the case are given by the editor of the Clemens-Rogers letters: "On 28 July 1893, Mai Rogers had eloped with and married ... Mott at Sheepshead Bay on Long Island. They never lived together, and an annulment was secured in December 1895."[25]

Unless further evidence becomes available, we have no way now of knowing Mai's feelings, nor how willingly she complied in the speedy ending of the marriage. But the records of the court case that followed suggest that her father—acting as guardian of a daughter still below the age of legal consent (twenty-one)—wielded a heavy hand in the resolution of what was to him, presumably, an unacceptable relationship.[26] The Rogers case was based on the "information and belief" that very shortly (in August or September 1893) after the elopement and marriage, "the defendant [Mott] committed adultery with a woman known as Frankie Stewart and with ... diverse other women whose names are unknown to this plaintiff."[27] It is clear from evidence given by one woman (Frances Adams) that a private detective was following Mott at this time and that the case against him—despite his denial of the allegations—was convinc-ing. Thus one interchange when Adams was questioned ran as follows:

Q. Did Mott on these occasions [when he came to Adams's house] visit [Nina Mann, another woman involved] in any particular room?

A. Always in her own room. I mean by that her bedroom.

Q. How long did he remain with her? . . .

A. Sometimes half an hour, sometimes an hour, sometimes longer.

Q. What was Mott known there as? . . .

A. He was known as Nina Man's friend; her particular friend . . . At this time I kept this house as a private place, for the purposes of accommodation of my friends . . .

Q. House of prostitution, that is the plain English of it?

A. Yes; I suppose so.[28]

There is some suggestion in the court records of the strength of Rogers's response to the news of the elopement. When Mai was asked whether her father threatened to disinherit her after he heard news of the marriage, an objection was immediately entered and sustained. In turn, Mott denied knowledge of any "demand for money on Mr. Rogers" having been made. There is also evidence of intransigence on Rogers's part as the case proceeded. Mr. Hummell (Mott's lawyer) told the court that "I may have made a suggestion to this effect: If Mr. Rogers would discontinue this action for divorce on the ground of adultery and bring an action in some other State on any other ground for divorce, that Mr. Mott would consent to it, if his counsel fee and expenses were paid."[29] If this suggestion was indeed made, Roger's evident refusal to countenance it paid off. For he must have achieved all he wanted in bringing the action on Mai's behalf. His daughter was declared "entitled to a decree of absolute divorce . . . with alimony during her lifetime, together with the costs of this action." She was also given the right "to resume her maiden name of Mary H. Rogers."[30] Whatever his bad faith (which he denied), Mott was made to pay heavily for his attempt to take Mai from her family, and Rogers's money and reputation can only have helped in achieving that result. Despite the lack of any hint of Mai's own feelings in the matter, it is tempting to read into the court case evidence of a strong Victorian father exercising his power on behalf of what he considered his daughter's—and his immediate family's—best present and future interests, whatever her personal stake.[31]

We see something here of the pressures and anxieties of parent-daughter—but most especially father-daughter—interaction among the upper social classes in the period. We also see the (sometimes claustrophobic) protectiveness and emphasis on the inviolability of the family that would bring, in Clemens's and Howells's cases, the extremes of grief that follow from the early deaths of their daughters. Rogers, too, lost a daughter, Millicent, in her teens but there is no record of the impact this had on him. His building of a library (the Millicent Library at Fairhaven) dedicated to her memory suggests, though, that it was considerable.[32]

There is growing interest in the processes of grief and mourning, and how they operated in a late Victorian world.[33] As Tony Walter points out, such practices are not just individual and private, but depend on their social context: "personal grief and the culture in which [people] live are intimately bound up together."[34] And in the post-Civil War and late-Victorian period core cultural changes radically affected mourning practices. For reasons of space, my argument is necessarily reductive. There are, however, two major shifts in cultural sensibility bearing on this issue that we can identify. The first is the decline of sentimentalism and accordingly an increasing emphasis on the "'privatization' of grief."[35] The second (which interacts symbiotically with the first) is the increasing secularization in the period, and the resulting "social and spiritual isolation and cultural shock" for those bereaved who could no longer give allegiance to traditional faiths or to the "concept of an afterlife" that those faiths endorsed.[36]

Mid-nineteenth-century American culture was shaped by sentimentalism, seeing the individual's existence not as an isolated one, but in sustaining relationship with both family and larger community (which that family represents). A strong affection and mutual sympathy bound the links in this chain, working to "resist the dissolving power of death and distance."[37] Sentimentalism, then, emphasized bonds of strong feeling and connectedness that countered any sense of individual "anomie, alienation, and disaffection." So when death and loss occurred they could be faced through the strength of an existing "network of family and friends."[38] It is this network that made the life of the individual meaningful in binding her or him to the larger communal whole, but also to God. For a shared religious sensibility provided compensation for individual loss in the belief in a restored relationship with the deceased—in God's presence—in the hereafter.

As the nineteenth century progressed, so sentimentalism, and its undoubted attractiveness as a way of making sense both of life and of death, declined.[39] The very notion of collaboration inherent in sentimentalism—with individual, family, local community, and nation engaged in a mutual "exchange of sympathy" that guaranteed participation in a "common cultural...project"—was under increasing challenge in a number of ways.[40] First, there was new emphasis placed on the individual separate subject and the immediate nuclear family in a larger social order defined by the conditions of (competitive) capitalism and by rapid mobility, both of which led to increasing social fragmentation. In such conditions the sense of loss that death brought tended to result in "isolated 'I's' and 'you's' rather than a mutually supportive 'we.'"[41] Accordingly, grief became a more private matter, shared by "a few isolated individuals" rather than by a mutually sustaining "coherent...group."[42] Moreover, the very idea of a supportive and sympathetic link between family and larger community was being increasingly undone by the recognition that the nation was not a type of extended family in which social complicity and the promptings of the heart were in exact correspondence. Rather, America was being increasingly seen as an "intrinsically corrupt and self-serving society," and one which ran on principles of social division rather than of cohesion: "The valence of sentimentalism shifted so that rather than being understood as a way of coming to grips with reality...it became a way to avoid harsh realities and to practice deceptive manipulations."[43]

Changing attitudes to religion also affected this sentimental model. In an increasingly secular age, religion lost its capacity (for at least some proportion of those bereaved) to bring solace. The assumption of "sympathy from God," and of a final reunion with the lost loved one "within the heavenly domesticated space dominated by the parental Jesus," became difficult to sustain.[44] Many continued to believe in immortality, the "resurrection of the soul" that was such an important factor in its ability to "reconcile many Victorians to death." But "for those Victorian agnostics who doubted the existence of God and were unconvinced by the concept of an afterlife, the trauma of the death of a loved one could be overwhelming."[45] Tony Walter argues that traditional modes of mourning have disappeared in our contemporary Western world as new ones have had to be negotiated and established—often on an individualistic level—by the bereaved.[46] This move away from established and shared models brought with it a potential "increase in chaos, anomie and uncertainty."[47] In the cases of both Clemens and Howells, we see—in different ways and to different extents—men who (and families that) had "abandoned the belief system and the set of rituals which their society normally used in dealing with death," and were struggling to discover a meaningful alternative.[48]

Howells was of an unusual "Quaker-Swedenborgian" religious background. Around the time of Winny's death, he attended a number of churches of different denominations and started to read Swedenborg again.[49] But, like many in his period, he seems to have been stranded between belief and unbelief. He wrote to Howard Pyle on December 22, 1890: "I believe in nothing, though I am afraid of everything. I do not always feel sure that I shall live again, but when I wake at night the room seems dense with spirits."[50] His biographers comment: "'O God, if there is a god, save my soul, if I have a soul.' The Victorian witticism about religious uncertainty speaks to Howells's own doubts in these years."[51]

Howells took Winifred's death hard. He wrote to his father on March 22, 1889, that "when I am alone I recall and reclaim all I did, and reconstruct the past from this point or that, and dramatize a different course of events in which our dearest one still lives. It is anguish, anguish that rends the heart and brain."[52] Two months later, he told Clemens that he and Elinor were taking up summer residence, "just beyond Cambridge, not far from Winny's grave, beside which I stretched myself the other day, and experienced what anguish a man can live through."[53]

In some of the letters written at the time Howells looks for consolation in the idea of an afterlife, but it is a struggle for him to do so: "I am trying, as I can, to imagine her well and happy somewhere . . . But at the end, I come back sore from head and to foot and grovel in the mere sense of loss."[54] His June 7, 1889, letter to Henry James gives perhaps the clearest idea of his thoughts and feelings. Looking to respond to condolences, he is unable to find the words to do so. Personally crushed in spirit, he again alludes to the possibility of an afterlife but in an entirely conditional way: "I wished to make you the intimate of our sorrow, and I found that in the letters which I did write I was breaking my heavy heart into mere rhetoric. In every way the expression of our bereavement escapes me ... I wonder we live; it seems monstrous ... It's no use; I might as well stop. For a time I felt like a wretched worm that had been trodden on; I could only writhe.—About the future we profess to know nothing. If I could believe I was to meet her again I should be the lightest hearted man alive."[55]

One way in which "many Victorian mourners found consolation" was in writing a memorial—"a precious recollection of the life and death of the deceased." This might be entirely personal to the writer (and act as a form of therapy for her or him) or could serve for a larger family or even public audience.[56] So Howells wrote an eighty-five-page sketch of Winny's life "almost a year" after her death—presumably as part of his mourning process, and an attempt to make sense and come to terms with the family tragedy.[57]

Pat Jalland suggests that the "idealization of the dead" is a "common human response to the loss of a loved one in the earlier stages of grief." As the mourning process continues, however, so there is "a more realistic assessment of the day-to-day reality of the relationship including its negative aspects."[58] But we should tread carefully here in the assumptions and judgments we make as to how mourning works, and what is or is not normal or abnormal in each particular cultural context. It does seem, though, that both Howells and Clemens (in their idealization of their dead daughters), and Clemens (in the unusual, and extreme, nature of some of his family's mourning practices), may have leant toward the "abnormal" side of the late Victorian cultural line.[59]

Winifred Howells is idealized in her father's memoir. He does not gloss over the form of depression from which she suffered, her "nature so inclined to melancholy introspection" (but not without "the uplift of brighter moods"). Howells uses her poetry as a way of illustrating this melancholy. "Literature," he writes, "was her life ... [H]er ambition was 'to be a great writer.'" But in her last year she was swamped by "pain and despair." "[T]oo sick to complete anything; she had to give up her reading, in great measure, and often she could not bear to talk, to think. Life withdrew itself more and more." He quotes the "broken lines" of the last poem she wrote, a poem reminiscent of Emily Dickinson in its self-reflexivity, figurative work and sense of abrupt disconnection:

> Then pondering rhymed she of her introspection,
> Till like a spider lost in her own web,
> She suddenly stopped, and ceased to rhyme at all.[60]

In representing Winny's "tortured nerves" and "long mysterious" illness, Howells converts his daughter into a type of innocent infant, an angelic presence broken by the "slow martyrdom of her malady," and let down by her parents well-intentioned but flawed attempts to understand and help her. Howells says that Winny "often said that she would rather be always a child," and the motif of the innocent child runs throughout his memoir, one unable to accept a knowledge of the adult world: "She wished to remain a child; it puzzled, it hurt, it stupefied her to find what men and women were." Though Howells then deleted his two adjectives (the words here emphasized), he initially described his daughter in terms of her "*angelic* Beauty and gentleness, . . . *heavenly* patience and courage, . . . wisdom and . . . goodness." "I can see nothing to blame in her," Howells concluded, then added the quotation, "To be young and gentle and do no harm; and to pay for it as if it were a crime."[61]

As he describes Winny's poetry and her artistic abilities, Howells does give some sense of his daughter and her life. But for the most part he converts her memory into a standard Victorian trope—the beautiful and sensitive child who is too good for this world. Winny's own words as she reflects on her condition (in the poem quoted above) are strikingly less conventional and more powerful than her father's. Howells—caught within the patterns and expectations of the prose elegy form—seems to find it difficult, despite the undoubted intensity of his feelings, to get all that far from "mere rhetoric." Indeed, idealization does tend to have that effect.

Pat Jalland writes that "the emphasis on the value of memory as a source of consolation in grief was increased for some," in the period, "by the growth of religious doubt."[62] And we get something of that sense in Howells's memorial tribute. The language of religious consolation is almost entirely absent from the piece—though he does allow for the possibility that death is not the final parting when he writes, "if it should be my lot to behold her again, in any sphere. . . ."[63] Howells's memory of his daughter's poems prompts an intimate sense of physical reconnection: "they bring her again to our knees, we feel the soft push of her tender form."[64] His elegy works, in part, to keep his (and Elinor's) emotional wounds open, and in that way helps to keep the memory of their daughter's physical and feeling presence alive. He accordingly remembers and cherishes the loss in an immediate and tactile sense rather than focusing (as traditional Christian mourning would do) on any sense of future reconnection and reunion.[65]

Clemens, too, would idealize Susy, his dead daughter. Even before her death, she would provide the "physical model" for *Joan of Arc* (1896)—his "literary idealization of a life of female purity and inviolate maidenhood."[66] In his *Autobiography*, Clemens portrays Susy as an exceptionally sensitive and thoughtful child, "much given to retiring within herself and trying to search out the hidden meanings of the deep things that make the puzzle and pathos of human existence."[67] And, reporting there—in a highly restrained manner—on the "thunder-stroke" of her unexpected death, he concludes with the words: "On the 23rd [August] her mother and her sisters saw her laid to rest—she that had been our wonder and our worship."[68]

When Susy died, Clemens poured out his heart to Olivia in the letters he sent across the Atlantic. His first response was to empathize with his wife, his "heart-broken darling," but not to regret Susy's death: "I wish I could see her, & caress the unconscious face & kiss the unresponsive lips—but I would not bring her back—no, not for the riches of a thousand worlds. She has found the richest gift that this world can offer; I would not rob her of it."[69] This response is in line with a repeated strand of Clemens's thinking (especially in his later years) about death's merciful quality.[70] But it also fits his particular gender conceptions—the retaining, through such an early death, of womanhood's ideal as "the innocent child-woman whose essential girlish nature remains unawakened, untransformed, that is, unsexualized."[71] Stoneley again comments perceptively:

> [Clemens] wrote of [Susy's] death as a "martyrdom," though the suffering is perceived egocentrically ... At the same time he found her death beautiful and unregrettable ... [H]e was later to remember [Susy] "lying white and fair in her coffin." Also in keeping with the myth of Joan, he shared his wife's sense of the supreme severity of their grief due to Susy's alleged uniqueness: ... "Others that are bereaved try to comfort us, & say Be patient, & wait—time will heal the wound. What do *they* know? They have not lost a Susy Clemens." The Clemens's hagiographic response to Susy's death reflected their perception of her as a "princess" and a "saint" in life, and their sorrow subsequently took precedence over the bereavements of other people.[72]

Writing about the age of (sexual) consent in 1903, Clemens speaks of the anxieties that "fathers of families—families with young girls in them, the treasures of their lives, the lights of their homes, the joy of their hearts" would necessarily feel about any destruction of "family ... bonds."[73] In Clemens's and Howells's mourning for their dead daughters (and despite Howell's gesture of connection toward the larger human family in his elegy for Winny), we see, I would suggest, the breakdown of the previous midnineteenth-century sentimental ethos, where it was taken for granted that sympathetic bonds linked the individual family to the larger community of which it was a part. Clemens's emphasis on the father, the family, and the young girl, all bound in intimate and heartfelt union, indicates a separating off of the nuclear family from the further extended family and from any local (and larger) community in this later time. If this was, in part, a product of the competitiveness between individuals and the transience that marked a modernizing capitalist economy, in the case of Clemens (and to lesser degree Howells) it took a particularly intense form. This was due to the particular conditions of the literary artist's life: working at home, emotionally reliant on the immediate family presence, and—in Clemens's case—often living abroad, in a series of temporary communities rather than in a deep-rooted and permanent one.

At the same time as such community bonds were weakening, so—as I have previously suggested—traditional religious consolations in the face of death were (for many) becoming less certain and effective. This was certainly true in Clemens's case. It seems that he did not completely reject traditional belief in some kind of hereafter.[74] But for the most part he would appear to have put little faith in such a notion. In the series of five letters written to Olivia between August 19 and 29, 1896 (following Susy's death on the 18th), nowhere does Clemens make reference to the possibility of an afterlife. All he can write in way of consolation is: "Be comforted, my darling—we shall have *our* release in time. Be comforted, remembering how much hardship, grief, pain, she is spared." Later, he reminds Olivia of the role she played in Susy's life as "the best friend she ever had, dear heart, & the steadfastest," and presents this as another form of relief: "Keep the thought of it in mind, & get from it the solace you have earned, dear Livy." In the same letter, he appears directly to reject the prospect of any type of future reunion: "Poor Susy, it is now eleven days. 'After life's fitful fever she sleeps well.' And will wake no more for me."[75]

In the first elegy Clemens wrote for Susy ("In Memoriam," written exactly a year after her death and published in *Harper's Monthly* in November 1897) Clemens does, though, appear to hold out hope of some kind of reunion with their lost daughter. He writes of "a spirit.../ Made all of Light!" The spirit here is Susy's, dwelling in the inner sanctum of a "temple" whose "altar" is attended by "adoring priests...submerged in [that light's] immortal glow." (These priests are clearly imagined as Clemens and his wife.) The poem describes the "vast disaster" that has occurred, metaphorically representing Susy's death in the loss of the temple and its giving way to "vacant desert." The poem then concludes with lines expressing the priests' "murmur":

> It knows our pain—it knows—it knows—
> Ah, surely it will come again.[76]

We might however read that "surely" in two ways: as a despairing attempt to assert the possibility of future meaning in the face of deep-rooted doubt, or simply as the marker of a conventional Christian belief. But there is certainly an open and ambiguous quality to this conclusion.[77]

Clemens and Olivia's grief over Susy's death was intense and long-lasting. The Christmas that followed its occurrence was "a desolate time...[T]he day came and went without mention. No presents were exchanged, and we studiously pretended to be unaware of the day."[78] And Fred Kaplan reports on the family reading: "The text of the fall and winter season [1896–97] was *In Memoriam*, which Livy read repeatedly from a collection of Tennyson that had belonged to Susy."[79] Olivia went into the deepest mourning for her daughter and suffered from chronic grief, writing to a friend that she had lost all her courage, and that "I long to be with Susy."[80] Clemens, meanwhile, immersed himself in his work, the expected route for Victorian men in such circumstances.[81] Olivia was still in mourning in December 1897, when Clemens wrote Twichell from Vienna, "We cannot persuade Livy to go out in society yet."[82] And, for years after the death, "wedding anniversaries and birthdays and holidays were observed only as they had some tenuous but harrowing connexion with Susy. The milestones had become gravestones, Clemens said."[83] Indeed, the couple "ritually observed the anniversary of Susy's death" until Olivia's own death eight years later.[84]

What we see here, I would argue, are all signs of the individualization of grief. Clemens and his wife, largely cut off—other than by letter—from any day-to-day contact with close friends, resided in Europe, with their remaining two daughters, during the four years that followed Susy's death (until 1900). Their grieving related to conventional Victorian mourning patterns—Olivia's absence from society, for example—but seems entirely removed from the larger framework of the supportive community that generally gave such practices much of their meaning.[85] Instead, the couple seem to have worked out (perhaps each in their own way) an individualistic and private set of rituals that suited their need to memorialize their daughter, but which took place in something of a vacuum as far as the larger surrounding world was concerned.[86]

How, then, does all this relate to male friendships? The men on whom I have been focusing certainly corresponded with their friends about their losses and in some cases (as in the exchange of letters between Clemens and Howells on Susy's death) with considerable feeling and sympathy.[87] While grief may have been privatized, it did nonetheless extend to affect close friends, both of the family as a whole and of each person composing that unit. But, however deeply and genuinely that sorrow might have been shared, this was not the main source of emotional expression or release. The predominant impression given, in what we know of Howells's and Clemens's response to their respective loss, is of private suffering and solitude, a retreat to interior thought and feeling—and to the writings where such thought and emotion found some degree of representation. Their grieving, then, was mainly done alone, and/or within the family, rather than outside it and in close intimacy with their male friends.[88]

This connects with my larger thesis about male friendship in the period. I have suggested throughout this book that forms of male friendships changed in two main ways at this time. I have argued, following Stoneley, that a "mundane social logic" underpinned and gave final meaning to these friendships. This is *not* to deny (I would insist) the importance of the friendships to the men involved, nor the genuine pleasure—and emotional warmth—they felt in each other's company and expressed in their letters to one another. It is to say, however, that if the relationships were predicated on a personal liking and sense of strong (and intimate) connection, they also depended on the social and professional interests held in common and the benefits in such areas that the friendships brought with them. This is not to suggest any type of cynical motivation on the men's parts but rather to remind us, to return to Sarah Cole's words quoted earlier, that friendship "is shot through with social meanings ... Like the family, against which it is often set as an alternative, friendship will be constructed in such a way as to reflect a culture's position on sexuality, gender, hierarchy and power."

The friendships then certainly did not preclude strong emotional connection and empathy. Indeed this is exactly what these men showed in response to each other's joys and tragedies. But—and this is the second strand of my analysis—what also occurs in this same period and changes the context for male friendships is an increasing sense of individuation and separateness in relation to the larger social whole. This brought with it, partly as a correlative, a new emphasis on nuclear family bonds; an increasing move to companionate and family-centered marriages (especially for men like Clemens, Howells, and Twichell whose work was often conducted within a domestic setting); and a stronger emphasis, in terms of masculine self-definition, on the roles of husband and father. When these men underwent family tragedies—and especially the deaths of these daughters ("the treasures of their lives, the lights of their homes, the joys of their hearts")—their male friendships were of limited help to them. In such extreme situations they were thrown back by and large on their own inner resources and (in Clemens's case certainly) on the internal family unit for what sustenance and support they could gain there. The group of male friendships I have explored—with Clemens their center—helped give these men their sense of social identity, provided support and camaraderie in both personal and professional terms, and were of enormous importance in their lives. At the same time, the altered conditions of a late-nineteenth and early-twentieth-century American world meant that such friendships had narrower limits and were less consuming in their personal and emotional effects than in an earlier sentimental age.

# Notes

## Introduction

1. William Dean Howells, "Storage," in *Literature and Life* (New York: Harper & Brothers, 1902), 303–5.

2. See too the letter to brother Orion of the same date. Both are in Michael B. Frank and Harriet Elinor Smith, eds., *Mark Twain's Letters*, vol. 6: *1874–1875* (Berkeley and Los Angeles: University of California Press, 2002), 308–12.

3. For this sequence of letters, see ibid., 6:312, 316, 499, and 584.

4. See ibid., 6:586–87, and also Henry Nash Smith and William M. Gibson, eds., *Mark Twain-Howells Letters: The Correspondence of Samuel L. Clemens and William D. Howells, 1872–1910* (Cambridge, Mass.: Harvard University Press, 1960), 183–84.

5. See Mark Seltzer, *Bodies and Machines* (New York: Routledge, 1992), 3–21.

6. W. D. Howells, *My Mark Twain: Reminiscences and Criticisms* (New York: Harper & Brothers, 1910), 5.

7. Ibid., 30, 13, 24, 34, 38, and 100.

8. One of Clemens's faults was, however, played down. For Howells "agreed to delete a reference to Twain's overimbibing after his editor pointed out that half the newspapers in the country would make it a headline and Howells its sponsor." Susan Goodman and Carl Dawson, *William Dean Howells: A Writer's Life* (Berkeley and Los Angeles: University of California Press, 2005), 399.

9. Though note, too, Goodman and Dawson's comment that "*My Mark Twain* is a meditative work, its subject both a record of friendship and a measuring of [Howells's] own life," *William Dean Howells*, 400.

10. William C. Fischer and Christopher K. Lohmann, eds., *W. D. Howells, Selected Letters*, vol. 5: *1902–1911* (Boston: Twayne, 1983), 317 and 326.

11. See, for instance, Clemens to Twichell on August 29, 1880, and Twichell to Clemens on June 13, 1905, the Mark Twain Papers at the University of California at Berkeley (henceforth MTP). I start the main section of my book with Twichell rather than Howells: the friendship may have started slightly later but it had the more immediate impact.

12. The letters written by Twichell during the Civil War are an extraordinary record (especially given his relative youth at the time) both of his chaplain's role and its larger wartime context. See Peter Messent and Steve Courtney, eds., *The Civil War Letters of Joseph Hopkins Twichell: A Chaplain's Story* (Athens: University of Georgia Press, 2006).

13. MTP. Twichell and Clemens's favorite walk together was to Talcott Mountain. Katy Leary, the Clemens's long-term family servant, remembered: "Mr. Twichell and Mr. Clemens was just devoted to each other, and Mr. Twichell used to influence him a great deal, I think—more than anyone else, except Mrs. Clemens. They used to have the grandest times together, tellin' stories and laughing, and every fall when Mr. Clemens got back from Elmira, he and Mr. Twichell . . . used to take a long walk together. They'd walk right up Talcott Mountain. 'Twas a ten-mile walk and they'd rig themselves all up good and walk out there and back to that old mountain every fall. Mr. Clemens said they'd have to take that long walk at least once a year, just to see if they were holdin' their own! Of course, they enjoyed it and they talked all the way, I'll bet!" Mary Lawton, *A Lifetime with Mark Twain: The Memories of Katy Leary, for Thirty Years His Faithful and Devoted Servant* (New York: Harcourt, Brace, 1925), 205.

14. Harmony fell ill after Twichell had left Hartford for Clemens's funeral at Brick Presbyterian Church on New York's Fifth Avenue, and her death quickly followed, following an operation for ulceration of the bowels. Twichell's journal entry explains what happened: "After the funeral service . . . I was to have accompanied the family to Elmira where at a furthur [*sic*] service I had been asked to make an address. But I had to change my plan. The summons home—it was by *telephones* from Joe [Twichell's son] to the Schoonmaker [hotel?]—reached me immediately *before* the service—which was at three oclock [*sic*]. I took the 4 o'clock train for Hartford. She died that night—soon after midnight at the Hartford Hospital. I had gone to New York with not the least apprehension of her peril." The newspaper report about Clemens's funeral, here pasted into Twichell's journal, takes on added resonance with this knowledge: "[I]t was no wonder that when [Twichell] came to deliver a prayer at the death of his friend his voice should fail him. Throughout the short service he had sat with bowed head to conceal the fact that tears had found their way to the surface. Now he made a determined effort to control himself, and finally was able to say what he had to say." This, and many of the archive materials relating to Twichell in this book (including his *Journals* ) are from holdings (the Twichell Papers) in the Yale Collection of American Literature in the Beinecke Rare Book and Manuscript Library, henceforth cited as Beinecke.

15. Twichell's *Journals*, Beinecke.

16. Its title, though, is misleading, for this is a biography, not a study of domestic architecture and space or any kind of family memoir.

17. Elbert Hubbard, *Little Journeys to the Homes of Great Business Men: H. H. Rogers* (East Aurora, Erie County, N. Y.: The Roycrofters, 1909), 127–30.

18. Email correspondence. Coe emphasizes, however, that Rogers was a "split . . . personality," whose business rapacity has to be set against the fact that he was also "an exceptionally kind and generous man to his friends, family, and to those (such as Booker T. Washington) whose causes he backed."

19. Quoted in Earl J. Dias, *Henry Huttleston Rogers: Portrait of a "Capitalist"* (Fairhaven, Mass.: The Millicent Library, 1974), 13.

20. Peter Krass, *Ignorance, Confidence, and Filthy Rich Friends: The Business Adventures of Mark Twain, Chronic Speculator and Entrepreneur* (Hoboken, N. J.: John Wiley & Sons, 2007), 191–92.

21. Gregg Camfield, *The Oxford Companion to Mark Twain* (New York: Oxford University Press, 2003), 519.

22. See Lewis Leary, ed., *Mark Twain's Letters to Mary* (New York: Columbia University Press, 1961).

23. See in "Mark Twain's Christmas letter," http://www.plantingfields. com/09_03/collection.cfm (accessed March 25, 2009). Planting Fields is an estate on Long Island formerly owned by William Robertson Coe, who married Rogers's daughter Mai in 1900. Coe deeded the estate to the State of New York in 1949.

24. See Albert Bigelow Paine, *Mark Twain: A Biography* (New York: Harper, 1912) 3:1491.

25. Victor Fischer and Michael B. Frank, eds., *Mark Twain's Letters*, vol. 4: *1870–1871* (Berkeley and Los Angeles: University of California Press, 1995), 50. And see Theodore Hornberger, ed., *Mark Twain's Letters to Will Bowen: "My First, & Oldest & Dearest Friend"* (Austin: University of Texas Press, 1941).

26. Smith and Gibson, *Mark Twain-Howells Letters*, 235.

27. On the Harte relationship, see especially Peter Stoneley, "Rewriting the Gold Rush: Twain, Harte and Homosociality," *Journal of American Studies* 30, no. 2 (1996): 189–209. See, too, Leland Krauth, *Mark Twain & Company: Six Literary Relations* (Athens: University of Georgia Press, 2003), 14–48.

28. I refer to Samuel Clemens rather than Mark Twain throughout this book (except, for obvious reasons, in the title). Sometimes, as here, there are good reasons instead to use Twain's name. When I quote other critics, I retain their individual use.

29. According to Peter Krass, "At its peak it would sell more than 50,000 copies a year; over six months in 1878 it made a profit of $12,000; by 1901, at least 57 different types of his albums were available; and in total Clemens would pocket a tidy $50,000," *Ignorance, Confidence, and Filthy Rich Friends*, 94.

30. And see ibid., 108–16.

31. In terms of place, see for instance Kenneth R. Andrews, *Nook Farm: Mark Twain's Hartford Circle* (Cambridge, Mass.: Harvard University Press, 1950); Howard G. Baetzhold, *Mark Twain and John Bull: The British Connection* (Bloomington: Indiana University Press, 1970); and Carl Dolmetsch, *"Our Famous Guest": Mark Twain in Vienna* (Athens: University of Georgia Press, 1992).

32. The Clemens-Fairbanks letters are collected in Dixon Wecter, ed., *Mark Twain to Mrs. Fairbanks* (San Marino, Calif.: Huntingdon Library, 1949).

33. The most recent biography of the later years, Karen Lystra's *Dangerous Intimacy: The Untold Story of Mark Twain's Final Years* (Berkeley and Los Angeles: University of California Press, 2004) presents Lyon, Clemens's secretary and housekeeper, as a schemer whose "most treasured goal [was] to walk down the aisle with America's greatest literary celebrity" (100), and who played a damaging role in terms of Clemens's relationships with his two remaining daughters. The scenario Lystra presents (a lonely and confused famous old writer controlled by a manipulative spinster gold digger) smacks somewhat of melodrama. It is likely a more balanced version of this undoubtedly complicated story remains to

be told, for a reading of Lyon's diary suggests her good faith, and that she may have been as much sinned against as sinning. (Laura Skandera Trombley, in "Mark Twain's *Annus Horribilis* of 1908–1909," *American Literary Realism* 40, no. 2 [Winter 2008]: 114–36, offers a rather more sympathetic version of her.] Some mention should also be made of Clemens's friendships with young girls (his "Angel Fish") in his last years. Hamlin Hill speaks of Clemens gathering this group around him in a "more than avuncular" and "even...latently sexual" way, *Mark Twain: God's Fool* (New York: Harper & Row, 1973), xxvii. Lystra is less provocative, reading the Angel Fish in terms of a "compensatory function," Clemens seeking to fill "a deep emotional hole" with these "surrogate children." For the young girls may have reminded him of the dead Susy, and perhaps "recalled his own lost youth or fed some lifelong nostalgia for the honesty and simplicity of childhood" (132). David Leverenz—in a book that moves between fiction and social reality—comments on *Sister Carrie* in a way that resonates, especially given Clemens's relations with daughters Clara and Jean (and despite Clemens's older age): "men such as Hurstwood [the lead male protagonist of Dreiser's novel] turn to daddy's girl fantasies when their sense of themselves as adored and adoring fathers starts to run up against the reality of maturing daughters heading out the family door. Daddy's girl fantasies compensate for midlife male anxieties about powerlessness....: aging men's fears of formerly dependent daughters' unresponsiveness or uncontrollability," *Paternalism Incorporated: Fables of American Fatherhood, 1865–1940* (Ithaca, N.Y.: Cornell University Press, 2003), 14–15. See too John Cooley, ed., *Mark Twain's Aquarium: The Samuel Clemens Angelfish Correspondence, 1905–1910* (Athens: University of Georgia Press, 1991).

34. Further bibliographical information appears in the later chapters.

35. There is one short book by Earl J. Dias (a scholar from Fairhaven, Rogers's home town) on *Mark Twain and Henry Huttleston Rogers: An Odd Couple* (Fairhaven, Mass.: The Millicent Library, 1984), and a chapter on "Rogers and Clemens" in Dias's earlier *Henry Huttleston Rogers: Portrait of a Capitalist*. The quote here is from *Henry Huttleston Rogers*, p. 185. In this same book, Diaz speaks of "the splendid Rogers Collection" at the Millicent Library (one of the many public buildings Rogers gifted to the town). "The collection," he continues, "includes personal papers and correspondence of Rogers and his family, diaries, journals, and various memorabilia from almost every stage of Rogers' career. It includes also an enormous file of newspaper and periodical articles about Rogers" (12 and 185). As Carolyn Longworth, the Library Director confirms, the collection is considerably more modest than this, with no diaries or journals. Diaz may, she writes, "have been alluding to some papers that have long ago been returned to the family" (email correspondence). Emails and letters sent to the remaining family did not, however, uncover the existence of any such papers.

36. William Merrill Decker raises many of the theoretical issues and problems concerning the use of letters as cultural objects in the early sections of *Epistolary Practices: Letter Writing in America before Telecommunications* (Chapel Hill: University of North Carolina Press, 1998). I put these to one side here, given my wider use of source materials for this book.

37. Smith and Gibson, *Mark Twain-Howells Letters*; Lewis Leary, ed., *Mark Twain's Correspondence with Henry Huttleston Rogers, 1893–1909* (Berkeley and Los Angeles: University of California Press, 1969).

38. The most complete record of the Clemens-Twichell correspondence is held at the Mark Twain Papers (University of California at Berkeley).

39. Harold K. Bush Jr., *Mark Twain and the Spiritual Crisis of His Age* (Tuscaloosa: University of Alabama Press, 2007); Richard Lowry, *"Littery Man": Mark Twain and Modern Authorship* (New York: Oxford University Press, 1996).

40. This is not quite as mechanical or as discrete as I may suggest here. So, for instance, I raise issues about class in my opening "biographical" chapter on the Twichell-Clemens friendship before moving to the subject of religion in the next chapter. And in all three chapters where I offer the larger overview and history of these relationships, I indicate the connection between the functioning of friendship and the larger social order to which it belongs.

41. Alan Trachtenberg, *The Incorporation of America: Culture and Society in the Gilded Age* (New York: Hill & Wang, 1982), 193.

42. The organization of the book differs in the Clemens-Rogers case. I start there with a chapter on the cultural context of their friendship and the relationship between literature and business, and follow with my wider overview chapter, since it suits the logic of the material to do so.

*Chapter 1*

1. Lewis Leary, ed., *Mark Twain's Correspondence with Henry Huttleston Rogers, 1893–1909* (Berkeley and Los Angeles: University of California Press, 1969), 658. See, too, Clemens's letter to Dorothy Sturgis, quoted pp. 647–48. The Railroad was merged with Norfolk and Western Railway (later Norfolk Southern) in 1959. Further information can be found in H. Reid, *The Virginian Railway* (Milwaukee, Wisc.: Kalmbach Publishing, 1961).

2. Paul Fatout, ed., *Mark Twain Speaking* (Iowa City: University of Iowa Press, 1976), 642–43.

3. Bryce Traister's essay on "Academic Viagra" (*American Quarterly* 52, no. 2 [June 2000]) questions the amount of energy recently "devoted to the 'problem' of masculinity as it manifests itself through the literary canon [etc.]" (298). Such writing, the author suggests, "does not sufficiently recognize the historical features of an American masculinity remarkable for its satisfied ego, its imperial drive, its individual power, its sexual aggression, and its assumption of citizenship as a matter of birth and God-given right" (299). I would argue that, even in the nineteenth century, Clemens and Howells showed an awareness in their writing of such "features." I also look to take account of them in my own analysis.

4. Eve Kosofsky Sedgwick, *Between Men: English Literature and Male Homosocial Desire* (New York: Columbia University Press, 1993 [1985]), 1. I slightly alter the context of her words.

5. The strength of Kosofsky Sedgwick's work lies in the way she connects sexuality to a broader set of social relationships (including gender). In this book, sexuality remains by and large a side issue. I recognize that, accordingly, Kosofsky Sedgwick's model is diluted. The whole issue of sexuality, and its relation to these friendships, deserves further critical attention.

6. Sarah Cole, *Modernism, Male Friendship, and the First World War* (Cambridge: Cambridge University Press, 2003), 4. My use of Cole is a reminder that the subject of male friendship has transatlantic, not just

national, dimensions. Clemens himself had close male friends in the United Kingdom.

7. Dana D. Nelson, *National Manhood: Capitalist Citizenship and the Imagined Fraternity of White Men* (Durham, N.C.: Duke University Press, 1998), ix.

8. Ibid., 181.

9. Ibid., x.

10. Ibid., 132.

11. Ibid., 136. My reading of Nelson (and other critics here) is necessarily reductive, tied to my immediate and limited critical purpose.

12. Personal intimacy, in other words, "bleeds into" larger public realms of culture and power, and vice-versa.

13. Any one of these men's relationship with Washington may have influenced the others.

14. I omit Twichell at this point, though he too worked for racial justice, writing about the education of African Americans in the South in religious journals and acting as a trustee for Atlanta University, one of the first post-Civil War colleges established for African Americans (Edmund Asa Ware, married to Twichell's sister Sarah Jane, was its first President). He also knew Washington, who spoke at his Asylum Hill church in 1896 and 1904.

15. See Shelley Fisher Fishkin, *Lighting Out for the Territory: Reflections on Mark Twain and American Culture* (New York: Oxford University Press, 1996), 101–7 (quotation on p. 101). On Clemens, his writings, and his critique of dominant assumptions about whiteness, see Richard S. Lowry, "Mark Twain and Whiteness," in Peter Messent and Louis J. Budd, eds., *A Companion to Mark Twain* (Oxford: Blackwell, 2005), 53–65. On the intricacies of his position regarding issues of race, class, and gender, see Randall Knoper, *Acting Naturally: Mark Twain in the Culture of Performance* (Berkeley and Los Angeles: University of California Press, 1995).

16. Louis R. Harlan and Raymond W. Smock, eds., *The Booker T. Washington Papers*. Open Book Edition, 14 vols. (Champaign: University of Illinois Press, 1972–89), 10:349 ("A Tribute to Mark Twain") and 6:303, online edition http://www.historycooperative.org/btw/ (accessed 3.24.2009).

17. Shelley Fisher Fishkin, *Was Huck Black? Mark Twain and African-American Voices* (New York: Oxford University Press, 1993), 106 (with photo). And Harlan and Smock, *Booker T. Washington Papers*, 8:508.

18. Susan Goodman and Carl Dawson, *William Dean Howells: A Writer's Life* (Berkeley and Los Angeles: University of California Press, 2005), 401. As it turned out, Washington did not speak. Howells himself was a founder member in 1910 of the NAACP (National Association for the Advancement of Colored People)—see Edwin H. Cady, *The Realist at War: The Mature Years of William Dean Howells, 1885–1920* (Syracuse, N.Y.: Syracuse University Press, 1958), 161.

19. Harlan and Smock, *Booker T. Washington Papers*, 1:165. The cautious nature of Washington's racial politics is suggested in the précis of his speech on that occasion: "BTW . . . said that there was a consensus North and South that blacks should receive an industrial education, and he rested his belief that blacks would advance by laying a foundation based on property, intelligence, and thrift" (Harlan and Smock, *Booker T. Washington Papers*, 5:284). Howells's literary friendship with Paul Dunbar is a better known example of his interracial connections, though Dunbar came to see Howells's emphasis

on his dialect poems alone as damaging. Howells's belief in "a precious difference of temperament between the races" suggests the limits to, and contradictions in, his racial vision. For more on Howells and race, the contradictions in his vision, and the fact that "'Whiteness' for Howells... [was] the standard by which 'human unity' is defined" (my emphasis), see Daniel G. Williams, *Ethnicity and Cultural Authority: From Arnold to DuBois* (Edinburgh: Edinburgh University Press, 2006), 103–14 (quoted passage on 109) and 176–89.

20. The image of Rogers giving out notes of such a large denomination prompts a connection with Clemens's short story, "The £1,000,000 Bank-Note" (1893).

21. Harlan and Smock, *Booker T. Washington Papers*, 10:122–26.

22. I am reminded here of David Leverenz's comment that: "Booker T. Washington's fund-raising makes each Yankee donor feel like a big strong daddy whose hand 'uplifts' the entire black race," *Paternalism Incorporated: Fables of American Fatherhood, 1865–1940* (Ithaca, N.Y.: Cornell University Press, 2003), 10.

23. Nelson, *National Manhood*, 16. Clemens's interracial "friendship" (described in Fishkin, *Lighting Out for the Territory*, 96) with John T. Lewis is also relevant here. Lewis was the African American tenant farmer in Elmira whom Clemens came to know following Lewis's risking of his life in August 1877 to prevent a possibly fatal accident, as he stopped a runaway horse and carriage carrying members of the Langdon family. I am not, again, questioning the fact of such a companionate relationship, but would look to position it in its larger social and racial context. That Lewis was both a tenant of Quarry Farm (owned by members of Olivia Clemens's family)—thus of a much lower social class than Clemens—as well as an African American would have meant that opportunities for fraternization, the places where it could occur, and the forms it might take, would necessarily have been strictly limited, and any intimacy between the two men restricted in its type.

24. Harlan and Smock, *Booker T. Washington Papers*, 10:122.

25. We might recall at this point some of Clemens's other writings on racial and gender relations. In an 1898 notebook entry, Clemens describes a dream where a "rounded and plump... negro wench" sells him "a pie; a mushy apple pie—hot," and then makes "a disgusting proposition to me." Clemens's dream self brushes her suggestion aside and asks for a spoon with which to eat the pie: "She had but the one, and she took it out of her mouth... and offered it to me. My stomach rose—there everything vanished." In *Which Was It?* (1899–1903), a mulatto (and thus, by the southern racial codes of the time, "black") ex-slave, Jasper, blackmails the white male protagonist, his former master, and forces him—while they are alone—to exchange places in a reversal of conventional racial power relations. Intimacy with an African American protagonist, in other words, in both these cases, rests not on any (supposed) spontaneous or unmediated basis but is constructed according to patterns of desire and threat buried deep within the American racial unconscious. In the first case this takes the shape of an "inadvertently erotic fantasy... driven in some degree by... persistent upwellings of errant, inter-racial desire." In the second, "Jasper is a projection of unresolved guilt,... a collective guilt for the national hypocrisy of slavery and, more pointedly, of the post-Emancipation reinstitution of slavery in the form of legalized segregation." Intimacy here works as its correlative, friendship, does, "constructed in such a way

as to reflect a culture's position on sexuality, gender, hierarchy and power" (Cole, *Modernism*, 4). My quotations are from Forrest G. Robinson, *The Author-Cat: Clemens's Life in Fiction* (New York: Fordham University Press, 2007), 178–79, and Susan Gillman, *Blood Talk: American Race Melodramas and the Culture of the Occult* (Chicago: University of Chicago Press, 2003), 128–29. Jim and Huck's much-discussed relationship in *Adventures of Huckleberry Finn* (1885) also occurs within this same interracial framework. Rather than entering the debate here about the meaning and resonance of that relationship, it is enough to quote Peter Stoneley's comment that: "Although Jim and Huck's relationship is usually seen as the most important [in the novel], their *de facto* inequality is never less obvious than the difference between black and white," "Rewriting the Gold Rush: Twain, Harte and Homosociality," *Journal of American Studies* 30, no. 2 (1996):203 n. 24. My range of reference to Clemens's writings is necessarily selective here.

26. Lauren Berlant, ed., *Intimacy* (Chicago: University of Chicago Press, 2000), 7.

27. I am here following lines suggested in a discussion on this topic on BBC Radio 4 some years ago.

28. Cole, *Modernism, Male Friendship, and the First World War*, 4. Cole is interested in the way that "comforting male relations" are in increasingly tense counterpoint with forms of "corporate comradeship" in the late Victorian period through to the trauma of the First World War years, and the sense of alienation, mechanization, and rupture increasingly associated with the forms of public meaning (6 and 18). The images of warfare and personal alienation in Clemens's *A Connecticut Yankee* (1889) and of solipsistic disconnection in the final section of *No. 44, The Mysterious Stranger* (written in 1904) reinforce such an understanding, especially given the male companionships earlier detailed in each book. The relationship between Cole's argument about British literature and the development of American literature in the period bears further consideration.

29. I am aware of the dangers of making general remarks about forms of friendship while rooting my study in the particularities of one historical period. I suggest that, while cultural and historical specificity is a crucial factor in my analysis, it nonetheless forms one part of a larger narrative of modern western male friendship.

30. E. Anthony Rotundo, *American Manhood: Transformations in Masculinity from the Revolution to the Modern Era* (New York: Basic Books, 1993), 1. See Michael Kimmel, *Manhood in America: A Cultural History* (New York: Free Press, 1997), on the multiple "masculinities" existing in America, and depending on "class, race, ethnicity, age, sexuality, region of the country" (5). Kimmel continues, though: "At the same time . . . all American men must also contend with a singular vision of masculinity, a particular definition that is held up as the model against which we all measure ourselves."

31. These brief working definitions are from John W. Crowley, "Howells, Stoddard, and Male Homosocial Attachment in Victorian America," in Harry Brod, ed., *The Making of Masculinities: The New Men's Studies* (Cambridge, Mass.: Unwin Hyman, 1987), 302.

32. Caleb Crain, *American Sympathy: Men, Friendship, and Literature in the New Nation* (New Haven: Yale University Press, 2001), 4, 35, and 159–60.

33. Rotundo, *American Manhood*, 77. Lillian Federman describes the intensity of women's friendships in nineteenth-century America in a similar way, but as a direct contrast to male friendships and the "emotions that

manly men had to repress in favour of 'rationality.'" See *Surpassing the Love of Men: Romantic Friendship and Love Between Women from the Renaissance to the Present* (New York: Perennial, 2001 [1981]), 159. The work of Crain and others has undermined such a binary, though undoubtedly male and female friendships did differ in kind according to gender and cultural circumstance. On women's friendships in the period, see also Caroll Smith Rosenberg, *Disorderly Conduct: Visions of Gender in Victorian America* (New York: Alfred A. Knopf, 1985).

34. Robert K. Martin, "Knight-Errants and Gothic Seducers: The Representation of Male Friendship in Mid-Nineteenth-Century America," in Martin Duberman, Martha Vicinus, and George Chauncey Jr., eds., *Hidden From History: Reclaiming the Gay and Lesbian Past* (London: Penguin, 1991 [1989]), 170.

35. Stoneley, "Rewriting the Gold Rush," 208. And Kosofsky Sedgwick, *Between Men*, 133.

36. Stoneley, "Rewriting the Gold Rush," 208. Stoneley uses Alan Sinfield to explain further: "Sinfield ... explains this shift in perception as being like the difference between stealing things, 'which any child might do, and being labelled a "thief": with the latter, thievishness seems to pervade the whole personality.'" There is still critical disagreement and ambiguity about the drawing of exact lines between intense friendship and its sexual expression, between quite was "taboo" and what was not, and about when, historically, such boundaries changed. David Deitcher's book, *Dear Friends: American Photographs of Men Together, 1840–1918* (New York: Harry N. Abrams, 2001), illustrates "the comfortable display of mutual [physical] affection between men" as evidenced in photographs throughout the *whole* of the nineteenth century (13). John Ibson, too, in *Picturing Men: A Century of Male Relationships in Everyday American Photography* (Washington, D.C.: Smithsonian Institute, 2002), suggests that "homoeroticism and intense homosocial bonds are a more important part of male culture [in the late nineteenth and early twentieth centuries] than has previously been imagined" (27). Deitcher sees the British 1885 Labouchère Amendment as a crucial turning point in terms of cultural change in this area: "As it prohibited all acts that men might engage in together, including many that were previously practiced with impunity by "romantic friends," the new law contributed to the social construction of the homosexual as explicitly criminal," *Dear Friends*, 11.

37. Stoneley, "Rewriting the Gold Rush," 208.

38. Donald Yacovone, "Abolitionists and the 'Language of Fraternal Love,'" in Mark C. Carnes and Clyde Griffen, eds., *Meanings for Manhood: Constructions of Masculinity in Victorian America* (Chicago: University of Chicago Press, 1990), 95.

39. Though Deitcher matches Yacovone's argument by suggesting that "the homosocial warmth of comradely love" provided a counter to "the soulless rivalry of the marketplace," *Dear Friends*, 94. This was clearly, however, a transitional period when the bonds of intense male intimacy were loosened. Even though he tends to date the process historically somewhat later, Ibson's comment that "*it is clear that the modernization process ... radically altered the nature of close relationships outside of marriage*" gets to the heart of this change; *Picturing Men*, 9 (my emphasis).

40. See, for instance, the letter from Charles Brockden Brown to William Wood Wilkins written at the end of the eighteenth century and quoted in Crain, *American Sympathy*, 67.

41. See Drury Sherrod, "The Bonds of Men: Problems and Possibilities in Close Male Relationships," in Brod, ed., *The Making of Masculinities*, 221.

42. Peter Messent and Steve Courtney, eds., *The Civil War Letters of Joseph Hopkins Twichell: A Chaplain's Story* (Athens: University of Georgia Press, 2006), 121, 144, 153, and 255.

43. See, too, Yacovone, "Abolitionists," 85–95. Twichell's letter to his close Yale friend, Edward Carrington Jr., during the Civil War, is another example of such expressiveness. Beginning, "Dearest of Eds," Twichell continues: "I *certainly* never loved you so much as I do now. You have never seemed more admirable to my eyes, more desirable to my bosom. . . . The sensation of being forcibly dragged away has marked every mile I have traveled. . . . The wheels clacking against the rails have kept time for me to a mournful monody of good-bye and true love crossed. . . . It came to me a hundred times, that of all things it would be sweetest to go back and stay at your side night and day till the war or your fighting ended. . . . Do write to me, darling." The letter closes, "Yours in true love." See Steve Courtney, *Joseph Hopkins Twichell: The Life and Times of Mark Twain's Closest Friend* (Athens: Georgia University Press, 2008), 107.

44. The Mark Twain Papers at the University of California at Berkeley (henceforth MTP).

45. The word "soft" might also be read as carrying a (latent) sexual meaning and charge.

46. The Yale Collection of American Literature in the Beinecke Rare Book and Manuscript Library.

47. MTP.

48. Crowley, "Howells, Stoddard, and Male Homosocial Attachment," 301–24. For a perceptive chapter on Howells's *The Rise of Silas Lapham* (1885) and the way in which "[r]omance and desire between men in [the novel's] homosocial world is sublimated into the rhetoric of business," see Graham Thompson, *Male Sexuality under Surveillance: The Office in American Literature* (Iowa City: University of Iowa Press, 2003), 21–45 (quotation from 35).

49. Crowley, "Howells, Stoddard, and Male Homosocial Attachment," 305–6.

50. Ibid., 307 and 317. See, too, 305. Anthony Rotundo argues that passionate male friendships in the period were most common in the interval between boyhood and manhood, and provided an early substitute for parental (and even future marital) relationships. See "Romantic Friendship: Male Intimacy and Middle-Class Youth in the Northern United States, 1800–1900," *Journal of Social History* 23, no. 1 (1989): 1–25.

51. A friendship he held in common with Clemens. Stoddard, to repeat, accompanied Clemens on his 1873–74 visit to England in the role of secretary and companion. Clemens evidently referred to him as "such a nice girl." See Lin Salamo and Harriet Elinor Smith, eds., *Mark Twain's Letters*, vol. 5, *1872–1873* (Berkeley and Los Angeles: University of California Press, 1997), 456.

52. Crowley, "Howells, Stoddard, and Male Homosocial Attachment," 311 and 313. Crowley relies on Kosofsky Sedgwick here and uses her words (see *Between Men*, 173 and 177).

53. So Clemens, in a September 21, 1876, letter to Howells, would describe him as "[p]oor, sweet, pure-hearted, good-intentioned, impotent Stoddard," a man with "no worldly sense." See Henry Nash Smith and

William M. Gibson, eds., *Mark Twain-Howells Letters: The Correspondence of Samuel L. Clemens and William D. Howells, 1872–1910* (Cambridge, Mass.: Harvard University Press, 1960), 154. Crowley sums up the description as representing Stoddard, "in short," as "a child"; "Howells, Stoddard, and Male Homosocial Attachment," 314.

54. Crowley, "Howells, Stoddard, and Male Homosocial Attachment in Victorian America," 317 and 320.

55. Ibid., 323–24. See too Howell's relationship with Edmund Gosse as described in Goodman and Dawson, *William Dean Howells*, 227–29 ("Howells...must have been aware that his...terms of endearment [toward the bisexual Gosse] went beyond the ordinary," 229).

56. Stoneley's words in "Rewriting the Gold Rush," 207.

57. Ibid., 192–93. I slightly change the terms of Stoneley's argument to reflect my own understanding of the subject. For an explicitly homosexual reading of the sketch, and of the Clemens-De Quille friendship, see Andrew Jay Hoffman, "Mark Twain and Homosexuality," *American Literature* 67, no. 1 (March 1995): 23–49.

58. John Ibson writes that: "it seems clear that the 'boys' in mining camps often shared an intense bond. Comely young miners...might be given a woman's name...Susan Lee Johnson has pointed out that although men's sleeping together was common enough throughout nineteenth-century America, doing so in the mining camps might have a singular significance, 'one characterized by the presence of curious young men and lonely husbands, by close dancing and hard drinking, by distance from customary social constraints and proximity to competing cultural practices,'" *Picturing Men*, 129–30.

59. Stoneley, "Rewriting the Gold Rush," 207.

60. Ibid., 201. And Mark Twain, *Roughing It* (New York: Oxford University Press, 1996 [1872]), 414–16.

61. Stoneley, "Rewriting the Gold Rush," 201.

62. Ibid., 200. Stoneley's perceptive remarks on Clemens's late-career "renegotiation of [homosexual, homosocial, and heterosexual] borderlines" (209) lead in the direction of the considerable number of texts Clemens wrote not just with male-male relationships at their center, but where, too, gender roles between male and female are in flux. For one such set of examples, see Mark Twain, *How Nancy Jackson Married Kate Wilson and Other Tales of Rebellious Girls & Daring Young Women* (Lincoln: University of Nebraska Press, 2001). Despite Stoneley's important work, there is certainly more to do on Clemens's fictional representations of masculinity and male friendship. The short story "The Belated Russian Passport" (1902) would be one place to start. For useful discussion on Clemens and gender roles, see especially Shelley Fisher Fishkin, "Mark Twain and Women," in Forrest G. Robinson, ed., *The Cambridge Companion to Mark Twain* (Cambridge: Cambridge University Press, 1995), 52–73; Susan K. Harris, "Mark Twain and Gender," in Shelley Fisher Fishkin, ed., *A Historical Guide to Mark Twain* (New York: Oxford University Press, 2002), 163–93; and Peter Stoneley, "Mark Twain and Gender," in Messent and Budd, eds., *A Companion to Mark Twain*, 66–77; and the bibliographical references in these essays.

63. Stonely, "Rewriting the Gold Rush," 193.

64. Ibid., pp. 197 and 209. Stoneley thinks it probable that "Harte was not 'homosexual' at all," but "that his own engagement with same-sex relationship was very much 'nascent and fluid,'" pp. 208–9.

65. Ibid., 196 (Stoneley quotes Twain's *Autobiography* here).

66. Stonely, "Rewriting the Gold Rush," 197. Louis J. Budd notes similarly: "Clemens...had always preferred [wearing] bright colors, partly because of recurring ambitions to rate as a dandy in the contemporary lingo of fashion (and to compete with Bret Harte)," "Mark Twain's Visual Humor," in Messent and Budd, eds., *A Companion to Mark Twain*, 470.

67. Stoneley, "Rewriting the Gold Rush," 198.

68. Crowley, "Howells, Stoddard, and Male Homosocial Attachment," 308.

69. In this later chapter, too, I undermine too-firm a construction of the late-nineteenth-century masculine world in terms of a set of "business" values, fundamentally opposed to a sentimental and domestic "female" world. I am also reminded here of Wilson Carey McWilliams's comment (quoted in Ibson, *Picturing Men*, 10) on contemporary male friendship becoming "less a relation of whole personalities than a situation based on discrete roles and attributes. We learn to modify them by adjectives ('business friends')...." Rogers was more than just a "business friend" for Clemens, but this description nonetheless clearly relates to the various dimensions of Clemens's subjectivity.

70. Peter Filene, "The Secrets of Men's History," in Brod, ed., *Making of Masculinities*, 108–9.

71. See, for instance, Mary Chapman and Glenn Hendler, eds., *Sentimental Men: Masculinity and the Politics of Affect in American Culture* (Berkeley and Los Angeles: University of California Press, 1999).

72. "Mark Twain and Gender," 173–74.

73. T. J. Jackson Lears, *No Place of Grace: Antimodernism and the Transformation of American Culture 1880–1920* (New York: Pantheon, 1981), 15–17.

74. Cole, *Modernism, Male Friendship, and the First World War*, 24. In "Separate Spheres, Female Worlds, Woman's Place: The Rhetoric of Women's History," *The Journal of American History* 75, no. 1 (June 1988), Linda K. Kerber unpacks the ambiguous meanings of the phrase "separate spheres" as it has been applied to a "women's culture" in America.

75. The quote is taken from Kerber (explicating Ryan's argument) in "Separate Spheres, Female Worlds, Woman's Place," 24. Such a retreat was accompanied by a sharp drop in the number of children born into marriage. Rotundo sees in nineteenth-century marriage as a whole "the growing presence of [an emotionally and sexually expressive] marital intimacy": "As the purpose of sex was changing from procreation to intimacy, the purpose of procreation itself was changing from an embodiment of lineage to the embodiment of love." See *American Manhood*, 163 and 158.

76. Margaret Marsh, "Suburban Men and Masculine Domesticity, 1870–1915," in Carnes and Griffen, eds., *Meanings for Manhood*, 112–13. For more on this "ideology of domesticity," see 113.

77. Ibid., 115 and 113.

78. Ibid., 117.

79. Ibid., 116.

80. Rotundo, *American Manhood*, 143 and 146.

81. See ibid., 256–62, and E. Anthony Rotundo, "Boy Culture: Middle-Class Boyhood in Nineteenth-Century America," in Carnes and Griffen, eds., *Meanings for Manhood*, 17. On American nervousness see, for instance, T. J. Jackson Lears, *No Place of Grace*, 49–57.

82. Cole, *Modernism, Male Friendship, and the First World War*, 23.

83. Rotundo, *American Manhood*, 146. Rotundo continues to make the connections between boyhood and manhood here, but there were other models for such forms of manliness readily at hand—in a past chivalric tradition, or the contemporary frontier experience, for instance.

84. W. D. Howells, *My Mark Twain: Reminiscences and Criticisms* (New York: Harper & Brothers, 1910), 13 and 10. He explains his necessary qualification, "from the outside," as follows: "Marriages are what the parties to them alone really know them to be." Family servant Katie Leary saw the marriage more from the inside and described it similarly: "Mrs. Clemens...was a lovely woman and there never was a happier couple lived in this world than they was." See Mary Lawton, *A Lifetime with Mark Twain: The Memories of Katy Leary, for Thirty Years His Faithful and Devoted Servant* (New York: Harcourt, Brace, 1925), 58.

85. The description of Olivia that Kenneth R. Andrews gives, as he writes about the family's life in Hartford's "Nook Farm" community, reinforces Howells's: "The virtues appealing to her friends were those of the ideal woman of the period—unassuming beauty, limitless devotion, grace in hospitality, intellectual anonymity—and as a result she sometimes seems to us hard to characterize as an individual, so little do we know of her passions," *Nook Farm: Mark Twain's Hartford Circle* (Cambridge, Mass.: Harvard University Press, 1950), 89. Susan K. Harris, among others, has started to develop a fuller picture of Clemens's wife, and of the intellectual as well as emotional qualities she revealed in their relationship. In her "Mark Twain and Gender," for instance, she writes that: "Though she herself conformed to the image of a True rather than New woman, Olivia Langdon was sympathetic to the suffrage movement and had many women friends who were actively engaged in public life," 182. More remains to be written on the Clemens marriage and inner family life. Despite his close involvement with domestic life, Clemens nonetheless could tend to play out the role of "overbearing paterfamilias," especially where his daughters were concerned.

86. Salamo and Smith, *Mark Twain's Letters*, vol. 5, 508. In other letters Clemens would heavily cancel that same last phrase (probably at a later date, after the letter had been received and saved). In the view of the *Letters'* editors, it "had acquired a private significance for the Clemenses, perhaps one that they were unwilling, on reflection, to allow posterity even to guess at," 509.

87. Kerber, "Separate Spheres, Female Worlds, Woman's Place," 16. On Clemens's identity as heavily dependent "upon values embedded in home and hearth," see Michael Kiskis, "Mark Twain and the Tradition of Literary Domesticity," in Laura E. Skandera-Tromley and Michael J. Kiskis, eds., *Constructing Mark Twain: New Directions in Literary Scholarship* (Columbia: University of Missouri Press, 2001), 13–27 (quoted passage, 15).

88. Andrews, *Nook Farm*, 92.

89. Ibid., 84 and 82. Twichell was a fellow member of this community, and his and Clemens's close friendship was not gender-exclusive, for it included their wives too: "Livy and Harmony Twichell were as intimate as [Clemens] and Joe.... Doors were always unlocked and residents of the Farm walked in and out of each other's houses at any time of day without knocking," ibid., 89 and 84.

90. See, for instance, Victor A. Doyno, "Samuel Clemens as Family Man and Father," in Skandera-Tromley and Kiskis, *Constructing Mark Twain*, 32–33 and 46.

91. Ibid., 35.

92. Andrews, *Nook Farm*, 83. I focus here on the Hartford years, when the Clemens children were young. The family would, in the longer term and for a number of reasons (professional, financial, medical, and educational), spend much time abroad. This must further have meant that— even despite the presence of nursemaids and tutors when the children were young—the needs of, and interrelationships within, the nuclear family played and would continue to play an unusually significant part in shaping Clemens's day-to-day life.

93. Harold K. Bush Jr. lists papers given to the Monday Evening Club, including the thirteen delivered by Clemens and the nineteen by Twichell, in *Mark Twain and the Spiritual Crisis of His Age* (Tuscaloosa: University of Alabama Press, 2007), 114–19.

94. See Andrews, *Nook Farm*, 104–5.

95. Rotundo, "Boy Culture," 16. Stoneley reads Clemens's boyishness (and Howells's own, when they were together) as only a "very cautious and partial defiance on the parts of both men" against the realm of "wives or mothers." He sees it much more as the mark of an ultimate submission "to 'adult' or established authority," "Mark Twain and Gender," 74. For another approach, via Clemens's fictions, to masculine domesticity— and the portrayal of female authority and irrationality and male incompetence in such family space—see his three "McWilliams" stories. Ruth Schwartz Cowans argues that changes in "household technology" (with men no longer having to chop wood, etc.) meant that the home became for them a place of leisure while for women it remained a place of work (see Kerber, "Separate Spheres, Female Worlds, Woman's Place," 32). That viewpoint, though, is skewed in these texts where the husband is rendered comically incompetent—in a way that James Thurber would have recognised—by new household technology, the whole household consequently turned upside-down ("The McWilliamses and the Burglar Alarm," 1882). Meanwhile his sufferings at the hands of his wife's anxieties seem related to the fact that she has handed over many of her domestic tasks to the servants. Clemens's self-representation here acts, though, as another way of partially distancing himself from the domestic sphere.

96. Susan K. Harris writes: "Happy to play the paterfamilias to his wife and three daughters, he was also happy to be called to the lecture circuit, where, despite slow trains and grubby hotels, he was freed from the constraints of Victorian gentility and the demands of property ownership," "Mark Twain and Gender," 176.

97. See Gregg Camfield, *The Oxford Companion to Mark Twain* (New York: Oxford University Press, 2003). Camfield comments that such clubs "were a strange variant of domesticity," with their emphasis on dining, the bedrooms they usually provided for members, and "their congenial company at most any time of the day or night." "Thus, they served the putative function of domesticity as a 'haven in a heartless world' of work, and cut out the familial responsibilities of home life as well. This . . . helped to make [them] attractive; absent women and children, members could relax conventional decorum of speech . . . , addressing topics taboo in mixed company," 119–21.

98. Andrews, *Nook Farm*, 83. For other such trips taken by Twichell away from the scan of family responsibilities, see Courtney, *Joseph Hopkins Twichell*, 137–39, 151–57, 193–95, 214, and 257–58. And see also pp. 222–23.

99. MTP.

100. On Clemens and sentimentalism, see Gregg Camfield, *Sentimental Twain: Samuel Clemens in the Maze of Moral Philosophy* (Philadelphia: University of Pennsylvania Press, 1994) and Mary Louise Kete, *Sentimental Collaborations: Mourning and Middle Class Identity in Nineteenth-Century America* (Durham, N.C.: Duke University Press, 2000), 142–79. See, too, my final chapter.

101. Stoneley, "Mark Twain and Gender," 72.

102. Ibid., 75–76.

103. Rotundo, *American Manhood*, 64.

104. Nelson, *National Manhood*, 178.

105. Ibid., 132.

106. The phrase is taken from Mark C. Carnes, "Middle Class Men and the Solace of Fraternal Ritual," in Carnes and Griffen, eds., *Meanings for Manhood*, 51.

107. Kimmel, *Manhood in America*, 83.

108. Nancy F. Cott, "On Men's History and Women's History," in Carnes and Griffen, eds., *Meanings for Manhood*, 210.

109. Dorothy Hammond and Alta Jablow, "Gilgamesh and the Sundance Kid: The Myth of Male Friendship," in Brod, ed., *Making of Masculinities*, 256. Although the authors write of the contemporary period, their argument applies to the conditions of the postbellum American world, when the "modern society" of which they speak is first taking shape. The focus on "social and geographical mobility" is certainly pertinent in Clemens's case, and their commentary on the way male friendships range from the "affective" to the "instrumental" or "expedient" is also useful (244). Drury Sherrod, discussing the impact of "affectionate marriages" in relation to work relationships, says: "the new marriages allowed men to rely on women for emotional support, at the same time that the changing nature of work was making it harder for men to receive that support from other men," "The Bonds of Men," in Brod, ed., *Making of Masculinities*, 232.

110. Sherrod, "Bonds of Men," 231–32. This process had been occurring certainly from the Jacksonian period, but its pace increased at a spectacularly rapid rate in the postbellum period.

111. Cole, *Modernism, Male Friendship, and the First World War*, 5.

112. Ibid., 47. Cole is referring to the British writer John Symonds here.

113. Clyde Griffen, "Reconstructing Masculinity from the Evangelical Revival to the Waning of Progressivism: A Speculative Synthesis," in Carnes and Griffen, eds., *Meanings for Manhood*, 191.

114. Berlant, ed., *Intimacy*, 2 and 3–4.

115. Figures for another group of workers (bookkeepers, cashiers and accountants) were 2 percent, 5.7 percent and 17.4 percent respectively. See Margery W. Davis, *Woman's Place Is at the Typewriter: Office Work and Office Workers 1870–1930* (Philadelphia: Temple University Press, 1982), appendix, table 1.

116. Just as are (and this applies with particular force to Clemens, Twichell, and Howells) the borders between the first two areas.

117. Rotundo, *American Manhood*, 199–200. We should remember, too, the "team" aspects of corporate culture: one is not in competition with everyone all of the time, but rather looks to forge affective bonds with some to compete with others. There was certainly a sense fostered in late-nineteenth-century corporate America that the corporation or business organization itself could, at times, be "like family" or "like friends."

118. Nelson, *National Manhood*, 136. Nelson focuses on white manhood as an entire group, but is aware of the way class (and other) lines mean that white "working class," for instance, can—in the overall spectrum of white manhood—be itself positioned within an "othered" category.

119. Ibid., 137.

120. Ibid., 178.

121. Ibid., 178–79.

122. The notion of individual competition in itself conceals the operations of what Nelson calls an "uneven economy" (*National Manhood*, 182). In other words, for the majority, American success ideology was already fatally compromised by hardening social and economic structures.

123. Rotundo, *American Manhood*, 87.

124. See Camfield, *Oxford Companion to Mark Twain*, 119–21. Due to his celebrity, his business bankruptcy in 1894 did not alter such socialization patterns to any major extent.

125. The assumption that Clemens's steamboat and frontier years were (historically earlier) exceptions to the capitalist business model is now generally discredited.

126. She is using David Leverenz's terms from *Manhood and the American Renaissance* (Ithaca, N.Y.: Cornell University Press, 1989). See Harris, "Mark Twain and Gender," 175.

127. Harris, "Mark Twain and Gender," 179.

128. And see Stoneley, "Mark Twain and Gender," 76–77 n. 7.

129. Nelson, *National Manhood*, 7.

130. This does not mean that such relationships cannot have a culturally competitive edge.

131. Stoneley, "Mark Twain and Gender," 75. As is clear here, my argument is strongly influenced by Stoneley's essay.

132. Ibid., 73.


*Chapter 2*

1. "Muscular Christianity" was a generic term in the second half of the nineteenth century, but was used to describe Twichell himself in the Hartford *Courant* of May 26, 1873. The phrase is introduced in the context of his advice to the Yale graduating class of that year relating "to the care of their health": "he illustrated his subject by testimony concerning his own boating experiences, which had laid up for him a reserved deposit of strength from which he had drawn in hard exigencies of his ministry to signal advantage." Twichell was himself a Yale man and a member of its first crew to beat Harvard (in 1859): see Steve Courtney, *Joseph Hopkins Twichell: The Life and Times of Mark Twain's Closest Friend* (Athens: Georgia University Press, 2008), 48–49.

2. See March 2, 1875, letter from Clemens to Howells, in Michael B. Frank and Harriet Elinor Smith, eds., *Mark Twain's Letters*, vol. 6: *1874–1875* (Berkeley and Los Angeles: University of California Press, 2002), 401–2, n. 1. Gage was a fellow local Congregationalist minister.

3. Pasted in Twichell's *Journals*. The Yale Collection of American Literature in the Beinecke Rare Book and Manuscript Library, henceforth cited as Beinecke.

4. Quoted in Courtney, *Joseph Hopkins Twichell*, 220–21.

5. Kenneth R. Andrews, *Nook Farm: Mark Twain's Hartford Circle* (Cambridge, Mass.: Harvard University Press, 1950), 10. Peter Messent

and Steve Courtney, eds., *The Civil War Letters of Joseph Hopkins Twichell: A Chaplain's Story* (Athens: University of Georgia Press, 2006), 16–18.

6. General Hooker's Division (of which the Excelsior Brigade was a part) was to lose 772 men killed, wounded, and missing in a single day on May 5, 1862, in the brigade's first real engagement, in McClellan's Peninsula Campaign. While Twichell's own regiment was not engaged that day, the other four in his brigade were. He noted his response to this event on viewing the battlefield after the conflict was over: "there I saw sights that can never fade from my memory. 'Sin entered into the world and death through sin' kept ringing through my brain as I wandered among the slain unburied." Messent and Courtney, *The Civil War Letters of Joseph Hopkins Twichell*, 124.

7. One of Twichell's daughters would also be named Harmony and would (ironically, given his breaking of its rules) marry the composer Charles Ives.

8. For more on Bushnell, see Courtney, *Joseph Hopkins Twichell*, chapter 3, "The Soul Streaming into the Eyes and Ears," 19–25, and William E. Phipps, *Mark Twain's Religion* (Macon, Ga.: Mercer University Press, 2003), 120–26.

9. "What is true manhood? A many-sided thing indeed. . . . I assume . . . that its consummate feature is *moral* —that it has its coronation in what we call *character*. . . . [N]o other character was ever brought forth to view on earth that has obtained such an acceptance as presenting the glory possible to Manhood as that of Jesus Christ," *The Coming Man*, dated May 24, 1885. Twichell's sermons, Beinecke.

10. Paine's version of the story appeared in his *Mark Twain: A Biography* (New York: Harper, 1912) 1:371, but also in *Harper's Magazine* of May 1912. Courtney doubts its truth: see *Joseph Hopkins Twichell*, 125.

11. See Harriet Elinor Smith and Richard Bucci, eds., *Mark Twain's Letters*, vol. 2: 1867–68 (Berkeley and Los Angeles: University of California Press, 1990), 144–45 ("Henry Ward is a brick") and 160. The Hookers were also good friends of the Langdons, Clemens's Elmira future in-laws, whose daughter Olivia he had already met and would soon be courting. Isabella's full brother (Henry Ward Beecher was her half-brother) was Thomas K. Beecher, pastor of the Langdons' Elmira church. For more on this unconventional minister, see Phipps, *Mark Twain's Religion*, 93–100.

12. Smith and Bucci, eds., *Mark Twain's Letters*, 2:161 and 166.

13. See, for instance, Justin Kaplan, *Mr. Clemens and Mark Twain* (Harmondsworth, Middx.: Penguin 1967 [1966]), 19–24.

14. Pasted in Twichell's *Journals*, Beinecke. Some of this archive material has been published elsewhere (in the present instance, see Leah A. Strong, *Joseph Twichell: Mark Twain's Friend and Pastor* [Athens: University of Georgia Press, 1966], 68). I use the original source where possible.

15. October 18, 1868, Smith and Bucci, eds., *Mark Twain's Letters*, 2:267–68.

16. March 13, 1869, Victor Fischer and Michael B. Frank, eds., *Mark Twain's Letters*, vol. 3: *1869* (Berkeley and Los Angeles: University of California Press, 1992), 173.

17. Beinecke. The letter is published in Albert Bigelow Paine, *Mark Twain's Letters*, vol. 2 (New York: Harper & Brothers, 1917), 640. Throughout this book, where possible, I use archive material to avoid transcription errors and editorial changes (Paine tended to omit sections of the letters).

18. Twichell's *Journals*, Beinecke.

19. Mark Twain, *Roughing It* (New York: Oxford University Press, 1996 [1872]), 329–338. Clemens read "Buck Fanshawe's Funeral" at the Annual meeting of the Yale Alumni Association of Hartford (where he was introduced by Twichell) in 1888. See Asylum Hill Church Parish Memorabilia, a "year to year Scrapbook" kept by Twichell for much of the Hartford pastorate (Connecticut State Library). Again the piece may in part have been chosen for its relevance to its author's relationship with his eastern, elite audience. A significant element in the friendship between Clemens and Twichell lay in the humor both men found in their interactions with those who lacked the sophistication and social status that they in fact shared. It is as though Clemens's own rawer edges ("bark") could be sublimated and effaced in the comedy released by much clearer cases of social and cultural inequality. So see Twichell's October 22, 1878, letter to Clemens about his shipboard experiences as he returned to America from the *Tramp Abroad* trip, and his description of Beilstein, a butcher from Pennsylvania, and his appearance, colorful language, etc.: "I can't begin to report all the entertainment he afforded me. . . . He used to go to the cooks [*sic*] galley and . . . stand for half an hour whetting his pocket knife and looking dreamily out upon the sea, as if [he] had a vision of slaughtered beeves that he [was] soon to enjoy the heavenly rapture of cutting up." The appreciation Twichell shared with Clemens in such "salt of the earth" types—perhaps the more condescending on the former's part—is clear when he says that, "[t]here were plenty of highly civilized people on board, clergymen and such like, but none of them gave me half the pleasure he did with his talk of butchering" (MTP). Clemens responded: "Well, your butcher is magnificent. He won't stay out of my mind. I keep trying to think of some way of getting your account of him into my book without his being offended." January 26, 1879 letter, MTP.

20. August 23, 1878. Twichell's letter to his wife when he was in Europe with Clemens on the *Tramp Abroad* trip: "Another feature of [Mark] is his extreme *sensitiveness* in certain directions. He has coarse spots in him. As he says Howells says he has a sewer running through him. But I never knew a person so finely regardful of the feelings of others in some ways," Beinecke.

21. This, despite the odd behavioral eccentricity that provided a reminder of his previous background, and continued to separate him from those (like the Aldriches) who might otherwise be judged his social peers. See, for instance, Kaplan, *Mr. Clemens and Mark Twain*, 221–22 and 265–66.

22. Unpublished in Clemens's lifetime but evidently written circa 1897.

23. See "Wapping Alice," in Mark Twain, *How Nancy Jackson Married Kate Wilson and Other Tales of Rebellious Girls & Daring Young Women* (Lincoln: University of Nebraska Press, 2001), 81–104. "Tom" (who replaces "The Reverend Joe . . . off on his vacation" in the fictional version of the narrative), is a thinly disguised version of Thomas Kennicut Beecher, pastor of the Elmira church to which the Langdons, and later, Clemens and Olivia, belonged. Beecher and Twichell were the attending ministers at Clemens's wedding in 1870. The two men thereafter would indeed occasionally swap parishes during the summer vacation period. See also, Mark Twain [Samuel Clemens], *"Wapping Alice." Printed for the First Time, Together with Three Factual Letters to Olivia Clemens; Another Story, "The McWilliamses and the Burglar Alarm"; and Revelatory Portions of the Autobiographical Dictation of April 10, 1907, Comprising the Evidence in the Curious Affair of Lizzie Wills and Willie Taylor*, with an Introduction

and Afterword by Hamlin Hill (Berkeley: The Friends of the Bancroft Library, 1981).

24. Letters of July 17–18, 1877, the Mark Twain Papers at the University of California at Berkeley (henceforth MTP).

25. Twichell's *Journals*, Beinecke, July 17, 1877.

26. Letter to James M. Tuohy, November 10, 1898, MTP (photocopy).

27. Clemens's letter to Olivia, July 17–18, 1877, MTP.

28. "Wapping Alice," 83 (*How Nancy Jackson Married Kate Wilson*). The letter to Tuohy of November 10, 1898 (see n. 26 above), reads: "I've always been a little sore over this cussed adventure, & I couldn't bring myself to substitute my own name for 'Jackson's' if I should try."

29. "Wapping Alice," 84. Clemens was always fascinated by slippages of identity, and of gender too—by women with "masculine" traits and by weakly "feminine" men. Cross-dressing is also a recurrent motif in his work.

30. Ibid., 99.

31. Interview with Twichell's son, Rev. Joseph Hooker Twichell (1883–1961), dated August 14, 1957, the Mark Twain Library and Memorial Commission, Hartford (copy in MTP). We cannot place too much reliance on accuracy here, as the details come from the recollection of much, much earlier events.

32. Twichell described Clemens's meeting with the Prince of Wales in Baden Baden in 1892 in an interview ("Mark Twain and 'Dear Old Joe'" by Robert Hugh Morris) in the *Continent* on December 4, 1913. He calls Clemens "a kind of rough diamond in some ways," "shambling along, bobbing around like a sailor fresh from a voyage" beside the Prince of Wales who "was dignity personified...walk[ing] as though he owned the earth and didn't care who knew it." Pasted in the Twichell Family Scrapbooks, Beinecke.

33. Beinecke.

34. August [1?], 1878, Beinecke.

35. See Manuscript of *Innocents Adrift* in MTP, 107–17. A different version of the story, taken from the *Life on the Mississippi* manuscript, appears in *Mark Twain in Eruption*, ed. Bernard De Voto (New York: Harper & Brothers, 1940), 366–72. Some of the 1890s travel sketches were published in magazines at the time, some posthumously in *Europe and Elsewhere* (New York: Harper, 1923). My thanks to Michael Frank for information on "The Profane Hostler" history.

36. Twichell *Journals*, Beinecke. Elsewhere Twichell writes to Clemens of "bathing our souls and bodies in the delicious tinted light of the wood paths of Talcott Mountain...and, having a *talk*, old fellow," letter of October 22, 1878, MTP.

37. From the Windham *County Transcript*, December 2, 1874. Cutting in Twichell's *Journals*, Beinecke. For more on Weston see running history and memorabilia Web site http://www.runningpast.com/pedestrian.htm (accessed March 25, 2009).

38. Interview with Clemens ("written for the Boston *Times*") pasted in Twichell's *Journals*, Beinecke.

39. November 13, 1874, Frank and Smith, *Mark Twain's Letters*, 6: 281.

40. Pasted in Twichell's *Journals*, Beinecke.

41. Twichell's *Journals*, November 16, 1874, Beinecke. Howells commented on Clemens's condition on arriving at his Boston party: "I never saw a more used-up, hungrier man....It was something fearful to see him

eat escalloped oysters." See George Arms, Christoph K. Lohmann, and Jerry Heron, eds., *W. D. Howells. Selected Letters*, vol. 2: *1873–1881* (Boston: Twayne, 1979), 76.

42. Twichell's *Journals*, November 17, 1874, Beinecke.

43. "Fastidious friend," a variant of "purist," is crossed out in the manuscript pages of *The Innocents Adrift*, MTP, 107, 107A and 107B. Beside "my friend who was a clergyman," Clemens put a note (dated 1894), "Rev. Joseph H. Twichell of Hartford."

44. Ms. of *The Innocents Adrift*, MTP, 107B–14. Clemens then adds "a neat little sequel" to the story. For at breakfast the next day is "a New England woman of fifty...[with] a face with a religious cast, & refined withal—the true New England type" and a "gentle & quiet little miss" of eleven or twelve. The "dominie" lets out a "deep sigh from a grateful heart" for the "protection" thus offered against "the unspeakable hostler." The hostler then tears in, carrying a sheet of ice and telling how "the whole pond's froze solid, & the geese's legs are froze tight *in* it," and bursting "like a Johnstown Dam...turn[ing] loose a spraying & tossing flood of profane expletives...." Neither woman nor child turns a hair, being totally accustomed to his "breed of talk" (115–17).

45. Mark Twain, "Some Rambling Notes of an Idle Excursion," in *The Stolen White Elephant, Etc.* (New York: Oxford University Press, 1996 [1882]), 36. The narrative was based on the two men's trip to Bermuda in May 1877.

46. Ibid., 67. Howells wrote to Clemens that on reading his "Bermuda papers" aloud to his wife, this joke "about killed us." See Henry Nash Smith and William M. Gibson, eds., *Mark Twain-Howells Letters: The Correspondence of Samuel L. Clemens and William D. Howells, 1872–1910* (Cambridge, Mass.: Harvard University Press, 1960), 185.

47. "Some Rambling Notes of an Idle Excursion," 87–88.

48. Another of the colorfully unconventional but good-hearted characters in whom both Clemens and Twichell took delight. Clemens first met Wakeman on the steamship *America* on the first leg of his journey back east from California in 1866. Twichell (coincidentally) met him on a trip to Peru eight years later. Twichell's appreciation of the eccentric captain is clear in the letter he wrote to Clemens from on board the S. S. "Colon" on August 22, 1874: "I never was more entertained in my life....What a delicious old misanthrope he is—what an entertaining denunciator! And, oh Mark, what a titanic commentator on the Old Testament!!", MTP.

49. Mark Twain, *A Tramp Abroad* (New York: Oxford University Press, 1996 [1880]), 17. See Courtney, *Joseph Hopkins Twichell*, 182 and 201, on the way Twichell acted as Clemens's "agent" in another way, too.

50. Russell Banks, "Introduction" to *A Tramp Abroad*, xxxii–iii.

51. *A Tramp Abroad*, 116–21. This incident was in fact based on one which occurred in Munich, with Olivia Clemens as the other party involved: "I...transferred the adventure to our big room in the hotel in Heilbronn, & got it on paper a good deal to my satisfaction." Letter to Twichell, January 26, 1879, MTP.

52. *A Tramp Abroad*, 299.

53. Ibid., "Afterword," 5.

54. Beinecke.

55. All quotations in this section of the chapter are from Twichell's *Journals*, Beinecke.

56. See the Yale University Web site, http://www.yale.edu/publicart/woolsey.html. Accessed March 25, 2009.

57. For more on this incident, see Steve Courtney, "Afterword: The Lee Ivy," in Messent and Courtney, *Civil War Letters of Joseph Hopkins Twichell*, 311–18.

58. Earlier, in June 1878, he had attended an Army of the Potomac reunion in Springfield ("a three days feast of military delights mixed with thrilling memories and much patriotic emotion"). In the summer of 1888 (June 29–July 5), he and Harmony attended the Grand Reunion of the Army of the Potomac and Army of Northern Virginia at Gettysburg where Twichell gave an address "at the laying of the corner stone of the Excelsior Brigade monument." Twichell's *Journals*, Beinecke.

59. Twichell and Clemens were radically opposed in their views of Roosevelt. Clemens would characterise him as "all bluster, all pow-wow, all gas," in a June 24, 1905, letter to Twichell.

60. The former was a major transcultural initiative managed by an American-educated Chinese man and Hartford resident, Yung Wing, whose work was strongly supported by Twichell. Yung Wing and his boys (sent from China to New England to educate, and Christianize, them) would figure repeatedly in Twichell's Journals. Clemens would facilitate and attend a meeting with General Grant in December 1880 to get his help in an attempt (temporarily successful) to urge the Chinese not to close down the mission. Despite Grant's intervention the mission soon collapsed, perhaps because of internal conflicts between Wing and other interested Chinese parties. And in the United States, in 1882, the Chinese Exclusion Act was passed. For more on Twichell, Yung Wing, and the mission, see Courtney, *Joseph Hopkins Twichell*, 144–48 and 201–207.

61. Only one other minister in the community—a noted Episcopalian civic reformer—spoke against Blaine.

62. Details and quotations here are from Courtney, *Joseph Hopkins Twichell*, 217–19.

63. Letter in Twichell's *Journals*, dated March 14, 1887. Both men seem to have put the scandal in which Beecher was involved (the 1875 court case concerning the accusation of adultery with Elizabeth Tilton, the wife of his religious associate Theodore Tilton) behind them by this point. When Beecher died (on March 8), Twichell wrote: "To me an occasion of inexpressible sorrow.... So passes the greatest man I ever knew.... No mind has had such influence on mine, unless it be Dr. Bushnell; and no character, unless it be my father." *Journals*, Beinecke.

64. Clemens to Twichell, January 25, 1889, Beinecke.

65. See Courtney, *Joseph Hopkins Twichell*, 205–6.

66. See ibid., 102–5.

67. Clemens evidently read this, when Twichell sent it to him, and was apparently generous in his response, for Twichell wrote, "I am delighted and proud...that you managed to pull through 'John Winthrop,' and could say that you found it interesting." See letters from Twichell to Clemens, November 18, 1891, and February 2, 1892, MTP. Clemens describes Twichell's talents as an oral performer but his weakness in terms of written expression in Smith and Gibson, eds., *Mark Twain-Howells Letters*, 380–81.

68. Twichell's *Journals*, Beinecke.

69. Twichell's *Journals*, June 26, 1880, Beinecke.

70. Twichell's *Journals*, Beinecke.

71. Courtney, *Joseph Hopkins Twichell*, p. xv. There is little information available on Harmony—in contrast to the considerable archive material on her husband. Courtney gives evidence of a good degree of intimacy with Olivia Clemens, when—"probably in June 1881 at the beginning of her seventh pregnancy," she wrote to Olivia in heartfelt (and negative) terms about it, and—by implication—about Joe's unwillingness to consider easing off on this reproductive front. Toward the end of the pregnancy she asked (secretly) to borrow money from Olivia for her household needs, but it is likely that it was given instead as a gift ("Livy I have had a good *'joyful'* cry over your goodness to me"). Olivia also offered to "nurse [Harmony] through the final month of her pregnancy and the birth of Sarah Dunham Twichell [in February 1882].... [I]n August she was pregnant again," pp. 223–24. Annie Moffett Webster (on reading Dixon Wecter's 1948 book, *Mark Twain in Three Moods*) would later comment: "Someone once asked Uncle Sam how many children Mr. Twichell had. He said 'I don't know. I haven't heard from him since morning'" (MTP).

72. All from Twichell's *Journals*, Beinecke. See Andrews for a fascinating account of the same 1876–77 New Year's Eve events at Isabella Beecher Hooker's house (also attended, early on, by Clemens), *Nook Farm*, 59–61.

73. Twichell's *Journals*, Beinecke.

74. Twichell's *Journals*, May 8, 1882, Beinecke. Clemens and his wife also offered to pay for Julie's education at Smith College (see *Journals*, May 25, 1887). They also helped the Twichells financially on a number of occasions. When members of his church gave Twichell the deeds to his house (previously rented) and four thousand dollars toward its improvement, as a fiftieth birthday gift, the Clemenses were among the major contributors. In July 1905, Clemens gave the Twichells—always apparently on the brink financially—$1500. He told Joe this was "conscience-money" after a Wall Street profit (see July 13 letter, Beinecke) though in fact it was Rogers who had secretly stepped in to help. Joe and Harmony were rendered "dazed like" by "the avalanche": "You have paid every earthly cent we owe.... [Y]ou have put us financially where we never were before.... [T]he thoughts of our hearts toward you and upon you are quite unspeakable" (July 15 letter, MTP).

75. July 21, 1903, letter, MTP. In May 1907, Harmony would go to work in the Henry Street settlement in New York (see Twichell's *Journals*, Beinecke).

76. See October 21, 1904, telegram, Twichell Family Scrapbooks, and October 23 letter (Beinecke). Despite—and perhaps because of—the apparently close, religious, and wholesome quality of the Twichell family circle, not all the children adjusted easily to life's demands outside it. Daughter Sally suffered debilitating illness (with "overtaxed...nerves"), while David suffered a "nervous breakdown resulting from overwork" and would later commit suicide. Twichell's *Journals*, July 4–6, 1903, and Twichell Family Scrapbooks, March 1913, Beinecke.

77. As Joseph Hooker Twichell told Dixon Wecter in July 1947, MTP. And see Clemens's July 21, 1903, letter to Twichell (Beinecke).

78. MTP. Similarly Clemens is "Uncle Mark" throughout David C. Twichell's 1910 memoranda on his mother's death, Beinecke. See Dixon Wecter, ed., *The Love Letters of Mark Twain* (New York: Harper, 1949) for other indications of such closeness (313, for example).

79. One wonders how Clemens reacted to Twichell's making the meetings of the Monday Evening Club alcohol-free when held at his house: "At the supper [which accompanied the meeting] we observed the rule we

have now for a good while followed as part of our Total Abstinence faith and furnished no alcoholic drinks—not even beer. It was something of a trial to us to do so... as ours is the only house where the Club is entertained that is 'dry' in this way" (Twichell's *Journals*, December 3, 1877). On the Stanley dinner, see the *Journals*, December 8, 1886, Beinecke. For information on the baseball banquet, see the cutting in Asylum Hill Church Parish Memorabilia, Connecticut State Library: "One of the features of the occasion was a witty speech by Mark Twain. The Rev. J. H. Twichell of Hartford, Conn., said a prayer."

80. November 18, 1874, Twichell's *Journals*, Beinecke. Twichell had recently returned from Peru investigating the condition of Chinese laborers there with Yung Wing.

81. April 2–5, 1886, Twichell's *Journals*, Beinecke.

82. Letter to Clemens, August 26, 1881, MTP. In 1898, reporting on the family holiday, he gives a good idea of their day-to-day activity: "We did the customary things, climbing mountains, making excursions into the woods, fishing (but not much) and, (some of us) playing a good deal of golf.... [W]e did much bathing in the fine pool below the 'Waldrushe' [?] cliff," Twichell's *Journals*, Beinecke. Twichell associated the "lonesome wilderness" with a "sense of the nearness of God" (See his "Pastor's Letter to the Sunday School from 'The Adirondacks,'" August 1871, Asylum Hill Church Parish Memorabilia, Connecticut State Library).

83. Letter to Clemens from Franconia, New Hampshire, September 8, 1883, MTP.

84. July 21, 1875, Hartford *Courant* clipping pasted in Twichell's *Journals*, Beinecke.

85. MTP photocopy (original, Vassar College, Poughkeepsie, N.Y.). An earlier part of the letter reads, "We had a noble good time in the yacht [H. H. Rogers's *Kanawha* ] and caught a China missionary & drowned him."

86. May 20, 1877, Twichell's *Travel Diaries*, Beinecke.

87. August 9, 1878, *Travel Diaries*, Beinecke.

88. *Travel Diaries*, Beinecke.

89. Twichell's *Journals*, Beinecke.

90. January 4, 1907, *Travel Diaries*, Beinecke. Twichell evidently "warned her that she was making Clemens too lazy, but Lyon was undeterred. "'I'm glad I can spoil the King,' she concluded, 'that is all my meat and drink and life in these days,'" quoted in Karen Lystra, *Dangerous Intimacy: The Untold Story of Mark Twain's Final Years* (Berkeley and Los Angeles: University of California Press, 2004), 102. "The King" was what Lyon generally called Clemens.

91. Isabel Lyon, *Diary* entries January 3–7, 1907, MTP. Hamlin Hill quotes a further entry: "He can scarcely tolerate Mr. Twichell, who does reminisce over the trivial ones of the earth until the King begins to show a blue flame out of him," *Mark Twain: God's Fool* (New York: Harper & Row, 1973), 160. Back in America, on April 13, 1907, Lyon writes: "Mr. & Mrs. Twichell arrived and [I am] so tired—so tired. They are nice & dear, but killingly hard to entertain, for Mr. Twichell's deafness is increasing" (Lyon *Diary*, MTP). As early as April 1880, Clemens notes Twichell's tendency not to hear what others (in this case Olivia) are saying, though at this point it seems to have to do with selective attention rather than deafness. He writes Howells how Twichell is "so unbearably aggravating to Mrs. Clemens when her voice ceases from an animated narrative, & Joe responds 'Well, Livy, how are they all at Elmira?' (not having heard a word of her

yarn.)," *Mark Twain-Howells Letters*, 300–1. As far as Lyon's comments about Twichell go, it is of course possible that, as Courtney implies, Lyon's "fiercely possessive" attitude toward Clemens affected her perception of the two men's relationship: see *Joseph Hopkins Twichell*, 258.

92. Twichell's *Journals*, Beinecke. Twichell pasted in a newspaper clipping, presumably from the *Courant*: "TWO HUNDRED AND FIVE DOLLARS REWARD—At the great base ball match on Tuesday, while I was engaged in hurrahing, a small boy walked off with an English-made brown silk UMBRELLA belonging to me, and forgot to bring it back. I will pay $5 for the return of that umbrella in good condition to my house on Farmington avenue. I do not want the boy (in an active state) but will pay two hundred dollars for his remains—SAMUEL L. CLEMENS."

93. Twichell's *Journals*, Beinecke. A newspaper clipping in the Twichell Family Scrapbooks (undated but placed alongside later 1896–97 material) reads: "Mark Twain and Rev. Joseph H. Twichell of Hartford, who were enthusiastic bicycle riders, were pedalling along side by side one day, when the author of "Roughing It" suddenly took a 'header.' Mr. Twichell slowed up and was about to dismount to aid his friend, when Mr. Clemens said: 'Don't stop, Joe; go right along. I think I'll stop here awhile and swear,'" Beinecke.

94. Letter to Twichell, July 20, 1883, MTP (photocopy).

95. Twichell to Clemens letter, July 22, 1883, MTP. And see the August 22 letter to Howells, *Mark Twain-Howells Letters*, 438–39.

96. Letter to Clemens, September 8, 1883, MTP.

97. See Courtney, *Joseph Hopkins Twichell*, 185–86.

98. Beinecke. Twichell himself occasionally shows a bawdy note as he writes to Clemens, though he steers clear of sexual innuendo. Speaking of his sponsor, Mr. Case, and his bladder problems, on an 1882 Europe visit, Twichell writes of the extreme temperature in the Swiss mountains, "so cold that my moustache froze solid,—and as for the old gentleman he lost his 'holt' on his bladder entirely. My sakes, how it *did* fetch the urine out of him. I thought he'd make a new glacier." Letter of September 20, 1882, MTP.

99. Beinecke.

100. *A Tramp Abroad*, "Introduction," p. xxxv.

101. Letter to Harmony Twichell, August 23, 1878, Beinecke.

102. Letter of June 25, 1877, MTP.

103. Letter of June 8, 1878, MTP.

104. Joseph Hooker Twichell, told to Dixon Wecter, July 1947, MTP.

105. Letter of November 20, 1893, Beinecke.

106. Joseph Hooker Twichell to Dixon Wecter, July 1947, MTP.

107. See the final section of chapter 1.

108. See chapter 1, n. 102.

109. I am not suggesting deliberate intent here, but rather giving an underlying cultural explanation for the friendship and the way it worked.

110. Harold K. Bush Jr., *Mark Twain and the Spiritual Crisis of His Age* (Tuscaloosa: University of Alabama Press, 2007) 161–62.

111. Twichell's *Journals*, clipping with others marked "[v]arious things that may some day be of interest to my children," Beinecke.

112. Twichell Family Scrapbooks, Beinecke. Taken from a report of "M.T's 'Pilgrim's' dinner" (London, July 1907) by Professor Norton of Hartford.

113. Mary Lawton, *A Lifetime with Mark Twain: The Memories of Katy Leary, for Thirty Years His Faithful and Devoted Servant* (New York: Harcourt, Brace, 1925) 207.

114. A "Tribute" to Olivia Clemens in the Hartford *Courant* pasted in Twichell's *Journals*. After Olivia's death, Isabel Lyon would take (for a time) something of her place.

115. Twichell's *Journals*.

116. July 11, 1904, Twichell's *Journals*.

117. In Twichell's Family Scrapbooks, Beinecke.

118. David C. Twichell, "Memoranda on His Mother's Death, 1910," Beinecke. Clemens's letter of June 18, 1904, read: "Dear Joe; It is 13 days. I am bewildered and must remain so for a time longer. It was so sudden, so unexpected. Imagine a man worth a hundred millions who finds himself suddenly penniless & fifty millions in debt in his old age. I was richer than any other person in the world, and now I am that pauper without a peer. Some day I will tell you about it, not now. Mark" (MTP). The notion of reciprocity mentioned here, of two men sharing a friendship of some intensity, took a peculiarly physical form in the similarity they came to share in their appearance and manner. In a letter of February 2, 1892, Twichell tells Clemens how a visiting missionary saw a portrait of Clemens and turned to Twichell to say "that is an excellent likeness of you. It is lifelike; and reproduces one of your characteristic expressions perfectly," MTP. Clara Clemens too would note the two men's similarities: see Smith and Gibson, eds., *Mark Twain-Howells Letters*, 816 n. 1. This is a touch eerie given Clemens's literary obsession with twins and doubles. Or do some friends, like dogs and their owners, grow more and more alike over time?

*Chapter 3*

1. This latter "diminishing belief" was particularly the case for Clemens. And see William E. Phipps, *Mark Twain's Religion* (Macon, Ga.: Mercer University Press, 2003), 355–56.

2. See Harold K. Bush Jr., who lists some of the reasons for the "emerging spiritual crisis" of the period in *Mark Twain and the Spiritual Crisis of His Age* (Tuscaloosa: University of Alabama Press, 2007), 2–4.

3. "The Revised Catechism," in Mark Twain, *Collected Tales, Sketches, Speeches, & Essays 1852–1890* (New York: Library of America, 1992), 539. William ("Boss") Tweed was New York's Commissioner of Public Works accused in 1871 of massive financial corruption and misdealing.

4. Stanley Brodwin, "Mark Twain's Theology: The Gods of a Brevet Presbyterian," in Forrest G. Robinson, ed., *The Cambridge Companion to Mark Twain* (Cambridge: Cambridge University Press, 1995), 220–48 (this quotation is on 221).

5. Ibid., p. 231. Recent analysis of Clemens and religion includes Harold K. Bush Jr., "'A Moralist in Disguise': Mark Twain and American Religion," in Shelley Fisher Fishkin, ed., *A Historical Guide to Mark Twain* (New York: Oxford University Press, 2002), and his book, *Mark Twain and the Spiritual Crisis of his Age* (2007). Bush takes a very different perspective from my own, insisting that Clemens's "literary and public career" be seen "as a profoundly moral and religious one," and affirming his "truly spiritual legacy" (*Mark Twain and the Spiritual Crisis of his Age*, 19 and 284). I find a tendency in his work to collapse the difference between "religion" and ethics. Nonetheless he does balance the picture I present by reminding us that Clemens seems never to have completely rejected conventional Christian rhetoric and even, perhaps, beliefs ("A Moralist in Disguise," 67–68 and 84). He also gives a valuable account of liberal Protestantism

in the period and of Clemens's place in the American jeremiad tradition. William E. Phipps's *Mark Twain's Religion* (2003) contains much useful information on religion in the period (the sections on the Langdon family background and on Thomas Beecher, and their joint influence on the Clemenses, are especially illuminating) and pays close attention to the way Clemens's language and thinking are imbued with religious ideas. Like Bush, he tends to equate Clemens's "religious" qualities with his compassionate nature (see 373). My emphasis is rather on that "utter rejection of institutional religion and biblical orthodoxy in general" to which Bush also refers ("A Moralist in Disguise," 79).

6. Bush and Phipps both discuss Clemens's relationship with Twichell, as does Courtney in *Joseph Hopkins Twichell: The Life and Times of Mark Twain's Closest Friend* (Athens: Georgia University Press, 2008), Dwayne Eutsey's essays on Clemens and liberal religion also refer to Twichell. See "The Influence of Liberal Religion on Mark Twain," *The Journal of Liberal Religion* 1, no. 2 (April 2000) at http://www.meadville.edu/journal/ 2000_eutsey_1_2.pdf (accessed March 25, 2009), and "Was Huck a Unitarian? Christian Liberalism, Joseph Twichell, and Mark Twain's *Huckleberry Finn,*" *Soundings* 88 (Spring–Summer 2005) pp. 43–70.

7. Twichell to Clemens, March 13, 1905. MTP.

8. See, though, n. 12.

9. Clemens's letter of December 29 or 30, 1875, is inserted into Twichell's *Journal.* Clemens adds: "Joe, you can sell the above to some religious paper...." And see Michael B. Frank and Harriet Elinor Smith, eds., *Mark Twain's Letters*, vol. 6: *1874–1875* (Berkeley and Los Angeles: University of California Press, 2002), 600–1, n. 1, and 606.

10. See, for instance, Leland Krauth, *Proper Mark Twain* (Athens: University of Georgia Press, 1999).

11. Leah A. Strong, *Joseph Twichell: Mark Twain's Friend and Pastor* (Athens: University of Georgia Press, 1966), 70.

12. Brodwin notes Clemens's "partiality to clergymen" and speculates: "Surely [he] found in these good men a part of himself, a function he could never fulfill—to make those sinners howl—and to carry the essence of Christianity sans 'ceremonies and wire-drawn creeds,'" "Mark Twain's Theology," 223. Twichell's style fits better the final part of the description: he was not one to make sinners howl. On Clemens's relation with clergymen and the changing nature of American Protestant beliefs, see too "Religion" in Gregg Camfield, *The Oxford Companion to Mark Twain* (New York: Oxford University Press, 2003), 489–94.

13. See Harriet Elinor Smith and Richard Bucci, eds., *Mark Twain's Letters*, vol. 2: *1867–68* (Berkeley and Los Angeles: University of California Press, 1990), 145–46, n. 3.

14. Ibid., Introduction, xxiii.

15. See Susan K. Harris, *The Courtship of Olivia Langdon and Mark Twain* (Cambridge: Cambridge University Press, 1996), for a fuller—and penetrating—account of the courtship (quotation from 72). See also Laura Skondera-Trombley, *Mark Twain and the Company of Women* (Philadelphia: University of Pennsylvania Press, 1994).

16. David C. Twichell, "Memoranda on His Mother's Death, 1910," Beinecke.

17. Victor Fischer and Michael B. Frank, eds., *Mark Twain's Letters*, vol. 3: *1869* (Berkeley and Los Angeles: University of California Press, 1992), 153 (March 8 and 9, 1869).

18. Smith and Bucci, *Mark Twain's Letters*, 2:xxiv. James D. Wilson reaches similar conclusions concerning "the depth and sincerity of [Clemens's] quest for religious faith" in his "Religious and Esthetic Vision in Mark Twain's Early Career," *Canadian Review of American Studies* 17 (1986): 155–72 (this quotation 167). He suggests, though, that Clemens's "reformation" started earlier, tracing it back to the *Quaker City* trip and the influence of Mrs. Fairbanks (166). He only mentions Twichell in passing. See too Bush, *Mark Twain and the Spiritual Crisis of his Age*, 61–63, and Phipps, *Mark Twain's Religion*, 100–107.

19. October 30, 1868. Smith and Bucci, *Mark Twain's Letters*, 2:271.

20. December 29, 1868. Ibid., 357. In this same letter, there is comment on the character references, from those who had known him out West, that Jervis Langdon had apparently asked Clemens (as "an almost entirely unknown person" to his future in-laws) to provide. See 358–59, 360–61 n. 2, 362 n. 5.

21. November 28, 1868. Smith and Bucci, *Mark Twain's Letters*, 2:293–94.

22. "A 'tiger' being a student shout at a regatta victory, a shrieked *T-I-I-I-I-I* followed by a roared *GER!* " Courtney, *Joseph Hopkins Twichell*, 129.

23. December 4, 1868. Smith and Bucci, *Mark Twain's Letters*, 2:305–6. Here Clemens repeats Twichell's words in a letter to Olivia.

24. See, too, ibid., 318–19, 331–32, 336; and Fischer and Frank, *Mark Twain's Letters*, 3:101, 102–3, etc.

25. December 9 and 10, 1868. Smith and Bucci, *Mark Twain's Letters*, 2:318–19.

26. See Fischer and Frank, *Mark Twain's Letters*, 3:439; and Victor Fischer and Michael B. Frank, eds., *Mark Twain's Letters*, vol. 4: *1870–1871* (Berkeley and Los Angeles: University of California Press, 1995), 125, 127, 144, 162, 167, and 169, n. 7. The Twichells had two young children (of their eventual nine) at this point, Edward Carrington (born August 1867) and Julia Curtis (born January 1869).

27. See, for instance, Fischer and Frank, *Mark Twain's Letters*, 3:97 n. 5, 195–96 and 265–66.

28. Ibid., 103. A letter to Twichell on the previous day reads: "my future wife wants me to be surrounded by a good moral & religious atmosphere (for I shall unite with the church as soon as I am located,) & so she likes the idea of living in Hartford," 101.

29. Fischer and Frank, *Mark Twain's Letters*, 4:xxviii.

30. The Hartford house was not put on the market till 1902, but the death there of daughter Susy and the deaths of other local friends made thoughts of a return to the town after the intervening years of foreign travel unbearable: "A Hartford with no Susy Clemens in it—& no Ned Bunce—& no Libbie Hamersley! It is not the city of Hartford, it is the city of Heartbreak" (Clemens to Twichell, January 3, 1899, Beinecke).

31. See Albert Bigelow Paine, *Mark Twain: A Biography* (New York: Harper, 1912) 2:631–32.

32. Kenneth R. Andrews in *Nook Farm: Mark Twain's Hartford Circle* (Cambridge, Mass.: Harvard University Press, 1950) 72; Courtney in *Joseph Hopkins Twichell*, 199. Courtney does however add: "But it is wrong to dismiss Paine's story entirely. Clemens was thinking about the issues of life, death, and eternity in 1878, and could well have had arguments about religion with Twichell.... Clemens was growing increasingly impatient with the hypocrisy of conventional religion."

33. Beinecke. Undated, but from internal evidence—and according to Twichell's biographer, Steve Courtney (email correspondence)—written on Sunday, August 11, 1878 (see, too, Bush, *Mark Twain and the Spiritual Crisis of His Age*, 7–9). In Clemens's *Tramp Abroad* notebook, he wrote: "I keep a clergyman, to remonstrate against my drinking—it gives zest and increase of appetite" (quoted in Andrews, *Nook Farm*, 70–71).

34. David C. Twichell, "Memoranda." This might just refer to the years up to the *Tramp Abroad* trip, but the grammar of the sentence suggests something more regular and extended. I rely considerably, in this chapter and the last, on Twichell's journals and letters, and am aware of their subjective nature.

35. Andrews says that most members of this close-knit community met "two or three times a week . . . for religious exercises or secular programs," and that Clemens "usually attended services when he and his family were in Hartford" (*Nook Farm*, 50). His overview of religious activity in the Hartford of the time (25–77) is invaluable. Phipps dates the renting of the pew until 1891 in *Mark Twain's Religion*, 116.

36. Pasted in the Asylum Hill Congregationalist Church Parish Memorabilia, Connecticut State Library. See, too, Courtney, *Joseph Hopkins Twichell*, 143–44.

37. For more on Clemens and tramps see Peter Messent, "Tramps and Tourists: Europe in Mark Twain's *A Tramp Abroad*," in David Seed, ed., *Yearbook of English Studies*, 34 (2004): 138–54. The Hawley lecture took place on January 31.

38. Lin Salamo and Harriet Elinor Smith, eds., *Mark Twain's Letters*, vol. 5, *1872–1873* (Berkeley and Los Angeles: University of California Press, 1997), 287–90. Clemens repeated his "Sandwich Isles" lecture on this occasion. Net proceeds were 1,500 dollars. Courtney describes an earlier example of Clemens's engagement with Twichell's work for the Hartford poor. In October 1868, the two men visited the almshouse on the Town Farm in the fields north of Asylum Hill. Clemens listened while Twichell preached to those citizens of Hartford who, with no other help or support, had been forced to take refuge there. The two men sang hymns. "Heaven & earth, what a sight it was!" Clemens reported to Livy. "Cripples, jibbering idiots, raving madmen; thieves, rowdies, paupers; little children, stone blind; blind men & women; old, old men & women, with that sad absent look in their faces that tells of thoughts that are busy with 'the days that are no more.'" Only in the leper hospitals of Honolulu and Damascus had he seen worse than here in wealthy Hartford, he wrote. *Joseph Hopkins Twichell*, 128. For more on Hawley and Nook Farm charity see Andrews, *Nook Farm*, 130–32.

39. See Courtney, *Joseph Hopkins Twichell*, 151–57.

40. Twichell's *Journal*, quoted in Frank and Smith, *Mark Twain's Letters*, 6:393 and 403.

41. Pasted in Twichell's *Journal*. As with all such reports we cannot rely on an accurate transcription of Clemens's words, though the style of the humor is clearly his. Kenneth Andrews gives details of another prize the Clemenses donated in *Nook Farm*, p. 50. For a full transcription of the *Courant* article, see Frank and Smith, *Mark Twain's Letters*, 6:659–63.

42. Asylum Hill Church Parish Memorabilia, Connecticut State Library. And see Andrews, *Nook Farm*, 50.

43. Twichell's *Journals*, Beinecke (and see Frank and Smith, *Mark Twain's Letters*, 6:497).

44. Letter from Twichell to Clemens, MTP.

45. Letter from Twichell to Clemens, March 25, 1880, and note from Clemens to Twichell, February 16, 1881, MTP. Clemens's note follows a letter from Charles Dudley Warner (forwarded by Clemens to Twichell) where Warner speaks of going "to talk tonight to the Young Men of Dr. Storr's church [in Brooklyn]—same such lecture humbug as Joe gets up in his." Clemens signals his preference for unadvertised appearances (presumably to keep the occasion low-key and relatively small) on a number of Hartford occasions.

46. As previously mentioned, Julia's trip was funded by the Clemens family. Twichell's *Journal* for May 8, 1882, reads: "H[armony] is heroic, as usual, in accepting her lot as a stay-at-home while I am off at liberty. How I wish she were free to go too," *Journals*, Beinecke.

47. Letter from Twichell to Clemens, July 11, 1882, MTP.

48. Strong, *Joseph Hopkins Twichell*, 92. Harold K. Bush Jr., too, says that Clemens "regularly participated in the social and religious activities of the Asylum Hill Congregational Church, pastored by Twichell, throughout his major period from 1871 to 1889," "A Moralist in Disguise," 72. And see Bush, *Mark Twain and the Spiritual Crisis of His Age*, chapters 3 and 4.

49. Letter from Twichell to Clemens, MTP. Twichell does mention Clemens's recent absences from church in this same letter ("I was thinking that . . . you . . . were feeling enough better to begin wishing you had gone to Church more of late . . ."), though he notes a report in the paper of his friend having suffered from rheumatism and malaria: "But if you have had the rheumatism—*and* malaria—It is too bad; indeed it is—and I won't moralize, at least not this time."

50. Twichell's *Journal*, Beinecke (the reception took place on May 27, 1888).

51. In the Twichell Papers (Beinecke), there is a notebook marked "Contributors of the Gift of 125 Woodland St.," with "Givers of the Testimonial to the Rev. Joseph H. Twichell May 27, 1888" written inside its cover. Clemens is named here as a donor.

52. Andrews, *Nook Farm*, 70. Clemens was ridiculing conventional religious beliefs regarding the Biblical representation of God by the early 1870s. See Howard G. Baetzhold and Joseph B. McCullough, *The Bible According to Mark Twain* (Athens: University of Georgia Press, 1995), 313–17.

53. Beinecke.

54. Stanley Brodwin in "Mark Twain's Theology" argues, however, that Twain's early religious environment would always affect him. Pointing to "Hannibal's Presbyterian ethos" and its effect on the young Clemens, he suggests that the author "never quite shook off the literalism of frontier Christianity" (233). Andrews points out (crucially) the changed nature of religion and especially the development of liberal Congregationalism in Hartford in the period. Talking of three local ministers (including Twichell) he says: "They were instinctively adapted to the new post-War atmosphere. . . . Their status derived almost entirely from the strength of their personal hold on their fellows. . . . Their churches became institutions for community good works and centers of information and appropriate recreation. . . . The individual's right to determine his own relationship to God would not be contested so long as personal morality, necessary for a secure society, was not threatened and public morality not undermined." Clemens, he notes, "did not ever feel called upon to conceal the true nature of his religious views from his neighbors, or, for example, from the full

membership of the Monday Evening Club [to which Twichell also belonged], upon which he often practised his heresies" (*Nook Farm*, 49, 69, and 70).

55. Letter from Twichell to Clemens, October 2, 1881, MTP.

56. Letter to James M. Tuohy, Vienna, November 10, 1898, MTP (photocopy). After Clemens's 1902 sixty-seventh birthday dinner in New York, Twichell pasted into his journal a newspaper clipping reporting a part of Clemens's speech: "It would have been better for me spiritually and financially if I had stayed under (Twichell's) wing." Twichell added, "said M. T.—(or something like it) and a good deal more in praise of an ancient friendship." Twichell's *Journal*, Beinecke.

57. See Andrews, *Nook Farm*, 69.

58. That quote was taken from a Review of Albert Bigelow Paine's edition of *The Letters of Mark Twain*, "Editor's Easy Chair," *Harper's Magazine* (March 1918), p. 603. The typescript of this piece (with handwritten corrections) is in the Houghton Library, Harvard University, bMS Am 1784.2 (36), and used with its permission. Variants in that typescript include the following: "the prevailing scientific agnosticism and negation" rather than "the prevailing scientific agnosticism"; and "his church-going became absolutely hollow and meaningless," rather than "his church-going became a meaningless form." Howells's identification of Calvinism with the 1870s seems off-target. It was certainly true however of Clemens's boyhood world.

59. Andrews argues that Clemens was gradually alienated from Hartford even as he resided there, especially in his later years: *Nook Farm*, 124–26. On November 17, 1899, Clemens would write to Twichell from London, apparently regarding the prospect of a return to Hartford: "Livy says she is going to attend your church, whether I do or not. I think she'd like me to, for it is a principle with her to manufacture as many hypocrites as she can, where its [*sic*] a hypocrisy that's smug and respectable." MTP.

60. Despite Howells's words, quoted at the start of this chapter, about doubt hardening into denial, Clemens, it seems, accepted the existence of God, but a very different God from the one represented in conventional Christianity. One version of this God was as cruel and capricious: "...the swindle of life and the treachery of a God that can create disease and misery and crime—create things that men would be condemned for creating—that men would be ashamed to create" (quoted in Isabel Lyon's *Journal*, February 2, 1906: http://www.twainquotes.com/God.html. This Web site with quotations, newspaper collections, and related Mark Twain resources, is run by Twain scholar, Barbara Schmidt, and was accessed March 25, 2009). Another was of a God operating on a cosmic level, and thus giving little or no consideration to earth and the human race inhabiting it. See Phipps, *Mark Twain's Religion*, 263–77, for more on Clemens's changing and often contradictory views on this topic. He did, though, come to deny the value of formal religious belief, and Phipps quotes an 1885 letter to Charles Stoddard that reads, "I have found... perfect peace...in absolute unbelief," (1). Like many of those living at the turn of the century, he seems to have wavered from belief to unbelief on the subject of an afterlife: see ibid., 299–304.

61. Letter from Twichell to Clemens, August 24, 1900, MTP.

62. Letter from Clemens to Twichell, Beinecke. For Clemens, the "risk" was in terms of the time and trouble it would take him to prepare such a critique for publication in a form that would suit him ("I have a family to support, & I can't afford this kind of dissipation"). But public reputation and

Clemens's sense of his position within the larger American community must also have figured here. See too the important April 17, 1909, letter to Howells (quoted at the start of this book) where Clemens speaks of his three main friendships in terms of the pouring out of his inmost and most extreme thoughts in unsent letters: "I will fire the profanities at Rogers, the indecencies at Howells, the theologies at Twichell," Smith and Gibson, *Mark Twain-Howells Letters*, 845. Often, in Twichell's case, such letters *were* sent.

63. Courtney writes in *Joseph Hopkins Twichell* that: "In 1869 Twichell considered a Middle Eastern mission, possibly to Turkey, where there was a strong New England Congregational presence established by the American Board for Foreign Missions.... But for now, especially with three small children and demanding and affectionate friends and parishioners, ... it was getting harder for Twichell to think about going anywhere else. Asylum Hill Church, after all, was a mission of sorts, if a mission to the well-to-do," 142.

64. Twichell "was proud of his pamphlet-length accounts of the lives of two English missionaries [Ion Keith-Falconer and John Coleridge Pattison] that had been reprinted and widely circulated," ibid., 265.

65. MTP.

66. Letter from Clemens to Twichell, August 12, 1900, Beinecke. Clemens does not, at this time, seem to have been so concerned about missionary activity elsewhere (and see his June 1901 letter to Twichell where he writes, "Whenever you ask people to support [foreign missions], Joe, *do* bar China"). Later, however, he widens his attack on this "criminal industry": "Joe, where is the fairness in the missionary's trade? His prey is the children: he cannot convert adults. He beguiles the little children to forsake their parents' religion & break their hearts.... To my mind the Christian missionary is easily the most criminal criminal that exists on the planet" (April 19, 1909, MTP). Twichell was a keen supporter of the missions, and (as Courtney points out) Clemens's "reference to beguiling little children—which Twichell and Yung [Wing] had been quite frank about doing when the Chinese students were in Hartford—was particularly cutting," *Joseph Hopkins Twichell*, 266.

67. January 29, 1901, MTP. See also Clemens's letter to Twichell of November 4, 1904, on the latter's public political interventions: "Oh, dear! get *out* of that sewer—party-politics—dear Joe..." (Beinecke).

68. Letter of January 27, 1900, in Paine, *Mark Twain's Letters* 2:695.

69. MTP. William M. Gibson quotes more of this letter in his Introduction to Mark Twain, *The Mysterious Stranger* (Berkeley and Los Angeles: University of California Press, 1969). There is an interesting early letter to Olivia of October 30, 1868, where Clemens reports his and Twichell's discussion of how those who *"think in words"* communicate with those born deaf and dumb, who "knew no *words* at all" (Twichell's church was just up the road from the American Asylum, the first school for the deaf in the United States). In Twichell's response to this question, framed in terms of a positive spiritual vision, we may see the germ for Clemens's later, secular and bleakly solipsistic vision: "He said we *didn't* always think in words—that our highest, grandest, most brilliant thoughts were far beyond our capacity to frame into words, & that we *had* no words that would express them....And he said something like this—I have the substance I think, but I have forgotten his language: But some day this tramelling flesh will be stripped away, this prison-house thrown open & the soul set

free—free to expand to its just magnitude—& *then* what thoughts we shall have! what visions!" In Smith and Bucci, *Mark Twain's Letters* 2:272.

70. Letter from Twichell to Clemens, September 5, 1901, MTP. Brodwin allows that Clemens's later determinism may have been, in part, "a secular version of Calvinistic predestination." He points out, however, that Clemens's "scientific theory of mechanical causality most likely derived from his early readings in eighteenth-century thought . . . reinforced by his familiarity with nineteenth-century concepts of determinism," "Mark Twain's Theology," 233.

71. Letter to Twichell, January 8, 1900, MTP.

72. "Public Meeting under the Auspices of the American Academy and the National Institute of Arts and Letters, held at Carnegie Hall, New York, November 30, 1910, in Memory of Samuel Langhorne Clemens (Mark Twain)," American Academy of Arts and Letters, 1922 (MTP).

73. November 4, 1904, as previously quoted (n. 67), Beinecke. The cancellation (and what then follows) does not figure in the Paine version of the *Letters*.

74. Twichell to Clemens, September 28, 1902, MTP.

75. This section of Twichell's speech comes from a newspaper report of the Memorial Meeting in the Twichell Family Scrapbooks (Beinecke).

76. Though see my comments at the end of chapter two.

77. Letter from Twichell to Clemens, MTP.

78. Letter from Twichell to Clemens, August 17, 1904, MTP.

79. David C. Twichell, "Memoranda," 1910. Twichell's son alludes to the short letter of June 18, 1904 (see n. 118, chapter 2). This act is an unusual one, and perhaps suggests a further dimension to the two men's relationship—that, for Twichell, Clemens was someone whose considerable verbal skills and ability to articulate emotion could be appreciated and used, but not matched.

80. David C. Twichell, "Memoranda," 1910.

81. Letter from Twichell to Clemens, March 13, 1905, MTP.

82. Paine, *Mark Twain's Letters* 2:767–70.

83. The words are William James's on the advance of liberal Christianity (see Phipps, *Mark Twain's Religion*, 122). On July 16, 1900, Clemens would (conversely) write to Twichell from Dollis Hill (England): "And look at South Africa—that black blot upon England. Let us hope there is no hereafter; I don't want to train with any angels made out of human material. Europe is going to sup in hell, there in China, I think, and will richly deserve it. . . . I believe the human race is filthier today than it ever was before; & that is saying much," MTP.

84. While wary of an identification of author with character, Daniel G. Williams notes that: "In Howells's novel, *The Rise of Silas Lapham*, Bromfield Corey argues in an Arnoldian vein that "[a]ll civilisation comes through literature now, especially in our country. Once we were softened, if not polished, by religion, but I suspect that the pulpit counts for much less now in civilising," *Ethnicity and Cultural Authority: From Arnold to DuBois* (Edinburgh: Edinburgh University Press, 2006), 89–90.

*Chapter 4*

1. Howells to Clemens, November 25, 1908, Henry Nash Smith and William M. Gibson, eds., *Mark Twain-Howells Letters: The Correspondence of Samuel L. Clemens and William D. Howells, 1872–1910* (Cambridge,

Mass.: Harvard University Press, 1960), 838. My epigraph, Clemens to Howells, the opening greeting in a letter headed "'Artford, Hapril 19/81," is from Smith and Gibson, *Mark Twain-Howells Letters*, 363.

2. In his March 24, 1874, letter to Thomas Bailey Aldrich, Clemens gives Twichell's response to the Aldrich family's recent Hartford visit: "Old Joe Twichell, that born prince of men, was in last night, & he is still gloating over the joys of that time. He says that next to being great one's self, is the luxury of meeting the great, face to face." Michael B. Frank and Harriet Elinor Smith, eds., *Mark Twain's Letters*, vol. 6: *1874–1875* (Berkeley and Los Angeles: University of California Press, 2002), 90.

3. In his *My Mark Twain: Reminiscences and Criticisms* (New York: Harper & Brothers, 1910), Howells calls his friend Clemens since "Mark Twain . . . seemed always somehow to mask him from my personal sense" (4). But Goodman and Dawson comment incisively: "The tribute [Howells's book] of course bears the title *My Mark Twain*, as though claiming for Howells alone the private man in his public role. To stretch another of his own metaphors, Howells offers a double exposure, two superimposed photographs of a complicated and sometimes baffling man. If Twain is a separate entity, the creation and alter ego of Samuel Clemens, Clemens himself often forgot or elected to blur the distinction, and so did Howells." Susan Goodman and Carl Dawson, *William Dean Howells: A Writer's Life* (Berkeley and Los Angeles: University of California Press, 2005), 151.

4. Goodman and Dawson, *William Dean Howells*, 150. At five feet, eight-and-a-half inches, Clemens was not, in fact, tall.

5. Kenneth E. Eble, *Old Clemens and W. D. H.: The Story of a Remarkable Friendship* (Baton Rouge: Louisiana State University Press, 1985). Budd's incisive essay is in *American Literary Realism*, 38 (Winter 2006): 97–114.

6. Leland Krauth, *Mark Twain & Company: Six Literary Relations* (Athens: University of Georgia Press, 2003), 49–86.

7. Goodman and Dawson, *William Dean Howells*, 148–73. Gregg Camfield's brief account of the friendship in *The Oxford Companion to Mark Twain* (New York: Oxford University Press, 2003), 267–72, is also useful.

8. January 31, 1882, Smith and Gibson, *Mark Twain-Howells Letters*, 391.

9. Quoted in Smith and Gibson, *Mark Twain-Howells Letters*, 782. Though see, too, the final comments in this chapter.

10. Krauth, *Mark Twain & Company*, 69. See 69–77 for an overall consideration of the *Letters*.

11. Goodman and Dawson, *William Dean Howells*, 158.

12. I am not ignoring the personal closeness between the two men, the easy and good-natured flow of their talk and feelings, and especially their responses to each other's domestic tragedies. I am suggesting, however, that it was their similar social and professional positioning that was the foundation allowing such other forms of intimacy free play.

13. "The Innocents Abroad" (December 1869). Reprinted in W. D. Howells, *My Mark Twain*, 112.

14. *My Mark Twain*, 3–4.

15. Ibid., 4.

16. Camfield, *The Oxford Companion to Mark Twain*, 269.

17. *My Mark Twain*, p. 6.

18. November 2, 1871. See Victor Fischer and Michael B. Frank, eds., *Mark Twain's Letters*, vol. 4: *1870–1871* (Berkeley and Los Angeles: University of California Press, 1995), 484 and 485–86, n. 3. James T. Fields and writer

Thomas Bailey Aldrich were also both present. On Howells and the *Atlantic* editorship, see Goodman and Dawson, *William Dean Howells*, 138–47 etc.

19. Goodman and Dawson, *William Dean Howells*, 153.

20. Budd, "W. D. Howells and Mark Twain," 101.

21. Goodman and Dawson, *William Dean Howells*, 167.

22. Budd recognizes a certain "coziness" and cronyism in the promotional work that Howells was always to do, both in the *Atlantic* and as a free-lancer, on his friend's behalf, "W. D. Howells and Mark Twain," 111. The line, though, between Howells's personal friendship and professional role was necessarily a narrow one, especially given his commitment to—and belief in—Clemens's literary importance and merit. See, too, Goodman and Dawson, *William Dean Howells*, 166–67.

23. Howells, *My Mark Twain*, 47.

24. From the February 1901 *North American Review* essay, "Mark Twain: An Enquiry" (*My Mark Twain*, p.181).

25. January 30, 1879, Smith and Gibson, *Mark Twain-Howells Letters*, 248.

26. August 5 and 10, 1889, Smith and Gibson, *Mark Twain-Howells Letters*, 608–9. Clemens also "gave Howells carte blanche to make corrections on the proofs of *Huck Finn*," Goodman and Dawson, *William Dean Howells*, 167.

27. And see Clemens's letter to Howells of March 23, 1878: "I owe as much to your training as the rude country job printer owes to the city boss who takes him in hand & teaches him the right way to handle his art," etc. Smith and Gibson, *Mark Twain-Howells Letters*, 226.

28. See Peter Messent, *The Short Works of Mark Twain: A Critical Study* (Philadelphia: University of Pennsylvania Press, 2001), 77–80.

29. Smith and Gibson, *Mark Twain-Howells Letters*, 42–43.

30. For instance, in Smith and Gibson, *Mark Twain-Howells Letters*, 441–42. See too the way he worked around Clemens when the latter vehemently opposed Bret Harte's consular appointment in Germany: ibid., 185, 186 n. 3, 235; and Howells's April 9, 1878, letter to President Hayes (a distant relation of wife, Elinore), George Arms and Cristoph K. Lohmann, eds., *W. D. Howells, Selected Letters*, vol. 2: *1873–1881* (Boston: Twayne, 1979) 194–95. Louis J. Budd comments: "WDH was heroically tolerant of friends" (email correspondence).

31. Goodman and Dawson, *William Dean Howells*, 167.

32. Isabel Lyon wrote in her diary (April 22, 1905): "Mr. Howells is down stairs. . . . How fine the appreciation of those two men—the one for the other—and the best of it is—that they lay their homage at each other's feet—a noble gift—& are the more lovely for the giving.—They look into each others' [*sic*] eyes & their speech is—'Oh noble you—' and it is enough," MTP.

33. January 9, 1898 Smith and Gibson, *Mark Twain-Howells Letters*, 668. And, of course, following Clemens's death, Howells would end *My Mark Twain* by calling Clemens "the Lincoln of our literature," 101.

34. January 21, 1879, Smith and Gibson, *Mark Twain-Howells Letters*, 245–46.

35. November 21, 1875, ibid., 110–11.

36. October 22, 1889, ibid., 616.

37. October 9, 1899, ibid., 707.

38. June 11, 1899, ibid., 701.

39. October 23, 1898, ibid., 680. Clemens admitted as much in his answering letter, but added the rider, "nor anywhere near half as much as I want to; still I read you all I get a chance to," 684.

40. "William Dean Howells," in *Mark Twain: Collected Tales, Sketches, Speeches & Essays 1891–1910* (New York: Library of America, 1992) 722. Peter Stoneley says of this essay: "while [Clemens's] praise is fervent, it is pitifully limited," "Mark Twain and Gender," in Messent and Budd, eds., *A Companion to Mark Twain* (Oxford: Blackwell, 2005), 75.

41. As Budd says (quoting Edward Wagenknecht), this is "all the more intriguing because . . . 'Howells wrote the kind of fiction that, when it was written by others, he often claimed he disliked,'" "W. D. Howells and Mark Twain," 110.

42. January 21, 1879, Smith and Gibson, *Mark Twain-Howells Letters*, 245.

43. March 1, 1883, ibid., 427.

44. July 21, 1885, ibid., 533.

45. Eble, *Old Clemens and W. D. H.*, 126.

46. If Clemens often disguised such critique behind his humor, and through the use of indirection.

47. Budd, "W. D. Howells and Mark Twain," 106.

48. On the professionalization of literature in the period, see my next chapter. On Clemens's financial concerns see chapter 6. Howells, despite what Eble calls his "remarkably orderly . . . career" (*Old Clemens and W. D. H.*, 161), showed an obsessive concern with money matters. Augusta Rohrbach examines this, and discusses the "canny business sense . . . inextricably bound up with his . . . literary success," in the chapter, "William Dean Howells without his Mustache," in *Truth Stranger than Fiction: Race, Realism and the U.S. Literary Marketplace* (New York: Palgrave, 2002) 73–97 (quotation, 83).

49. Robert C. Leitz III, Richard H. Ballinger, and Christoph K. Lohmann, eds., *W. D. Howells, Selected Letters*, vol. 3: *1882–1891* (Boston: Twayne, 1980) 86. The number of these schemes and the gold mine mentality behind them are—to a degree—reminiscent of Howells's father, who was "full of inventions" and proposed business schemes like the manufacturing of "paper from milkweed pods" (Goodman and Dawson, *William Dean Howells*, 93). Clemens himself became involved in one of William Cooper Howells's inventions, grape-scissors "for gathering grapes . . . with one hand and convey[ing] them without bruising to the basket. . . ." See Smith and Gibson, *Mark Twain-Howells Letters*, 437–38 etc.

50. Smith and Gibson, *Mark Twain-Howells Letters*, p. 415.

51. Ibid., quoted on 392.

52. July 13, 1875, ibid., 95.

53. September 15 and 17, 1879, ibid., 269–70. One sign of Orion's general unpredictability was his frequent changes of religious belief.

54. See Smith and Gibson, *Mark Twain-Howells Letters*, 717–18 and 818–19. And see June Howard, *Publishing the Family* (Durham, N.C.: Duke University Press. 2001).

55. For Howells's brief comments on the book, see *My Mark Twain*, 17–18.

56. April 25, 1880, Smith and Gibson, *Mark Twain-Howells Letters*, 303.

57. For Howells's description of both incidents, see *My Mark Twain*, 39–41 and 22–27.

58. April 18, 1882, Smith and Gibson, *Mark Twain-Howells Letters*, 403. The reference to "outside interference" refers to Howells and Clemens's saving of the (threatened) consular position Howells's father held in Toronto by meeting with, and relying on the influence of, Ulysses S. Grant.

59. May 5, 1886, ibid., 556. Clemens would eventually get to have the play staged in late 1887 but it quickly flopped. *The American Claimant* (1892) makes use of the play's material.

60. May 13 [15, 17], 1886, Smith and Gibson, *Mark Twain-Howells Letters*, 559–63.

61. May 19, 1886, ibid., 566. The "turn again" reference is to Howells's giving of his side of the story, and suggesting that Clemens was also partly to blame for the situation.

62. Arms and Lohmann, *W. D. Howells, Selected Letters* 2:93.

63. Ibid., 123.

64. Quoted in Goodman and Dawson, *William Dean Howells*, 379. The authors speak, too, of "the Howellses' unending quest for the perfect house," 357. That such restlessness may have originated with Elinor rather than her husband is suggested in the October 10, 1908, entry in Isabel Lyon's diary, referring to Clemens's house (Stormfield) and grounds in Redding, Connecticut: "The King [Clemens] . . . & I took a most lovely walk this morning around what we call Howells Hill, for to the Westward there is a lot that the King would gladly give to Mr. Howells, if only he would come here and build. But he can't do that for Mrs. Howells wont [*sic*] hear of his settling anywhere," MTP.

65. See too Lawton, *A Lifetime with Mark Twain: The Memories of Katy Leary, for Thirty Years His Faithful and Devoted Servant* (New York: Harcourt, Brace, 1925), 39, 92–93, 316–17, 326 and passim.

66. See Smith and Gibson, *Mark Twain-Howells Letters*, 87 and 88 n. 1.

67. October 4, 1875, ibid., 103.

68. November 30, 1876, ibid., 165. Clemens was officially staying at the Parker House. On this visit and Clemens's "lawlessness and [the Howells's] delight in allowing it" (Clemens's going for walks in muddy Cambridge in evening dress and slippers, but with "a pair of rubbers over them"), see p. 166, n. 5.

69. Goodman and Dawson, *William Dean Howells*, 148.

70. August 17, 1870, and February 13, 1903, Smith and Gibson, *Mark Twain-Howells Letters*, 324 and 764. Howells would occasionally respond in (somewhat gentler) kind: see for instance his letter to Clemens on February 21, 1907, 822–23.

71. See ibid., photo facing 719, and 723. "The thing that gravels [Howells] is, that the camera caught his private aspect, not giving him time to arrange his public one. . . . Compare this one with the impostor which he works into book-advertisements. They say, Notice this smile; observe this benignity; God be with you. . . . *This* one says, Bile! Give me more bile; fry me an optimist for breakfast." Clemens astutely caught a certain truth about his friend here as I later suggest.

72. Howells to his father, July 20, 1879, Arms and Lohmann, *W. D. Howells, Selected Letters* 2:233.

73. February 14, 1904, Smith and Gibson, *Mark Twain-Howells Letters*, 781.

74. Howells, *My Mark Twain*, 33. And see Smith and Gibson, *Mark Twain-Howells Letters*, 661–62.

75. *My Mark Twain*, 90. In a letter to Charles E. Norton of October 12, 1902, though, Howells gives a different version of the meetings, with more emphasis on the changes that age and the passing of time had brought: "My mainstay for talk, this summer, has been Mark Twain, only forty trolley minutes away. But how sad old men are! We meet, and strike fire and flicker up, and I come away a heap of cold ashes," William C. Fischer and Christoph K. Lohmann, eds., *W. D. Howells, Selected Letters*, vol. 5, *1902–1911* (Boston: Twayne, 1983), 37.

76. See Smith and Gibson, *Mark Twain-Howells Letters*, 768.

77. Clemens to Howells, January 22, 1898, ibid., 670.

78. Howells, *My Mark Twain*, 99.

79. Peter Stoneley, "Mark Twain and Gender," 74–75. Stoneley argues "that friendship is constituted by regressive moments, as though, by passing through...infantile pleasures together, men...then seem to share a longer and naturalized history: they create a sense that they were children together" (74). I am reminded here of a December 6, 1893, letter from Clemens to Aldrich, recalling "the town of my boyhood—with all which that implies & compels: the bringing back of one's youth, almost the only time of life worth living over again, the only period whose memories are wholly pathetic—pathetic because we see now that we were in heaven then...." By permission of the Houghton Library, Harvard University, BMS Am 1429 (1165). Stoneley (importantly) adds that "[t]he relationship may have had a boyish element, but it was also a first and last testing-ground for their most keenly held ideas and beliefs" (75).

80. See Clemens's letter to Howells of October 4, 1875: "I 'caught it' for letting Mrs. Howells bother & bother about her coffee when it was 'a good deal better than we get at home.' I 'caught it' for interrupting Mrs. C.... I caught it once more for personating that drunken Col. James ...," Smith and Gibson, *Mark Twain-Howells Letters*, 103–4.

81. See Eble, *Old Clemens and W. D. H.*, 16.

82. Goodman and Dawson, *William Dean Howells*, 154.

83. Ibid., quoted pp. 82 and 67.

84. Ibid., quoted p. 136.

85. Arms and Lohmann, *W. D. Howells, Selected Letters* 2:29. On August 16, 1875, he would write (ironically) to Clemens of their summer stay in Shirley Village, Massachusetts, and of the good the country air "has done Mrs. Howells, who has gained an ounce and a half since she came, and would easily turn the scales at 65 pounds," Smith and Gibson, *Mark Twain-Howells Letters*, 97.

86. March 7, 1875, Arms and Lohmann, *W. D. Howells, Selected Letters* 2:92. Howells's own health, and belying his physical solidity, was not of the strongest. In his late teen years (the summer of 1854) he suffered what he would, on a later and comparable occasion, call a "vastation"—in Goodman and Dawson's words "a terrifying dissolution of self"—marked especially by a fear of rabies, or hydrophobia. He suffered a collapse on a visit to New York in 1871. And he had a serious illness (confined to his bed for seven weeks and losing twenty-six pounds in weight) from November 1881 onward that may well have been a type of breakdown, due to overwork and worry about his daughter's health. See Goodman and Dawson, *William Dean Howells*, 25–26, 200–1, and 215. In 1904, he is again writing Clemens that he is "rather run down nervously," Smith and Gibson, *Mark Twain-Howells Letters*, 781. Clemens himself seems to have verged on the over-sensitive—see Howells's letter to sister Aurelia of October 18, 1903, speaking of the Clemens family move to Florence: "He goes first for his wife's health, and then because he can't stand the nervous storm and stress here. He takes things intensely hard, and America is too much for him," Fischer and Lohmann, *W. D. Howells, Selected Letters* 5:71.

87. October 22, 1889, Smith and Gibson, *Mark Twain-Howells Letters*, 616.

88. Fischer and Lohmann, Introduction to *W. D. Howells, Selected Letters* 5: 3.

89. December 12, 1904, Fischer and Lohmann, *W. D. Howells, Selected Letters* 5:113.

90. October 1, 1880, Smith and Gibson, *Mark Twain-Howells Letters*, 328. See Clemens's letter to Elinor: "O dear, I never imagined you were drifting into invalidity as a settled thing," and what then follows (323). When, in the summer and autumn of 1881, daughter Winny was clearly in a seriously deteriorating condition, Elinor also suffered from crippling back pain as well as from her nerves. So Howells wrote to Edwin D. Mead on July 8: "Winny and Elinor are at Dio Lewes's, Arlington Heights, for their Nerves," Arms and Lohmann, *W. D. Howells, Selected Letters* 2:288.

91. August 2, 1898, Smith and Gibson, *Mark Twain-Howells Letters*, 672.

92. Ibid., 673.

93. Ibid., 816.

94. December 11, 1910, Fischer and Lohmann, *W. D. Howells, Selected Letters* 5:337.

95. Louis J. Budd comments: "In [the 1988 book, *If Not Literature: Letters of Elinor Mead Howells*] . . . she comes across as keenly intelligent, witty, decisive and mentally collected" (email correspondence). Thus Howells's representation of her to Clemens may be one-sided, to say the least.

96. Again, I am strongly influenced by Stoneley and his discussion—in this case—of Clemens's fiction, "Mark Twain and Gender," 73. So, too, in the correspondence, Clemens's occasional obscenities and stretchings of the limits of good taste are the private face of a (usual) public restraint, especially and deliberately directed against Howells's Boston-influenced sensitivities. (The movements between Clemens's role as socially successful citizen and his public and performative reputation as humorist "Mark Twain" does, though, complicate such an apparently straightforward pattern.) His response to Howells's *Atlantic* review of *Roughing It*—"I am as uplifted . . . as a mother who has given birth to a white baby when she was awfully afraid it was going to be a mulatto" (June 1872, Smith and Gibson, *Mark Twain-Howells Letters*, 10–11)—is intended, one can speculate, to intentionally unsettle his friend. Howells was himself, though, occasionally capable privately of a similar breadth of expression: he riffs on Clemens's words in a September 4, 1875, letter to Charles Dudley Warner: "I can only forgive myself for writing novels at all on the ground that the poor girl urged in extenuation of her unlegalized addition to the census: it was such a very *little* baby!" Quoted in "Introduction" to Arms and Lohmann, *W. D. Howells, Selected Letters* 2:8.

97. July 1874, Smith and Gibson, *Mark Twain-Howells Letters*, 20.

98. November 17, 1874, ibid., 41. For another example of Clemens's joking about Olivia's "baneful habit of underhanded swearing," see 294–95.

99. February 11, 1884, ibid., 469.

100. Ibid., 63–64. See too Clemens's letter about some (probably minor) offence committed during a Boston visit to Howells, and Olivia's consequent "measureless scorn & almost measureless vituperation," April 16, 1882, 400–402.

101. January 10, 1875, ibid., 57.

102. May 6–7, 1880, ibid., 305–6.

103. Goodman and Dawson, *William Dean Howells*, 155.

104. Budd, "W. D. Howells and Mark Twain," 105.

105. By permission of the Houghton Library, Harvard University, bMS Am 1429 (1187).

106. By permission of the Houghton Library, Harvard University, bMS Am 1429 (306).

107. Though both Clemens and Howells could be very slighting when it came to, say, Irish immigrants.

108. February 2, 1890, Leitz, Ballinger, and Lohmann, *W. D. Howells, Selected Letters* 3:271. The idea of Olivia Clemens as a "theoretical socialist" seems particularly far from the truth.

109. April 20, 1873, Arms and Lohmann, *W. D. Howells, Selected Letters* 2:24. He is referring to the Granger movement here, and to its campaign against extortionate railroad rates for farmers' produce.

110. Choosing one who may have been guilty of financial irregularity over one (Cleveland) who had been found definitely guilty in the public eye of unacceptable sexual behavior (fathering an illegitimate son): "I voted for a man *accused* of bribery . . . . I would not vote for a man *guilty* of what society sends a woman to hell for," August 15, 1884, to Thomas S. Perry, Leitz, Ballinger, and Lohmann, *W. D. Howells, Selected Letters* 3:108. In fact, Cleveland may not have been the father of the child in question, but rather—as a then-bachelor—protecting the interests of other, married men involved with the same woman.

111. Howells to Thomas S. Perry, August 15, 1884, Leitz, Ballinger, and Lohmann, *W. D. Howells, Selected Letters* 3: 108.

112. Goodman and Dawson, *William Dean Howells*, 197.

113. Ibid., quoted 271.

114. October 10, 1888, Leitz, Ballinger, and Lohmann, *W. D. Howells, Selected Letters* 3:231.

115. I follow in part the fuller narrative in Goodman and Dawson, *William Dean Howells*, 275–89.

116. Quoted in Goodman and Dawson, *William Dean Howells*, 282.

117. See ibid., 283–84. There is another long November 23 letter to the editor of the New York *Sun*, which also seems to have gone unsent. In this, he answers the accusation of his being a socialist by writing: "Every citizen of a civilized State is a socialist. You are yourself a socialist if you believe that the postal department, the public schools, the insane asylums . . . are good things; and that when a railroad management has muddled away in hopeless ruin the money of all who trusted it, a Railroad Receiver is a good thing. . . . Yesterday afternoon . . . I saw a decently dressed man stoop and pick up from the [New York] pavement a dirty bit of cake or biscuit, which he crammed into his mouth. . . . [T]he conditions in which he came to such a strait seemed to me Christless, after eighteen hundred years of Christ." Leitz, Ballinger, and Lohmann, *W. D. Howells, Selected Letters* 3:236–39.

118. Howells to Henry James, December 25, 1886, Leitz, Ballinger, and Lohmann, *W. D. Howells, Selected Letters* 3:176.

119. Smith and Gibson, *Mark Twain-Howells Letters*, 626–27.

120. Howells to sister Aurelia, June 21, 1896, Thomas Wortham, Christoph K. Lohmann, and David J. Nordloh, eds., *W. D. Howells, Selected Letters*, vol. 4: *1892–1901* (Boston: Twayne, 1981) 128. He adds, "I might as well vote for McKinley, and the State Socialist ticket."

121. Howells to Aurelia, November 7, 1896, ibid., 133.

122. December 27, 1897, ibid., 161.

123. Goodman and Dawson, *William Dean Howells*, 359–60.

124. Howells too Aurelia, April 17, 1898, Wortham, Lohmann, and Nordloh, *W. D. Howells, Selected Letters* 4:170.

125. Ibid., 182.

126. See Goodman and Dawson, *William Dean Howells*, 361–62.

127. A related type of accommodation was in the way he retained his personal friendships with men like Theodore Roosevelt and John Hay despite major political differences. See Goodman and Dawson, *William Dean Howells*, 362–63. He judged Roosevelt privately, "a wretched Jingo," Wortham, Lohmann, and Nordloh, *W. D. Howells, Selected Letters* 4:188.

128. See Goodman and Dawson, *William Dean Howells*, 362. Clemens spoke of how England and America had "always been kin...in blood,... religion,...ideals [etc.]...; and now we are kin in sin, the harmony is complete, the blend is perfect, like Mr. Churchill himself, whom I now have the honor to present to you."

129. See Smith and Gibson, *Mark Twain-Howells Letters*, 729.

130. Goodman and Dawson, *William Dean Howells*, 165.

131. Krauth, *Mark Twain & Company*, 83.

132. Eble, *Old Clemens and W. D. H.*, 168.

133. To his father, October 17, 1880, Arms and Lohmann, *W. D. Howells, Selected Letters* 2:268.

134. Budd, "W. D. Howells and Mark Twain," 104. For more on Clemens's sociopolitical views, see, for instance, Louis J. Budd, *Mark Twain, Social Philosopher* (Bloomington: Indiana University Press, 1962); Robert E. Weir, "Mark Twain and Social Class," in Shelley Fisher Fishkin, ed., *A Historical Guide to Mark Twain* (New York: Oxford University Press, 2002), 195–225; and James S. Leonard, "Mark Twain and Politics," in Peter Messent and Louis J. Budd, eds., *Companion to Mark Twain* (Oxford: Blackwell, 2005), 94–108.

135. Howells, *My Mark Twain*, 81.

136. May 12[–13], 1899, Smith and Gibson, *Mark Twain-Howells Letters*, 697. And see too his "Knights of Labor—The New Dynasty" speech to the Hartford Monday Evening Club (March 1886), described in ibid., 597–98.

137. See, for instance, Clemens's relationship with his father-in-law, Jervis Langdon, prior to Langdon's death in August 1870. On the one hand, he would send him an article he had written attacking miners' unions that "stripped [mine-owners] of their independence and converted them into the servants of their own employees." On the other he would ironically comment on the harsher human costs of the Langdon family coal business. See Victor Fischer and Michael B. Frank, eds., *Mark Twain's Letters*, vol. 4: *1870–1871* (Berkeley and Los Angeles: University of California Press, 1995) 105–6 and 544–47; and Justin Kaplan, *Mr. Clemens and Mark Twain* (Harmondsworth, Middx.: Penguin 1967 [1966]), 144–45. Kaplan comments of Langdon: "like Henry H. Rogers,...[he] was able to combine rectitude and benevolence in his personal affairs with a certain *laissez-faire* rapacity in business. Neither [man] felt fettered by the conflict between private and business morality," 117. In *The Oxford Companion to Mark Twain*, Gregg Camfield explains Clemens's attitude to labor in terms of his own "guild labor" background, 317–21.

138. *Old Clemens and W. D. H.*, 224–25. Eble also points out—and this must crucially be taken into account in any consideration of both men's relationship to their larger society—that, "both Howells and Mark Twain became capitalists, though on a small scale compared with the big capitalists of their time," 192.

139. He refers to both Clemens's letters and his published works here. The words come from the typescript of his "Easy Chair" review of *The*

*Letters of Mark Twain* in the Houghton Library, but do not then appear in the published piece.

140. Budd, "W. D. Howells and Mark Twain," 99.

141. April 2 [–13], 1899, Smith and Gibson, *Mark Twain-Howells Letters*, 689.

142. Leitz, Ballinger, and Lohmann, *W. D. Howells, Selected Letters* 3:314.

143. Fischer and Lohmann, *W. D. Howells, Selected Letters* 5:54. To some degree, this recalls Clemens's "Some Learned Fables for Good Old Boys and Girls," which Howells rejected for the *Atlantic* some thirty years previously, in 1874. Leland Krauth sets Clemens's *Mysterious Stranger* manuscripts against *A Traveler from Altruria* to find similar "flirts with . . . solipsism," and a "dark and critical" late humor on the part of both writers, suggesting "a kind of giving up on the comic itself," *Mark Twain & Company*, 85. While Lawrence I. Berkove links Howells's story "A Difficult Case," with its "respect [given] to a fatalist and a pessimist," to Clemens's (later) works, claiming that "[Howells] appears to have assimilated Twain more deeply than has hitherto been realized. . . . 30 years of friendship . . . had to have left an impression on [him], at least in terms of some of Twain's values, ideas, and ways of thinking," "'A Difficult Case': W. D. Howells's Impression of Mark Twain," *Studies in Short Fiction* 31, no. 4 (1994): 613. Paul Abeln, in *William Dean Howells and the Ends of Realism* (New York: Routledge, 2005), focuses on Howells's 1916 novel, *The Leatherwood God*, to note "an active integration of Clemens's personality and aesthetic into Howells's late fiction" (see especially 87–89). See, too, my following chapter.

144. I run together two letters of June 9, 1910, one to brother Joseph, the other to Henry James. Fischer and Lohmann, *W. D. Howells, Selected Letters* 5:321–22. Howells suggests something of the two men's difference in temperament when he writes of Clemens: "The sorrows which time accumulated upon [Clemens and his wife] were those which life brings. They were of the common lot, and no special tragedy. . . . [B]ut the death of his children would seem to have struck him with a sort of dismay, as if no one else had known the like, and it finds naïve utterance in the letters." Review of *The Letters of Mark Twain*, "Editor's Easy Chair," *Harper's Magazine* (March 1918): 603. For a wider sense of this same temperamental trait, see Howells on Clemens's "elemental" nature, in "Mark Twain: An Enquiry," *My Mark Twain*, 178. Howells did, however, at times lose such poise. Thus he writes to Henry James soon after Winny's death: "'All happiness is alike, but every sorrow has its own physiognomy,' and every trait of anguish is in this experience. I wonder we live; it seems monstrous . . . ," June 7, 1889. Leitz, Ballinger, and Lohmann, *W. D. Howells, Selected Letters* 3:253.

145. Howells's "Editor's Easy Chair" review of *The Letters of Mark Twain*, 602.

146. We might remember here, Clemens's half-jocular, half-serious remark of 1909 about the sifting of his letters to his three best male friends into different categories (profanities, indecencies, and theologies): "[T]he *scheme* furnishes a definite target for each letter, & you can choose the target that's going to be the most sympathetic for what you are hungering & thirsting to say at that particular moment," Smith and Gibson, *Mark Twain-Howells Letters*, 845. Similarly, we should also keep in mind the status of a literary recollection of a friendship, like Howells's *My Mark*

*Twain*, written primarily in the spirit of memorial and tribute rather than as objective record or critique.

147. December 22, 1890, Leitz, Ballinger, and Lohmann, *W. D. Howells, Selected Letters* 3:299.

148. Howells, *My Mark Twain*, 29.

149. And see my next chapter.

150. I take for granted that the gap between one self and another can never fully be bridged. I am suggesting a significant change in the matter of degree around this period. So, to give another instance, in 1906 Howells could still speak of an alternative homosocial world in which "men [might] marry men." This type of casual mention would, however, become rarer and more problematic with the changes in sexual and social mores following the Wilde case.

151. Howells, *My Mark Twain*, 9.

152. August 2, 1907, Fischer and Lohmann, *W. D. Howells, Selected Letters* 5:224. Henry James would note the "depression" he saw in Howells existing at a remove from "his '*operative* self,'" quoted in Goodman and Dawson, *William Dean Howells*, 30. And see note 71 above.

153. July 3, 1902, Fischer and Lohmann, *W. D. Howells, Selected Letters* 5:32.

154. Goodman and Dawson, *William Dean Howells*, 384.

155. Forrest Robinson, "Mark Twain, 1835–1910: A Brief Biography," in Fishkin, ed., *Historical Guide to Mark Twain*, 26–27.

156. April 15, 1907, Fischer and Lohmann, *W. D. Howells, Selected Letters* 5:222.

*Chapter 5*

1. Susan Goodman and Carl Dawson, *William Dean Howells: A Writer's Life* (Berkeley and Los Angeles: University of California Press, 2005), 301.

2. George Santayana, "The Genteel Tradition in American Philosophy" (1911), in Cleanth Brooks, R. W. B. Lewis, and Robert Penn Warren, *American Literature: The Makers and the Making*, vol. 2 (New York: St. Martin's Press, 1973), 1545 and 1550.

3. Though (and this follows my previous argument in this book) there was often a separation here between these men's roles and behavior as private citizens and their artistic insights.

4. Brander Matthews, "Of Mark Twain's Best Story," in *Americanisms and Briticisms Etc.* (New York: Harper, 1892), 160–61.

5. Ibid., 153–54.

6. Michael Davitt Bell, *The Problem of American Realism: Studies in the Cultural History of a Literary Idea* (Chicago: University of Chicago Press, 1993), 45.

7. Sarah B. Daugherty, "William Dean Howells and Mark Twain: The Realism War as a Campaign that Failed," *American Literary Realism* 29, no. 1 (1996): 15.

8. Edwin H. Cady (ed.), *W. D. Howells as Critic* (London: Routledge & Kegan Paul, 1973), 170.

9. Ibid., 393. See Daniel H. Borus on the distinction between picturing and mapping, and some of the paradoxes then raised, *Writing Realism: Howells, James, and Norris in the Mass Market* (Chapel Hill: University of North Carolina Press, 1989), 93–96. Cady defines Howells's view of the photographic as "what *realism* is not because realism is not mechanical or cartographic but an art like painting," *W. D. Howells as Critic*, 5.

10. Matthews, "Of Mark Twain's Best Story," 155 and 153.

11. Cady, *W. D. Howells as Critic*, 233.

12. Clara Marburg Kirk and Rudolf Kirk, eds., *Criticism and Fiction and Other Essays by W. D. Howells* (New York: New York University Press, 1959) 51. I approach my topic indirectly, by way of Brander Matthews, since the critical language he uses so clearly accords with realist practice. Howells himself wrote extensively on Clemens, and in "Mark Twain: An Enquiry" (1901) he recognized both the importance of the vernacular in *Huckleberry Finn*, and the essentially democratic nature of the book: "The probable and credible soul that the author divines in the son of the town-drunkard is one which we might each own brother, and the art which portrays this nature at first hand in the person and language of the hero, without pose or affectation, is fine art." But the problems Howells would always have in fitting Clemens into his preferred critical scheme of things are clear here. He first tentatively defines Clemens as a "romancer," then talks about this particular novel as picaresque rather than romance, only to qualify further: "Still, it is more poetic than picaresque, and of a deeper psychology." Once more revealing his definitional uncertainties, he continues: "In the boy's history the author's fancy works *realistically* to an end as high as it has reached elsewhere, if not higher" (All above quotes in Howells: *My Mark Twain*, 173—my emphasis in final quote). Borus identifies realist writing with "dialect rendered as exactly as possible," and uses *Huckleberry Finn* as his primary example, *Writing Realism*, p. 23.

13. Leland Krauth, *Mark Twain & Company: Six Literary Relations* (Athens: University of Georgia Press, 2003), 23.

14. See, for example, the analyses of "Lucretia Smith's Soldier" (December 1864) and "The Launch of the Steamer 'Capital'" (November 1865) in Peter Messent, *The Short Works of Mark Twain* (Philadelphia: University of Pennsylvania Press, 2001), 21 and 16–18. Clemens's comedy, however, also undermined realist assumptions of stable subjectivity, representational authority, and ontological certainty, right from the start of his writing career.

15. David E. Shi, *Facing Facts: Realism in American Thought and Culture, 1850–1920* (New York: Oxford University Press, 1995), 3. This raises the issue of how we distinguish realism as a broad and sweeping intellectual movement from the literary movement linked specifically to the career and influence of William Dean Howells, "the center and circumference of realism in America" as Eric J. Sundquist calls him in "Realism and Regionalism," in *Columbia Literary History of the United States*, ed. Emory Elliott (New York: Columbia University Press, 1998) 503. Though I focus here on the Clemens-Howells connection, I suggest answers to this question as I proceed.

16. My argument here generally runs counter to that of Michael Davitt Bell in *The Problem of American Realism*. I would resist the narrow limits of Bell's definitions and conclusions as he argues, to my mind perversely, that it is in *A Connecticut Yankee*, and not *Huckleberry Finn*, that Clemens identifies most strongly with realist values.

17. Sundquist, "Realism and Regionalism," 502. Though Clemens would often fail to conform to such principles in his own fiction. I return to this later.

18. Cady, *W. D. Howells as Critic*, 231.

19. "A Cure for the Blues," in Mark Twain, *Merry Tales* (New York: Charles L. Webster, 1892), 83 and 90.

20. Ibid., 80, 83, and 89.

21. Ibid., 99.

22. Quoted in Alan Trachtenberg, *The Incorporation of America: Culture and Society in the Gilded Age* (New York: Hill & Wang, 1982), 186.

23. Quoted in "Introduction" to William Dean Howells, *A Hazard of New Fortunes* (London: Oxford University Press, 1965), ix.

24. Twain, "A Cure for the Blues," 78.

25. Brook Thomas, *American Literary Realism and the Failed Promise of Contract* (Berkeley and Los Angeles: University of California Press, 1997), 196, 5, and 229.

26. Richard H. Brodhead, "Literature and Culture," in *Columbia Literary History of the United States*, ed. Emory Elliott, 474.

27. Bell, *The Problem of American Realism*, 58.

28. Sundquist, "Realism and Regionalism," 512.

29. Daugherty, "William Dean Howells and Mark Twain," 12.

30. Phillip Barrish, *American Literary Realism, Critical Theory and Intellectual Prestige, 1880–1995* (Cambridge: Cambridge University Press, 2001), 39.

31. Shi, *Facing Facts*, 107.

32. Lee Clark Mitchell, "Naturalism and the Languages of Determinism," in *Columbia Literary History of the United States*, ed. Emory Elliott, 531.

33. Richard S. Lowry, "*Littery Man: Mark Twain and Modern Authorship*" (New York: Oxford University Press, 1996), 46.

34. Louis J. Budd, "W. D. Howells and Mark Twain Judge Each Other 'Aright,'" *American Literary Realism*, 38 (Winter 2006): 103 and 108.

35. Amy Kaplan, *The Social Construction of American Realism* (Chicago: University of Chicago Press, 1988), 9.

36. Ibid., 15. Howells's own critical vocabulary is full of large-scale abstractions and troublingly paradoxical statements that hinder as much as they help is in constructing a working definition of the "realism" for which he argued. "The novelist's main business," he writes in a particularly unenlightening sentence, "is to possess his reader with a due conception of his characters and the situations in which they find themselves" (Cady, *W. D. Howells as Critic*, 67). Other phrases scattered through his essays— "good form without formality" (77), "fidelity to experience and probability of motive" (83), "the faithful representation of life" (87), "to know and to tell the truth" (115)—either raise questions as to their exact meaning or leave the reader with a series of unanswerable questions: if all artists (surely), in one way or another, look to know and tell the truth, what then is so distinctive about the realist project? For the crucial paradox in his version of realism, see the final section of this chapter.

37. Richard H. Brodhead, *The School of Hawthorne* (New York: Oxford University Press, 1986), 86.

38. Ibid., 83 and 103.

39. Krauth, *Mark Twain & Company*, 24. And see elsewhere in this book, especially its Coda.

40. Ibid., 37–38. Gregg Camfield was the first to explore this area in depth in *Sentimental Twain: Samuel Clemens in the Maze of Moral Philosophy* (Philadelphia: University of Pennsylvania Press, 1994). And see too Mary Louise Kete, *Sentimental Collaborations: Mourning, and Middle Class Identity in Nineteenth-Century America* (Durham, N.C.: Duke University Press, 2000), 145–86. And see chapter 1, n.100.

41. Philip Fisher, *Hard Facts: Setting and Form in the American Novel* (New York: Oxford University Press, 1986), 93.

42. Ibid., 93–94.

43. June Howard, *Form and History in American Literary Naturalism* (Chapel Hill: University of North Carolina Press, 1985), 11–12.

44. Barrish, *American Literary Realism, Critical Theory and Intellectual Prestige, 1880–1995*, 29.

45. Though we should note Lowry's reading of the novel as an "ideological drama of literacy": "Huck resists the incorporating fictions of others by empowering himself as the subject of his own discourse, yet his autobiographical strategy is itself the product of his submission to an education that reforms him into a literate subject," *"Littery Man,"* 119.

46. Lee Clark Mitchell, *Determined Fictions: American Literary Naturalism* (New York: Columbia University Press: 1989) xii.

47. The problem of individual moral responsibility in a world where the subject's engagement within the larger determining social network had become increasingly binding was one that haunted realist authors. And it often becomes very difficult to separate out independent moral action from dependent social conditioning. Thus the end of Howells's *Silas Lapham* is commonly read in terms of Lapham's "moral rise . . . the victory of self-regulation over temptation, of rural values over urban," as he refuses to act dishonestly in business (Sundquist, "Realism and Regionalism," 506). But this can be viewed differently, and more deterministically, with Lapham as the "victim of his own premodern ideology." His Boston years then become "an anomaly, a period where the decentralized production of goods by small, family-owned concerns momentarily had access to major urban markets. . . . [T]his moment soon [necessarily] passed, as American industry entered an age of mass production and distribution." See Stanley Corkin, *Realism and the Birth of the Modern United States: Cinema, Literature, and Culture* (Athens: University of Georgia Press, 1996) 47 and 49. See also note 113 below.

48. Jane Tompkins, *Sensational Designs: The Cultural Work of American Fiction 1790–1860* (New York: Oxford University Press, 1985), 175.

49. Borus, *Writing Realism*, 17.

50. See Lowry, *"Littery Man,"* 4–5.

51. Kaplan, *The Social Construction of American Realism*, 6.

52. Borus, *Writing Realism*, 9 and 19.

53. Lowry, *"Littery Man,"* 7.

54. Brodhead, *The School of Hawthorne*, 87.

55. Borus, *Writing Realism*, 38.

56. Augusta Rohrbach, *Truth Stranger than Fiction: Race, Realism and the U.S. Literary Marketplace* (New York: Palgrave, 2002), 76.

57. See ibid.

58. Lowry, *"Littery Man,"* 46.

59. Ibid., 85.

60. And see Corkin, *Realism and the Birth of the Modern United States*, 25.

61. Trachtenberg, *Incorporation of America*, 193.

62. Borus, *Writing Realism*, 113, 172 and 133.

63. Corkin, *Realism and the Birth of the Modern United States*, 24–25.

64. Kirk and Kirk, eds., *Criticism and Fiction and Other Essays by W. D. Howells*, 308.

65. Corkin, *Realism and the Birth of the Modern United States*, 26.

66. Trachtenberg, *Incorporation of America*, 199.

67. Borus, *Writing Realism*, 57–58.

68. Corkin, *Realism and the Birth of the Modern United States*, 26.

69. Borus, *Writing Realism*, 58.

70. Trachtenberg, *The Incorporation of America*, 197.

71. Mark Twain, "A Curious Experience," *Merry Tales*, 139 and 141.

72. A further irony lies in the fact that Clemens's most famous novel, *Huckleberry Finn*, was attacked by at least one early reviewer as "being no better in tone than the dime novels which flood the blood-and-thunder reading population." See Joe B. Fulton, *Mark Twain's Ethical Realism* (Columbia: University of Missouri Press, 1997), 54. Fulton's Bakhtinian analysis of Clemens's "ethical realism," and its search "for a nonsystemic, nonrelativistic ethics that would serve as a kind of ... practical morality" (7), provides another useful approach to the topic.

73. Borus, *Writing Realism*, 88, and Lowry, "*Littery Man*," 45.

74. Sundquist, "Realism and Regionalism," 507.

75. Mark Twain, "About Play-Acting." In *The Man That Corrupted Hadleyburg and Other Stories and Essays* (New York: Harper, 1900), 242–43.

76. Ibid., 248–51.

77. Kirk and Kirk, *Criticism and Fiction and Other Essays by W. D. Howells*, 48.

78. See Mark Twain, *Early Tales & Sketches, Volume 1, 1861–1864*, ed. Edgar Marquess Branch and Robert H. Hirst (Berkeley and Los Angeles: University of California Press, 1979), 543.

79. Krauth, *Proper Mark Twain* (Athens: University of Georgia Press, 1999), 6.

80. See Messent, *The Short Works of Mark Twain*, 117. Leland Krauth gives a slightly different version of the letter and continues quoting to show that later in it Clemens "endorses the idea of literature [for the masses] as a way to cultural improvement" (*Proper Mark Twain*, 15).

81. Sundquist, "Realism and Regionalism," 504.

82. Cady, *W. D. Howells as Critic*, 113.

83. And see Krauth, *Mark Twain & Company*, 232.

84. I have written elsewhere on Clemens's links with naturalism, and the limited nature of that fit. See, for example, "Toward the Absurd: Mark Twain's *A Connecticut Yankee, Pudd'nhead Wilson* and *The Great Dark*," in Robert Giddings (ed.), *Mark Twain: A Sumptuous Variety* (London and Totowa, N.J.: Vision and Barnes & Noble: 1985), 176–98.

85. Sundquist, "Realism and Regionalism," 520. Keeping Clemens's works in mind, I would modify Sundquist's "effects of capitalism" to "changing conditions and social relationships" (of which the effects of capitalism would be one crucial part). In his essay on "Mark Twain, 'Hadleyburg,' and the Performance of Redemption," David Zimmerman shows how the signifying properties of money and language are bound together in "The Man That Corrupted Hadleyburg," and how the story as a whole works to challenge the very premises of realism. This essay contributes significantly to the debate about Clemens and realism. *ESQ* 48 (2002): 275–98.

86. Barrish, *American Literary Realism*, 8.

87. Daugherty, "William Dean Howells and Mark Twain," 21.

88. Cady, *W. D. Howells as Critic*, 83.

89. Corkin, *Realism and the Birth of the Modern United States*, 27.

90. Borus, *Writing Realism*, 93 and 95.

91. Kaplan, *Social Construction of American Realism*, 22. See, too, Daniel G. Williams: "Realism for Howells is an art form that resolves and

reconciles.... There is thus a contradiction ... between the passive realist narrator, who simply observes contemporary life, and the interventionist novelist, who seeks to educate and inform his readers," *Ethnicity and Cultural Authority: From Arnold to DuBois* (Edinburgh: Edinburgh University Press, 2006), 88 and 90.

92. See Borus, *Writing Realism*, 154.

93. Kaplan, *Social Construction of American Realism*, 23.

94. Trachtenberg, *Incorporation of America*, 192.

95. Kaplan, *Social Construction of American Realism*, 9.

96. The "top-down" nature of Howells's work, the fact that he wrote for a particular class audience that did not include the working-class "mass," further and necessarily compromised his intentions. For another version of the argument about the contradictions in Howells's vision, though one that also emphasizes the way he distanced himself from the New England cultural tradition (so powerful in the previous decades), see Williams, *Ethnicity and Cutural Authority*, 72–114.

97. Krauth, *Mark Twain & Company*, 81.

98. Kaplan, *Social Construction of American Realism*, 46.

99. Howells, *Hazard of New Fortunes*, 285.

100. Kaplan, *Social Construction of American Realism*, 57.

101. Ibid., 63.

102. Ibid., 61.

103. If, as Kaplan suggests, the fissures can (just about) still be contained within "realist" space, the novel is very close to falling apart at its seams. In her words, "[b]y the end of the novel, the paint threatens to fly off the surface of Howells's largest novelistic canvas," *Social Construction of American Realism*, 63.

104. Barrish, *American Literary Realism*, 5.

105. Ibid., 31 and 38–39.

106. Ibid., 36.

107. Ibid., 43.

108. Ibid., 47 and 40.

109. Daugherty, "William Dean Howells and Mark Twain," 22 and 13. Both Barrish and Daugherty (see my next paragraph) make a bridge from realism to post-structuralism/postmodernism. One could equally connect Clemens's use of irony and of defamiliarization techniques with modernism, his spiralling relativism with the postmodern. Such connections are valid in their suggestion that both writers saw beyond the limits of realism; also in linking the instabilities and uncertainties of a late-nineteenth-century world to more recent social and intellectual preoccupations. The readings of Howells I follow here present one particular view of his artistic development.

110. Quoted in Daugherty, "William Dean Howells and Mark Twain," 23.

111. And see chapter 4, n. 145.

112. Thomas, *American Literary Realism and the Failed Promise of Contract*, 224.

113. Though the antebellum setting of the text masks its contemporary relevance, the picture of racism and racial division in the novel is nonetheless unrelenting. Brook Thomas's discussion of "the question of agency" (*American Literary Realism and the Failed Promise of Contract*, 270) in the work of Clemens and other realist writers is a stimulating one and suggests the individual capacity for meaningful engagement even in a world where surrounding and conditioning social and economic forces press

increasingly on the human subject. He relies here on Hannah Arendt's distinction between sovereignty ("the ideal of a free will, independent from others") and freedom (which "resides not in control over action but in action itself"), 272. "Free agents," in Thomas's view, "retain the capacity to produce actions that are not totally controlled by the forces that create the conditions in which action occurs," 279. *Pudd'nhead Wilson* remains for Thomas a realist text, largely (it seems) due to Clemens's own authorial role: "even though Twain works with material and voices made available to him by his culture, when that material passes through his imagination it is translated [a key word for Thomas] into a different form," 280. While this may be true, the internal message of the text is less positive. Thomas's statement that "the realists...work to find a form that will be true to the contingency of events" (275) matches Barrish's view of the later Howells, but shares, to my mind, something of its "often paralyzing" implications (*American Literary Realism*, 47). See, too, my later comments on *Huckleberry Finn*.

114. Thomas, *American Literary Realism and the Failed Promise of Contract*, 281 and 283.

115. Henry Nash Smith and William M. Gibson, eds., *Mark Twain-Howells Letters: The Correspondence of Samuel L. Clemens and William D. Howells, 1872–1910* (Cambridge, Mass.: Harvard University Press, 1960), 710.

116. Though see Krauth, *Mark Twain & Company*, 78–86, for a useful comparison and contrast of the two writers' use of the figure of the stranger (Howells's in *A Traveler from Altruria*) to launch "grim and angry assaults on the ills, wrongs, and injustices they learned to see in life at the very beginning" (78). Krauth, as this last implies, sees their shared western backgrounds as helping to shape their final visions.

*Chapter 6*

1. Justin Kaplan, *Mr. Clemens and Mark Twain*, (Harmondsworth, Middx.: Penguin 1967 [1966]), 463.

2. Hamlin Hill, ed., *Mark Twain's Letters to His Publishers, 1867–1894* (Berkeley and Los Angeles: University of California Press, 1967), 343 and 355 (I fuse two separate passages from June 2 and July 30, 1893).

3. Letter to Clemens of June 9, 1893. See Peter Messent, *The Short Works of Mark Twain*, (Philadelphia: University of Pennsylvania Press, 2001), 243.

4. See Lewis Leary, ed., *Mark Twain's Correspondence with Henry Huttleston Rogers, 1893–1909* (Berkeley and Los Angeles: University of California Press, 1969), 11.

5. "Well, whatever I get out of the wreckage will be due to good luck,—the good luck of getting you into the scheme—for, but for that, there wouldn't *be* any wreckage; it would be total loss," ibid., 115. Clemens is referring to the Paige Compositor Manufacturing Company, but the comment has a wider truth.

6. Ibid., 24.

7. Ibid., 389.

8. There is an echo here of *A Connecticut Yankee in King Arthur's Court* (1889) where different kinds of power and authority collide and Hank Morgan's "magic of science" battles—but finally fails to defeat—Merlin's "magic of folderol." Rogers's skills in business matched, for Clemens, those of Thomas Edison (popularly known as "the wizard of Menlo Park") in science and technology.

9. Gail Bederman, *Manliness & Civilization: A Cultural History of Gender and Race in the United States, 1880–1917* (Chicago: University of Chicago Press, 1996 [1995]), 10–11. Commenting on the "crisis" thesis, she continues: "there is no evidence that most turn-of-the-century men ever lost confidence in the belief that people with male bodies naturally possessed both a man's identity and a man's right to wield power," 11.

10. Again, see ibid., chapter 1, "Remaking Manhood through Race and 'Civilization,'" 1–44. A continuing belief in the ideology of self-made manhood, despite this, remained strong.

11. Amy Kaplan, *The Anarchy of Empire in the Making of U.S. Culture* (Cambridge, Mass.: Harvard University Press, 2002), 18–19.

12. Mary Ryan, writing on this subject in 1981 in her book about the middle-class family in Oneida County, New York, from 1790 to 1865, says that "[a]ny cultural construct that achieved such popularity bore some semblance to social reality." Quoted in Margaret Marsh, "Suburban Men and Masculine Domesticity, 1870–1915," in Mark C. Carnes and Clyde Griffen, eds., *Meanings for Manhood: Constructions of Masculinity in Victorian America* (Chicago: University of Chicago Press, 1990),1 13. This continues to hold true as the century advances.

13. Mark C. Carnes, *Secret Ritual and Manhood in Victorian America* (New Haven, Conn.: Yale University Press, 1989), 123 and 114–15. Carnes does go on to show how Masonry's "Royal Secret" recognized ultimate divinity in a God who had both male and female characteristics. This is, in turn, was to affirm that Victorian men "were of a 'double nature': a unity of assertion and nurturance, of aggression and conscience, and of male and female" (see 147–50).

14. Bederman, *Manliness & Civilization*, 6, and Carnes and Griffen, *Meanings for Manhood*, 132. I am aware of my different uses of terminology, from manhood to manliness and masculinity. This is inevitable given my critical sources. I will return to the distinction between the last two terms. I would further recognize that Clemens's own individual sense of manhood was not necessarily coherent and unified.

15. Gregg Camfield, *The Oxford Companion to Mark Twain*, (New York: Oxford University Press, 2003), 517. See Leary, *Mark Twain's Correspondence with Henry Huttleston Rogers*, 5, n. 2, and the prefacing quotation to the next chapter, for a list of some of Rogers's corporate positions.

16. Marsh, "Suburban Men and Masculine Domesticity," 111. See, too, E. Anthony Rotundo's definition of a late-nineteenth-century "passionate manhood": "competitiveness and aggression were exalted as ends in themselves. Toughness was now admired, while tenderness was a cause for scorn," *American Manhood: Transformations in Masculinity from the Revolution to the Modern Era* (New York: Basic Books, 1993), 5 and 6. While, in part, I challenge this verdict later, I still recognize its general truth. Manhood was, and remains, a site of ideological contradiction.

17. I recall material from my first chapter here.

18. Marsh, "Suburban Men and Masculine Domesticity," 112, 117, and 121. Despite her endorsement of Mary Ryan's words (n. 12 above), Marsh contends that "the doctrine of separate spheres [for men and women] began to break down after the Civil War," 113. I see this breakdown as both inconsistent in application and subject to ambivalent response.

19. But note what I say elsewhere about the limits of such an "unfolding."

20. Sandage, "Gaze of Success," 183.

21. Leary *Mark Twain's Correspondence with Henry Huttleston Rogers*, 108 (December 22, 1894). Clemens's financial collapse stretched out over a significant period, as did Rogers's intervention in the Paige debacle.

22. December 27, 1894, reflecting on the "despairing day" just mentioned when Rogers's news arrived, ibid., 112. Clemens tells Rogers of his attending, that same night, a masked ball in Paris (where he was then residing) "blacked up as Uncle Remus." There is surely significance in his assuming, at such a carnivalesque event, the mask of an ex-slave—though one who had a certain authority as a storyteller—at this low point of his life. If masculine identity is in part tied to economic success and social status, this act may well have been an unconscious reflection of Clemens's deepest anxieties and ambivalences.

23. Letter of July 20–22, 1895, ibid., 172. This refers to claims against Webster & Co.

24. Ibid., 98 and 574.

25. Ibid., 229.

26. Bederman, *Manliness & Civilization*, 16 and 11–12. She refers to middle-class manhood here, but the argument can be extended. Again, conceptions of manhood clearly filter across different male groupings.

27. Ibid., 16–17. See too Rotundo, *American Manhood*, chapter 10 ("Passionate Manhood: A Changing Standard of Masculinity"), 222–46, for similar ideas.

28. Bederman, *Manliness & Civilization*, 18.

29. Interview in the *New York Times*, August 17, 1895, quoted in Leary, *Mark Twain's Correspondence with Henry Huttleston Rogers*, 182. We should, however, be realistic about the motives behind Clemens's actions and rhetoric. It was his wife Olivia who insisted on such "honorable" behavior when Clemens was initially ready to take such financial advantages as the laws for bankruptcy allowed. Rogers advised (shrewdly) that taking this ethical position would pay off best in the long run. On this, see, for example, Fred Kaplan, *The Singular Mark Twain* (Doubleday: New York: 2003), 524.

30. Quoted in Leary, *Mark Twain's Correspondence with Henry Huttleston Rogers*, 306.

31. Ibid., 306. Letters from creditors were sent to Rogers's secretary, Katharine Harrison. They were, however, mostly addressed to K. I. Harrison, Esq. or Mr. K. I. Harrison. Katharine Harrison's business role and part in the Clemens's correspondence was significant, and her own challenge to Victorian gender conventions deserves further attention. On April 12, 1894, writing to Rogers, Clemens directly refers to press interest in Harrison, and her (considerable) salary: "The Boston sketch has just arrived and I thank that ten-thousand-dollar secretary of yours for sending it: the one I have read so much about, recently as being as unpumpable as the Sphynx, and the only secretary of her sex that either earns that salary or gets it" (562).

32. See ibid., 293.

33. George Santayana, "The Genteel Tradition in American Philosophy," in Cleanth Brooks, R. W. B. Lewis, and Robert Penn Warren, *American Literature: The Makers and the Making*, vol. 2 (New York: St. Martin's Press, 1973), 1545.

34. Daniel H. Borus, *Writing Realism: Howells, James, and Norris in the Mass Market* (Chapel Hill: University of North Carolina Press, 1989), 38 and 33.

35. Richard S. Lowry, *"Littery Man: Mark Twain and Modern Authorship* (New York: Oxford University Press, 1996), 46. And see chapter 5 of this book.

36. Leary, *Mark Twain's Correspondence with Henry Huttleston Rogers*, 545.

37. Camfield, *Oxford Companion to Mark Twain*, 137 and 140.

38. Here, as so often, Clemens refuses any too firm a categorization. Any glance at his speeches, letters, and other activities shows his prodigality with his time and energy. In Louis J. Budd's words he was "too impulsive and irrepressible ever to rein himself in entirely for the cash register" (private correspondence).

39. July 14, 1895, Leary, *Mark Twain's Correspondence with Henry Huttleston Rogers*, 167.

40. Ibid., 24.

41. There are some hints of the difficulties Rogers faced as he worked on Clemens's behalf. So he writes firmly, when Clemens is looking, even in 1906, to adjust the Harper arrangements: "Don't allow yourself to think of anything that will vitiate the Harper contract.... I look upon [it] as being so valuable that they would seize the opportunity of breaking the arrangement if it were possible, and then you know you promised me you would not do anything in that line without consulting me," June 4, 1906, Leary, *Mark Twain's Correspondence with Henry Huttleston Rogers*, 608.

42. See ibid., 466, n. 2, for evidence of "Clemens's increasing dependence on Rogers" at this time (Summer 1901). Fred Kaplan says that Rogers became "for all practical purposes, [Clemens's] literary agent and money manager," *Singular Mark Twain*, 541.

43. March 6, 1896, Leary, *Mark Twain's Correspondence with Henry Huttleston Rogers*, 197–98 (my emphasis).

44. June 11, 1895, ibid., 151.

45. See ibid., 289. The reference is to the New York *Herald* announcement (June 1, 1897) of a subscription fund for his financial relief. Clemens's own attitude to this fund was ambivalent, but following Olivia's strong opposition he eventually requested that it be closed and any money collected returned. *The Chap-Book* noted that Clemens's "legitimate business losses" came about "due largely to the fact that Mr. Clemens could not force himself to be content with one trade only—that of author." But see Richard H. Brodhead, *Cultures of Letters: Scenes of Reading and Writing in Nineteenth-Century America* (Chicago: University of Chicago Press, 1993) 2–3 and 5–6, for pertinent remarks on this magazine's cultural assumptions and constituency.

46. "The $30,000 Bequest," in Mark Twain, *Collected Tales, Sketches, Speeches, & Essays, 1891–1910*, (New York: Library of America, 1992), 598.

47. Ibid., 20.

48. April 12, 1898, ibid., 340.

49. November 2, 1898, ibid., 372.

50. March 17–20, 1898, ibid., 327. Clemens later enthusiasm for an "invention...[that] makes blankets and other cloth out of peat" (342–43), and for the health food Plasmon (he became an elected director of the Plasmon Syndicate in April 1900), continued this pattern. Clemens does accept that "I am afraid you [Rogers] will not care for this" (343) in the former case!

51. March 17–20, 1898, ibid., 328.

52. Ibid., 329–30.

53. Though, as I indicate, his role had effectively changed. He was not "in business" in the same way as previously.

54. November 7, 1898, Leary, *Mark Twain's Correspondence with Henry Huttleston Rogers*, 375.

55. December 27, 1894, ibid., 112.

56. And see chapter 7.

57. See Leary *Mark Twain's Correspondence with Henry Huttleston Rogers*, 486.

58. Ibid., 591. He did though, in 1894, write to his wife Olivia that Rogers was one of the "two men who make me laugh without any difficulty." See Camfield, *Oxford Companion to Mark Twain*, 519. And Rogers would surprise his fellow guests at his Fairhaven School reunion in early 1902 by reading his own comic composition, "The Hen Roasted, or Truth Fricasseed" (see Leary, *Mark Twain's Correspondence with Henry Huttleston Rogers*, 481).

59. I expand on this in my next chapter. Bederman, in *Manliness & Civilization*, sees (middle-class) leisure as an arena where male identity could be realized in response to "narrowing career opportunities" (13): In Rogers and Clemens's case, it seems rather that it was money and time (and the leisure then released) that allowed a reconnection with their younger (bachelor) male selves. See Kaplan, *Singular Mark Twain*, 477–82, on Clemens's earlier enjoyment of "bachelorizing" in New York in the late summer of 1893, when he had left his family in Paris in an attempt to resolve his various financial problems.

60. Rotundo, "Boy Culture," in Carnes and Griffen, *Meanings for Manhood*, 19. That I draw my quote from this source is to once more recognize a continuity between boyhood and manhood and a shared positioning in relation to the codes and conventions of the domestic sphere.

61. Leary, *Mark Twain's Correspondence with Henry Huttleston Rogers*, 522–23.

62. Ibid., 627. "Sodomy" could refer at this time to "wanton lust of any sort." See Donald Yacovone, "Abolitionists and the 'Language of Fraternal Love,'" in Carnes and Griffen, *Meanings for Manhood*, 94.

63. In early 1900, Clemens writes to Rogers from London, wishing him there "to pilot me over a crossing or two," Leary, *Mark Twain's Correspondence with Henry Huttleston Rogers*, 434. This is particularly significant in its reflexive reference to Clemens's own early career as a steamboat pilot, the very symbol for him of self-sufficient masculine authority.

64. See his writing block, which he described in terms of being "broke down—in my head" (September 9, 1894, ibid., 73); and his high anxiety levels (see 111, n. 2, and 265–66).

65. Ibid., 550 and 552. The court hearings were in a case brought against Rogers and William Rockefeller's Consolidated Gas Company. On February 8, Rogers—referring to the same case—admits he is "head over heels in trouble," 555.

66. Ibid., 590. Rogers would suffer a stroke in the summer of 1907.

67. See ibid., 7.

68. Isabel Lyon measures the costs of the strain Rogers had been under, and the illnesses suffered, when she reports on the Clemens-Rogers Bermuda trip commencing February 22, 1908: "Mr. Rogers came feebly onto the boat, a sick sick man." Quoted in Leary, *Mark Twain's Correspondence with Henry Huttleston Rogers*, 645.

69. April 8–9, 1900, ibid., 440.

70. And see Clemens's previously quoted distinction between "cold business" and "sentimental bellyaches."

71. Harris, "Mark Twain and Gender," in Shelley Fisher Fishkin, ed., *A Historical Guide to Mark Twain* (New York: Oxford University Press, 2002), 179. Scott A. Sandage's work on the "vernacular genre" of the begging letter—letters, written by men whose "economic impotence and dependency" resulted from their failure to succeed in the competitive marketplace, to those (like Rogers) who had notably succeeded—is also of interest here. For Sandage, the genre (and the assumptions underlying it) illustrate a widely held belief that, in fact, "sentiment was not out of place in the competitive sphere of market capitalism." See "Gaze of Success", 181–201.

72. See, for instance, Camfield, *Oxford Companion to Mark Twain*, 519. Fred Kaplan does, however, say that: "If Rogers had attached himself to a much-loved humorist to mitigate the unpopularity of monopolistic wealth, such ulterior motivation escaped Twain. Rogers also paid far more in labor and energy than any public relations advantage could amount to," *Singular Mark Twain*, 499.

73. See Leary, *Mark Twain's Correspondence with Henry Huttleston Rogers*, 22. The over-insistent quality of Clemens's voice here may suggest that the Rogers friendship involved him in some shameful compromises, which adversely affected his sense of manliness. Such a reading would qualify other aspects of my argument here. On Clemens's general hostility to "the new American plutocracy" and on his knowledge and resentment of the fact that "he was partly in the pocket of the wealthy and partly under the spell of their example," see Camfield, *Oxford Companion to Mark Twain*, 515–17. And see my next chapter.

74. March 4, 1894, Leary, *Mark Twain's Correspondence with Henry Huttleston Rogers*, 38.

75. July 27, 1906, ibid., 613.

76. Ibid., 498. See, too, Clemens's reference on September 24, 1902 to Roger's "infinitely touching" letter, expressing himself "grateful beyond any words" (508). The letter itself is now missing.

77. I would recall here what Drury Sherrod says about same-sex male friendships and their "inferred" and "low-intimacy" nature, an intimacy often based on "shared pursuits and shared risks, rather than the shared disclosures of women." Sherrod refers to contemporary relationships here but it is reasonable to apply these words to the earlier period too. See "The Bonds of Men: Problems and Possibilities in Close Male Relationships," in Harry Brod, ed., *The Making of Masculinities: The New Men's Studies* (Cambridge, Mass.: Unwin Hyman, 1987), 220–22, 231–32, 236. Again, see my next chapter for more detail.

78. August 12, 1907, Leary, *Mark Twain's Correspondence with Henry Huttleston Rogers*, 632.

79. See ibid., 648.

80. Ibid., 711.

81. Leary, *Mark Twain's Correspondence with Henry Huttleston Rogers*, 309.

82. See June 6 and August 18, 1904, ibid., 569 and 580.

83. September 24, 1902, ibid., 509. Clemens does, though, in the same letter, describe Olivia's ceding of her authority (over her own body) to professional medical male expertise. For she recognizes the "merit and masculinity" of two new specialists and defers to them accordingly. After Olivia's death, Clemens's daughters and Isabel Lyon, his secretary, tended to replace her domestic role for him. Thus daughter Jean is "the executive

head and manager" (June 8, 1904, ibid., p. 570) soon following the death. Later, on May 29, 1907, Clemens notes that "Miss Lyon runs Clara, and Jean, and me, and the servants, and the house-keeping, and the house-building, and the secretary-work, and remains as extraordinarily competent as ever," ibid., 625.

84. John Cooley, "Mark Twain, Rebellious Girls, and Daring Young Women," in Mark Twain, *How Nancy Jackson Married Kate Wilson and Other Tales of Rebellious Girls & Daring Young Women* (Lincoln: University of Nebraska Press, 2001), 235. See, too, Susan K. Harris's brief though illuminating comments on "Men" in "Mark Twain and Gender," in Fishkin, *A Historical Guide*, 174–79.

85. Sandage, "Gaze of Success," 83 and 186. Though "Which Was the Dream?" is set in the 1850s that does not prevent the identification of a (refracted) concern with later historical issues.

86. Twain, "Which Was the Dream?" 222.

87. Ibid., 222.

88. Rotundo, "Boy Culture," 19 and 16.

89. Twain, "Which Was the Dream?" 225–26. There may be a suggestion here that the lauding of Tom's male identity is premature.

90. See Rotundo, *American Manhood*, 232–38. Forrest G. Robinson reads such military and political references in terms of Clemens attempting "to submerge his own life in a fictionalized portrait of his friend and great moral hero, Ulysses S. Grant, and thereby to earn a kind of absolution for his own failures in war and business. But once the nightmare of personal ruin has commenced, there is no return; instead, the narrative is left unfinished, as if to concede that the moral acquittal of an awakening into Grant's reality is imaginatively beyond reach," *The Author-Cat: Clemens's Life in Fiction* (New York: Fordham University Press, 2007), 195.

91. Twain, "Which Was the Dream?" 225.

92. "These are lovely days . . . with these busy little tykes for comrades. I have my share of fun with them. We are great hunters, we. The library is our jungle . . . I am the elephant, and go on all fours, and the children ride on my back, astride" (ibid., 231).

93. Margaret Marsh, "Suburban Men and Masculine Domesticity, 1870–1915," 122.

94. Twain, "Which Was the Dream?" 226.

95. Ibid., p. 227.

96. This is not quite a natural disaster, but verges on one in the part fire plays (and the elemental force with which it is associated). The sense of vulnerability identified here is also one of Clemens's larger habits, relating to a repeated sense of catastrophe and personal damage, perhaps originating with brother Henry's dramatic 1858 riverboat death.

97. Susan Gillman notes that many of the details of Tom's narrative of decline "are recognized as roughly parallel to the agonizing Clemens family history during the later 1890s," *Dark Twins: Imposture and Identity in Mark Twain's America* (University of Chicago Press, 1989), 173.

98. Twain, "Which Was the Dream?" 239.

99. Ibid., 250.

100. There is a strong echo here of *Pudd'nhead Wilson* (1894) and its concern with identity and difference. Tom and Jeff (like Tom and Valet in the earlier novel) are twinned figures. Individual difference, depending on conventionally authoritative markers (fingerprints and autographs), collapses in both cases.

101. Twain, "Which Was the Dream?" 239.

102. Such concerns also uncannily predict Clemens's later disputes with Isabel Lyon and Ralph Ashcroft. See Karen Lystra, *Dangerous Intimacy: The Untold Story of Mark Twain's Final Years* (Berkeley and Los Angeles: University of California Press, 2004).

103. Twain, "Which Was the Dream?" 249 and 252.

104. I take these last terms from Harris, "Mark Twain and Gender," 175. In the final section of the narrative, this representation of Tom's complete fall from public male grace is slightly modified as we learn that some friends "stood by" the family, that the newspapers "used [him] generously," and that his fellow army officers believed his story: Twain, "Which Was the Dream?" 258.

105. Twain, "Which Was the Dream?" 253.

106. No narrative explanation is given for the move from Washington and the change of name.

107. Twain, "Which Was the Dream?" 253 and 258.

108. See Bederman, *Manliness & Civilization*, 41.

109. Quoted in Michael S. Kimmel, "The Contemporary 'Crisis' of Masculinity in Historical Perspective," in Brod, *Making of Masculinities*, 147.

110. I would not downplay another side of Clemens that can, in his narratives of cross-dressing, also playfully upset traditional gender roles. His representation of gender is complex and, as so often in the various aspects of his work and thought, difficult to pin down in a single interpretative whole. His anxieties about male identity can, then, coexist with—and be displaced by—that "secret admiration for spirited women" found in his depiction of female cross-dressers (Harris, "Mark Twain and Gender," 182). See, too, Shelley Fisher Fishkin's discussion of Clemens's use of the male cross-dressing traditions of the American stage, and his representation of Widow Tillou, in her edition of Mark Twain, *Is He Dead? A Comedy in Three Acts* (Berkeley and Los Angeles: University of California Press, 2003), 191–96 and 202–3. Linda A. Morris, in *Gender Play in Mark Twain: Cross-Dressing and Transgression* (Columbus: University of Missouri Press, 2007) is another valuable source on this topic.

*Chapter 7*

1. For a reproduction of the painting see the National Gallery of Art (Washington) Web site, http://www.nga.gov/fcgi-bin/timage_f?object=30667&image=5043&c=gg71 (accessed March 26, 2009). For the original title of the painting, see MarianneDoezema, *George Bellows and Urban America* (New Haven: Yale University Press, 1992), 105.

2. Doezema, *George Bellows and Urban America*, 106. Doezema suggests Bellows's painting was inspired by "explosive...tensions" in late 1909 "surrounding [Jack] Johnson's continuing claim to the heavyweight title." A *New York Times* editorial commented: "It is really a serious matter that, if the negro wins [against Jim Jeffries, "the great white hope"], thousands and thousands of other negroes will wonder whether, in claiming equality with the whites, they have not been too modest...," quoted in ibid., 106. For Doezema's full discussion of this racial issue, see 104–13.

3. Robert Haywood, "George Bellows's 'Stag at Sharkey's': Boxing, Violence, and Male Identity," *Smithsonian Studies in American Art* 2, no. 2 (Spring 1988): 6.

4. Doezema, *George Bellows and Urban America*, 103.

5. Robert Haywood, "George Bellows's 'Stag at Sharkey's,'" 7, and see Doezema, *George Bellows and Urban America*, 68–72 and 94. Doezma writes that: "during the decades surrounding the turn of the century... forces of feminization were perceived on several fronts.... S. Weir Mitchell complained that 'the monthly [magazines] are getting so lady-like that naturally they will soon menstruate,'" 70. Both Haywood and Doezema, and especially the former, focus on the homoeroticism of Bellows's painting, and associated more generally with boxing as a sport (see, for instance, Haywood, "George Bellows's 'Stag at Sharkey's,'" 8–14).

6. Doezema, *George Bellows and Urban America*, 78 and 80.

7. I take my term here from Robert H. Murray, "Henry H. Rogers—The Man," *Young Life: A Magazine of Today* 3, no. 1 (April 1906): "Our premier humorist, Mark Twain, is Rogers' most intimate chum. Rogers' funny stories gain wide circulation through Mark Twain, who knows more people. Mark is a better mixer than Rogers.... Rogers' circle of cronies is very small. He is never seen in society, or at big public dinners. The theatre has no especial charm for him. He doesn't care for fishing or hunting. He is as methodical in his habits as a bachelor; probably he is never happier than when he and Mark Twain and one or two others sit down to a game of euchre," 3. If this portrait of Rogers is true, it would seem that Clemens's friendship did draw Rogers, to at least some extent, out of a relatively narrow social shell (though see the quote from Camfield that follows).

8. Gregg Camfield, *The Oxford Companion to Mark Twain* (New York: Oxford University Press, 2003), 517. Doezema comments in relation to boxing: "The all-male company at Sharkey's represented not merely the absence of women but everything associated with the feminine—social constraints, marriage, responsibility, civilization," *George Bellows and Urban America*, 88.

9. Fred Kaplan, *The Singular Mark Twain* (Doubleday: New York: 2003), 478.

10. Lewis Leary, ed., *Mark Twain's Letters to Mary* (New York: Columbia University Press, 1961), 11.

11. Clemens to wife Olivia, December 25, 1893, quoted in Peter Krass, *Ignorance, Confidence, and Filthy Rich Friends: The Business Adventures of Mark Twain, Chronic Speculator and Entrepreneur* (Hoboken, N. J.: John Wiley & Sons, 2007), 198–99. And see Lewis Leary, ed., *Mark Twain's Correspondence with Henry Huttleston Rogers, 1893–1909* (Berkeley and Los Angeles: University of California Press, 1969), n. 3.

12. See Leary, *Mark Twain's Correspondence with Henry Huttleston Rogers*, 464 and 474, n. 1.

13. See the Lotos Club Web site at http://www.lotosclub.org/ and the *New York Times* report of the dinner at the Web site dedicated to Twain quotations, newspaper pieces about him, and related resources, http://www.twainquotes.com/19001117.html (both sites accessed March 25, 2009). An article in the New York *World Telegram* (March 20, 1940), "Ghosts Gather for Feast of Lotos Eaters," reports on the club's seventieth anniversary and recalls Clemens as "a frequent visitor to the clubhouse, where he enjoyed playing billiards and discussing the issue of free silver at inordinate length, delivering expositions on the subject which confused everyone, including himself." This may indicate that Clemens had only a partial grasp of one of the most complex political issues of the day.

14. Information provided by Nancy Johnson, Archivist, The Lotos Club (email correspondence). When I wrote to ask whether the Club had any

African American members at this time, or—if not, as I assumed—when such members first joined, I received no reply. Debbie Charpentier (archivist at the Millicent Library) lists the clubs to which Rogers belonged at the time of his death: Union League Club; Metropolitan; Engineers Club; New York Yacht Club; Lotos Club; and Seawanhaka Corinthian Yacht Club (email correspondence).

15. Camfield, *Oxford Companion to Mark Twain*, 120. There is a chapter by Clemens in Aaron Watson, *The Savage Club* (London: T. Fisher Unwin, 1907), for he was also a member of this famous London club. Clemens joked, "he didn't feel fit for civilization,... but might feel more at home among savages," 128. The club in fact has a figure wearing an American Indian headdress featured on its current Web site.

16. "New Stories and Anecdotes of Famous Writer Revealed in Picture of Clemens by His Friend and Physician," Boston *Sunday Globe*, November 29, 1925.

17. Ibid. Rice may be presenting his friend in the best light he can here for it is clear that at times Clemens did drink a lot. Miss Lyon, for example, records in her diary (January 17, 1908): "At 2:30 I wakened to hear the billiard-bang, & went down to find the King playing in a drunken haze. He was trying to drown out the chill—& couldn't move without reeling.... It was wonderful to see the King pick up a ball & fondle it—& then try to hit it with his cue & be unable to touch it; but he swore splendidly.... I gently took the King's cue away, & led him to his room. He staggered & hit his head against one of the little angels on his bed post, & grabbed his dear head with a volley of oaths," the Mark Twain Papers at the University of California at Berkeley (henceforth MTP). Or it may be that Clemens exercised considerably more restraint outside his home—a home we should remember where he was frequently desperately lonely once Olivia had died. Rice is interesting too on the (possibly) depressive side of Clemens's personality, and its longstanding nature: "Mark Twain was at times a very sad man, a pathetic figure, and this, too, before death came into his family, and before his financial worries. When he read of the death of a friend or an acquaintance I frequently heard him say, 'There is a mighty lucky man.'"

18. Clemens reported on this boxing match in a letter to Olivia dated January 4, 1894, reprinted in Dixon Wecter, ed., *The Love Letters of Mark Twain*, (New York: Harper, 1949) 287. References to the "Coffee Cooler" are scattered through Leary, *Mark Twain's Correspondence with Henry Huttleston Rogers*: see index under Craig, Frank.

19. Letter to Olivia Clemens, January 28, 1894, MTP. Clemens's reference to Corbett being "the most perfectly and beautifully constructed human animal in the world" reminds us of "boxing's eroticism...[its] muscular primal performance," Haywood, "George Bellows's 'Stag at Sharkey's,'" 14 and 10.

20. I am again aware of Clemens's own role as one whose status lay (in part) in his own ability to entertain both his wealthier companions and a wider audience. And I am reminded of the crowd's reaction to Clemens when he and Rogers attended the match between the American Ora Morningstar and the Frenchman Louis Cure at an international billiards championship at Madison Square Garden in 1906. The *New York Times* report of April 10 reads: "[Mark Twain] was alive with keen appreciation of the good shots, and soon attracted the attention of the crowd. He left a few innings before the close of the match. Cure was at the table shooting when

he went out, and the spontaneous outburst of cheering on the part of the crowd puzzled the Frenchman. Mark Twain saluted the spectators by throwing kisses to them, and when Cure saw this he waved his hand to the retiring humorist and resumed his play," http://www.twainquotes. com/19060410.html (see n. 13 above: Web site accessed March 26, 2009). Clemens himself attributed his conspicuousness at the event to "two reasons." One was that he and Rogers "were the only men in evening clothes." The other was because of "our old white heads." Isobel Lyon's diary, MTP.

21. Shelley Fisher Fishkin, "Mark Twain and Race," in Fishkin, ed., *A Historical Guide to Mark Twain* (New York: Oxford University Press, 2002), 154 and 150.

22. MTP.

23. April 24, 1896, Leary, *Mark Twain's Correspondence with Henry Huttleston Rogers*, 210.

24. Typescript of "Winter-end Excursion to the Sutherd," 2, 6, and 7. MTP.

25. Clemens provides the majority of letters in the correspondence, and the most intense, though this may just mean that many of Rogers's letters are now missing.

26. Fairhaven, Mass.: Millicent Library.

27. Camfield has a short section on Rogers in *Oxford Companion to Mark Twain*, 517–520.

28. February 20, 1898, MTP.

29. *Mark Twain's Autobiography*, ed. Albert Bigelow Paine (New York: Harper, 1924), 1:250.

30. MTP.

31. See, for instance, Leary, *Mark Twain's Correspondence with Henry Huttleston Rogers*, 57, 59, and 398.

32. Leary, *Mark Twain's Letters to Mary*, 45.

33. I am also thinking of his "Angel Fish" here. On April 1, 1908, during the trip Clemens took with Rogers to Bermuda (February-April), Isabel Lyon notes: "[The King—Clemens] has his aquarium of little girls—& they are all angel fish . . . Off he goes with a flash when he sees a new pair of slim little legs appear; & if the little girl wears butterfly bows of ribbon on the back of her head then his delirium is complete," Isabel Lyon's Diary, MTP.

34. Leary, *Mark Twain's Letters to Mary*, 27. In her October 1, 1906, diary entry, Isabel Lyon writes: "The King has come back. . . . He was so beautiful, so gay, so full of his trip & of Santissima's [Clara's] Concert and of his playings at Fairhaven. There is no one who can play so successfully as the King can—He is so fond of Mrs. Harry Rogers—& calls her his 'Pal.' He made a badge or a coat of arms for the "pals" while he was in Fairhaven this time—a bottle of saccharine & a candle on a shield with "Sweetness & Light" for the motto. Their partnership was to torment—or to provide entertainment for those who were playing cards—Bridge or Poker—by throwing in remarks, personal remarks—and this they'd keep up until one of them would be thrown from the room," MTP.

35. Leary, *Mark Twain's Letters to Mary*, 38.

36. By permission of the Houghton Library, Harvard University, bMS Am 1784.1 (75). Clemens was apparently unable to interact with Clara as she followed her career without upstaging her with his own celebrity: see, for instance, the account of Clara's September 1906 recital in Norfolk (Connecticut) in Leary, *Mark Twain's Letters to Mary*, 64–67. See, too, the manner in which "Clemens . . . managed simultaneously to recognize and diminish" Clara in his speech following her and Gabrilowitsch's

performance to raise funds for the Redding Mark Twain Library on September 21, 1909, Laura Skandera Trombley, "Mark Twain's *Annus Horribilis* of 1908–1909," *American Literary Realism* 40, no. 2 (Winter 2008): 126.

37. Leary, *Mark Twain's Letters to Mary*, 78.

38. Ibid., 37–38. For more on Clemens's relations with his two youngest daughters, see Karen Lystra, *Dangerous Intimacy: The Untold Story of Mark Twain's Final Years* (Berkeley and Los Angeles: University of California Press, 2004).

39. Kaplan, *Singular Mark Twain*, 617–18.

40. Leary, *Mark Twain's Correspondence with Henry Huttleston Rogers*, 650. On Rogers's visits, see Paine, *Mark Twain: A Biography* (New York: Harper, 1912) 3:1337, and Mary Lawton, *A Lifetime with Mark Twain: The Memories of Katy Leary, for Thirty Years His Faithful and Devoted Servant* (New York: Harcourt, Brace, 1925), 280 ("I told you what a wonderful friend he was to [Mr. Clemens], all his life . . . Mr. Rogers could never do enough. . . . He'd come every morning in his car to the Fifth Avenue house, just to see Mr. Clemens"). Isabel Lyon, too, gives a good impression of the time the two men spent together in diary entries like that of Saturday March 10, 1906: "Mr. Rogers came at 12.30 and took [Clemens] off to luncheon & to the matinee—'Abbysinia' [sic] at the Majestic Theatre. . . . [O]ut again this evening to play billiards with Mr. Rogers," MTP.

41. See Leary, *Mark Twain's Correspondence with Henry Huttleston Rogers*, 647.

42. Ibid., 659.

43. Summer 1906, ibid., 613. All misspellings here are as in the original letter.

44. August 31, 1906, ibid., 616.

45. Ibid., quoted 616.

46. Peter Stoneley, "Mark Twain and Gender," in Messent and Budd, eds., *A Companion to Mark Twain* (Oxford: Blackwell, 2005), 77.

47. Though he did continue to carry responsibility for his daughter Jean.

48. Henry Nash Smith and William M. Gibson, eds., *Mark Twain-Howells Letters: The Correspondence of Samuel L. Clemens and William D. Howells, 1872–1910* (Cambridge, Mass.: Harvard University Press, 1960), 833.

49. "Summer Excursion to the Nutherd," typescript, 2, MTP. There is also a variant and fuller version of this document in Clemens's handwriting.

50. Handwritten version of the log, 7, MTP.

51. "Summer Excursion to the Nutherd," typescript, 6.

52. "Winter-end Excursion to the Sutherd," typescript, 6.

53. Ibid., 16.

54. Ibid., 18. Clarence Rice gives a rather different picture of Clemens as standing a little apart from his companions and hints at his corrosive wit when he refers to Thomas Reed having "brought some of his famous rum on board": "Mr. Clemens didn't need a stimulant to play cards, because I don't remember that he ever played in our games. . . . [He] was always reading during the card games. He read anything that came to hand." Rice speaks of Reed being annoyed one day when Clemens declined his hospitality; "I don't remember how Mr. Reed expressed his displeasure at Mr. Clemens' behaviour, but I do recall that Mr. Clemens observed that he didn't require any artificial stimulant to compete with the intellectual output of the rest of the party," "New Stories and Anecdotes of Famous Writer Revealed." Rice was recalling events over twenty years later so his words must be treated with a degree of caution.

55. Paine, *Mark Twain's Autobiography*, 2:204 and 206.

56. Though he is wrong regarding Clemens's previously "negligent" dress sense.

57. "To the Person Sitting in Darkness," in Mark Twain, *Collected Tales, Sketches, Speeches, and Essays: 1891–1910* (New York: Library of America, 1992), 457.

58. "Edmund Burke on Croker and Tammany," in *Mark Twain, Collected Tales, Sketches, Speeches, and Essays: 1891–1910*, 492. My examples are highly selective. Clemens was also of course concerned about racial matters, especially the rising numbers of lynchings in the United States in the period. And his concerns about child and female labor conditions in America are indicated in *No. 44: The Mysterious Stranger* (1902–8), if we accept the argument that one of his intentions in this text was to address American matters through a European lens. The latter case is made in Peter Messent, "The Chronicle of Young Satan and *No. 44, The Mysterious Stranger*: A Transnationalist Reading," in Joseph Csicsila and Chad Rohman, eds., *Centenary Reflections on Mark Twain's "No. 44, The Mysterious Stranger"* (forthcoming).

59. Quoted in Milton Meltzer, *Mark Twain: A Pictorial Biography* (Columbia, Mo.: University of Missouri Press, 2002), 205. And see Dan Beard's illustration of Gould as the slavedriver in *A Connecticut Yankee* (1889).

60. See Ron Powers, *Mark Twain: A Life* (New York: Free Press, 2005), 491 and 530. Camfield suggests that throughout his life, and especially in the later years, Clemens "was partly in the pocket of the wealthy and partly under the spell of their example, and he knew and resented it." This, for him, helps to explain the "scathing denunciations of various plutocrats" (especially Gould and John D. Rockefeller, Jr.) in the autobiographical dictations. Given these were not to be published until after his death, Clemens could here release feelings otherwise suppressed. See *Oxford Companion to Mark Twain*, 516. To my mind the situation was more complex than this, depending on judgments of individual personalities as well as their professional activities.

61. Leary, *Mark Twain's Letters to Mary*, p. 47. Clemens heads a continuation of the same letter, "3 p.m.—in bed," and writes: "I have resumed my habits, you see. When I am not away from home I live in bed, to beat the lonesomeness," 48. Clemens's liking for, and dependency on, the company of others is in good part explained in this statement.

62. Kaplan, *Singular Mark Twain*, 482. See too the section on "Henry H. Rogers" in Paine, *Mark Twain's Autobiography*, 1:250–65. This portion of the *Autobiography* was written by Twain in Florence in 1904.

63. Ibid., 262–63.

64. "The Plutocracy," *Mark Twain in Eruption*, ed. Bernard De Voto (New York: Harper & Brothers, 1940), p. 99. Clemens here takes a position against the representations of Rogers's company generally found in the press ("For some years now . . . the Standard Oil Company . . . has been freely and volubly charged with every crime and every villainy known to commercial oppression and misconduct," 98).

65. See Leary, *Mark Twain's Correspondence with Henry Huttleston Rogers*, 478–79.

66. See Kaplan, *Mr. Clemens and Mark Twain*, 591. In the "Corporate America" section of "Becoming Multicultural: Culture, Economy, and the Novel 1860–1920," Susan L. Mizruchi puts this more bluntly: "In 1908,

Mark Twain made a speech at the Aldine Club...in support of the Rockefellers. This was less Twain's betrayal of an earlier democratic impulse than his embrace of plutocratic leanings he had always had," *The Cambridge History of American Literature*, vol. 3: *Prose Writing 1860–1920*, ed. Sacvan Bercovitch (Cambridge: Cambridge University Press, 2005), 682.

67. Clarence Rice writes of the period when Olivia was still alive: "As all [Clemens's] friends knew...[h]e depended on [Mrs. Clemens's] judgment in all decisions....When Mrs. Clemens was away and Mr. Clemens was alone in New York and a question of importance came up for decision it was a habit of his to say: 'I'm no more competent than a child to settle this matter; if Mrs. Clemens were only here she would know the right answer instantly. God gave very few people her wisdom. He certainly could not bestow that large gift on two members of the same family,'" "New Stories and Anecdotes of Famous Writer Revealed." The degree of such difference is, though, debatable as Olivia was—as her background suggests—(and in Louis J. Budd's words) "a fully pro-laissez-faire conservative" (private correspondence).

68. So Allan Nevins claims, in a statement that (one has to say) is more than a touch debatable, that "had our [American] pace been slower and our achievement weaker, had we not created so swiftly our powerful industrial units in steel, oil, textiles, chemicals, electricity and the automotive vehicles, the free world might have lost the First World War and most certainly would have lost the Second." Quoted in Jack Beatty, *Age of Betrayal: The Triumph of Money in America, 1865–1900* (New York: Alfred A. Knopf, 2007), 390.

69. I am reminded here of Peter Stoneley's remarks on American masculinity in the period and the way that "the priority of 'potency' makes difficult the idea of partnership, which is founded on 'parity,'" "Rewriting the Gold Rush: Twain, Harte and Homosociality," *Journal of American Studies* 30, no. 2 (1996): 206. Rogers and Clemens's parity was based exactly on the fact that they were not in economic competition with one another, possessed fame and cultural authority of very different types (as businessman and literary artist/celebrity respectively).

70. See Clemens's letter to Emilie Rogers of November 26, 1896, Leary, *Mark Twain's Correspondence with Henry Huttleston Rogers*, 253–54.

71. Elbert Hubbard, *Little Journeys into the Homes of Great Businessmen: H. H. Rogers* (East Aurora, Erie County, N. Y.: The Roycrofters, 1909), 157 and 161–62. Clemens spoke at the dedication of Fairhaven town hall on February 22,1894, and at the laying of the cornerstone for the Unitarian church on August 5, 1901. He also sent inscribed copies of his books and other memorabilia to the Millicent Library (named after Rogers's dead daughter).

72. See extracts from Lawson's book on the Fairhaven Millicent Library Web site (accessed March 26, 2009), http://www.millicentlibrary.org/lawson.htm.

73. Powers, *Mark Twain*, 553.

74. Beatty, *Age of Betrayal*, 384–85. Beatty comments, "Carnegie's pacificism was no match for his greed," 384.

75. See ibid., 347–59 (quotation on 349).

76. Powers, *Mark Twain*, 562. Though Howells, too, as we have seen earlier, if he avoided friendships of quite this kind, made similar types of accommodation himself.

77. Earl J. Dias, *Mark Twain and Henry Huttleston Rogers: An Odd Couple* (Fairhaven, Mass.: The Millicent Library, 1984), 160. The "eyes blazing" detail may well, however, be Dias's elaboration.

## Coda

1. Twichell is the odd man out here, though he was with Susy Clemens (while her parents were abroad) when her fatal illness first set in, and—after her death—he came from his Adirondacks holiday "to New York on the sad errand of meeting Mrs. Clemens coming from England, to tell her that Susy was dead—one of the most distressing duties I ever had to perform" (quoted in Steve Courtney, *Joseph Hopkins Twichell: The Life and Times of Mark Twain's Closest Friend* [Athens: Georgia University Press, 2008], 246). He also officiated at both Susy and Jean's funeral services. I might also have focused on these men's responses to their wives' deaths here, but space prevents me from doing both.

2. Susan Goodman and Carl Dawson, *William Dean Howells: A Writer's Life* (Berkeley and Los Angeles: University of California Press, 2005), 295.

3. And deeply upsetting. Pat Jalland writes that "[i]n the nineteenth century, parental grief for adult children may have been greater than that for very young children for two reasons. People were well aware that child mortality was highest in infancy and the first five years in life [see the figures that follow], so that the death of a very young child . . . was a terrible loss but not one that was entirely unexpected. . . . Deaths of adult children between twenty and middle age were entirely unexpected and untimely, while they were also harder to cope with because of greater emotional investment, a stronger bonding process, and half a lifetime of memories," *Death in the Victorian Family* (New York: Oxford University Press, 1996), 334–35.

4. http://www.cdc.gov/nchs/data/vsushistorical/vsush_1890_4.pdf (pp. 8 and 10). This, the Centers for Disease Control and Prevention Web site, has copies of Dept. of the Interior Census Office Reports: accessed March 27, 2009. The comparative rise in the twenty to twenty-five-year-old group may possibly relate to death in childbirth.

5. Journal entry, September 25, 1891. The Yale Collection of American Literature in the Beinecke Rare Book and Manuscript Library, henceforth cited as Beinecke.

6. Letter to Clemens, February 2, 1892. The Mark Twain Papers at the University of California at Berkeley (henceforth MTP). Twichell's biographer, Steve Courtney, speaks of "the element of the charmed family circle of mother, father, and nine children experiencing its first rift, which Twichell expresses in [the quoted] letter. . . . At any rate, he loved the insularity of the family. The 'Lost Boys (and Girls)' aspect of Twichell's lengthy two-month vacations in the Adirondacks are of interest to the history of Victorian family life, I think. . . . [W]hen sent out into the world on their own, the Twichell children didn't always do all that well setting up families that could reproduce this childhood idyll." Private correspondence.

7. Letter to Clemens, January 5, 1909, MTP.

8. Letter dated July 20, [1907], MTP. For a report of Marjory Rice's wedding (which took place on 14 November 1907) see archive on the *New York Times* Web site (accessed March 27, 2009): http://query.nytimes.com/mem/archive-free/pdf?res=9F00EFD8103EE033A25756-C1A9679D946697D6CF. Clemens and Henry H. Rogers were among the invited guests.

9. See too Peter Stoneley, *Mark Twain and the Feminine Aesthetic* (Cambridge: Cambridge University Press, 1992), for valuable material on Susy Clemens.

10. Andrew Hoffman, *Inventing Mark Twain: The Lives of Samuel Langhorne Clemens* (London: Weidenfeld & Nicolson, 1997), 362.

11. August 1893, from Florence (Italy), MTP. Susy's parents had taken her there in part (it seems) to lessen Louise's influence. Susy started to call herself Olivia (her actual first name) at Bryn Mawr: see Hoffman, *Inventing Mark Twain*, 364. The best acount of the Susy-Louise friendship is in Linda Morris, *Gender Play in Mark Twain: Cross-Dressing and Transgression* (Columbia, Mo.: University of Missouri Press, 2007), 12–20.

12. Hoffman, *Inventing Mark Twain*, 367.

13. When Clemens, in Guildford, was separated from his wife Olivia (who had travelled to America on hearing of Susy's illness), he wrote to her on August 29, 1896—just after Susy's death—that "such a little time ago we had three daughters, now we have lost two. Susy goes out of our life to something better; Clara goes out of it to a doubtful change—& one which I would have prevented if I could have done it," MTP. Hoffman describes Clara's problems in breaking away from the family to live her own life and pursue a career. Writing of a later period in 1903—with Clemens and his wife in Europe and Richard Watson Gilder acting as Clara's chaperone back in the United States—he says that "[t]hough Clara had celebrated her twenty-ninth birthday earlier that summer, [Clemens] did not believe that she was free to make her own choices about what to do with her life. . . ." Hoffman, *Inventing Mark Twain*, 451.

14. Letter of February 28, 1893, MTP. And see Morris, *Gender Play in Mark Twain*, 118–23.

15. Letter of January 25, 1904, MTP.

16. Hoffman, *Inventing Mark Twain*, 383. Hoffman also quotes a college friend who described her as "very emotional, high-strung, temperamental," 364. Edith Colgate Salisbury, who attempted to recreate a collage of the voices of the Clemens family and others closely associated with them in *Susy and Mark Twain: Family Dialogues* (New York: Harper & Row, 1965), has Madame Marchesi—Susy's Paris singing teacher—speak of her "voluntary self-starvation," 339.

17. Karen Lystra, *Dangerous Intimacy: The Untold Story of Mark Twain's Final Years* (Berkeley and Los Angeles: University of California Press, 2004), 44.

18. For more on Clemens's relationships with Jean and Clara and particularly on the latter's 1906–8 scandalous relationship with (the already married) Charles Edwin Wark, the "extraordinary speed of events" surrounding her October 1909 marriage to Ossip Gabrilowitsch (127), and Clemens's (possibly) manipulative hand in both these affairs, see Laura Skandera Trombley, "Mark Twain's *Annus Horribilis* of 1908–1909," *American Literary Realism* 40, no. 2 (Winter 2008): 114–36.

19. See Goodman and Dawson, *William Dean Howells*, 210.

20. Ibid., 214.

21. George Arms and Cristoph K. Lohmann, eds., *W. D. Howells, Selected Letters*, vol. 2: *1873–1881* (Boston: Twayne, 1979), 292.

22. Robert C. Leitz III, Richard H. Ballinger, and Christoph K. Lohmann, eds., *W. D. Howells, Selected Letters*, vol. 3: *1882–1891* (Boston: Twayne, 1980), 194.

23. Ibid., 245.

24. Ibid., 293–95. Winifred may have had some kind of congenital defect or been affected by some childhood disease. The autopsy report on an (unnamed) organic problem, and Howells's comment in a March 10, 1889, letter that "I feel as if she were a child again; and since our loss we have learned that in some things she was indeed never otherwise," suggest some issue concerning her physical development (248). The illness however may have been both physical and psychological—and may (in part) have taken the form of what we would now know as anorexia. Howells's grief must have been compounded by the fact that his wife Elinor had evidently been against his decision to put Winifred in Weir Mitchell's care (see 249). Weir Mitchell, it seems, believed he was locked in a "tussle of wills" (the words here are Howells's) with what he—and evidently her father too—saw as Winny's "hypochondriacal illusions and obstinacy in believing her symptoms physical rather than mental" (Goodman and Dawson, *William Dean Howells*, 295).

25. Lewis Leary, ed., *Mark Twain's Correspondence with Henry Huttleston Rogers, 1893–1909* (Berkeley and Los Angeles: University of California Press, 1969), 195. The detail about the annulment does not seem to be entirely correct—see below.

26. The material here comes from a 161-page transcript of the trial that took place to end the marriage, headed: *Supreme Court Appellate Division. Mary H. Mott, by Henry H. Rogers, her guardian ad litem Plaintiff-Respondent against Joseph C. Mott—Defender-Appellant, New York, 1896* (copy in Millicent Library, Fairhaven, Connecticut).

27. Ibid., 2–3.

28. Ibid., 37–38.

29. Ibid., 27, 105, and 130–31.

30. Ibid., 14 and 20. It was also "ordered . . . that it shall be lawful for the said plaintiff, Mrs. Mary H. Mott, to marry again in the same manner as if the said defendant, Joseph C. Mott, were dead, but that it shall still not be lawful for the said defendant . . . to marry again until the said plaintiff be actually dead. . . ." This seems an extraordinary judgment.

31. It may, of course, be that Mai's wishes were in entire accord with his by this point.

32. In the ornate sixteen-foot-high stained-glass window in the Library, one pane "shows a female form—the gentle muse of poetry herself in softly draped robes—her face, pure and lovely, raised in a sort of adoration. The spectator knows at once that this is a real face, the actual likeness of a flesh and blood maiden. The face is that of Millicent G. Rogers, in whose memory the window was mounted—and, indeed, the whole building was raised," http://www.millicentlibrary.org/history.htm (the "story of the Millicent Library [Fairhaven]" Web site, accessed March 27, 2009). Pat Jalland writes that "[m]emorial church windows" were "high on the list" of "commemorative objects" that "late nineteenth-century mourners . . . favoured," *Death in the Victorian Family*, 291. Rogers's memorial took a more secular form, and (as befitted his wealth) a grander one too, in comprising the whole building as well as that specific window.

33. See, for example, Mary Louise Kete, *Sentimental Collaborations: Mourning and Middle Class Identity in Nineteenth-Century America* (Durham, N.C.: Duke University Press, 2000). In "'Broken Idols': Mark Twain's Elegies for Susy and a Critique of Freudian Grief Theory," *Nineteenth-Century Literature* 75, no. 2 (2002): 237–68, and in his later *Mark Twain and the Spiritual Crisis of His Age* (Tuscaloosa: University of Alabama Press,

2007), Harold K. Bush Jr. looks to apply contemporary grief theory to Clemens's case (though I find his conclusions unconvincing).

34. Tony Walter, *On Bereavement: The Culture of Grief* (Maidenhead, Berks.: Open University Press, 1999), xv.

35. Ibid., 31.

36. Jalland, *Death in the Victorian Family*, 339.

37. Kete, *Sentimental Collaborations*, 35. I follow Kete's argument here, though heavily elide it.

38. Ibid., 75.

39. Though it certainly did not disappear. Kete is right to point to Clemens as one who was himself "indebte[d] to the sentimental ethos," but who was also critically aware of its "dangers and faults," *Sentimental Collaborations*, 183. She tends, though, to read this "dual stance toward sentimentality" in a gap between Clemens's attitude toward the events of his own life and the representations given in his fictions. I rather see such ambiguity operating in both realms. My discussion here builds back into my prior comments on sentimentality in chapters 1 and 5.

40. Kete, *Sentimental Collaborations*, xv.

41. Ibid., 81.

42. Walter, *On Bereavement*, 75. Walter is discussing modern modes of grief and mourning, identifying a move away from "the Victorian celebration of the bond between living and dead" to "a more muted, more private grief...that found it hard to incorporate the dead into the ongoing life of increasingly secular families and societies," 104. I argue that Clemens's and Howells's grief should be viewed in terms of just such a transition, but one already well underway in the late-nineteenth-century Western world.

43. Kete, *Sentimental Collaborations*, 160.

44. Ibid., 76 and 6.

45. Jalland, *Death in the Victorian Family*, 339.

46. Walter, On Bereavement, 125. "Bereavement becomes a psychological experience of the individual, rather than the shared experience of the group; individual grief replaces group mourning," 34.

47. Ibid., 125.

48. I am here reapplying what Jalland says about Charles Darwin (a self-described agnostic) and his father in *Death in the Victorian Family*, 344.

49. Goodman and Dawson, *William Dean Howells*, 27 and 308–9.

50. Leitz et al., *W. D. Howells, Selected Letters* 3:299.

51. Goodman and Dawson, *William Dean Howells*, 248.

52. Leitz et al., *W. D. Howells, Selected Letters* 3: 262.

53. May 21, 1889. Henry Nash Smith and William M. Gibson, eds., *Mark Twain-Howells Letters: The Correspondence of Samuel L. Clemens and William D. Howells, 1872–1910* (Cambridge, Mass.: Harvard University Press, 1960), 603.

54. To Edward E. Hale, April 5, 1889, Leitz et al., *W. D. Howells, Selected Letters*, 3:249.

55. June 7, 1889, Leitz et al., *W. D. Howells, Selected Letters* 3:253.

56. Jalland, *Death in the Victorian Family*, 287.

57. Howells names the audience for his sketch as Winny's "own family, first; and then...the family in which we are all brethren and sisters," "A Sketch of Winnie's Life," quoted by permission of the Houghton Library, Harvard University, bMS Am 1784.16 (19), 1 and 3. I do not know whether the sketch was in fact published—and suspect not—but it seems this was Howells's intent. The vocabulary here is a reminder of (and possible

leftover from) the culture of sentimentalism previously discussed. The sketch's title gives a variant of Howells's normal spelling of his daughter's name.

58. Jalland, *Death in the Victorian Family*, 336.

59. Walter, *On Bereavement*, 165. My conclusions, in Howells's case, are tentative. I suspect that, in the period, an ongoing idealization of the dead was more common than Jalland suggests. My claim of (some) abnormality is despite an awareness of modern grief theory's notion of "continuing bonds"—one replacing an earlier Freudian model where "healthy mourning" means the working through of grief until the dead are "sooner or later left behind." Ibid., 22 and 104–5.

60. Howells, "A Sketch of Winnie's Life," 40, 52, 59, 45 and 59.

61. Ibid., 6–8, 47, 24, 34, 1, and 60.

62. Jalland, *Death in the Victorian Family*, 286.

63. Howells, "A Sketch of Winnie's Life," 63. See, too, n. 76 below on that "in any sphere."

64. Howells, "A Sketch of Winnie's Life," 14.

65. I am partly prompted here by what Karen Sánchez-Keppler says about memorial photographs in "Then When We Clutch Hardest: On the Death of a Child and the Replication of an Image," in Mary Chapman and Glenn Hendler, eds., *Sentimental Men: Masculinity and the Politics of Affect in American Culture* (Berkeley and Los Angeles: University of California Press, 1999), 68. I also adapt one of her phrases.

66. Gillman, *Dark Twins: Imposture and Identity in Mark Twain's America* (University of Chicago Press, 1989), 110–11. Stoneley gives a strong reading of the parallels (unacknowledged by Clemens) between Joan's story and Susy's own "mental and physical maturation." He describes Susy as "a typical example of a woman who could neither accept, nor establish herself outside, the values that informed her upbringing." Clemens, Stoneley asserts more generally, "seems to have regarded [Susy] with a romantic possessiveness that one would more readily associate with a husband," though he sees this as a larger cultural, as much as an individual, problem. *Mark Twain and the Feminine Aesthetic*, 96 and 98.

67. *Mark Twain's Autobiography*, ed. Albert Bigelow Paine (New York: Harper, 1924), 2:37.

68. Ibid., 34 and 37.

69. August 19, 1896, MTP.

70. Two entries in *Pudd'nhead Wilson's Calendar* read: "All say, 'How hard it is that we have to die'—a strange complaint to come from the mouths of people who have had to live," and "Whoever has lived long enough to find out what life is, knows how deep a debt of gratitude we owe to Adam, the first great benefactor of our race. He brought death into the world," *The Tragedy of Pudd'nhead Wilson* (New York: Oxford University Press, 1996 [1894]), 121 and 40. In this case, the calendar entries clearly square with Clemens's own feelings.

71. Gillman, *Dark Twins*, 111. Quoting Clemens, "Susy died at the right time, the fortunate time of life, the happy age—twenty-four years," Gillman comments: "Quite apart from the grieving father's need somehow to justify his daughter's untimely death, the time was right because, though well past adolescence, she was still a child in his eyes," 106.

72. Stoneley, *Mark Twain and the Feminine Aesthetic*, 101–2. And see especially chapter 4, n. 144.

73. "Why Not Abolish It?" In Mark Twain, *Collected Tales, Sketches, Speeches, and Essays 1891–1910* (New York: Library of America, 1992) pp. 551 and 552.

74. See, for instance, Bush, "Broken Idols," 262–68, and chapter 3 of this present book. But Howells's words in his *Harper's* review of *Mark Twain's Letters* ("Editor's Easy Chair," *Harper's Magazine*, March 1918) are pertinent. Writing of Clemens's "denial of a conscious creator," he continues: "Almost to the very last he steadfastly denied himself the hope of life hereafter, though before the very last, but then only at the entreaty of those who stood nearest him, he is said to have permitted this hope, with a murmur, a look," 603.

75. Letters of August 19 and 29, 1896, MTP.

76. "In Memoriam," *Collected Tales, Sketches, Speeches, and Essays 1891–1910*, 218–19. The elegy's use of the word "immortal" may be a way of referring metaphorically to the intensity of the parental memory of the dead daughter. This would be in accord with a poem where Clemens consistently uses a quasi-religious vocabulary (temple, spirit, altar) to describe feelings of immediate and worldly family loss. We should too allow for Clemens and his wife's interest in spiritualism as an alternative to traditional religious belief, even though (as Gillman reminds), "during séances when he and his wife Livy tried futilely to contact the dead Susy's spirit," Clemens remained "the sceptic malgré lui," Gillman, *Dark Twins*, 10. And see Hamlin Hill, *Mark Twain: God's Fool* (New York: Harper & Row, 1973) 33–34. It is of course possible (though to my mind unlikely) that in his elegy Clemens reverts to traditional Christian belief. Alternatively, he may follow a standard model of reconciliation found within the form itself.

77. A second elegy, "Broken Idols," dated 1898, is altogether bleaker, concluding: "We miss them [our younger family members whose 'earlier selves' are now lost] as we miss the dead, / We mourn them as we mourn the dead." See Bush, "Broken Idols," 255–57.

78. Clemens to Rogers, January 4, 1897. Leary, *Mark Twain's Correspondence with Henry Huttleston Rogers*, 259.

79. Fred Kaplan, *The Singular Mark Twain* (Doubleday: New York: 2003), 535.

80. To Grace King, March 8, 1897, quoted in ibid., 536.

81. "I am working, but it is for the sake of the work—the 'surcease of sorrow' that is found there. I work all the days; & trouble vanishes away when I use that magic. . . . I am well protected; but Livy! She has nothing in the world to turn to. . . . She sits solitary; & all the day, wonders how it all happened, & why." Clemens to Twichell, January 19, 1897, Beinecke.

82. December 10, 1897, Beinecke.

83. Justin Kaplan, *Mr Clemens and Mark Twain*, (Harmondsworth, Middx.: Penguin 1967 [1966]), 520.

84. Gregg Camfield, *The Oxford Companion to Mark Twain* (New York: Oxford University Press, 2003), 108.

85. See Jalland, *Death in the Victorian Family*, 301–2.

86. "[O]n the first anniversary of Susy's death, Clemens and Livy spent the day apart from each other. She took the steamer up Lake Lucerne and spent the day alone at an inn. He sat under some trees and wrote a memorial poem," Kaplan, *Mr Clemens and Mark Twain*, 520.

87. Twichell also wrote, but his letter is no longer extant, though Clemens responded at some length. See too Henry James's letter to Howells on Winny's death.

88. The balance between grief expressed within and outside the family is, to a degree, difficult to judge. Howells's memoir on Winny was originally meant for a larger audience than that of his immediate family, and Clemens's emotions about Susy found public expression in the first of the poems he wrote in elegy to her and in the passages about her he prepared for his *Autobiography*. I am nonetheless reminded of William Merrill Decker's account of Henry Adams and his correspondence, and the move Decker outlines from bereavement, in Adams's case, as a condition met by "a community of sufferers, a secret society . . . that unites humanity across the social and political barriers of a nearly unsalvageable public life," to a later emphasis on "insularity," "the silence and suffering that encompass the sufferer—the failure of language to address pain and the inaccessibility of the sufferer to comfort." See Decker, *Epistolary Practices: Letter Writing in America before Telecommunications* (Chapel Hill: University of North Carolina Press, 1998), 181, 221, and 223.

# Index